# CLASSICS IN MURDER

# CLASSICS IN
# *MURDER*

## True Stories of Infamous Crime as Told by Famous Crime Writers

EDITED WITH AN INTRODUCTION
AND NOTES BY

## Robert Meadley

UNGAR • NEW YORK

1986
The Ungar Publishing Company
370 Lexington Avenue, New York, NY 10017

This Selection and Introduction Copyright ©
Robert Meadley 1984

Originally published 1984 by Xanadu Publications Ltd.
5 Uplands Road, London N8 9NN

Printed in the United States of America

**Library of Congress Cataloging-in-Publication Data**

Classics in murder.

   1. Murder—Miscellanea.   I. Meadley, Robert.
HV6515.C42   1986      364.1'523'09      86-16058
ISBN 0-8044-5643-7

# Contents

8   CONTENTS

# ROBERT MEADLEY

# Introduction:
# Crippen, or, Is the Reader
# Sinister?

Consider:

An irritable little man inadvertently—I can find no better word—
murders his landlady. He manages, without arousing suspicion, to
dismiss the maid, to put off the landlady's lover, and to persuade his
fellow lodger that she has gone to Bristol. He then begins the tedious
and unsatisfactory process of dismembering the body and attempting
to conceal its parts. Suddenly two friends arrive at the front door.
Imagining him to have been scurvily abandoned by his landlady,
whom they presume to have been his mistress, they have brought a
bottle and a prostitute to cheer him up ...

And again:

Mr Clay, manager of the Catalonian Cork Cutting Company, is
at the rear of his premises when shots are heard in an adjacent house.
Mr Clay is untroubled, the occupant of this house has recently been
given to domestic pistol practice, but then a florid gentleman, flourishing an umbrella and a broken pair of tongs, appears at a second
storey window evidently determined to hurl himself into the street. Mr
Clay warns him against the spiked area railings below and asks what
is the matter. Murder is the matter, shouts the stranger, and jumps.
As the confusion and bustle ripen, the local window cleaner arrives,
bearing a linnet in a cage and brandishing threepence change ...

It would be a dull sort of reader who did not wish to know the
upshot of such promising events. Mercifully for our sense of reality—
and all these accounts describe real events—not all the cases in this
collection are elaborately ornamented with baroque detail, but all
are curious. Even the Rowland/Ware case, which as a murder is both
sordid and dull, but which I have included because, like seasoning, it
has its place in the overall flavour.

Most murders are commonplace affairs; domestic quarrels or trifling
robberies heightened by that momentary frisson of *memento mori* that all
fatal accidents produce in us. It is a commonplace that murder must
fascinate, but ask yourself: In any one year, how many murders reach
the national news, and of those how many do you remember? But

some murders do fascinate. And a few, a very few, become symbols for a whole generation and are enshrined in the folk memory, the facts of the case appearing dim and incomplete like palimpsest beneath some potent and distorted image, a lurid cartoon sketched over almost indecipherable copy. For my father's generation it was Crippen, for my own the mystic words were 10 Rillington Place. I am sure I could picture Crippen before I really knew what murder was: a little man with a small moustache and small, evil spectacles; as real if not as large as Robin Hood, King Arthur and Buffalo Bill. I heard of other murderers as a boy—they are associated in my mind with long car journeys, keeping us entertained while going on holiday, which perhaps explains my rather cheerful attitude to murder. There was G. J. Smith drowning his successive brides in assorted baths; Rouse, who burnt an unidentified man in his car not far from the house where my brother was born; the Brighton Trunk murders and the Acid Bath murders. But these were somehow more curiosities than horrors, the doings of lesser devils in the shadow of Crippen. These were merely murderers while Crippen was a symbol. Yet there was nothing in his single murder that made Crippen more horrific than these others, so it was not the horror of what he did that made Crippen's reputation.

That he lived in a dark basement, painted throughout a dingy pink; that he poisoned his wife, then chopped her up and buried her in the cellar; these facts were important but somehow atmospheric. The point of the story as I remember my father telling it was the drama of the arrest at sea and how the suspicious captain had trapped Ethel Le Neve, disguised as Crippen's son, into revealing her true sex. He tossed a penny into her lap, and being accustomed to wearing skirts she spread her legs to catch it instead of closing them as a boy would.

This story of the penny and the legs is apocryphal, one of those curious common-figures that recur in folk myth, replacing truths that are often more interesting, and in this case more pathetic. I shall give you the facts in a moment but they need not trouble us here. My father was only six months old when Crippen was hanged, but the elements of the drama were the stuff of his boyhood, the shadow of murder making vivid the excitement of the captain's radio messages to shore and the pursuit by the detectives in a newer, faster ship; a technological excitement, belonging to a period when boys made crystals sets at school and waited for the first aeroplane to cross the Atlantic, that established Crippen in such a way that when the importance of the details was forgotten the name remained, enshrined as somehow more than a murderer.

I have developed this little exercise in memory because the point seems to me worth making that our interest in murder is as much if not more curious and dramatic than morbid. Where we might seem to relish the details of dismemberment in a murder, few of us would care for the same details in the report of a car accident, so it is not the dismemberment that fascinates us. The details only interest us in so far as they are constituents of a drama.

I do not wish to be coy about this. There is much that is despicable in our most innocent-seeming interests, but in the matter of an interest in murder we tend to treat ourselves unjustly. True, our attention is first caught by the morbid element. It is the same instinct that draws our attention to a street accident or a headline shouting '10 Dead . . .' It is an instinct about which most of us, quite rightly, have ambiguous feelings, and if our sole interest is to dwell on heads battered in, corpses sexually molested and bits of bodies turning up in the dustbin, then we certainly need tranquillizers and probably advice, but on the whole we judge ourselves unkindly. We assume, as in the case of Crippen, that if a case is particularly famous it must be because it was particularly gruesome, and probably that the more famous the murderer the more murders he committed. We assume, unless we know the details of the case, that the Acid Bath murders were committed with baths of acid, that the Brighton Trunk murders were a series of killings and not just a curious coincidence, and that our only interest in such matters is to dwell upon the horrors, to feed the cannibal hunger of our lower natures. Certainly, to judge by their covers, many books on murder are offered to us on this assumption, despite the prefaces inside that tell us they are sociological treatises or exercises in literary elegance.

But, while the gruesome first captures our attention, it is not generally sufficient to hold us for very long, and the literature of murder, considering the number it has to choose from, discusses very few examples. All but the most dedicated student of the subject, offered five continents and a thousand years of history would be hard put to name more than a couple of hundred cases—which is as many as the UK currently produces in a year—and of those no more than half would be cases of genuine interest, the remainder memorable only for some occasional detail, curious in itself or analogous to some more interesting crime.

To avoid the tedium of general comments, let us consider the Crippen case as an example of what we are looking for. Broadly, it satisfies all quarters of the popular imagination with vanity, sex, violence and sentiment in equal parts. Specifically, it has all the small components of a classic murder: curious names, a novel poison, a dismembered corpse, domestic hypocrisy, a crucial clue and a remarkable effort at concealment marred by acts of astonishing stupidity. It is also a compact and complete drama.

Cora Crippen, born Kunigunde Mackamotzki, and given to posing with theatrical pretensions under the name Belle Elmore, is, like many in classic murders, an unattractive victim; miserly in small domestic matters, at home a slattern and a shrew, yet for the outside world extravagantly dressed and jewelled, tyrannizing her husband and taunting him continually with the admiration, if not more intimate attentions, of other men. But this is a portrait of her after seventeen years of theatrical disappointment and domestic failure. Probably she appeared sprightly and attractive when Crippen first admired her as the teenage mistress of a stove manufacturer in Brooklyn. At 34, with her dreams in rags, the bohemian domestic chaos and the artist's temperament showed the raw bones of slovenliness and spite.

In the early years Crippen adored her. He paid for her to study for the opera, and when it became evident she had no future there, he subsidised her vain attempt to establish a career in the music halls. Unfortunately she lacked even that little talent which will allow a predominantly male audience, mellowed with alcohol, to watch a plump, pert woman sing a sentimental song. Even though Crippen was more than willing to pay managements to let her perform, she managed only a few appearances at very minor halls. Her last appearance was in London, during a strike of music hall performers, when she was hissed off the stage.[1] It is said that when pickets tried to prevent Cora going on, Marie Lloyd told them to let her pass since her singing would drive out the audience.

The limit of her success as a thespian was that by cultivating theatrical friends and acquiring a reputation for lavish entertainments, she managed eventually to be elected honorary treasurer of the Music Hall Ladies' Guild, a charitable support for the less fortunate members of the profession. Filson Young, in *The Trial of H.H. Crippen*, remarks that her enthusiasm for this work is the best thing we know of Belle Elmore. Considering that this was the last ditch of her ambitions in this quarter, it is not an impressive epitaph.

All this time Crippen was paying out like a good 'un. He bought her jewels and furs to an astonishing value, considering his income. He paid for numerous elaborate costumes and for writers to provide

[1] An artiste with the unlikely name of Weldon Atherstone appeared on the same bill and got a similar reception. Three years later, in the same week in which the papers reported the discovery of Cora's mutilated remains, he was found shot dead in the garden of his flat in Battersea. The coincidence was remarked on by the coroner, who himself died a few days later. Curious.

songs and sketches to sustain her theatrical ambitions, and for a steady turnover of expensive *toillettes* to support her roles as theatrical hostess and hon. treasurer to the Music Hall Ladies' Guild. Right up to the end he was considered by her friends as a model of kindness, considerateness, and, most important, generosity. No doubt he relished the applause his stream of gifts received, since there was much domestic by-play in public to make sure his generosity and her resultant splendour were properly appreciated, but the worm was in the apple, and these once-fond essays in domestic theatre eventually deteriorated into mechanical observances, the futile charades of vanity pursued by habit.

At his trial, Crippen was vague about the exact date of their marriage, but thought it was about 1892. At the beginning of the new century, when Crippen returned briefly to America on business, Cora contracted an intimate friendship with a fellow expatriate and music hall performer, Bruce Miller, an ex-prizefighter, now an exponent of the 'automatic orchestra'. At the trial, Miller stoutly if unconvincingly denied that there was anything improper about their relationship or clandestine about his visits to Cora after Crippen's return. It does not matter whether we believe him or not. What is important is that Cora boasted to Crippen of her new admirer and it so happened subsequently that whenever Miller called on Cora, Crippen was always absent. And this went on not just for a few months but for several years until Miller returned to the U.S.A.

It is possible that the liaison was quite innocent, that Cora engineered it so that she could play at having a lover as she played at being an artiste, but either way one can understand that Crippen found it galling, the more so since a photograph of Miller adorned the piano, while two more hung in large frames on the parlour wall. By the time of Miller's return to America in 1904, according to Crippen's evidence at the trial, Crippen found it intolerable to share a bedroom with his wife, and shortly thereafter they moved from their small Bloomsbury flat to 39, Hilldrop Crescent, a small semi-detached house where they could occupy separate rooms.

This double loss of her apparent lover and her husband's affections, especially as her failure on the halls was now quite manifest, must have been a severe blow to Cora. Despite her boasts to Crippen of other and more affluent admirers, there is no evidence of a successor to Bruce Miller, while Crippen now became increasingly attached to Ethel LeNeve, his typist and general assistant. The burden of failure dragged at Cora's wobbling chariot of fantasy. Her bursts of hasty temper and harridan demands upon her husband became increasingly more frequent and more shrewish. However hard she played at being an artiste, however hard she struggled to be cute and lively for her little audience of ageing thespians, at some level of reality she had to live with the humiliating truth: where she was once plump, she was now lumpish—a late photograph shows her coarse-featured and a monument to corsetry—and her shrill vanity had earned her only theatrical and domestic failure.

Crippen himself is an enigmatic character. His ability to maintain an amiable and unruffled mask throughout both his public career as a husband and the investigations following the disappearance of his wife, is the one characteristic that is remarked on by all who had any dealings with him. He was a doctor of sorts with an American diploma, and he had various jobs of a quasi-medical nature, principally as U.K. agent for Munyon's, an American firm promoting patent medicines. He also ran a small mail-order business, compounding homeopathic remedies, failed to promote a patent cure of his own, and had a half share in Yale Tooth Specialists, a one-room dentistry. For a short while at Hilldrop Crescent he catered to four lodgers, doing such chores as boots and laying breakfast before going to his office, but Cora's laziness and her flirtations with the lodgers discouraged him. He was industrious, in a Yankee style, but seems to have dispersed his energies—tempted by schemes that were a little flashy and often more than a little seedy—too much to be substantially successful.

Crippen met Ethel LeNeve when he was working for Drouet's, another firm dealing in dubious remedies, and took her with him when he went back to Munyon's. Gradually, it seems, propinquity and Ethel's quiet contrast to the shrewish Cora drew them into an affair. Ethel was 19 when she first met Crippen, he was turning 40. She had already left home and was living in lodging in Hampstead, where she seems to have had an affectionate and confiding relationship with her landlady. She is described as a quiet, modest girl; lovable and affectionate, with a playful sense of fantasy; but prone to anaemia and neuralgia. There is a curious motif of names in this story. She was born Ethel Neave but changed it to LeNeve as more romantic.

Crippen's letters make it clear that it was in December 1906 that he and Ethel finally became lovers, and the affair continued for the next three years without ostensibly disturbing anyone's domestic arrangements, but there is no doubt that Cora objected strongly to Crippen's liaison, the more bitterly since the gander was now in sauce while the goose had none. Increasingly alcoholic, she was frequently unpleasant about Ethel and repeatedly threatened to go off to Bruce Miller, whom, she claimed, was eager and able to take care of her. However, she must have known, if Crippen did not, that Miller was now settled with a wife and family and a flourishing business as an estate agent in Chicago. It was another fantasy.

You may ask why Crippen did not simply leave. The problem was that all their savings were in Cora's name. Crippen's business affairs were not flourishing as they once had, and if Cora, complete with savings and a small fortune in her jewelry, far from fleeing to America, were to sue for separation citing Ethel as co-respondent, there would not only be an unpleasant scandal, but she would be able to continue living on a substantial part of whatever income Crippen had left.

There is a further point, overlooked by the prosecution and by subsequent commentators, but which may have proved crucial. Cora, both Catholic and vindictive, could do all this without agreeing to a full divorce; she could punish Crippen, not only financially and socially, but also by preventing him from marrying Ethel; and it seems clear from Crippen's last letters that marriage to Ethel had become important to him.

We cannot know, but I suspect that is what she eventually threatened—in the poisonous atmosphere of Hilldrop Crescent it seems all too likely—and if she did, then murder was the only way that Crippen could finally be rid of her. Certainly by now he hated her enough to do it. For whatever reason, it may be only as a gesture, in December 1909 Cora applied to withdraw the £600 of their savings. On the 1st of January 1910, Crippen signed the poisons register and invested in enough hyoscin to poison a dozen Coras.

He took delivery of the hyoscin on the 19th of January, and may, with the murder in mind, have suggested to Ethel that they should cool the outward appearance of their relationship for a while. Perhaps he hinted darkly that he might have to go away for a while. If he made some such suggestion, it is easy—since she was almost certainly ignorant of the murder right up to the time of her arrest—to imagine her misconstruction of it. This would explain not only her landlady's evidence that Ethel was distraught about this time, but also, a desire to reassure Ethel once the deed was done might explain some of Crippen's subsequent indiscretions.

After taking delivery of the poison Crippen waited until the 1st of February before applying it. He then told Cora's friends that she had been called suddenly to America on business in connection with a will, and told Ethel that she had at last left him as she had so often threatened. He disposed of almost all the body without trace—there is an apocryphal story that he took her head with him in a hatbox when he went to France with Ethel for a week, and dropped it from the ferry—and told her friends that she had caught pneumonia in America and died. They were surprised she had not written either during the journey or the preliminary illness, but not yet suspicious, although with what may have been bravado but was certainly stupidity he had already set tongues wagging by parading Ethel, wearing Cora's jewelry, at the dinner and ball of the Music Hall Ladies' Benevolent Fund on the 20th of February. On the 24th of March he announced Cora's death and went off to France with Ethel. (If he did take Cora's head with him in a hatbox, it would have been two months old and more than a little ripe.) It might have been wise to exercise a little tact, but on his return from France Crippen continued to parade Ethel in front of Cora's friends, wearing Cora's furs and jewels, and rubbing continually at any uneasy feelings they may have had. Finally, on the 30th of June, a Mr Nash requested Scotland Yard to investigate Cora's disappearance.

The police were not particularly impressed by Mr Nash. It was a week before they interviewed Crippen (now living with Ethel at Hilldrop Crescent), and although Crippen changed his story, saying that Cora had walked out after an argument, that he presumed she had gone to her lover in America, and that he had invented her death to avoid a scandal, Inspector Dew was satisfied—as he subsequently told Filson Young—that there was no more in the affair than Crippen had suggested. He told Crippen that Cora's whereabouts would have to be eventually established, but this was a formal fiction, one suspects: an officer liking to appear conscientious. This was on Friday.

On Monday, having nothing else pressing, Dew dropped in at Crippen's office to clear up one or two small details for his report. He found that Crippen had written to two colleagues winding up his affairs and announcing that he was going away for a while. At Hilldrop Crescent Dew gained access and made another search of the house without finding anything incriminating. But Dew was persistent; he searched again on Tuesday, and on Wednesday turned up some loose bricks in the coal cellar. Buried not far beneath he discovered human remains, quite well preserved since, being close packed in clay, putrefaction had been delayed. Crippen, otherwise so conscientious, who had left no other trace of that messy, gruesome business of dismemberment that has defeated so many murderers, had been sadly lazy. Perhaps he sickened at his task and shovelled the last few bits under the cellar floor to be done with them. But after all his effort—and one would dearly love to know how he disposed of most of it—he left, in what was little more than a small sack of scraps, a piece of skin with an identifiable scar, a hank of hair dyed à la Cora, the viscera still charged with poison, and a piece of pyjama jacket demonstrably his own. He had damned himself as thoroughly as he had done the other parts of the business.

From here the story turns into a tragic farce. Crippen, hoping to hide his trail, sailed for Canada via Antwerp. In doing so he delayed long enough for the captain of his proposed ship to read not only the police circulars but also the London papers with details of the discovery. He then tried to pass Ethel off as his son, although male clothes do not in general disguise the female form, and Ethel's ample bottom split the trousers so that they had to be fastened up the back with safety pins. Crippen, in gaol, insisted that this ludicrous disguise was his idea and there is a curious echo of Cora, alias Belle Elmore, in the bathos and the tragic unreality of it. Had Crippen carried on in London the affair would have died in a forgotten file. Had he escaped quickly and unobtrusively he would probably have got away. But by his crazy ruses and hideously misguessed timing he first got himself suspected and then caught as inevitably as the few choice scraps of Cora that he shovelled under the cellar floor brought him to the scaffold.

That, briefly, is the affair of the Crippens and LeNeve, a perfect little drama in which each person, simply by being what they were, converged inexorably upon the tragedy. I have not space to develop it more fully, and it is not the place of an introduction to steal all the best material, but even briefly sketched the Crippen case exemplifies what I find interesting in the study of classic murders. By 'classic' murder I mean one which satisfies us as a drama. There are other ways of approaching the subject: with the emphasis on legal or forensic science, on psychology in the clinical sense, or on the merely gruesome; these aspects are all present but they are not my first concern in compiling this collection.

Murders may interest us for many reasons, as puzzles or mysteries, studies in atmosphere, tragedies or curiosities or farce, and I have tried, within the limits of availability and space, to include examples of all these, and to represent the major writers in the genre.[1]

There is one other point—a warning to the unwary—that I must make while I still have hold of your lapel. This collection is intended as an introduction to the genre for the general reader, and obviously it was impractical to include more than one version of each case, or, unfortunately, to overwhelm the text with notes, but some of these cases are still controversial, and though naturally I have included those versions with which I tend to sympathize, none of these accounts should be considered the last word on its subject.

This is particularly so in the Hanratty case, which is still fiercely

[1] Some may remark upon the absence of F. Tennyson Jesse. Frankly, I find her indigestible; sententious, and a snob.

debated. In general I agree with Charles Franklin that Hanratty was guilty and that Valerie Storie's unshakeable evidence is damning, but I sometimes wonder if this is because the case reminds me of a delightful early melodrama about Thurtell in which the corpse miraculously recovers for just long enough to identify his murderer. I am not being callous or flippant. With truth such an elusive quantity and our judgement too easily coloured, it is important to ask whether we might *want* to believe a particular version of events. Much of the argument about Hanratty is coloured by the emotions that ran high during the debate preceding the abolition of hanging. In the aftermath of the war there was a succession of questionable or emotive hangings—Rowland, Bentley and Ruth Ellis—the most famous being that of Timothy Evans for the murder that Christie almost certainly committed. I believe it was the memory of these that persuaded so many people that Hanratty was unjustly hung, and that it was this cumulative unease that swung the balance in favour of abolition. I am an abolitionist myself, but I find it interesting to speculate whether abolition would have got through if Brady and Hindley, the Moors murderers, had been convicted in 1962 instead of 1966.

Think on these things. I have discussed murder as drama, and I am not ashamed to do so, but I do not forget that these same murders were all real events.

Apart from a few minor amendments (the deletion of cross-references which make no sense out of context, and the correction of some obvious misprints), the texts which follow are exactly as they were written. No attempt has been made to regularize spelling or punctuation; the pieces span a century, and many of them reflect the time and place of their composition. The authors' own notes, where they occur, are printed in roman type while the few that I have added, to explain points that would otherwise be puzzling or to add information that seemed to me to be of interest, are printed in *italics*.

Leeds, 1984

# C. E. VULLIAMY

# *A Corpse for Company*

We are all, to use De Quincey's phrase 'curious in homicide'. The reasons are complex. We like to read of achievements which are beyond our capacity though by no means beyond our inclination. We sometimes feel a private sympathy with a murderer's impulse. Perhaps we know that we are all potential murderers, and ready to become real murderers in a moment of aberration, encouragement or despair. And there is always the extraordinary interest of the doubtful cases: the cases where we do not know if we are dealing with a genuine act of murder as legally defined, 'of malice aforethought', or with an act of temporary panic, or with a mere accident.

The strangely gruesome though ironical history which I have chosen is that of Theodore Gardelle. It is a true history, and one of the most oddly mysterious of London crimes. I had at first thought of including a very brief account of this affair in my essay on hanging[1]; but the story is so good in itself, and of a sort so commendable to those who delight in the problems of crime, that it seems worth relating in detail.

Moreover, the case of Theodore Gardelle is probably unknown today, except to those who are more then usually 'curious in homicide'. It belongs to the doubtful class and is one of the most problematical affairs in the whole history of private murder. The story might have been squalid, were it not for the strange variety and action of the characters, the weird intricacy of events and the complex irony of its different stages. The scene is set in that murky world of grim little houses which, in the first half of the eighteenth century, lay between Leicester Fields (now Leicester Square) and the Haymarket.

Theodore Gardelle was a harmless and industrious little man, with the irritable nature which is commonly found in the artist; a man of good education and of pleasing manners. He painted miniatures, providing 'likenesses' for the humbler sort of client. These miniature painters occupied, at that time, the position which is now occupied by the photographer.

[1] *In* Rocking Horse Journey (*London: Michael Joseph, 1952*).

Whatever may be said of Gardelle, a man so gentle and so incon-spicuous, I think it may certainly be said that he was the last man in the world who could have been suspected of a deliberate murder. He was timid and unobtrusive, presumably not robust, and honestly engaged in a very ordinary profession.

Of his personal history very little is known. He was born in Geneva, and it is said that he studied for some time in Paris. If this is true it shows that he took his profession seriously, and there is no reason for supposing that he was not competent as well as industrious.

He appears to have come to London in 1760, where he found lodgings with a Mrs King in Leicester Fields.

Mrs King was not a woman of extravagant virtue, but she was not exactly a prostitute. There was no such person as Mr King, and she appears to have been unencumbered with friends or relatives. Various 'gentlemen' from time to time shared her bedroom and her parlour. The permanent lodgers, highly respectable, were Mr Gardelle and a man-servant who was employed by one of Mrs King's 'gentlemen'. The servant's name was Pelsey, and his master was a Mr Wright. There was also a maidservant, employed by Mrs King.

On the morning of Thursday the 19th of February 1761 Mr Gardelle, in 'a red and green nightgown' was at work in his room upstairs. He had recently painted a miniature of Mrs King, and she was not at all pleased with it. No doubt this worried him. Downstairs, the maid was attending to Mrs King, who slept on the ground floor in a bedroom with two doors—one leading to the 'fore parlour' and the other to the passage. These doors were bolted on the inside. The maid took the key of the street door from Mrs King and then went into the parlour to light the fire. Mrs King bolted the passage door, and the maid went upstairs to see if Gardelle wanted anything.

He did. He wanted two letters delivered, and he wanted a pennyworth of snuff. The letters were ready, and the empty snuff-box, and a guinea. But the maid, very properly, said that she would have to ask leave of Mrs King before setting out on these errands; for Mrs King was in bed.

Mrs King refused to let the maid go, as there would be nobody to answer a call at the street door; whereupon the maid suggested that Mr Gardelle would perhaps agree to sit in the 'fore parlour' until she came back. The maid went upstairs again and obtained the consent—unfortunately—of Mr Gardelle. (It was never denied that the maid alone was responsible for this arrangement.) She then went off on her errands. By this time Pelsey, the manservant, had already gone out to attend to his master, and so Gardelle and Mrs King were alone in the house.

Gardelle, taking a book with him, settled himself in the parlour.

Before long Mrs King appeared, whether fully dressed or not is uncertain. It is most probable that she wore a coat or dressing-gown over her shift. All that we have to go upon is the evidence of Gardelle himself.

A conversation began on the subject of Gardelle's inadequately flattering miniature of Mrs King. It was not handsome enough; indeed, it was not a protrait at all, said Mrs King. The colours were wrong. The nose and the eyes and the mouth and the teeth and the hair and the neck were all wrong. Everything was wrong. Let him say what he liked, it was the opinion of Mrs King that she knew her own face better than he did; and *that* was not her face; it was a stupid and impudent fraud, a bungled thing—and she would have none of it.

Now, the most inferior painter has at least one thing in common with greater men: he has a strong predilection in favour of his own work; and this, in turn, produces an abnormal sensitivity to criticism. The pride of Mr Gardelle was deeply injured. He bubbled with anger, he quivered, he jabbered, and at last—it would seem—he drove Mrs King back into the bedroom, shouting fiercely 'You are a very impudent woman!'

If this is what happened, it is quite likely that Mrs King was thoroughly scared. There may indeed have been something frightful in the aspect of this excited little man, something totally unforeseen. But her retort was ill-considered. She struck Gardelle so hard that she sent him staggering. You could never have believed, he said afterwards, that a woman had such terrible strength in her arms. He therefore 'pushed her away'.

Mrs King lost her footing; she fell, and her head struck against a corner of the bedstead. A trickle of blood flowed from her mouth, and she began to scream hideously. When Gardelle bent over her, doubtless intending to help, the screams became louder than ever, and she thrust him off.

It now occurred to the wretched man that the position was difficult and even dangerous. The appearance of Mrs King was alarming and it was rapidly getting worse. The noise, too, was getting worse. People in the adjoining houses would imagine that somebody was being murdered . . .

Murdered? He became obsessed, and then maddened, with one idea—he must somehow *stop the noise*.

Stop the noise! He spoke angrily; but it was no good. Then he lost the final vestiges of control. He saw 'an ivory comb with a sharp taper point continued from the back'. Using the comb as a dagger he struck again and again until there was no more noise; indeed, until there was no more Mrs King—only a corpse, and a lot of blood. He flung the bedclothes over the body of Mrs King; and then, aghast in the returning light of reason, he fell by her side in a 'swoon'.

When he came to himself, the frantic little man could hear the maid moving in the house. One door of the bedroom was already bolted on the inside. He tottered out through the door leading to the parlour, locked it from the outside and put the key in his pocket. Somehow, he got upstairs without the maid seeing him. She went into the parlour, and then up to Gardelle's room, which was deserted. Having seen that everything (as she imagined) was in order, she went down to the kitchen and had her breakfast. She then heard somebody walking about upstairs, and later, when she was tidying Gardelle's room, Gardelle himself came down from the garret. He had changed his clothes, was evidently embarrassed, and the maid, with considerable amusement, observed that he was blushing. He sent her off with a letter to a gentleman in Great Suffolk Street, and told her to wait for an answer. When she came back she found Gardelle in the parlour. He told her that Mrs King had gone out with a man in a hackney coach. This, of course, was a fatal blunder.

If Mrs King had been a respectable woman there might now have been some suspicion in the mind of the maid. But she had no illusions, and was fully persuaded that Mrs King and Gardelle had been in bed together. This, to be sure, was diverting, because Gardelle was a comical, unenterprising wisp of a creature; but it was not at all out of the ordinary.

The first serious complication arose when Pelsey came in and told the maid that she was to get the beds ready, since his master, Mr Wright, was coming to the house that evening. Shortly after hearing this, Gardelle sent the maid with yet another letter—this time to a friend of his called Broshet at the Eagle and Pearl in Suffolk Street. When Broshet had read the letter he asked the girl if she knew that Gardelle was to discharge her, after paying her wages, on the instructions of Mrs King.

Even this gave rise to no sinister thoughts. (You must remember that Gardelle appeared to be a man of almost ludicrous respectability.) A proper form was provided by Broshet, the wages were paid, with a gratuity from the now unhappy Gardelle, a porter came for the trunk, and the maid went off.

By seven o'clock Gardelle was alone in the house with a corpse for company. A corpse is company, but it may present the most horrible of problems. Murder, *per se*, is not, as De Quincey suggested ironically, a fine art; few things are more easy; but extremely fine art is usually required for the disposal of the body, and this is where the incautious and inartistic murderer comes to grief.

Whether Gardelle had intentionally murdered the woman or not, his only hope, after what he had said, was to dump the body somewhere outside the house. This would have been risky though not at all impracticable, for in those days we had no scientific method of criminal investigation. What Gardelle decided upon eventually was the disposal of the body inside the house by various methods and in various places. This has often been attempted, but is rarely successful.

And yet it seemed at first as though he might be fortunate. Pelsey came in and told him that Mr Wright was not coming after all. Upon hearing this, Gardelle said that Mrs King had not yet returned, and that he would sit up and let her in. He had already stripped the body and laid it on the bed. He then most unwisely put the bedclothes and one of the bed-curtains into a water butt in the back wash-house. The shift, and his own shirt, he concealed (also unwisely) in his room.

On the following morning he told Pelsey that Mrs King had returned and had gone out again, and when Pelsey returned in the evening it was agreed that Gardelle should sit up once more for Mrs King.

But this could not go on much longer. On Saturday morning, two days after the death of Mrs King, Pelsey was told by Gardelle that she had gone to Bath or Bristol. In the afternoon things took a turn for the worse. A friend of Gardelle's, Mr Mozier, called at the house. He had come to take Mrs King to the Opera. 'What a misfortune!' cried the witless Gardelle. 'She has gone ... to Bath or Bristol ... I don't remember very clearly ...'.

Supreme irony now stalks upon the scene, transforming the affair of Gardelle into one of the most whimsical of crime histories. It occurred to Mozier that Mrs King had treated his friend with abominable inhumanity. He had no doubt at all that she was Gardelle's mistress, that she looked after him and attended to his comforts; and now she had gone away, after dismissing the maid, leaving the poor little man to shift for himself as best he could. The kindly Mozier carried the story to another friend, and they decided upon the charitable course of providing Gardelle with an interim companion.

Strolling down the Haymarket, these worthy men selected a decent-looking prostitute, Sarah Walker, and brought her to the house. Now, they said with cheerful benevolence, now he could safely depend upon Miss Walker; she was a good girl and would make him both happy and comfortable.

Gardelle, secretly agonized, was afraid of showing ingratitude or reluctance. He put the best face on it—and a very odd face it must have been—and admitted the willing though unwelcome Miss Walker to the house.

Naturally the arrival of Miss Walker produced a frightful complication. It is doubtful whether Gardelle by this time had seriously got to work on the body, but he now realized that not a moment was to be lost. He therefore came down in the night, leaving Miss Walker (as he supposed) fast asleep, with the intention of getting on with his dreadful task. But the girl followed him downstairs. Whatever his excuses may have been, he had to go back to bed.

At half-past seven next morning (Sunday) he told Sarah not to get up, and she slept until ten o'clock. During this time he was 'employed on the body'. Later, he told Sarah to hire a charwoman; she went out and secured a Mrs Pritchard, and when she came back she 'found with Gardelle two or three men and two women'. This cheerful company, including Gardelle, presently left the house.

On Tuesday morning Pelsey noticed an odd smell: it was, in fact, the smell of roasted bones, and it came from the garret at the top of the house.

That evening, Gardelle again started the pantomime of 'sitting up for Mrs King'. Sarah was packed off to bed and the work of cutting up the body and of distributing the pieces of it in various parts of the house, though chiefly in the 'cock-loft', went on without interruption. Two days later—on Thursday—Gardelle said that he expected Mrs King home again that evening, and Sarah Walker was dismissed—with two of Mrs King's night-gowns. The charwoman, Pritchard, continued to work in the house by day.

Gardelle was now in a hopeless tangle, although, up to the afternoon of Thursday, no one appears to have had any suspicion of a crime. Then, looking for an extra supply of water, Pritchard and Pelsey found the bedclothes in the butt. Saying nothing, but obviously thinking a great deal, they put them back again. And then, next morning, Pelsey found the bed-curtain, stretched out as though to dry, on the bannisters of the kitchen staircase.

All was now prepared for the final scenes of the comical tragedy. By sheer chance Pelsey met the maid (Mrs King's maid) who had been dismissed by Gardelle. The maid swore that she had never put any clothes in the butt. On the deposition of this maid a warrant was issued by Mr Justice Fielding, the brother of Henry (who had died in 1754), for the immediate arrest of Gardelle on a charge of murder. This was on a Saturday, nine days after the death of Mrs King.

When he was arrested Gardelle denied the charge and at once fell in a 'swoon'. But a search of the house revealed things too gruesome to be described, and of an unbelievable clumsiness. Moreover, some cheap jewels belonging to Mrs King had been deposited in a box by Gardelle with 'one Perroneau, a painter in enamel', who understood that the box contained valuable colours: a very damaging revelation, though by no means conclusive. When he was faced with all this evidence Gardelle made a verbal confession, though apparently not a confession of murder, and he obstinately refused to sign a statement.

He was taken to the New Prison, where he swallowed a heavy dose of opium, followed by a dozen halfpennies. The eighteenth-century halfpenny was a massive coin[1], but neither halfpence nor opium had any effect whatsoever. After this, Gardelle was taken to Newgate, where he was kept under observation.

His trial took place at the Old Bailey on the 2nd of April. He pleaded, perhaps truly, that the death of Mrs King was the result of an accident. This plea was rejected, no time was lost, and he was hanged two days later 'amidst the shouts and hisses of an indignant populace in the Haymarket, near Panton Street, to which he was led by Mrs King's house, where the cart made a stop, and at which he just gave a look'. His body was then taken to Hounslow Heath, where it was hanged in chains.

There is a contemporary mezzotint of Gardelle which portrays him as a haggard, anxious little man in a nightcap. Did he deserve his fate? Only Gardelle himself could have given the true answer to this question. At the time of his execution he was described as 'an atrocious malefactor'. Such a description is clearly inappropriate. Andrew Knapp and William Baldwin, who compiled the *New Newgate Calendar*, evidently regarded the charge as not proven. 'How earnestly we would intreat the weaker vessel', they declared, 'not to run rashly upon the stronger; or, in other words, we would pray of females to let their tongues move in unison with the comfort which, by nature, they were formed to accord to man'.

Could Gardelle have got away with it—or rather, whether innocent or guilty of an intention to murder Mrs King, could he have avoided conviction, or even suspicion? I think this is quite possible. What would have happened if, for example, he had locked the bedroom door on the outside (as he did), thrown the key away, accounted for his absence, and said nothing whatever about Mrs King? Might it not then have been assumed that Mrs King had admitted an unknown murderer from the street? This would not have been at all improbable. And there are many other alternatives (for example, an escape to the continent), which I leave to the ingenuity of the reader. But one thing was essential—coolness; and of this Gardelle was incapable.

So there it remains; one of the grimmest and oddest of all the Newgate

---

[1] *It was also a copper coin, and the* Newgate Calender *expressed some surprise that twelve of them did not kill him 'because verdigrise, the solution of copper, is a very remarkable and active poison, and the contents of the stomach would act as a dissolvent upon them'.*

stories, and a mystery of the choicest order for those who are 'curious in homicide'. Also a warning to the vain female and the impetuous artist.

# WILLIAM ROUGHEAD
# *The Sandyford Mystery*

'Alas! I had na the wyte [blame] of it.'
—Last Words of the Master of Gowrie.

I am doubly in debt to Mrs Jessie M'Lachlan. She provided me with a case of high interest and importance; one which affords an instance unique in our juridical annals, namely, that of a person charged with murder, whose defence is that the crime was committed by the chief witness for the Crown! This surely is a situation sufficiently startling and dramatic to outgo even the most bold of fictionmongers. Then, my report of the trial being duly completed—not, as Mr Sapsea remarked of his famous Epitaph, without some little fever of the brow, for in fact it was a tough job—and the volume having taken its place in the series to which it belongs, it chanced to meet the eye of that fine connoisseur in matters criminal, the late H. B. Irving. He fell in love at first sight with my Jessie, and for her sake sought an introduction to her biographer, which effected, led to a friendship greatly prized by me and subsisting until his untimely death. My account of the case became for him a bedside book—his nerves were in such circumstances of the strongest; and he told me that it was the best murder he had ever read. This, from one of his wide acquaintance with the literature of the subject, was praise indeed and made me very proud. That was over twenty years ago, and in re-telling to-day the old story for a new audience I am heartened by the remembrance of his approval.

In the Glasgow of the early 'sixties the Sandyford Mystery (with a capital M) was the topic not only of the hour, but of the year. The Second City, in Mid-Victorian times, was singularly rich in wrongdoers of the most attaching type. There was the wonderful Miss Madeleine Smith in 1857, there was the poisonous Dr Pritchard in 1865; and between these twain, in 1862, a first-class case, bristling with sensation and strange surprises; possessing everything requisite to a great criminal drama and constituting, in my submission, an ideal murder. For to do one's self the deed of which by means of your evidence another is convicted, is a veritable triumph of naughtiness only to be compassed by a past-master of the art of homicide. Little wonder, then, that such of the public as credited James Fleming, that curious old gentleman, with having achieved this feat at the expense of his former maidservant, Jessie M'Lachlan, were lost in admiration of the veteran's prowess. But there was an opposing faction that held old Fleming to be the blameless victim of a wicked woman, seeking to cast upon his venerable shoulders the weight of her own blood-guiltiness. So the interest of the case resides in this condundrum: Which of these solutions is the right one?

## I

Sandyford Place is a respectable street in the West End of Glasgow, and in the summer of 1862 there lived at No. 17 a suitably respectable accountant named John Fleming, together with his respectable son young John, who occupied a stool in the paternal office. Mr Fleming was a widower; his house was presided over by his sister, and he had two young daughters. These ladies were also highly respectable. But there was in the background another member of the family whose respectability was not on a par with that of the rest. This was Mr Fleming's aged parent, James Fleming, who had been a hand-loom weaver in Cumbernauld and claimed to be eighty-seven, though it was afterwards averred that he was in fact but seventy-eight. The point is of importance in connection with his alleged activities. Now old Fleming, as he was familiarly known throughout the subsequent proceedings of which he may or may not have been the occasion, had failed to attain the high standard of respectability of which his descendants were in their own persons so justly conscious. Despite their rise in the social scale, the grandfather remained a man of the working class. He spoke broad Scots, his habits were homely, his manners rude and unpolished, and he was difficult to fit into the genteel middle-class circle of which the Fleming family was an ornament. His ways were not their ways; he took his meals in the kitchen, lived largely below-stairs, and consorted chiefly with the maidservants. Now it was not mere snobbery that caused the refined Flemings thus to relegate to the basement their unattractive progenitor: the old man's character exhibited certain traits abhorrent to his self-respecting issue. If drink were available he got drunk, and in his cups he was apt to be amorous after a fashion painful to his relations and most unseemly in one of his advanced years. Nay more, in 1852 he had a child by a domestic servant and in respect of this patriarchal lapse was rebuked by the Kirk Session of Anderston United Presbyterian Church, of which he was the oldest member, for 'the sin of fornication with Janet Dunsmore'. But having shewed becoming contrition, he was restored to the full fellowship of the

Church. This regrettable incident occurred ten years before the date of our story.

Mr John Fleming, like most prosperous Glasgow folk, had a country house on the Clyde, whither in the summer months the establishment removed, one servant being left in town to look after the house and attend to the grandfather, as also to the father and grandson during the week, the two Johns going down to Dunoon from Saturday to Monday. Thus at the week-ends the sole occupants of the house in Sandyford Place were old Fleming and the maid in charge. At the time in question this was a young woman named Jess M'Pherson, who had been for some years in Mr Fleming's service with complete satisfaction to her employer.

Friday, 4th July 1862, is the leading date in the case. That morning after breakfast Mr Fleming and his son left for the office in St Vincent Street as usual and went down to Dunoon by the afternoon steamer. They returned to town by 'the first boat' on Monday the 7th, going straight to the office in pursuance of their regular custom. At half-past four o'clock young John went home. The door was opened to him by his grandfather. This was quite unusual, and the lad exclaimed: 'Where is Jessie?' to which the old gentleman rejoined: 'She's away; she's cut. I haven't seen her since Friday, and her door's locked.' 'Why didn't you have it opened?' naturally asked young John, to which the patriarch replied that 'he thought she was away seeing her friends and would be back again'. Mr Fleming, arriving at the moment, was told by his son of the situation. 'She may be lying dead in her room,' said the lad, 'for anything he [the old man] knows.' So the three generations descended to the basement, the grandfather making no further comment. The maid's door was locked and the key missing. Mr Fleming tried that of the pantry adjoining; it opened the bedroom door and they all entered the room. It was in partial darkness; the blinds were down and the shutters half-shut. On the floor beside the bed lay the dead body of the unhappy maid, practically naked, with a piece of carpet covering the head. There was much blood about the room. With singular acumen the old gentleman touched at once the very kernel of the case: '*She's been lying there all this time,*' he exclaimed, holding up his aged hands, '*and me in the house!*' They then went upstairs, and Mr Fleming ran for the doctor, Dr Watson, who lived hard by in Newton Terrace. Dr Watson at once accompanied him back to Sandyford Place. Having looked at the body, he remarked, with respect to the injuries which he saw: 'This is evidently not a suicide; you had better call in the police', which was done; and Dr Joseph Fleming, surgeon of police, was promptly on the scene of the tragedy, arriving there before five o'clock.

The two doctors examined the body and then turned their attention to the condition of the basement flat. In the kitchen, which immediately adjoined the bedroom, a good fire was burning. Obvious blood-stains were seen upon the 'jawbox' (sink); upon the inside of the door; and on the door-post, four or five feet above the floor. The door-mat was soaked in blood and sticking to the threshold. Along the lobby, from the kitchen to the bedroom, was a trail of blood, suggesting that the body had been dragged from the one apartment to the other. There were many other blood-stains about the flat, notably in the bedroom, of which we shall hear again. But the strangest discovery made by the doctors was this: the floors of the kitchen and bedroom, respectively of stone and wood, and the flags of the lobby, as also the face, neck, and chest of the dead woman, *had all been washed.* 'The lobby was perfectly moist,' said Dr Fleming at the trial; 'it was very damp, as if it had been recently washed. The kitchen floor was drier, *but still there was a damp appearance.* They had the appearance of not having been done on the same day.' When that night at ten o'clock the superintendent of police and two detective officers made a thorough examination of the premises they found that the kitchen floor, though appearing to have been lately washed, *was then dry.*

Next day, 8th July, Dr Joseph Fleming and Dr (afterwards Professor) G.H.B. Macleod, by instructions of the Sheriff, conducted a post-mortem examination of the body, the results of which were embodied in a joint report. The doctors, *inter alia,* stated:

> The body was lying on its back on the floor, close to and in front of the bed, the clothes of which were heaped together and in many places deeply stained with blood. The lower limbs of the deceased lay fully exposed, and a piece of carpet was thrown carelessly over the head and trunk. On removing the carpet the body was seen to be dressed in a chemise and a knitted worsted jacket. *These clothes were all quite damp,* and much stained with blood. *The neck and chest appeared to have been partially washed.* The furniture of the room was in confusion. Large drops of blood were seen on the floor, and that even at a distance of 6 feet from the body. On further examination it became apparent that the body had been dragged from the kitchen (where evidence of a severe conflict was obtained) along the lobby to the apartment in which it was found, and also that imperfect attempts had been made to obliterate the traces of this removal.

The head was horribly mangled. There were three deep *transverse* wounds upon the face: one across the forehead and two across the bridge of the nose. On the right side of the head and neck were eleven distinct incised wounds. The right ear was destroyed and the right-half of the lower jaw broken into fragments. All these wounds, in distinction to the transverse wounds on the face, *sloped from above downwards and from behind forwards.* Both the hands and wrists were mutilated, there being nine distinct wounds on each. The body was otherwise healthy and free from disease or injury. From these appearances the reporters drew the following conclusions:

1. That this woman was murdered, and that with extreme ferocity.
2. That her death had taken place within three days.
3. That a severe struggle had taken place before death.
4. That such an instrument as a cleaver or a similar weapon was the most likely to have caused the fatal injuries found.
5. That the injuries had been inflicted before or immediately after death.
6. That all the wounds on the neck and head, with the exception of those on the nose and forehead, had apparently been inflicted by a person standing over the deceased as she lay on her face on the ground.
7. That the comparatively slight degree of strength shewn in the blows would *point to a female or a weak man* as having inflicted them; and
Lastly, that the body had been drawn by the head with the face downwards along the lobby from the kitchen to the front room.

As regards the lobby, there were spots of blood on the lower steps of the stair leading to the floor above, and on the *front* of the steps marks which seemed to have been made by blood-stained skirts. There were finger-prints on the corner of the wall; a blood-smear on the inside at the top of the press door beside the kitchen; and blood behind the back door to the yard. In a room used by the patriarch as a dressing-room—he slept in the flat above—there was upon the floor a mark of blood, and some of his clean shirts in a chest of drawers were spotted with blood. In the dead woman's bedroom there was blood on the basin-stand and blood-stained water in the basin; the servant's box lay open and rifled, 'as if some bloody hand had been working amongst the contents'. Strangest of all, on the bare floor, beyond the margin of the washed area, were plainly to be seen three several bloody imprints of a naked foot. Finally, in a drawer of the kitchen dresser was found a butcher's cleaver, eminently adapted to produce the injuries; clean, but as afterwards appeared, bearing traces of blood.

## II

There were missing from the servant's box two silk dresses, one black and one brown, a silk 'polka' or jacket, and other garments. There were also missing from the dining-room sideboard sundry silver and plated spoons, etc., which the maid had out for daily use. A valuable silver tea-service was left there untouched. The cruet bottles were upon the sideboard, but the cruet-stand was found near the body in the servant's room. Particulars of the missing articles were published in all the Glasgow newspapers and issued in official handbills.

Despite the *prima facie* appearance of burglary presented by these facts, old Fleming, as the last person to see the dead woman alive and having spent three days in this blood-stained house without raising any alarm, was very properly interrogated by the police; and so unsatisfactory did his account of his behaviour seem to the official mind, that on 9th July he was apprehended on a warrant from the Sheriff on the charge of being concerned in the crime. The Sheriff of Lanarkshire, before whom he was brought for examination, was Sir Archibald Alison, the distinguished historian, who justly observes of old Fleming's conduct after the murder that it was 'extremely suspicious'. His examination lasted for four hours and on its conclusion he was committed to prison. That is all we are permitted to know about the matter, though in view of later developments it were vital to have heard the old man's original version. In England he would, of course, have been a witness at the inquest and his evidence fully reported; in Scotland, however, the preliminary investigation into a criminal case is conducted in private by the Procurator-Fiscal, as Crown prosecutor, and the result is kept secret from the vulgar. While I consider that as a general rule our system is the better one, like all rules it is subject to exception, a fact of which the Sandyford case forms undoubtedly a flagrant instance. Superintendent M'Call, who apprehended Fleming, stated in cross-examination at the trial: 'He made a statement to me. He said he had been wakened by screams, *which he attributed to loose characters at the back of the house*; that he looked at his watch and saw that the time was 4 a.m.' Lord Deas stopped at this point the line of cross-examination, which he thought 'might lead to the contradiction of what had been said out of the box'!

The obvious difficulties of the patriarch's position were these: Having heard such screams in the night and finding the maid missing in the morning, with her bedroom door locked, he did nothing whatever about it, raised no alarm, made no inquiries, and carried on as if everything were all right. Yet he admitted noticing that morning the spots of blood on his shirts. In these circumstances he lived alone in the house for three days without saying a word about the matter to the several persons with whom he had occasion to talk, particularly an admirer of the maid, who called twice to see her! Finally, the noticeable blood-stains in and about the kitchen where he passed his time; and the *recent* washing of the kitchen floor and of the lobby.

Meanwhile the boards of the bedroom floor containing the bloody footprints were removed for skilled examination. Dr Macleod found that the impressions were totally different from the feet both of old

Fleming and of the deceased. In his judgment they were those of a female.

The advertisements speedily bore fruit. On the 9th the police learned from a pawnbroker in East Clyde Street that the missing plate had been pledged for £6. 15s. at midday on Saturday, the 5th, by a woman who gave a false name and address. On the 13th the police, acting upon information received—plainly from the patriarch—went to a house in the Broomielaw and took into custody a sailor named James M'Lachlan and his wife, Jessie M'Intosh or M'Lachlan, as being concerned in the crime. The apprehension of the mariner was merely a device of the authorities to get him to testify against his wife, seeing they were then aware that he had been in Ireland with his ship at the time of the murder. Mrs M'Lachlan, being judicially examined, denied that she had been at Sandyford Place on the night of 4th–5th July. She said that the plate in question had been given to her by old Fleming the day before, with instructions to pawn it as he was short of money. After she had done so, he called again, gave her £4 for her trouble in the matter, and received from her the balance. He warned her to tell no one of this curious transaction. She was examined at vast length on this and two subsequent occasions as to her own dresses and those of the deceased, and the tactics of the Fiscal were successful in involving her in a mass of falsehoods and contradictions. Strong objection was at the trial taken by the defence as to the manner in which these 'voluntary' declarations were extorted from the accused. Its gross unfairness is manifest from the shabby trick played upon her at her third examination. The Fiscal, having found the box in which she had sought to conceal the missing clothes, questioned her in detail as to Jess M'Pherson's wardrobe. She denied that she had lately seen any of the items referred to; whereupon the Fiscal confronted her with the recovered garments, which she then said had been given to her by the deceased to be altered and dyed. This official trap-laying would have seemed to Mr Sapsea 'un-English', and is certainly foreign to Scots practice. We shall hear the true history of the dresses later.

It was further ascertained by elaborate tests that hers was the foot which had undoubtedly left the bloody imprints in the dead girl's room, a fact held conclusively to prove that Mrs M'Lachlan had a hand—or rather a foot—in the affair. Now while her concern in the matter was obvious, this in nowise affected the 'extremely suspicious' behaviour of old Fleming, and in the circumstances both prisoners ought to have been indicted for the murder and jointly have been tried therefor. But the authorities took a different view—it was said at the time that the Fiscal was an intimate friend of the Flemings—so the old man was set at liberty to bear witness, whether true or false, against his fellow-prisoner. As was well observed by the *Spectator* in an admirable article on the case:

> Strange to say, the Glasgow authorities seem to have adopted at once, and with an almost personal bias, the latter, and to our minds we will not say the least probable, but the more improbable of these two hypotheses. The fact of Mr Fleming's innocence was assumed as an axiom, and the object of the prosecution appeared to be not so much to prove that Jessie M'Lachlan was guilty of the murder as that Mr Fleming had no concern with it whatever.

The Press on the whole, with the exception of the *Glasgow Herald*, which held from the first a brief for 'the old innocent', was of the same opinion.


## III

The case was set down for trial at the Glasgow Autumn Circuit. This course was highly prejudicial to the accused. The crime had aroused unprecedented excitement in Glasgow, and to meet the popular demand the local newspapers of the day anticipated the most unscrupulous methods of modern journalism. Detectives were dogged by reporters and the results of their discoveries regularly published; witnesses examined by the Fiscal were waylaid and their proposed evidence printed in full, with editorial comments; correspondents were encouraged to air the most fantastic theories as to how the accused committed the murder, to suggest all sorts of motives, and to asperse with irresponsible spitefulness her character and previous conduct. So profitable proved this scandalous campaign, that since the publication of the precognitions [witnesses' statements] began, the circulation of certain of the daily papers rose from 10,000 to 50,000! In these disgraceful circumstances it was manifestly impossible that the accused could have a fair trial in Glasgow. Six years earlier fortunate Miss Smith, and three years later pious Dr Pritchard, though their alleged crimes were committed in Glasgow, were each tried at Edinburgh. And *they* were both popular prisoners, courteously treated by the local Press. *A fortiori* Mrs M'Lachlan should certainly have been tried before the same Court, where, by the then existing practice, her case would have been presided over by the Lord Justice-Clerk and two Lords of Justiciary. As it was, it was dealt with by a hostile jury and a single Judge.

Unfortunately for his judicial reputation, it fell to the lot of Lord Deas to try the Sandyford murder case. His Lordship was a senator of strong character, high integrity, and great experience; powerful in personality, masterful in mind, learned in the law; but so far from being of counsel with Portia in the article of mercy as to be termed by the profane a 'Hanging Judge'. The prosecution was conducted by an Advocate-Depute—the chief law officers of the Crown do not attend the Circuit Courts—Adam Gifford (afterwards himself a Judge), assisted by a junior. Andrew Rutherfurd-Clark (later a well-known Senator of the College of Justice), with two juniors, appeared for the defence. The trial took place in the Old Court in Jail Square, and the proceedings lasted from 17th to 20th September 1862. As I have elsewhere devoted to these an entire volume,[1] in which the evidence and speeches are printed at length, together with the additional evidence taken as a subsequent inquiry, and other documents relative to this most amazing case, all that I need do here is to give the reader a brief narration of what happened at and after the trial.

The Court-house was besieged, and those concerned in the case had literally to fight their way into Court. The prisoner, who was quietly dressed and perfectly composed, was placed at the Bar. She pleaded Not Guilty to the charge, and her counsel lodged a special defence: 'that the murder alleged in the indictment was committed by James Fleming'. John Fleming and his son having given their account of the discovery of the crime, James Fleming entered the witness-box. Nothing could have been more respectable than the appearance presented by 'the old gentleman', as Lord Deas termed him. Of grave demeanour, attired in his best Sunday blacks, bald, aquiline, silver-whiskered, he looked a typical Free Kirk elder of the old school. He was wearing spectacles, but let out that they had only been given to him that very morning, and admitted that he could see 'gey weel' without them! So they may be regarded as part of his excellent make-up. The only infirmity of age to which he pleaded guilty was being 'a little dull o' hearing'.

The patriarch gave his evidence in broad Scots and his testimony is reported in the vernacular, tempered slightly by the shorthand writer for behoof of the Sassenach reader—the only instance of the kind known to me. He told the following tale. He was employed by his son to look after certain house property in the Briggate. He knew the deceased. On Friday, 4th July, he was alone with her in the house. He went to bed at half-past nine; the girl was still busy with her work in the kitchen: it was washing-day. At four o'clock next morning he was awakened by three loud 'squeals', which suggested to his mind that the maid had a sister spending the night with her! He slept again till six, from which hour he lay waiting for the servant to bring him his porridge according to her daily custom. She did not do so, and at nine he arose and dressed.

---

[1] *Trial of Jessie M'Lachlan.* Notable British Trials series, 1911; second edition, 1925; third edition, 1950.

On research, he found her bedroom door locked and 'gied three chaps' (knocks) which met with no response. The pantry window, giving upon the area, was open and he closed it. He made up the kitchen fire. His first caller was a maid from next door, who requested 'the len' [loan] o' a spade', with which he was unable to oblige her. This was at eleven, and he then noticed that the front door, though closed—'just snecked, ye ken'—was unlocked. The next person to call was the baker, from whom he accepted a half-quarter loaf. At twelve he repaired to the office, did some business in the Briggate, and so home by bus at two o'clock. He made himself a 'bit dinner'. At seven came a third ring at the bell. This was the maid's young man, who had arranged with her to call and was disappointed to learn from the patriarch that she 'wasna in'. Leaving his name he went his way. The old man then put away his clean shirts, which, since the maid had washed them, had been drying on a 'screen' before the kitchen fire. He noticed 'there was two marked with blood on them'. He supped at eight and retired at nine. 'On Sabbath morning the bell was rung by the milkman, *but I did not answer.*' After breakfast—tea and a boiled herring—he went to church as usual, speaking to a neighbour by the way. Fortified by a dinner of bread and cheese, he attended divine service in the afternoon. That evening the maid's young man repeated his call and was surprised to hear that she was out again. At half-past nine the patriarch sought his couch. Monday was a busy day, for then the tenants paid their weekly rents. The old man was up and doing by eight o'clock, went off to the office for his books, thence to the Briggate 'to lift what he could', returning to the office in the afternoon to lodge with the cashier the proceeds of his industry, and going home at two o'clock. It should be noted that to none of the several persons with whom he spoke on the Saturday, Sunday, and Monday did he say one word as to the mysterious disappearance of the servant. Having described the finding of the body and identified the pawned plate, which he denied giving to the accused, he said that he knew her when in his son's service three years before and had visited her once at her own house since. With that single exception he had never seen her after she left until confronted with her on his examination before the Sheriff—when, as was stated in the Press at the time, he denied that he ever knew her!

'Was your watch right that Saturday morning?' was Mr Rutherfurd-Clark's first question on rising to cross-examine the venerable witness, for this matter of *time* was to be the touchstone of the truth or falseness of his story. He stuck to it that he did not rise till nine and that the first person he spoke to was the girl for the spade, who called at eleven. The front door was not on the chain when he opened it to her. Then Mr

Clark put his crucial question, which in the sequel was to become historic: '*Did the milk come that Saturday morning?*' Surely an easy enough question for one of the witness's remarkable power of memory, though strange to say he found the greatest difficulty in replying to it. But Mr Clark would have an answer. Seven separate times the witness swore that the milkboy did *not* call that morning. Finally, he was brought to admit that the boy *did* call—'betwixt eight and nine', that he opened the front door 'on the chain' and said he did not need any milk, and that he was then dressed. Being reminded that he had sworn he did not rise till nine, the patriarch paused for a space and slowly replied: 'Whether I was dressed or not I cannot charge my memory.' To the next question: 'Why did you not let Jessie open the door as usual when the milkboy rang?' the old man returned the startling answer; 'ON SATURDAY MORNING, YE KEN, JESSIE WAS DEID; SHE COULDNA OPEN THE DOOR WHEN SHE WAS DEID!' Asked whether he then knew that she was dead? he replied, sharply and with emphasis, that he did not. In further cross-examination, being reminded of the cries of distress heard by him in the night, the servant missing, her door locked, and the blood upon his shirts, did he not suspect some evil had befallen her? he said he 'never thocht onything was wrang'—which, as we shall presently see, implies a lack of interest strangely at variance with his proved character. None of the significant appearances in the kitchen and lobby attracted his attention during that week-end; neither did it occur to him to inform the police or have the maid's door opened; nor to tell the milkboy, the baker, the servant from next door, Jessie's young man, his friends at church, or the people at the office that the maid had vanished. He never thought that she had run away; yet his first mention of her to anybody was: 'She's away, she's cut!' Old Fleming was the only witness in the case to whom the Judge put no questions; but his Lordship made many observations very helpful in relieving him from the undue pressure and inconsiderate persistence of Mr Rutherfurd-Clark.

Before leaving this branch of the case it may be convenient for the reader to know how far the evidence of the old gentleman was supported by the sworn testimony of other witnesses. I have summarized the proven facts as follows:

1. That old Fleming was notoriously of an abnormally suspicious and inquisitive disposition; that nothing could take place in the house without arousing his curiosity; that the door-bell could not be rung without his knowing the cause, and that he would even rise from his bed to look out of the window on such occasions; that if a servant left the house upon an errand he must know where she had been and what she did; that he devoted much attention to acquiring a full knowledge of such visitors as

came to see the servants, and if possible personally interviewed them; that he extended the sphere of his observations to the servants next door, so far as he had opportunity of spying upon their movements; and that in everything relating to the deceased girl, who enjoyed a special share of his attentions, he was known to be peculiarly interested.

2. That the milk was usually delivered at the house not later than twenty minutes to eight in the morning; that prior to the Saturday in question he had never answered the door to the milkman; that at 7.40 a.m. on that day the milkboy rang the bell once as usual; that there was no delay in answering his ring; that the boy heard the chain being taken off the door; that old Fleming, dressed in black clothes, himself opened the door, and said 'he was for nae milk'; and that never before that morning had milk been refused at that house.

It will thus be seen that not only was the patriarch uncorroborated, but that his evidence was in all vital points flatly contradicted.

The movements of the accused on that eventful night were proved by certain friends and neighbours. She made no secret of her intention to visit Jess M'Pherson that evening, and arranged with a woman to look after her young child during her temporary absence. Another woman, who chanced to call as she was dressing to go out, accompanied her part of the way to Sandyford Place. She left her own house at ten o'clock, remarking that she always went late so as to let old Fleming be in bed. She returned at nine o'clock next morning, carrying a large bundle, and was admitted by the neighbour who was attending to her child. She was then wearing a brown dress different from that in which she had gone out. That day she paid her arrears of rent: £4, and pawned the plate for £6. 15s. The clothes of the deceased she packed in a box and despatched by rail, addressed: 'Mrs Darnley, Ayr'. The clothes she herself had worn that night she sent off in a trunk, addressed: 'Mrs Bain, Hamilton'. Both were labelled: 'To lie till called for'. It need hardly be added that these apocryphal consignees had no existence. They were the creatures of Mrs M'Lachlan's imagination, as was the immortal Mrs Harris of Mrs Gamp's. The accused went later personally to Hamilton, uplifted the trunk, which she left at a saddler's to be repaired, and walked out into the country, carrying a bundle. Near where she was seen to go there were afterwards found in a hedge certain torn pieces of clothing, blood-stained, which were identified as the skirt and petticoat worn by her on the night of the murder. Finally, she had burnt her crinoline in the fire and given the wires thereof to a lady friend; these also, despite the cleansing process, retained traces of blood. So in addition to the footprints, there was clear evidence of the prisoner's presence in the house at the time of the crime.

Among other witnesses called for the Crown was the servant from next door, who had proposed to borrow a spade from old Fleming. She stated that she did so on the Saturday afternoon *between two and three o'clock*. The door was opened by the patriarch, whom she accompanied downstairs to the back door. He went out to the washing-house, and returning said that it was locked. She suggested searching the kitchen for the key, but he said he had looked there already, so she was not admitted to the kitchen. The deceased's young man stated that he called for her twice: on the nights of Saturday and Sunday. On the first occasion old Fleming, in reply to his questions, admitted that 'Jessie had been out a good while'; on the second, when witness said she was surely very often out, he made no reply. A fellow church member stated that he had a conversation with old Fleming on the Sunday, and the cashier at the office described his interviews with him on the Saturday and Monday. To neither of these witnesses did the patriarch make mention of the maid's disappearance. Mr Clark asked the elder if he were aware that the venerable adherent had been up before the Kirk Session, but Lord Deas, very jealous for the old gentleman's repute, disallowed the question. Of the medical evidence given by Drs Watson, Fleming, and Macleod we have heard the general purport. They spoke to the remarkable character of the wounds: the three *transverse* cuts across the face, the multiple injuries to the back of the head and neck, and the incisions upon the hands and wrists: all which could have been inflicted with the cleaver produced. They also described the extraordinary appearance of the body: the underclothing quite damp, the face, neck, and chest washed with water; and the partial washing as well of the bedroom and kitchen floors as of the lobby between them. The only expert from whom we have not yet heard was Professor Penny of the Andersonian University, who examined the remains of the accused's apparel, recovered from Hamilton as already mentioned; the crinoline wires; and the cleaver, upon each and all of which he found stains and clots of blood.

To the admission of the prisoner's declarations, which it was then proposed to read, Mr Clark strenuously objected as having been extorted from the accused by questions; in respect of the inordinate length of her examinations; and on account of the traps laid for her by the Fiscal as before narrated. Lord Deas repelled the objections, holding that there was no ground in law for refusing to admit these declarations. They were read to the jury accordingly; but in the legal journals of the day the soundness of his Lordship's ruling was questioned. Here endeth the case for the Crown.

## IV

The evidence of the witnesses for the defence, though brief, was cogent. George Paton, milkman, who had been long in use to supply the

Flemings' daily wants, stated that on Tuesday, the 8th, he heard of the servant's death. On the previous Saturday he stopped his cart as usual at No. 17 Sandyford Place between half-past seven and twenty minutes to eight in the morning. His boy Donald went up to the door and rang the bell. It was immediately answered, witness could not see by whom, as the door was only opened 'a small bit'. No milk was taken in. The same thing happened on the Sunday and Monday morning. These were the only occasions when milk had not been taken in at that door.

Donald M'Quarrie, the milkboy, stated that he went his rounds with his master's cart on the Saturday in question, reaching No. 17 at the accustomed hour: about twenty minutes to eight.

> I went up and rang the bell. Old Mr Fleming answered it. I did not ring more than once. I had not to wait any time before it was answered. The first thing I heard after ringing the bell was the chain coming off the door.

> Are you quite sure of that? Yes. After the chain came off, the door was opened by old Mr Fleming. I saw him. He was dressed. He had on black clothes. He said 'he was for nae milk'. Witness never knew of old Fleming answering the door before.

Mrs Mary Fulton or Smith stated that she had known the deceased intimately for some six years. She also knew the accused as a friend of the dead girl, who always spoke of her in most affectionate terms. She last saw Jess M'Pherson alive on 28th June, when walking in Sauchiehall Street with her husband, and noticed that she seemed unwell. 'I do not feel very happy or comfortable with old Mr Fleming,' Jess told her, 'for he is actually an old wretch and an old devil.' This she said very seriously. Witness remarked that she was looking ill and asked what was wrong with her. 'I cannot tell you what the cause is,' she replied, 'because Sandy is with you'; but she promised to come to tea next Sunday, the 6th, her day out. 'And then,' said Jess, 'there is something I would like to tell you.' The secret was plainly of a nature so delicate that it could not be communicated in the hearing even of a married man. What it was Mrs Smith never learned, for on her next Sunday out poor Jess was indeed gone out—for ever.

Mrs M'Kinnon, a sister of the deceased, stated that Jess and the accused were affectionate friends. A month before the murder witness called on her sister and asked why she never came to see her. She said she had too much to do, adding 'that her heart was broken by the old man, who was so inquisitive that the door-bell never rang but he must see who it was and know all about them.' Martha M'Intyre, another servant of Mr Fleming's, stated that the old man was most curious as to the maids' doings—particularly so in all that related to the deceased. Witness had known him get out of his bed to see who had rung the door-

THE SANDYFORD MYSTERY 41

bell. Ann M'Intosh, sister of the accused, stated that James M'Lachlan, her husband, earned 30s. a week, which he invariably gave to his wife. (He must have been an ideal husband.) The accused's brother also contributed to her needs; he gave her money after every voyage and had given her 25 sovereigns last November. (He must have been a model brother.)

Robert Jeffrey, criminal officer, who conducted a search of the premises after the murder, stated that he found in old Fleming's bedroom a canvas bag, having on one side of it a bloody mark. He also found under a chair a strip of cotton, spotted with blood. On Mr Rutherford-Clark asking what had become of these significant finds, of which the defence now heard for the first time, witness said they were handed by him to the Procurator-Fiscal, who gave him a receipt therefor. It seems that subsequently they disappeared from the case, presumably as not forming links in the chain where with the Crown sought to bind the prisoner to the crime. Lord Deas suggested that the marks might have been other than blood-stains, but witness declined to accept his Lordship's hint. Superintendent M'Call, who saw and examined the stains, corroborated.

The last witness examined was a police constable, who alleged that between 8.30 and 9 p.m. on Saturday, 5th July, he saw two women come out of the front door of 17 Sandyford Place. They stood talking together for five minutes; then one went away and the other re-entered the house. (He seems to have mistaken the night.) Here endeth the case for the defence.

## V

Before we glance at the addresses of the learned counsel and the charge of the presiding Judge, it were well to remind the reader of certain proven facts whereof the case for the prosecution, as presented, offered no explanation. Such were the washing of the body, the dampness of the clothes, and of the lobby and the kitchen floor, the three footprints—on which alone the Crown could prove the presence of the prisoner in the house—so considerately left intact by the criminal when washing the rest of the bedroom floor, the trifling value of the articles abstracted, and finally the inexplicable lingering of the accused on the scene of her alleged crime: the murder being committed, according to old Fleming, at 'exactly four o'clock—a bonny, clear morning', and Mrs M'Lachlan not going home with her bundle till nine. Should it be said that she did so in order to remove from the vigilant and then unspectacled eye of old Fleming the damning traces of the deed, it may be answered that while this might be so as regards the kitchen and the lobby, it is inapplicable to the cleaning up in the bedroom, the door of which was locked and the key missing. If that kitchen floor were washed by the accused before nine o'clock on the Saturday morning, how came it to be still moist at five o'clock on the Monday afternoon, though dry by ten that night? It was a stone floor and, we are told, would dry rapidly, there being a good fire. But for none of these anomalies could the prosecution satisfactorily account.

The Advocate-Depute handled his case delicately. In view of the obvious stumbling-blocks in the prosecutor's path caused by the peculiarities of his chief witness, it behoved him to emulate King Agag. He relied for a conviction mainly upon the footprints of the accused, her all-night absence from her home, her pawning of the plate, her dealing with the deceased's garments, and her disposal of her own blood-stained raiment. Mr Gifford's white-washing of old Fleming, essential to a verdict adverse to the accused upon the charges as libelled, was surprisingly half-hearted and inadequate. The old gentleman, said he, had been aroused at 4 a.m. by cries of distress, had lain awake from 6 to 8, and risen at 9—although it was clearly proved that he was up and dressed before 7.40! (As the accused did not leave the scene till 8.30, it would never have done for the patriarch to admit an earlier rising.) With reference to these facts, and to what Mr Gifford termed 'the extraordinary circumstances of this case, which distinguish it from all others': the presence of old Fleming in the house at the time of the murder and his behaviour during the ensuing three days: he justly observed that *'the gravest possible suspicion attached to such a person so acting'*, and the jury could not wonder that he was apprehended and charged with being concerned in the crime.

> But the guilt of James Fleming is not the subject of inquiry at all. It is possible, in crimes of this kind, that more than one person is connected with it. If guilt be brought home to one, it will not be enough to say: 'Somebody else had a share in it.' If there were more murderers than one, and if the prisoner was one of them, you must find a verdict against her. For the question is, and it is the only question: Is the prisoner guilty or is she not guilty?—not had she confederates, not was she alone?

Even the prosecutor could not put it higher than that. He spoke for over two hours; and at 7.30 p.m. on the third day of the trial, Mr Rutherford-Clark rose to address the jury. As a defending counsel in criminal causes, like his gifted successors, the late Lord Aitchison and Mr Macgregor Mitchell, he had no equal at the Scots Bar, and the fine fight which three years later he was to put up for wicked Dr Pritchard is still recalled with admiration. But in the M'Lachlan case, as we shall soon see, he was hopelessly handicapped by the tactics which the accused's advisers, in their mistaken attempt to do the best for their client, had seen fit to adopt; and his argument, though brilliant and resourceful, was vitiated by his knowledge of its essential hollowness. On the conclusion of his address, which occupied an hour and a half, the Court rose.

The fourth day of the trial, Saturday, 20th September, began with the Judge's charge to the jury. His Lordship's handling of the case was not the least of the remarkable features by which it is distinguished. The charge had a bad Press. 'The conduct of Lord Deas,' observed the *Law Magazine and Review*, 'has been almost universally censured ... Instead of maintaining a proper judicial equilibrium, and holding the balance of justice even, he put his foot fiercely into one scale and kicked at the other. We shrink from the unpleasant task of analysing his charge ... It lasted four hours, and from beginning to end of it there is not one observation favourable to the prisoner; not one fair consideration of a doubt in her favour; not one suggestion that any fact renders her guilt a matter of the least doubt. On the contrary, facts that in our humble opinion tell strongly in her favour are either quietly ignored or disposed of by reckless assertion of the most transparent sophistry ...' The grave censure thus expressed by this responsible legal journal is mild in comparison with the torrent of adverse criticism poured forth by the popular Press, always excepting the *Glasgow Herald*, which rejoiced at the judicial vindication of 'the old innocent'. His Lordship's treatment of the evidence incompatible with the innocence of Fleming was a conspicuous element of this singular charge: the patriarch was too stupid to notice the condition of the basement flat or to make any inquiries; the milkboy had mistaken the time; what the deceased meant by calling him an 'old devil' was that he might 'look a little sharply' after the maids, and so on, and so forth. But the masterpiece of this judicial gloss upon the proven facts was his Lordship's explanation of the secret which the dead girl could not tell her friend Mrs Smith in the presence of that lady's husband: '*What she might have to say was that she was going to emigrate!*' The fact that when Lord Deas took his seat that morning he carried in his hand and laid down upon the Bench before him the Black Cap, the symbol of the prisoner's doom, shewed plainly that he was prepared for the worst; and the jury, following his Lordship's lead, and having presumably weighed the three-day's evidence with that scrupulous care and caution requisite to a matter of life or death, *after an absence of fifteen minutes* returned to Court with a unanimous verdict of Guilty.

## VI

And now I am free to disclose an astonishing incident with which I have been longing to confound the reader, a surprise so unlooked for and dramatic as would make the fortune of any writer of fiction—although I do not expect that it will make mine. The Advocate-Depute moved for sentence; and while the verdict was being recorded and the Court hummed with suppressed excitement, the prisoner summoned her counsel and earnestly spoke with him for a space. Whereupon Mr Clark announced that his client wished to make a statement, either by her own or by his lips, and Lord Deas said she could do so. Then for the first time the voice of Jessie M'Lachlan was heard in that chamber. Throwing back her veil and standing up in the dock she said loudly and distinctly: 'I desire to have it read, my Lord. I am as innocent as my child, who is only three years of age at this date.'

Amid a thrilling silence Mr Rutherford-Clark rose to read one of the most remarkable documents ever read in a court of justice. I shall have much to say about it later; meantime the reader should note that it, the statement, was made by her to her law agents on 13th August, so soon as she learned that old Fleming had been set at liberty, and was by them taken down to her dictation and signed by her. She told how on that fatal night she set forth to visit her friend. Contrary to his custom and to her expectation, she found old Fleming still up and sitting with Jess in the kitchen. The patriarch hospitably produced a bottle and they had each a dram. Reference was made to Mr John Fleming having commented on the undue consumption of his whisky, which the patriarch had accounted for by saying it had been used by young John. 'However,' said he to Jess, 'if ye'll haud your ill tongue, I'll gi'e ye half a mutchkin, if ye'll sen' for't.' To which overture the girl replied: 'Aye, I've a tongue that would frighten somebody if it were breaking loose on them'—a dark saying. The bottle giving out, Fleming asked the visitor to have it replenished and handed her 1s. 2d. for that purpose. He let her out at the back door into the lane. It was then hard upon eleven o'clock, and when she reached the public house in North Street, she found it closed. Returning empty-handed to the house, she saw in Elderslie Street one Mrs Walker, whom she knew by sight, talking to a friend. She found the back door shut; none answered her knock, and she looked in at the kitchen window; the gas was lighted but she saw nobody. The more important passages of the statement must be given in her own words.

I rapped at the door with the lane door key, and after a little old Mr Fleming opened the door. He told me he had shut the door on 'them brutes o' cats'. I went into the kitchen, and put the money and bottle on the table. The old man locked the door and came in after me. I told him the place was shut and I could get nothing. I then said: 'Where's Jessie? It's time I was going home.' He went out of the kitchen, I supposed to look for her, and I went out with him. When in the passage, near the laundry [bedroom] door I heard her moaning in the laundry [bedroom] and turned and went past the old man, who seemed at first inclined to stop me. I found Jessie lying on the floor, with her elbow below her and her head down. The old man came in close after me. I went forward, saying: 'God bless us, what is the matter?' She was stupid or insensible. *She had a large wound across her brow and her nose was cut*, and she was bleeding a great deal. There was a large quantity of blood on the floor. She was lying between her chest and the fire-place. I threw off my bonnet and cloak, and stooped down to raise her head, and asked the old man what he had done this to the girl for? He said he had not intended to hurt her—it was an accident. I saw her hair all down, and she had nothing on but a polka and her shift. I took hold of her and supported her head and shoulder, and bade him fetch me some lukewarm water. He went into the kitchen. I spoke to her and said: 'Jessie, Jessie, how did this happen?' and she said something I could not make out. *I thought he had been attempting something wrong with her*, and that she had been cut by falling. He did not appear to be in a passion and I was not afraid of him. He came in again, bringing lukewarm water in a corner dish. I asked him for a handkerchief and some cold water, as the other was too hot. He brought them in from the kitchen, and I put back her hair and bathed away the blood from her face and saw she was sore cut. I said to the old man: 'However did he do such a thing to the girl?' and he said he did not know, and seemed to be vexed and put about by what had happened. I asked him to go for a doctor, but he said she would be better soon, and he would go after we had got her sorted. The old man then went ben the house again, and I supported her, kneeling on one knee beside her. In a little she began to open her eyes and come to herself, but she was confused. She understood when I spoke to her, and gave me a word of answer now and then, but I could get no explanation from her, so I just continued bathing her head. I bathed it for a long time, until she got out of that dazed state and could understand better. I asked her whether I would not go for a doctor, and she said: 'No, stay here beside me.' I said I would. While I was sorting at her head, the old man came into the room with a large tin basin and soap and water in it, and commenced washing up where the blood was all round about us, drying it with a cloth and wringing it into the basin. I had raised Jessie up and was sitting on the floor beside her. As he was near us, he went down on his elbow and spilt the basin with a splash. *He spilled the water all over my feet and the lower part of my dress, and my boots were wet through.*

Jess asked to be put into her bed, and as Mrs M'Lachlan was unable alone to lift her—she was a big, heavy woman—old Fleming lent a hand. As she seemed to be getting weaker Mrs M'Lachlan again begged him to let her fetch a doctor. He looked at the patient, and said: 'There was no fears; he would go for the doctor himself in the morning.' She lay with her eyes shut till the day was beginning to break—about three o'clock. The old man was in and out of the kitchen making up the fire and preparing tea. Mrs M'Lachlan took off her wet boots and stockings, and carried them 'ben' to the kitchen to dry. During old Fleming's absence Jess regained consciousness. She told her friend that some weeks before the old man had been out on the spree with a brewer of his acquaintance and came home at 11 p.m. 'gey tipsy'. During the night he entered her room and bed, and attempted to take advantage of her. Upon her 'outcry' he desisted, and withdrew to his legitimate couch. Next morning she threatened to tell his son, her master, of the outrage, but he begged her not to do so, attributing his lapse to drink taken, and promising not so to offend further. There had been 'words' between them about it ever since; old Fleming continuing in terror lest his backsliding should be revealed. That night, so soon as Mrs M'Lachlan had left for the half-mutchkin, there arose between them an angry scene, the patriarch construing her reference to her tongue breaking loose as a threat to disclose to her friend his naughtiness.

> She had given him some words in the kitchen, and he was flyting and using bold language to her in the lobby after she was in the room, and she was giving it him back while loosening her stays; when he was there and going to take them off she went and shut the door to in his face, and *he came back immediately after, and struck her in the face with something and felled her* ... She also asked me if she was badly cut, and I said she was, and she said when the doctor came in the morning she would need to tell some story or other how she got it.

Without telling old Fleming that she now knew the truth, Mrs M'Lachlan again asked him why he had struck the girl? He said he was sorry and would make it up to Jess, and that if she, Mrs M'Lachlan, would never mention what she had seen, he 'would not forget it to her', whereupon she justly observed that it was a great pity she had anything to do with it. Jess said she must tell what had happened to the doctor or to Mr John Fleming. 'No, no, Jess,' said the patriarch; 'ye'll no' need to do that,' adding that if they held their tongues he would 'put everything to rights'.

> He would not rest content till I would swear it, and he went upstairs and brought down the big Bible with a black cover on it, and he made me swear on the Bible by Almighty God that I would never tell to man, woman, or child anything I had seen or heard between him and Jess that night. He said that he would make her comfortable all her life. After this he sat at the bedside.

Jess having occasion to rise, the old gentleman was requested to leave the room. She was very stiff and weak, and complained of being cold; so Mrs M'Lachlan put a blanket round her, recalled the patriarch, and between them they got her into the kitchen and laid her on an improvised couch before the fire. Between four and five she grew rapidly worse and asked her friend to go for a doctor. The old man was then upstairs. Mrs M'Lachlan put on her boots and Jess's French merino dress over her own, which was 'all wet and draggled', and went up to the front door, but found it locked and the key removed. She asked old Fleming to let her out as the girl was dying. He refused. She then went into the back parlour and threw up the window to see if she could see anyone whose aid she could invoke, but saw no one.

> I was leaving the parlour to go into the dining-room to look out in front when I heard a noise in the kitchen. I turned downstairs as fast as I could, and as I came in sight of the kitchen door *I saw the old man striking her with something which I saw afterwards was the meat chopper. She was lying on the floor with her head off the pillow, and he was striking her on the side of the head.* When I saw him I skirled [shrieked] out and ran forward to the door, crying to him; and then I got afraid when he looked up, and I went back up part of the stair, where I could go no further, as I got very ill with fright and palpitation of the heart, to which I am subject.

Holding to the wall, without power of motion, she stood crying: 'Help! help!' The old man came to the stair foot and looked up at her. 'Oh, let me away, let me go,' she cried; 'for the love of God, let me go away!' He came up and took her by the cloak, and said; 'I kent frae the first she couldna live,' and that if any doctor should come he would have to answer for her death, as she would have 'told'. 'Don't be feart,' he continued; 'only, if you tell you know about her death you will be taken in for it as well as me. Come down, and it can never be found out.' She was terrified, alone in the house with the murderer and his dead victim, and knew not what to do. 'My life's in your power,' said the tempter, 'and yours is in mine'; if both would keep the secret, both were safe. But if she informed on him, he would deny the deed and charge her with the crime. He asked her to help him to wash up the blood upon the kitchen floor, but she was incapable of action.

> He took the body by the oxters [arm-pits] and dragged it ben into the laundry [bedroom], and took the sheet and wiped up the blood with it off the floor. When he took up the sheet I saw the chopper, all covered with blood, lying beneath it. I beseeched and begged of him to let me go away and I would swear never to reveal what I had seen, in case of being taken up for it myself as well as him. *He said that the best way would be for him to say that he found the house robbed in the morning, and to leave the larder window open.*

The old man then gave her certain of the dead girls' gowns, instructing her to send them by rail to some out of the way place to lie till called for. Afterwards he brought down the plated spoons, etc., and directed her to pawn them in a false name—all this to simulate a burglary.

> He got some water at the sink in a tin basin and washed himself. He had taken off his coat and was in his shirt sleeves since after the time he killed the girl. His shirt was all blood when he took it off to wash himself, so he put it in the fire. He put on a clean one off the screen, and went ben to his own [dressing] room and changed his trousers and vest. He went down to the cellar for coals, brought them up, and put them on the fire. *The bell rang. He bade me open, but I said: 'No, I'll not go to the door; go you.'* IT WAS THE MILKBOY. *The old man took up no jug with him. He was in his shirt sleeves when he went up, but in a coat when he came down again. He brought no milk with him.*

He presented her with £1. 7s., which she agreed to accept, together with the other articles, promising never to breathe a syllable of what had passed. He said he would never see her want and would set her up in a shop. About 8.30 he let her out at the back door into the lane, and she made her way home in safety. She declared that she never had any quarrel with Jess; they were always most affectionate and friendly.

The reading of this document, which occupied forty minutes, was listened to by the crowded audience with breathless and intense excitement. No one knew what would happen in a situation at once so surprising and unprecedented. But Lord Deas was equal to the occasion. Having narrated at length the manner in which he conceived she had done what he termed 'her bloody work' and barbarously butchered her bosom friend, his Lordship expressed his entire concurrence in the verdict. 'There is not upon my mind a shadow of suspicion that the old gentleman had anything whatever to do with the murder.' As counsel and Judge he had never known statements made by prisoners after conviction to be other than false. A person who had committed a crime such as that of which the prisoner had been convicted was capable of saying anything. 'Your statement,' said his Lordship in conclusion, 'conveys to my mind a tissue of as wicked falsehoods as any to which I have ever listened; and in place of tending to rest any suspicion against the man whom you wished to implicate, I think *if anything were awanting to satisfy the public mind of that man's innocence, it would be the most incredible statement which you have now made.*' Lord Deas then assumed the Black Cap and passed sentence of death, ending with the formal commendation of the prisoner's soul to the mercy of the Almighty. 'Mercy!' exclaimed the doomed woman in the dock, 'aye, He'll hae mercy, for I'm innocent!'

## VII

Lord Deas's dictum as to the effect of the Statement upon the public mind proved unsound. The Press, not only of Glasgow, but of London and the provinces, was loud in denunciation of the conduct of the trial, the verdict, and the attitude which the Judge had seen fit to adopt throughout, especially with reference to the prisoner's Statement. Only the *Glasgow Herald* rejoiced at the complete vindication of 'the old innocent'. Sir Archibald Alison, who as Sheriff of Lanarkshire had conducted the preliminary inquiries, has well observed: 'She had not a fair trial; the minds of the jury were made up before they entered the box.' And he comments on the indecency of a verdict returned in fifteen minutes after a judicial charge lasting four hours. In his judgment there was a miscarriage of justice. 'The Statement,' he points out, 'bore the mark of truth, coincided in a remarkable way with the evidence, and explained much in the case which was otherwise inexplicable.'

Immediately upon her conviction Mrs M'Lachlan's law agents, a reputable firm of Glasgow writers, addressed to the Press a letter describing the circumstances in which their client had made to them her Statement. From the time of her arrest she insisted 'that Mr Fleming would surely [certainly] clear her.' When she learned from them of the old man's release, she was so greatly astonished that she would not believe it, until she sent for her husband to confirm the fact. She then informed her agents that she had a communication to make to them, and on 13th August the famous Statement was made. *The indictment was not served till the 30th.* On the 13th, therefore, they knew not what evidence would be brought against her, nor had they seen any of the witnesses for the prosecution. They had nothing to go on but the newspaper reports, for Mrs M'Lachlan would give them no information whatever. The Statement was most anxiously considered by her counsel and agents; the former were of opinion that as the Crown might fail to prove her presence in the house that night, her admission to the contrary must at all costs be suppressed. But it was decided to lodge a special defence that old Fleming committed the crime. Before the Court met on the last morning of the trial Mrs M'Lachlan sent for her counsel and agents, and insisted that her Statement should be read aloud in open Court. Mr Rutherfurd-Clark's decision to suppress it was much blamed at the time, and as things turned out this was certainly a grave error in tactics; but it is easy to be wise after the event. The fact, however, greatly hampered him both in his cross-examination of old Fleming and in his address to the jury.

Now that the cat was out of the bag, public opinion ran strongly in favour of the condemned woman's story; and the demand was urgent that its truth or falsity must be determined before she was sent to her death. Memorials were addressed to the Home Secretary both by her counsel and agents and by the general public. Committees were formed, meetings were held, even sermons were preached, for the purpose of securing a reprieve. Deputations waited upon the Lord Advocate and the Home Secretary. Never in any trial before or since was there such an ebullition of public feeling. Sheriff Alison and the Lord Provost of Glasgow lent the weight of their authority to a petition for further inquiry; and the eminent Professor (later Lord) Lister wrote to the editor of the *Herald*—who must have been much annoyed— expressing his opinion 'that the medical features of the tragedy are in remarkable accordance with the prisoner's statement'. On 3rd October a respite was granted from Whitehall to allow of time for some further investigation; but it was intimated that if such failed to confirm the truth of the prisoner's Statement, '*no hope can be held out to her of commutation of the capital sentence*'.

Meanwhile the venerable cause of all this fuss was confined to the house by reason of the popular resentment. On leaving the Court he had been assailed by groans, hoots, and hisses from an angry crowd, and hardly escaped undamaged from their hands. He fled to the villa at Dunoon, where the *Herald* described him as reading with much interest the printed comments upon the trial; but other papers proclaimed him the object of hostile demonstrations, and on occasion, like an early martyr, he was even stoned. So late as November he was reported to be mobbed at Greenock. What Lord Deas thought about this treatment of his protégé is not recorded.

Mr George Young, who had been Solicitor-General the year before, and afterwards became a distinguished Judge, was appointed Crown Commissioner to conduct the investigation, which opened on 17th October. The proceedings, invidiously known as 'The Secret Inquiry,' were held in private; the Crown being represented by the Procurator-Fiscal and the prisoner by one of her agents, Mr Dixon. The Commissioner had no power to compel the attendance of witnesses nor to administer the oath to such as were called before him; and the order of their coming was arranged by the Procurator-Fiscal, who, as the offical instigator of the recent prosecution, seems hardly the ideal person to inquire into his own conduct.[1] The investigation was concluded on the 20th and the result communicated to the Home Secretary. On the 28th the convict was respited 'until further significance of Her Majesty's

---

[1] These Gilbertian conditions curiously anticipated those under which a similar Official Inquiry was, subsequent to the trial, held in the case of Oscar Slater by the Sheriff of Lanarkshire at Glasgow in 1914.

pleasure'. On 6th November the death sentence was commuted to penal servitude for life.

This illogical and anomalous conclusion pleased nobody. Had the case occurred to-day and been reviewed by the Court of Criminal Appeal, Mrs M'Lachlan could have been allowed to give evidence in her own behalf and been cross-examined as to its veracity; old Fleming, too, could in the witness-box have been treated with a freer hand than Mr Clark was able to use at the trial. But the patriarch remained in seclusion at Dunoon, and the Fiscal refrained from intruding upon his retirement. His law agents, however, were very indignant at the Secretary's decision, which they held—and justly—'led to the inference that, in his judgment, Mr Fleming was other than innocent of the murder'. The Secretary intimated that he 'must decline to express any opinion on that point', and the matter came to nothing. But when we remember that the first respite was granted on the express stipulation that unless the truth of her story were established the woman must be hanged, the commutation had indeed in his agents' words, 'brought suspicion on the hitherto unblemished character of Mr Fleming'! But I think that in the circumstances 'the old gentleman' did not do so badly after all. Whatever happened, having been accepted as a witness for the prosecution, he could never be arraigned at mortal bar. How it might fare with him at that of a Higher Tribunal does not concern us.

## VIII

The Sandyford Mystery was the subject of two long debates in the House of Commons, in the course of which the Home Secretary defended the action of the Crown. The Statement, he said, was corroborated in many respects by the subsequent inquiry; admittedly Mrs M'Lachlan was an accessory after the fact, and as such had now received suitable punishment. The Lord Advocate (Moncreiff) explained for the benefit of his English critics the reason why, according to Scots law, old Fleming could not be put on trial for the crime.

Subsequently the papers called for in the debate and ordered to be printed were laid before the House, and formed the subject of further discussion, not only in Parliament but in the Press. Seventy-six witnesses had been examined at the trial; sixty-nine were called at the inquiry. most of these had testified before, but some were new. The prisoner's law agents told how she made her famous Statement. They knew nothing of the milk episode until she mentioned it, and only then got into touch with the milkboy and his master. The Flemings, father and son, had nothing material to say; but they admitted that there were openly in the house two silver tea-services, which were untouched, and that the whisky had a habit of disappearing. Old Fleming's hour of rising was nine. The deceased never had anyone staying the night with her. Mr Stewart, their next-door neighbour, said that on the night of the murder he went to sleep at eleven and was awakened two hours later by a scream from the Fleming's house. Mrs Walker and friend said they saw the accused in a grey cloak go into the lane at a quarter past eleven. Another woman corroborated these twain, and further stated that on passing No. 17 thereafter, she heard a wailing cry, as of someone in great distress, and saw that the windows in the area—those of the servant's bedroom—were lighted. Three sisters, going home from a dance, saw the dining-room gas alight at four o'clock in the morning. The milkboy and the milkman repeated their former evidence. The man had looked at his watch while the boy was at the door: it was exactly twenty minutes to eight. They called as usual on the following Sunday and Monday mornings. On each occasion old Fleming answered the bell and refused to take delivery of the milk.

One of the most interesting of the new witnesses was Miss Mary Brown, aged sixteen years. She said the deceased used to employ her to wash the steps and go errands. She called by her appointment at nine o'clock on the Saturday morning. Old Fleming opened the door upon the chain, let her in, and put up the chain again. He was dressed in black and had on a 'Sunday' coat. He asked her to wash the upper hall near the head of the stair, and gave her a cloth and a pail of water for that purpose. The floor was dirty, 'as if trampled on by persons having *soot* on their feet'. She smelt soot at the time. She saw no marks of blood, but one mark of a naked foot. The old man stood beside her all the time, and when her job was done and she was going downstairs to empty the pail, he bade her leave it where it was. 'He spoke only once, when I was going away. *He catched a grip of me by the hand and put his hand on my waist, and said I was a nice girl.*' He then gave her sixpence for her trouble and dismissed her. She told her mother, who said she must hold her tongue 'for fear she might get into some hobble about it'. Mrs Jane Pollock or Brown corroborated her daughter's evidence. Now if, as the *Herald* averred, little Mary were telling lies, she was surely an artist in fiction: the passage which I have italicized, if invented, is a master-stroke.

The three Crown experts were re-examined with reference to the medical features of the Statement. These were entirely consistent with all the appearances observed by them. The wounds on the face might have been received while the deceased was standing; they would fell and stun her. The other injuries were inflicted while she lay on the floor. Dr Macleod still stuck to the evidence of a struggle, which he said he observed in the kitchen: there was nothing else he saw contradictory of the Statement. Certain of the Briggate tenants, from whom on the Monday old Fleming had collected rent, stated that he then wore his best black clothes, not those he wore 'for ordinary', that his manner was 'raised like', and they thought something had happened to agitate him. Daniel Paton, clothes dealer, denied the fact, sworn to by Fleming at the trial, that he had sold to him an old brown coat. Much evidence was given by the friends and neighbours of the prisoner to the effect that she was of a very mild, gentle, and kindly disposition, neither thriftless, extravagant, nor prone to drink; and that she was a woman who, in the quaint Scots phrase, 'enjoyed' but poor health.

Mrs Mary Smith, re-examined, said that the prisoner and the deceased were almost like sisters. Jess often told her how she was tormented by old Fleming and could not get quit of him. She frequently said he wanted to marry her; she seemed disgusted by his attentions. On the last occasion of their meeting, a fortnight before her death, witness said: 'She was looking very ill; I never saw her looking so melancholy ... She said: "I'm no' weel. You don't know how I am situated; I live a miserable life. He [James Fleming] is just an old wretch and an old devil." I said: "Tell me the right way of the story; what has he done to you?" She said: "I have something to tell you, but I cannot tell you just now before your husband." She made the remark that she was well enough when the family was at home, and that *her misery began when she was alone with him.*' Witness was positive there was something gravely wrong from the serious tone in which Jess spoke. It is reassuring, however, to know from Lord Deas that it only denoted a purpose of emigration.

Mrs M'Kinnon, sister of the deceased, said that a month before her death Jess told her that her heart was broken by old Fleming, whom she described as 'an auld deevil', adding that she intended to give up her place at the end of the six months. Witness never spent the night with her sister, and old Fleming had no reason to suppose so. A fellow-servant of the deceased stated that Jess spoke of the old man as '*a nasty, dirty body*'; witness understood he had behaved indecently to her. The gardener at Dunoon stated that Jess told him old Fleming was very anxious to marry her, 'and would give her all he had if she would do it'. The brewer friend, with whom the patriarch had a day out as already mentioned, denied that old Fleming went home tipsy: 'he was hearty and in good spirits.' But the cabman who drove him home said he was so drunk he had to be helped up the steps. The ministers and elders of that Presbyterian temple in which old Fleming was as a polished corner, deponed reluctantly to the patriarchal lapse before referred to. A sheriff-officer, who had sifted the ashes of the kitchen fire, stated that he found therein a shirt button. Many other witnesses were examined, but these are those who contribute chiefly to our knowledge of the facts.

The outcome of the inquiry was this: on each and every point in which Mrs M'Lachlan's statement was capable of confirmation, its truth was clearly established; in no single instance was it in any respect contradicted. It fitted the proven facts so perfectly as to render its fabrication incredible. If it were false, then in Mrs M'Lachlan we have lost a fictionist more marvellous than Defoe; one so adroit as to foresee and account for facts and circumstances which it is humanly impossible she could have known she would be called upon to meet. And this masterpiece of mendacity, this feat of fraudulence, this dexterity in deceit was achieved by the illiterate authoress of those clumsy and idiotic declarations, concocted in her early efforts to escape from the meshes of the net wherein she had been so cunningly entangled— which, as Euclid would say, is absurd. On literary grounds alone, apart from all question of corroboration, the statement, in my judgment and *pace* Lord Deas, warrants belief. Only a supreme artist could have supplied the numberless minute torches, the telling strokes, which produce the lifelike effect of the figured scene. If these be lies, then indeed, as an humble tiller of the field of letters, I admire Mrs M'Lachlan's genius as greatly as I do that of her so gifted sisters, Miss Austen and Miss Ferrier.

IX

For fifteen years Jessie M'Lachlan 'dreed her weird' within the gloomy precincts of H.M. General Prison of Perth. She was a model convict. Years afterwards the chaplain told me her conduct was exemplary, and that throughout the long term of her punishment she ceased not to proclaim her innocence of the deed for which she had been condemned. On 5th October 1877 the gates of her prison-house were opened and she was released on ticket-of-leave. For the leading of a new life she was provided with a sum of £30, the wages due to her in respect of her penitentiary labours. She was in her four-and-fortieth year. After the trial her husband had emigrated with her child, now a lad of eighteen, and was living in the United States.

At first she sought refuge with a cousin in Greenock, where she hoped gradually to recover the sense of a living world. Looking backward across the gulf that separated her from the dreadful past, it must have seemed to her impossible that those old dim happenings should be still remembered. So much was changed, so many things had since befallen, that none could yet bear in mind the memory of her tragedy. But she knew not the inexhaustible persistence of a public-spirited and resourceful Press! Word of her release 'transpired'; speedily she was pursued, run to earth, and taken captive by enterprising journalists in quest of copy. She was paragraphed and interviewed, and only escaped the camera's fire because it had not yet occurred to our reporters to shoot their prey. The victim of newspaper enthusiasm found life a burden to her; so, seeing that in Scotland there was no rest for even the relatively wicked, she fled her native country and rejoined her husband in America. How she fared in the Land of Freedom is not recorded. She died at Port Huron, Michigan, on New Year's Day 1899, as her son intimated to the Greenock cousin, in the sixty-sixth year of her pilgrimage. Her death was due to an old affection of the heart, from which in her Glasgow days she had been wont to suffer. Whether or not in another and a better world she met once more her ancient enemy, who had long preceded her beyond the veil, is a matter of conjecture.

Should this partial and imperfect outline of her most attaching case arouse in some sympathetic bosom any interest, I would counsel the owner thereof to read the verbatim report of the trial. No mere abridgment can do justice to its manifold attractions. Indeed, as regards the Statement, none can possibly appreciate its merits who has not studied it *in extenso*. To compare her story of the crime with the facts established at the trial and the inquiry, will furnish an intellectual pastime more entertaining and worthier the effort than the solving of many crossword puzzles. But in an age of short-cuts and substitutes, when the part is esteemed greater than the whole, I have small hope that anybody will take my advice. If not, why then so much the worse for us both: the loss is his, and mine—or rather, my publishers'.

Twice have I had occasion to call at Sandyford Place and, like the heroic milkboy, to ring the bell of No. 17. The first time was while collecting my material; the second, to introduce Mr Irving, who, having read my book, desired to view the *locus* of a crime which peculiarly appealed to him. He was bred to the Bar, and in such cases had the advantage of the popular criminologist: he was an expert in his subject. We were courteously received by a genial physician, for thirty years the tenant of the house, which despite its grisly history he deemed a most desirable abode. Although the surroundings were different the house itself was unaltered; just the same as when gazed at long ago by morbid-minded crowds, a twelve-months' wonder to the curious. The grim little kitchen, the narrow lobby, the ill-lit bedroom within the shadow of the area—all were unchanged since that fatal Friday night on which was staged by its three protagonists the dreadful drama of the murder. We were cautioned not to discuss the case before the maids when we explored the basement flat, as they were happily ignorant of its darker associations. Probably they took us for sanitary inspectors, which indeed, in a sociological sense, we were.

'H.B.' conceived the notion of having a play written upon the tragedy; but alas, it never came to birth. He himself was keen to impersonate the patriarch, in whom he perceived a character study after his own heart. Doubtless he could have done so to the life, as far as acting and make-up were concerned. But I am afraid that old Fleming's broad Scots would have proved too strong for him in the end. Someone has since made a fiction out of the old facts, transferring the scene and the actors to England, and raising the social status of the parties to a degree that would have been most gratifying to the Flemings. But I doubt whether Jessie gains anything from her enhanced gentility, while I am sure that 'the old gentleman' loses much by dressing for dinner.

EDMUND PEARSON

# *That Damned Fellow Upstairs*

Mr Pickwick knew an old man who said that the rooms in the Inns of Court were 'queer old places'—odd and lonely.

'Not a bit of it!' said a sceptical friend.

Then the sceptic, who lived by himself in one of these rooms, died one morning of apoplexy, as he was about to open his door. Fell with his head in his own letterbox, and lay there for eighteen months. At last, as the rent was not being paid, the landlords had the door forced, 'and a very dusty skeleton in a blue coat, black knee-shorts and silks, fell forward in the arms of the porter who opened the door'.

Years after Mr Pickwick's adventures were over, entrance was one day forced into another queer old room in a London house, and, with a tremendous clatter, out tumbled another skeleton, of a still stranger kind.

The noise it made was not heard in America, since we were completely absorbed, that summer, in the first Battle of Bull Run. The story would be forgotten in England today, were it not for the admirable essay published seven years ago by the late Sir John Hall, Bart. This gentleman is respected by all those who appreciate scholarly descriptions of curious events.[1] It is probable, however, that of all who see my retelling of the tale, only experts like Messrs. Alexander Woollcott and S. S. Van Dine will be familiar with Sir John Hall's work. And as it has been solemnly asserted, in print, that the names of both Mr Woollcott and Mr Van Dine are but pseudonyms of the writer of this piece, the circle is very much narrowed. So I feel moderately safe in going ahead, especially as I have unearthed one or two details on my own account.

Towards noon of a day in July, in that far-off year, Mr Clay, the manager of the Catalonian Cork-Cutting Company, was in the rear of his premises in Northumberland Street, London. He heard two pistol

[1] *Scholarly, but somewhat less than gripping; Pearson's account is much livelier, hence its inclusion here.*

shots from within the house, one shot following the other at a five-minute interval. He paid no attention, since he knew that one of the residents of the house had, for a month past, anticipated Sherlock Holmes in the eccentric custom of indoor pistol-practice.

After a few minutes, a rear window on the second floor was opened, and there appeared the hero of the story. His conduct, his accoutrement, and some of his speeches, have always recalled to me those half-demented and curious persons who flit through the novels of Mr G. K. Chesterton. He was a man in his forties; wearing, I think, side-whiskers, and carrying in one hand an umbrella, in the other, half a pair of tongs. He put one foot on the sill, and seemed about to jump twenty feet or more into the yard.

This horrified the Catalonian cork-cutter, not only because the stranger's face was covered with blood, but because of the flagstones and an area, with iron railings, directly below the window. He adjured the bearer of the umbrella, in the name of God, to do nothing desperate, but to tell him what was the matter.

'Murder is the matter!' replied the gory one, and continued his preparations for a desperate leap.

Mr Clay sent one of his employees for the police, and ran indoors to try to get into the second-floor apartment. While he was banging at the locked doors, he heard glass breaking, and on looking out again, found that the mysterious person had jumped into the yard; fought off a workman who tried to stop him; clambered over a high wall into the next yard – still armed with the umbrella; gained an alley between the houses; and made his way into the street.

Here, he was surrounded by a group of people who had come running from various directions. He complained that someone who lived at Number 16 had tried to murder him. One of the men in the street must have secured the umbrella—perhaps while the wounded man was adjusting his cravat, or brushing off his clothes—for the stranger asked for the umbrella again, and said that he must be getting to his office. This in spite of the fact that he had lost his hat; had a terrible wound in the back of the neck; another, which was bleeding freely, on his cheek; and that both his hair and whiskers were singed.

Duty was evidently the keynote of his character. He was an officer and a gentleman, and to introduce him by name, he was Major William Murray, late of the 10th Hussars, but a total stranger to all in the street. As it will appear presently, deception was in his eyes a far more grievous offence than personal violence, and to him unsportsmanlike conduct seemed the blackest of sins.

A man in the crowd reasoned with him about going to his office.

'You are badly wounded,' said this one.

'Am I?' replied the Major.

'Indeed, you are fearfully wounded.'

Then the Major remarked:

'It's that damned fellow upstairs—Grey.'

'There is nobody named Grey in that house,' the man returned. 'But if you mean the man I saw you go in with, about half an hour ago, *his* name is Roberts.'

Then, at last, the Major allowed a faint note of bitterness to creep into his tone.

'He told me,' he said, 'he told me, that his name was Grey.'

Meanwhile, much was going on in and about Number 16 Northumberland Street. The occupants of that and nearby houses had all heard the pistol shots, and one of them had heard other noises—as if someone were beating a mattress. But no one gave much thought to the reports, since they all knew the habit of their neighbour, Mr Roberts, of amusing himself by target practice. Roberts was, by profession, a solicitor; actually he accommodated people by lending money. This he did at no great disadvantage to himself—his idea of a proper rate of interest being 133⅓ per cent, per annum.

Inside the house, during the talk on the street, was a Mr Preston-Lumb, an engineer. To him came young Mr Roberts, son of the moneylender.

'Oh! Mr Lumb,' he cried—forgetting, in his excitement, the glories of the hyphenated name, 'Oh, Mr Lumb, someone has been and murdered Father!'

Thus, at last, we learn the real origin of the remark which Miss Lizzie Borden called up the stairs to Bridget Sullivan, on another warm and sanguinary noonday, many years afterwards.

Meanwhile, the man in the crowd, and most of the crowd, too, were escorting the wounded Major, first to a chemist's for immediate relief, and then to a bed in the Charing Cross Hospital. His injuries were serious, but he was able, as they walked along, to give the First Citizen a perfectly lucid account of the surprise attack which had been made upon him by the fellow who said his name was Grey.

When the police arrived, and began to search for Mr Roberts, another inquirer came upon the scene. This was one Timms, a man who had been engaged in washing down the back of the house. To him, shortly before the shots were fired, had come Mr Roberts, given him a shilling, and asked him to go to the top of St Martin's Lane, and buy a linnet. He added that the price of the bird was ninepence. Now, Mr Timms returned, and was left in possession of the linnet, and of the threepence change.

This, in a modern American murder trial, would have been a

winsome incident, to be repeated to the jury by the weeping lawyer for the defence, coupled with a demand for the instant acquittal of the prisoner, as one whose tender heart was solely concerned with feathered songsters of the air.[1]

The police, by means of ladders, at last effected an entrance to the rooms of Mr Roberts. To these locked apartments hardly anyone, not even the moneylender's son, had ordinarily been admitted.

The officers looked at an amazing sight. The rooms were elaborately overfurnished in the French style of the period of Louis Philippe. There were half a dozen good watercolour paintings, with heavy gold frames. Brackets and shelves were ornamented with statuettes and bric-à-brac, under glass covers. The floor space was crowded with ormolu tables and boule cabinets. Everything in the room was filthy with dirt and dust— the thick, black encrustation which follows years of neglect. On the floor was a great heap of crumpled papers, also powdered with dust, while the marble mantelpiece was scarred and chipped by the bullets from Mr Robert's pistol.

In the front room the ornate and dirty furniture was little disarranged, but the other room showed the marks of a terrific fight. Chairs and gilded tables had been upset. The dust had been beaten down; the inlaid cabinets were smeared by bloody fingers. There were splashes of blood on the walls, and a shower of drops of blood on the glass covers over the ornaments. In places, the room looked 'as if a bloody mop had been trundled round and round'.

The police found parts of the broken tongs, 'actually coated with bits of flesh and blood', and another weapon of the fight, a broken wine bottle, lying in a pool of blood. Near the wall in the front room, his head a shocking mass of wounds, lay the owner of all this: Roberts, the moneylender. He had a dozen or twenty injuries, any one of which looked as if it alone should have been instantly fatal. Yet he lived, and could talk.

He, also, was taken to the hospital, where, to the astonishment of the surgeons, he lived for six days. Most of this time he was conscious, but did not say much to help the police. He said that Murray, whom he met by accident in the street, had come to his rooms for a loan. And then, 'Murray shot himself in the neck, attacked me with the tongs like a demon, and hit me with a glass bottle.'

Aside from the improbability of this, the chief wound of the Major made the moneylender's story absurd, and indicated that Roberts had

[1] Or, perhaps, in an English trial, if the late Sir Edward Marshall Hall were defending. The recent publication of the life of this eminent defender of accused persons has done much to hearten American jurists, by revealing that our courts have no monopoly of oratorical flapdoodle.

done the shooting. The Major had said, from the start, that Roberts was an utter stranger, whom he had met in the street; that he had been asked to come to the house in Northumberland Street to discuss a proposed loan to a company, and that he had been shot and almost killed for no reason which he could imagine. He then defended his life with the weapons that came to hand.

Young Roberts was brought to his bedside, but still the name meant nothing.

'What Roberts?' said the Major.

'Why, the son of the Roberts who shot you,' was the reply.

Then the exasperation of Major Murray burst forth again.

'Why, damn him,' he said, 'he ought to be hanged for shooting a man on the ground!'

To the sporting Major, especially at a time of the year when the thoughts of all Englishmen were dwelling upon the approach of the grouse season, it was scandalous that Roberts had not flushed him before firing.

Since Roberts died without giving any reason for the fight, and since it was a mystery to Major Murray, the police continued to search the rooms for an explanation. At last, as in a detective story, they believed they had found it in a few marks on a bloodstained sheet of blotting paper. Holding this to the mirror, they deciphered the name 'Mrs Murray', and an address: Elm Lodge, Tottenham. There were also some fragments of letters from Mrs Murray to Mr Roberts.

The inquest was held ten days after the fight. The jury met in the hospital, where they could most easily inspect the battered remains of the man who lost the combat, and also question the winner of it. The so-called Mrs Murray appeared, heavily veiled. When she lifted this veil, she disclosed 'the features of a remarkably pretty woman' of about twenty-five. Her name was Anna Maria Moody. Seven or eight years earlier, she had left her family 'to live under Major Murray's protection', and she had called herself Mrs Murray for five years. The Major had taken Elm Lodge for her, and had always treated her in the most 'noble-hearted manner', in accordance with his disposition, which was 'amiable and kind'. When her baby was born, she was embarrassed for funds, and was unwilling to ask for more money from the Major, who, although apparently a bachelor, was 'under heavy expenses'.

Someone told her of Roberts; she went to him, and found him willing to lend her fifteen pounds, provided she signed a three-months' note for twenty pounds.

She had never been able to pay the debt, but had continued to make quarterly payments of five pounds, as interest. From the beginning, Roberts had tried to make love to her, and offered to release her from the debt, if she would leave Major Murray, and go to Scotland with him.

It was believed that Miss Moody told the truth; that she was faithful to the Major; and that she was forced to accept Roberts's company, and go with him—usually chaperoned by his wife—to church and to entertainments; and even to write affectionate notes to him; and that all this was the craft of a helpless woman who was badgered and threatened by a usurer. She said the two men had never met before the day of the fight, and Major Murray had not known of the other's existence.

The Major gave his testimony in the hospital ward; his throat bandaged, and his neck too stiff to let him move his head. He unfolded a tale which impressed everybody with its melodramatic qualities and caused Thackeray to refer to the affair in *Roundabout Papers*.

Roberts had accosted him in the street; introduced himself as 'Grey', and offered a loan of fifty thousand pounds to the Railway Palace Hotel, of which project the Major was a director. The two men went to Roberts's rooms, where the host left his guest alone for a few minutes. (He went on the errand about the linnet, in order to get rid of a possible witness.) He came back, stopped behind the chair in which the Major was sitting, and, under pretence of looking for some papers, held a pistol directly against the neck of his victim, and fired. The Major fell to the floor, paralysed. Roberts left the room again, and came back to see the Major beginning to move. He walked up and again fired at his right temple. The outrush of blood from this wound relieved the Major a little, and, as he said, 'I knew if I could get on my feet I could make a fight for it.'

He opened his eyes and saw the tongs. With these in his hands, he jumped up and attacked his intending murderer. Then occurred a fight which raged all over the room. The tongs were smashed against Roberts's skull, after which the Major found a large black wine-bottle and smashed that in the same manner. Both men were up and down, sprawled on the floor, and fighting desperately for whatever weapon the Major tried to employ. Once, Murray caught up a metal vase and threw it at the other's head—but missed. Two or three times, Roberts seemed to be down and out, but he would recover his feet, and—a hideous sight—come lurching towards the Major, who was trying to find an escape from the apartment. At last Roberts fell on his face as though dead; the Major pushed him through into the front room, shut the folding doors, and leaped out the window. He regarded the men in the back yard as possible enemies, because he thought that people who could listen to pistol shots and all the uproar of the fight, and take no notice of it, must be associate ruffians in a den of thieves and murderers.

Major Murray's story was corroborated by all the facts known to the jury, who brought in a verdict of 'justifiable homicide' – this amidst the applause of the crowd of spectators.

Roberts's motive for the attempt at murder seems absurdly inadequate but it is probable that, in his desperate infatuation for Miss Moody, he thought that with the Major out of the way he might somehow become the heir to her affections. How he planned to dispose of the body is not clear: perhaps, in the mass of other rubbish which filled his strange dwelling, he thought that the corpse of a retired officer would pass unnoticed.

Miss Moody, like Mr Timms's linnet, disappears from the history. Whether she was a member of the Major's family at a later date, I do not know.

If you should be eccentric enough to look at *The Times* for April 1, 1907, you will find this, under *Deaths*:

MURRAY. On the 28th March, at Ossemsley Manor, Christchurch, Hants, Major William Murray, late 97th Regiment, and 10th Hussars. Service Newmilton, 9 a.m., Wednesday. Cremation, Woking. No flowers, by his special request.

All the bullets of that damned fellow upstairs had not prevented the gallant Major from reaching the hearty old age of eighty-eight. But not even in the Crimea—if he was in that war, which is doubtful—did he ever come so near death as on that day when he fought 'like a demon' against a man whose name, and whose purpose, were alike, to him, a mystery.

# HORACE WYNDHAM

# *Maria Manning*

I

Maria Manning has two claims to notoriety. She murdered Patrick
O'Connor; and she destroyed the vogue of black satin for feminine
wear. In the former activity she was assisted by her husband; in the
latter one, she had no help.

Switzerland had the dishonour of being Mrs Manning's native
country. She was born there Marie de Roux, the daughter of a respectable couple, at Lausanne. With a laudable desire to 'better herself,' as
soon as she grew up she went to England, where her ambition was to
become a housekeeper. As a preliminary, she entered the service of
Lady Palk, in the more humble capacity of maid.

While thus employed, she appears to have given full satisfaction; and
when she left, it was with a batch of glowing testimonials, one of which
declared her to be of an 'affectionate and pious disposition.' Hence, she
was very soon offered a situation with the family of the Duke and
Duchess of Sutherland. This was in the establishment of their daughter,
lady Blantyre, then living at Stafford House. As before—being clever,
adaptable, and hard working—she acquitted herself in a fashion that
left nothing to be desired.

Although occupying no more exalted position than that of a lady's
maid, Marie de Roux was something of a 'catch.' She had been treated
liberally by her mistress and visitors; and, instead of squandering them,
had banked her wages and tips. Also, on the deaths of her parents, she
had inherited a few hundred pounds. Added to this, she was an
attractive-looking young woman, with a good figure and complexion,
and was always smartly dressed. Hence, it is not surprising that she
should have had a number of 'followers'.

One such, with whom her name was coupled, was a certain Patrick
O'Connor, a man employed as a gauger in the Customs Department
at the London docks. He had first met her (without the formality of an
introduction) while she was with her mistress at Boulogne, where he
himself happened to be spending a holiday. On his return to London,

he had kept up the acquaintance, and visited her at Stafford House. Marie de Roux, too, for all her demureness, also visited him at his lodgings. Before long, the pair were on such intimate terms that, if they happened to have had any strict regard for propriety, the purchase of a wedding ring would have been imperative. But O'Connor's intentions towards the attractive and well-dowered Swiss girl appear to have been strictly dishonourable. Indeed, if a shocked biographer is to be credited, they were 'nothing less than to obtain possession of her person without first accepting matrimonial responsibility.'

While Marie de Roux had shown herself not overburdened with a rigid morality, there were limits to the lengths to which she was prepared to go. This was one of them. When, however, she informed O'Connor that she expected to be led to the altar by him, he abruptly broke off the 'friendship' that had sprung up between them.

It was an action for which he was to pay; and to pay dearly.

Although she wrote him a reproachful letter on the subject, it is questionable if Marie de Roux had any real regard for Patrick O'Connor. What, however, she did have was a very real regard for his money. Her nature was essentially avaricious, and O'Connor had the reputation of being a 'warm' man. It was not undeserved, for, in addition to his job as a gauger, he carried on the more profitable business of money-lending as usury among his fellow employees in the Customs. Altogether, he was said to have amassed a capital of £10,000, the bulk of which he had invested in railway shares.

## II

Despite his scurvy treatment of her, Marie de Roux did not quarrel openly with O'Connor. Outwardly, at any rate, she remained on good terms with him. As it happened, too, she had a second string to her bow. This was one Frederick Manning, a guard in the service of the Great Western Railway Company, whose acquaintance she had made while she was living with Lady Palk in Devonshire. Having discovered that her weak point was money, he represented himself as occupying a much better position than was really the case. In this he was successful; and Marie de Roux, taking him at his own valuation (and incidentally wanting to show O'Connor that his defection had not troubled her), agreed to become Mrs Manning.

Her ideas being somewhat grandiose, the bride (who received from the Duke and Duchess of Sutherland their good wishes and a handsome present) resolved that the wedding should be a 'function,' and the ceremony took place at St James's Church, Piccadilly, in the summer of 1847. The bridegroom would have much preferred the simpler routine of a registry office, but he had no voice in the matter. He was a weak-willed person, with a fondness for alcohol, and then, as afterwards, despite the fact that she had promised to love, honour, and obey him, very much under his partner's thumb. Still, he did persuade her to do one thing. This was to change her baptismal name from Marie to Maria.

Shortly after his marriage, Manning left the railway company with which he had been employed. Perhaps it would be better put to say that the railway company left him. It appeared that a box of bullion was stolen in transit from a train; and, as he was on duty at the time as guard, he fell under suspicion of being concerned in this business, and also in several other thefts that had occurred.

Having lost his position with the railway company, Frederick Manning induced his wife to invest part of her capital in a public house at Taunton. As he drank more beer than he sold, the investment proved unprofitable. Returning to London, his thoughts still running on beer, he took a second public house at Haggerston. This, too, was a failure, and swallowed up another £100. The pair then moved to Bermondsey, where, in the summer of 1849, they rented an unfurnished house in Minver Place. Since it was larger than they could afford, they proposed to have a lodger.

Although she was now a wife, Mrs Manning was quite ready to resume her intrigue with Patrick O'Connor. He, too, declared himself of the same opinion, and agreed to become a lodger in her house. But when the time came to make the move, he announced that he had changed his mind and would stop where he was. Thereupon, Mrs Manning was so annoyed that she took out a summons against him in the Whitechapel County Court. Thinking that he had perhaps put her to some trouble, O'Connor voluntarily offered three weeks' rent, and the summons was withdrawn. Mrs Manning, however, had not really sustained any loss, for, during the interval, she had secured another tenant. This was William Massey, a medical student.

While she was crafty enough to hide it from him, Mrs Manning nourished a bitter grudge against Patrick O'Connor. First of all, he had jilted her. This was bad enough. What, however, was still more unforgivable was that she had lost some money in a speculation that he advised. Accordingly, she determined to be 'revenged' on him. He was to pay; and he was to pay with that which he most valued.

### III

Maria Manning set about her dreadful preparations with a cold-blooded callousness that can never have been equalled. As a preliminary, she got her husband (who was in her confidence) to buy a crowbar and shovel, and then to help her to dig a grave under the kitchen flagstones. Her next purchase was a sack of quicklime. When the shop assistant remarked on this, she declared that she wanted it 'to destroy slugs.'

With a view to remaining herself in the background as long as possible, Mrs Manning hit on an ingenious scheme for securing the presence of her intended victim. This was to get her lodger, William Massey, to ask him to dinner as his guest. Massey, under circumstances on which an odd construction might be put, agreed without demur, and despatched a cordial invitation, worded as follows:

> Dear O'Connor, I shall be happy to see you to dine with me and my sister, as she is coming from Derbyshire to stop a few weeks with me. She will be most happy to be introduced to you. Dinner will be ready at half-past five o'clock. If you are engaged, drop me a line. Trusting you are quite well,
>
> I am, dear O'Connor, yours truly,
> WILLIAM MASSEY.

O'Connor, scenting another 'conquest,' and unaware that William Massey had no sister in London, swallowed the bait. When he arrived at the house, he asked for Massey and his sister. Mrs Manning said they had not yet come in, and suggested that he should stop and talk to her. But O'Connor had other ideas. He wanted the dinner he had come to eat, and was so annoyed at the absence of his host that he refused to stay.

Directly he had gone, Mrs Manning upbraided her spouse for not doing his part in helping her to lure him into the kitchen. If his subsequent 'confession' is to be credited, she said to him, 'You cur-hearted villain, you have spoiled my scheme. I wanted to cook his goose, and now I am certain he will never come here any more.' Thereupon, so Manning declared, 'I asked her what would become of her immortal soul if she committed such a wicked act.'

Mrs Manning, whose views on psychological problems were ahead of her period, was undisturbed by the question. 'We have no soul,' she informed him. 'When we are dead, we are like a lump of clay. We shall not suffer hereafter if we kill that scoundrel.'

O'Connor had slipped through her fingers, but only for the time being. Mrs Manning's next step was to get rid of William Massey, to whom she gave notice, on the grounds that she and her husband were leaving London. When he had gone to lodge somewhere else, she sent her intended victim another invitation, this time written by herself:

Dear O'Connor, I shall be happy to see you to dine with us this day at half-past five. I trust you are quite well.

Yours affectionately,
MARIA MANNING.

This had the desired effect, and, on the evening of August 9th, the guest duly presented himself. After he had been in the house a few minutes, his hostess made the odd proposition that he should go downstairs and wash his hands. When he protested that he had done so before starting, he was told that 'a very particular young lady' was expected. Thereupon, and all unsuspiciously, he walked into the kitchen. While he stood with his back to her, Mrs Manning took a pistol from her pocket, and shot him through the head. 'I saw O'Connor,' said her husband afterwards, 'fall across the grave. He was moaning. As I never liked him very well, I battered in his skull with a chisel.'

Although her main object was now accomplished, Mrs Manning still had other business afoot. Leaving her husband in that grim kitchen, to solace himself with beer, and keep off inconvenient visitors, she hurried to O'Connor's address in the Mile End Road. She was so well known there that the landlady thought it quite natural that she should 'wait for him' in his bedroom. Making the most of her opportunity, she unlocked his trunks and took from them a packet of securities, consisting of bonds and shares, together with a few pounds in cash and a couple of watches. Having done this, she returned to Minver Place, and methodically proceeded with her dreadful preparations for disposing of the body and destroying the evidence of the crime. The first thing she did was to strip it naked and burn the clothes. As O'Connor was a tall man, she, helped by her husband, then doubled back the legs and secured them with a cord. Having done this, they sprinkled a gallon of vitriol over it, lowered it into the grave, and filled up the cavity with lime, afterwards shovelling in the earth and replacing the flagstones in position. Then, untroubled by either conscience or digestion, Mr and Mrs Manning sat down, as if they had not a care in the world, to a hearty meal of roast goose.

## IV

Patrick O'Connor was not the sort of individual who could disappear without some enquiry as to the cause being made. When he did not turn up to his work at the docks, a messenger was sent to his rooms. Miss Armes, the landlady, said that he had gone to dine on the previous Thursday with the Mannings, and suggested that they would know where he was to be found. Two of his friends, William Flynn and Pierce Walshe, called to ask for him at Minver Place. Mrs Manning, however, declared that he had not been there. This made the enquirers so suspicious that, when two more days had elapsed, they went to the police.

Although they did not at the moment suspect any foul play, the police thought it would perhaps be as well if they made some formal enquiries on the spot. But, when they got there, they were astonished to find the house shut up and empty, and every stick of furniture removed. Nor had the Mannings left any address behind them with the neighbours. This looked so curious that the callers felt uneasy. Yet, although they examined every nook and corner, there was no trace anywhere of Patrick O'Connor.

Constables Henry Barnes and James Burton were quite ordinary policemen; and the modern Scotland Yard official would probably have laughed at them and their rough-and-ready methods of investigations. Still, these methods secured results. The first thing they noticed was that, while the rest of the house was dirty, the kitchen was scrupulously clean. The occupants, too, had even taken the trouble to scrub the floor. This fact struck the pair so odd that they began to examine the flagstones. They were rewarded by finding that the cement joining two of them was much fresher than it ought to be. On lifting these flags, they found a mass of similarly soft cement. As no workmen would have done the job in such a clumsy fashion, they resolved to see what the cement covered. There was no necessity to dig far before they saw, lying huddled up in the cavity, the naked and decomposing corpse of what had once been Patrick O'Connor.

The remains of the murdered man presented a horrible spectacle. There was a bullet wound in the skull; the head and face were battered out of recognition; and much of the body was destroyed by the action of the quicklime that had been sprinkled over it. But identification was still possible, for a dentist positively declared that the false teeth in the mouth had been made by him for O'Connor.

The inevitable slip. The murderers had thought of most things, but not of this one.

A hue and cry for the two Mannings (against whom a coroner's jury returned a verdict of wilful murder) followed immediately. But they had left no visible traces. Still, as they had gone off with their luggage, it was obvious that they must have gone by cab. Since cabs were seldom hired in Bermondsey, the police had no difficulty in discovering that two cabs had been called to Miniver Place. One had driven Mrs Manning, first to London Bridge, and then to Euston, and the other had driven her husband to Waterloo. From these points the 'fares' had disappeared. Still, Mrs Manning's driver could give a little more information. She had, he said, left some boxes, labelled 'Mrs Smith, passenger to Paris,' in the cloak-room at London Bridge.

The fugitives had secured a good start; and the fact that they had disappeared separately increased the difficulty of tracking them. The newly organized detective force was on its mettle. But those entrusted with it handled the business in a fashion that redounded to their credit. The trail of Mrs Manning was picked up first. As a preliminary step, the boxes left at London Bridge, and labelled 'Mrs Smith,' were examined by Superintendent Haynes, who found in them a number of articles that had belonged to the unfortunate O'Connor, together with some linen that was identified as the property of Mrs Manning. She was thus connected with 'Mrs Smith.'

The telegraph wires sent messages flashing all over the country; and full descriptions of the 'wanted' couple, together with the numbers of the stolen bonds, were forwarded to every police-station throughout the provinces. A special watch was also kept on the Channel ports, as it was felt that an attempt would be made to leave England. In fact, the authorities were so convinced that one would be made that the Admiral at Portsmouth dockyard was instructed to despatch a frigate, H.M.S. *Fire Queen*, in chase of an emigrant ship bound for America. After overhauling a Prussian man-of-war in error, the pursuers, under cover of night, caught up with the other vessel. When, in response to a peremptory signal, the captain replied that he had two passengers on board named Manning, he was ordered to produce them. Having done so, it was discovered that they were a couple of maiden ladies of blameless reputation. As they were also of American nationality, apologies were demanded and given.

## V

The 'passenger to Paris' labels, on the trunks left by Mrs Manning at London Bridge Station, had merely been intended to throw the police off the scent. Where she had really gone to was Edinburgh. As soon as she arrived there. she took a bedroom in Leith Walk, calling herself 'Mrs Smith,' and announcing that she had come from Newcastle.

So far, Mrs Manning had exhibited a diabolical skill in covering her traces. She now, however, embarked on the series of false steps that was to prove her undoing. With incredible carelessness, she offered some of the stolen securities to an Edinburgh firm. They were quite prepared to buy them, but, as a business precaution, they enquired her name and address. When she said that she was Mrs Smith, and that her father was a Mr Robertson, of Glasgow, her accent struck the firm as so little suggestive of Glasgow or Scotland that making some excuse, they asked her to come back a couple of days later. They also mentioned their mysterious visitor's call to the Chief

Constable, and hinted that he should 'keep an eye' on her. He did better. He kept two.

The Edinburgh firm's next step was to telegraph to London, enquiring about the securities that had been offered them. As soon as they had got a reply, they went to the police; and the police went to the alleged 'Mrs Smith.' On being arrested her trunks were searched by Superintendent Moxey, who found in them, together with a volume of *Family Devotions for Every Day in the Year*, a packet of share certificates that had belonged to O'Connor. After this, having no doubt as to her identity (which Mrs Manning did not trouble to deny), he brought her before a magistrate.

'This is a very serious charge, madam,' said that official. 'It is my duty to tell you that you are not required to make a statement at this juncture.'

But Mrs Manning, who was always fond of the sound of her own voice, insisted on making one.

'It is absolutely ridiculous to suggest that I murdered Mr O'Connor,' she declared. 'He was the kindest friend I had in the world. If he had been murdered, it was done by that villain of a husband of mine, while I was out for a walk. I hope you gentlemen will catch him.'

The magisterial proceedings in Edinburgh only lasted a few minutes; and, on their conclusion, Mrs Manning was escorted to London. As her arrest was known, an immense crowd assembled at Euston to see her arrive in custody. But while she was being bustled into a cab, she disappointed the mob that swarmed round it by covering her face with a handkerchief.

The capture of Frederick Manning followed a few days later. Shortly before disappearing, he had disposed of some of the stolen bonds. With this money in his pocket, and a few pounds which he had raised by selling all his furniture, he then crossed from Southampton to Jersey. By a remarkable coincidence, one of the passengers on the steamer happened to be a young woman who lived next door to him. At the moment she had not heard of the murder. When, however, she read an account of it a couple of days later, she told the Jersey police that he must be somewhere on the island. After a vigorous search, he was discovered by them living in a cottage at St Heliers, under the assumed name of Jennings, and professing to be the London representative of a gin-distiller.

Keeping him under observation, the local police telegraphed to London for a detective who could identify him. One was despatched for the purpose. On being confronted by this officer, Manning, addled with drink, and abject with terror, cut a pitiable figure. Before he was even charged, he insisted on making a 'confession.' In this he sought to throw the whole responsibility on his wife, declaring that, from start to finish, he had acted under her 'influence.'

What the precious 'confession' amounted to was as follows:

'My wife said to me, "That old villain O'Connor has been the cause of my losing much money. As I am a living woman, I mean to be revenged on him." I said to her. "Do, in the name of God, abandon all such wicked thoughts." Her reply was, "Now I shall begin to get things ready to cook his goose." She then bought a shovel, and dug under the flagstones in the kitchen. When O'Connor came to dinner with us that night, no food had been prepared, but the table was laid with dishcovers. While he was in the kitchen, washing his hands, I was upstairs in my bedroom. Presently I heard the discharge of a pistol, and my wife came to me and said, "Thank God, I have finished him off at last. I think no more of what I have done than if I had shot a cat on the wall." I went into the kitchen, and saw O'Connor lying across the grave; he was moaning. As I never cared very much for him, I battered in his skull with a chisel. My wife cut off his clothes, and we put the body in the grave, covered it with lime, and trod down the earth. My wife said she was sorry she had not read prayers over the body. This will show you what sort of a woman she is.

'After the murder, my wife went to O'Connor's lodgings, and took away his shares and bonds. On the Saturday she asked me to sell some of the shares. I said I could not do this, as it would be committing a forgery. Still, I borrowed £100 on them, and gave most of it to her. On the Monday she told me that two men had called to enquire for O'Connor while I was out. When I said they were sure to be police officers, she said, "Pray, don't tell me that, or I shall faint." We planned to go to new York, and I went to sell the furniture to a dealer. As soon as I came back, I found my wife had gone. I do not know where she is, but I hope the wretch has been captured.'

Clearly, no love lost between the pair.


## VI


The trial of the Mannings took place on October 25th and 26th, 1849, at the Central Criminal Court, and was presided over by Chief Baron Pollock. Sitting with him were Mr Justice Cresswell and Mr Justice Maule. The Attorney-General, Sir John Jervis, conducted the prosecution; and Frederick Manning was defended by Sergeant Wilkins, and Mrs Manning by Sergeant Ballantine and Sergeant Parry. Altogether a strong team.

The trial was regarded with immense interest by the general public; and, the moment the doors were opened, a surging mob attempted to secure places from which to watch the proceedings. Only a limited number, however, could get into the gallery, for admission tickets had been issued by the sheriffs, just as if the court were a theatre. Among those specially favoured, and permitted to sit on the bench, were the Austrian Ambassador, the Spanish Minister, the Secretary to the Prussian Legation, Bishop Wiseman, Lord Augustus FitzClarence, and the Marquis of Hertford; while seats in the well were allotted to representative members of the worlds of art, literature, politics, and Society. But, even then, the accommodation was so taxed that, according to one account, 'several gentlemen of the first distinction, and two or three ladies, were glad to be given chairs in the dock itself, immediately behind the prisoners, but separated from them by the Governor of Newgate and various officials.'

Mrs Manning's toilet in the dock was apparently chosen to impress the jury. Thus, it consisted of a black satin gown, a cap and ruffles of white lace, a plaid shawl, and a pair of primrose yellow gloves. Mr Manning, for his part, did not aspire beyond a 'respectable suit of black.' This was regarded by the public as a delicate tribute to the memory of O'Connor. 'He struck us,' observes a reporter, 'as altogether repulsive, being a bullet-headed, thick-necked individual, with a half effeminate expression. Also, he semed nearly dead from terror.' The attitude of his companion, however, was very different. 'She walked into the dock with a firm, unfaltering step; and, during the whole time that she stood there, her countenance did not betoken the least symptom of agitation or alarm.'

Both the prisoners pleaded 'not guilty' to the indictment charging them with the murder of Patrick O'Connor. Mrs Manning also demanded, through her counsel, that, as a foreigner, she should be tried separately, and by a jury *de medietate linguæ*. It was a nice point. The court, however, refused the application, declaring that, having married an Englishman, she was no longer an alien, and, consequently, that an all-British jury was quite good enough for her.

A fact that had puzzled the authorities was that, while O'Connor's skull showed a bullet wound, no pistol had been found. An explanation, however, was furnished by a pawnbroker. This individual said that, a few days after the discovery of the murder, the male prisoner had pledged one at his establishment; and a marine store dealer in the New Cut was prepared to swear that he had sold him this identical weapon. As for that part played by Mrs Manning, a gunsmith said that he had instructed her in loading and firing a pistol; and it was also proved that she had accepted delivery of the quicklime and crowbar.

William Massey, the medical student who had lodged in Minver Place for three months, said that Frederick Manning had often asked him for information on anatomical subjects. A non-anatomical question, however, that had been put to him was 'if a murderer went to heaven.' In his, Mr Massey's opinion, this was not the probable destination of such people. Still, he could not say what it was. Nor could he explain the curious attitude he had observed all through the dreadful business, nor give any acceptable reason for not suspecting that something criminal was afoot and warning the authorities. Altogether, an unsatisfactory witness.

Evidence of the discovery and condition of the corpse was given by the police and doctors. The medical 'experts,' however, were not very reliable, for one of them positively declared that there was 'no known test for human bloodstains.' This astounding contention was unchallenged. Two of O'Connor's colleagues, David Graham and Pierce Walshe, said they had met him crossing London Bridge on the afternoon of August 9th, and that he had told them he was on his way to dine with Mrs Manning. Three days later, when they called at Minver Place, to enquire for him, Mrs Manning declared he had not kept the appointment. When they asked for her husband, she said he had gone to church. As this was a very unusual practice on his part, they felt suspicious.

Both Sergeant Wilkins and Sergeant Ballantine made strenuous efforts on behalf of their respective clients. Wilkins, who appeared for the male prisoner, had begun life as a clown in a circus; and his forensic methods were always a little suggestive of the sawdust. But they were the methods of the period, and went down with juries. He began by alluding to the reports of the case that had been printed in various Sunday papers, 'conjuring the jury to treat this depraved Press with ignominy and honest English indignation.' After this, he expounded his theory of the crime. 'My hypothesis,' he told the twelve men in the box, 'is that the female prisoner premeditated, planned, and concocted the murder, and made her husband her dupe. It is lacerating and agonizing for me,' he added, 'to depict a husband criminating a woman, and that woman his wife, yet my sense of duty and love of justice leave me no other alternative.'

Sergeant Wilkins had abused the Press. Sergeant Ballantine abused Sergeant Wilkins. He roundly dubbed his rhetoric as 'unnecessary and vulgar'; and, further, declared that the conduct of his learned friend 'in thus attempting to exculpate Frederick Manning at the expense of Mrs Manning—to blacken the character of a prisoner, and that prisoner a woman—was unparalleled in a Court of Justice.' He was prepared to grant that an 'illicit connection' had existed between his client and O'Connor, but this 'lubricious dalliance' did not, he argued, prove that she had murdered him. He even went so far as to describe her as 'a woman of frail but kindly feelings.' As for the certificates found in her possession, he held it a reasonable assumption that, in view of their equivocal relationship, they had been given her by O'Connor. The 'wages of sin,' in fact.

The Attorney-General, in his reply, made short work of these ingenious theories; and the Chief Baron summed up dead against both prisoners. They were represented by different counsel, he pointed out, and each protested that the crime was the act of the other. The male prisoner had admitted being present when the victim was done to death; and the female prisoner had possessed herself of the murdered man's property, and left London under a false name. It was for the jury to decide if such conduct were consistent with her innocence, and also if the murder could have been committed by one of the accused without the full knowledge and help of the other.

## VII

A British jury will forgive a woman most things. There is, however, one thing which they will not forgive. This is maltreating a corpse. Mrs Manning had maltreated that of O'Connor to a horrible extent, for, not only had she buried it in quicklime, but she had also poured vitriol over it. Thus, it was inevitable that, together with her husband, she should be found guilty.

When the verdict was delivered, the prisoners were asked if they wished to say anything before sentence was pronounced. Frederick Manning had nothing to say. His wife, however, had a great deal to say, and insisted on addressing the court.

'There is no justice nor fair treatment for a foreign subject in this country,' she declared passionately. 'I have had no proper protection from the judges, or from the prosecutor, or from my husband. I am wrongly condemned. My solicitors should have called witnesses to prove that the shares were bought with my own money. I have lots of letters from Mr O'Connor to show his regard for me. I think, too, that, considering I am a woman and alone, and have had to fight against my husband's statements, as well as against the prosecution, and that even the judge himself is against me—well, I think that I am not being treated like a Christian, but like a wild beast of the forest. The judge and jury will have it on their consciences for giving a verdict against me. I am not guilty. I have lived in respectable families, and can produce testimonials of character. If my villain of a husband, through jealousy and revenge, chose to murder poor Mr O'Connor, I really don't see why I should be punished. That is all I have to say just now, except that I wish I could express myself better in English.'

The court listened patiently to this harangue. But it was all to no purpose, and sentence of death was passed. This duty devolved upon Mr Justice Cresswell.

Scarcely, however, had he begun, 'George Frederick Manning and Maria Manning, you have been convicted of the crime of murder,' when he was interrupted.

'I have not been convicted my lord,' screamed Mrs Manning furiously. 'I will not stop here and let you say it. You ought all to be ashamed of yourselves!'

While the judge was continuing, she kept up a running commentary. Then, when the last solemn words, 'to be hanged by the neck until you are dead, and may the Lord have mercy on your soul!' had been uttered, there was another scene, for Mrs Manning clung to the ledge of the dock, and once more expressed her opinion.

'Base and shameful England!' she shouted at the top of her voice. 'There is no justice in this country!'

## VIII

From the Old Bailey dock the pair were removed to the condemned cells at Horsemonger Lane Gaol. As soon as she arrived there, Mrs Manning, always full of resource, wrote two letters, asking for a respite. These were addressed to the Queen and the Duchess of Sutherland. No replies were returned. What, however, were returned were the letters themselves. Still, if disappointed, Mrs Manning was not depressed. On the contrary, she appeared rather proud of the notoriety accorded her, and conducted herself with immense dignity towards the prison officials.

Despite the fact that he was briefed by her, Sergeant Ballantine appears to have had no delusions about the lady. 'Although she was my client,' he remarks in his *Reminiscences*, 'I suspect she was the power that really originated the deed of blood.' Still, he did his best to get her another trial, with a mixed jury in the box. The court, however, ruled that, having become a British subject on her marriage, she had lost her privileges as an alien, and thus had been properly tried by an all-British jury.

'On being told by the Rev. Chaplain the result of her appeal, Mrs Manning seemed much chagrined; and, when exhorted to confess, she flatly refused to do so, emphatically declaring that the crime had been committed by her unfeeling spouse.' The Established Church having failed, a Roman Catholic priest then tried his hand. But the result was no better, for 'she would not listen, and was rather rough in her refusal.' Nor would she see her husband.

'Tell him,' she said to the governor, 'that he has brought me here.

He is a liar and a coward. Until he learns to tell the truth as to what happened, I do not want to see him.'

Despite the strenuous efforts of the chaplain and a 'benevolent lady visitor,' to direct them to higher things, Mrs Manning's last thoughts were concerned with purely mundane matters. Thus, we read, 'on being told the exact date fixed for her execution, she calmly set to work and made a new pair of drawers, expressly for the purpose of being hung in.'

The Rev. Mr. Roe had better luck with the male prisoner, for Frederick Manning indulged in a veritable orgy of 'repentance.' At the chaplain's suggestion, he wrote several letters to his wife, begging her to 'repent.' They were all couched in the customary sanctimonious strain that marks the average epistle from the condemned cell; and were full of smug assurances that—despite his regrettable slip—he would join the unfortunate O'Connor in heaven.

A specimen letter was as follows:

I address you as a fellow sinner, and not as my wife ... We may already consider ourselves as cut off from the world. The consciousness of this truth does not, however, prevent me from expressing my earnest solicitude for the happiness of your soul, as well as for my own. I do therefore beseech and implore you to be truthful in all you utter, and that you may not be tempted to yield to any evil suggestion of the enemy of our souls' welfare, or to question for one instant that we shall shortly appear before our God in judgment ... I earnestly pray that you will look to God for the pardon you need (and of which I feel my own need also), through the merits of our crucified Redeemer.

Mrs Manning responded to this unctuous rigmarole with some dignity and logic, for she pointed out that it was only her husband's statements that had condemned her. This happened to be true; and, had she been tried separately, it is doubtful if she could have been convicted, since such statements would not then have been accepted.

On the Sunday preceding the execution, Maria Manning and her husband attended a special service in the prison chapel. It must have been a nerve-racking ordeal, for the Rev. Mr. Roe 'delivered a very impressive sermon, in the course of which he made frequent and pointed reference to the unhappy criminals, who wept bitterly. The reverend gentleman also took occasion to desire the prayers of the congregation on behalf of the two convicts, their wretched brother and sister, who had but a few more hours to live.'

## IX

The day fixed for the double execution was Tuesday, November 13th, 1849. As was the savage custom at that period, it was to be carried out in public. All through the previous night an immense crowd, attracted by the promised spectacle that the morning would offer them, gathered in the vicinity of the prison. Catering to the evil passions that such scenes invariably let loose, the tenants of the houses opposite the scaffold did a roaring business in letting 'seats to view.' A place at a window commanded a couple of sovereigns; and half a crown was the minimum price for a peep from a roof. Even the branches of the trees in the gardens had their occupants. But the great mass of would-be spectators had assembled immediately in front of the prison wall, pressing against the stout wooden barriers that prevented them coming too near. There they prepared to spend the long night, in ghoulish anticipation of what the next morning would bring. A mob composed of practically every section. The cream of Mayfair, and the scum of the New Cut. Smart young Guardsmen and contingents from the clubs; medical students and costermongers; shop assistants and navvies; errand boys and clerks; women and children; gutter-merchants selling 'last dying speeches and confessions'; pickpockets and prostitutes openly plying their trade; people fighting, and people fainting; everywhere drinking and gambling and debauchery; devilled kidneys and jorums of punch in the houses and on the stands; saveloys and beer in the booths under the flaring naphtha lamps; the air hideous with ribald songs and black-guardly obscenities; jeers and cat-calls without intermission. Altogether, the conduct of the mob suggested a Saturnalia. It formed the subject of a memorable letter in *The Times* from the pen of Charles Dickens:

> A sight so inconceivably awful as the wickedness and levity of the immense crowd collected at the execution this morning could be imagined by no man, and presented by no heathen land under the sun. The horrors of the gibbet, and of the crime which brought the wretched murderers to it, faded in my mind before the atrocious bearing, looks and language of the assembled spectators. When I came upon the scene at midnight, the shrillness of the cries and howls that were raised from time to time, denoting that they came from a concourse of boys and girls already assembled in the best places, made my blood run cold.
>
> ... When the day dawned, thieves, low prostitutes, ruffians, and vagabonds of every kind, flocked on to the ground, with every variety of offensive and foul behaviour. Fightings, faintings, whistlings, imitations of Punch, brutal jokes, tumultuous demonstrations of indecent delight, when swooning women were dragged out of the crowd by the police, with their dresses disordered, gave a new zest to the general entertainment.
>
> ... I am solemnly convinced that nothing that ingenuity could devise to be done in this city, in the same compass of time, could work such ruin as one public execution, and I stand astounded and appalled by the wickedness it exhibits. I do not believe that any community can prosper

where such a scene of horror and demoralization as was enacted this morning outside Horsemonger Lane Gaol is presented at the very doors of good citizens, and is passed by, unknown or forgotten. And when, in our prayers and thanksgivings for the seasons, we are humbly expressing before God our desire to remove the moral evils of the land, I would ask your readers to consider whether it is not a time to think of this one, and to root it out.

But the public conscience is stirred slowly; and, despite this spirited protest, public executions remained to blot the Statute Book and debauch spectators for another twenty years.

## X

The morning of November 13th. The last one she would ever know. At a quarter-past eight Mrs Manning, who was said to have slept soundly, was conducted to the chapel. There, for the first time since they had stood in the dock together, she spoke to her husband. 'I trust,' he remarked, 'that you are not going to depart this life with animosity towards me.' After the Sacrament had been administered, they were permitted to talk to one another for a few minutes.

'I hope we shall meet in heaven,' said Manning unctuously, when Mr Keene, the governor, announced that the interview must come to an end.

The two Mannings were to be 'turned off' by Calcraft. A thoroughly experienced practitioner in all connected with his grisly business, he stepped forward and deftly adjusted the pinioning straps.

Only in that moment did the woman's iron nerve fail her.

'Will it hurt me, Mr Calcraft?' she faltered.

'Not a bit, my dear madam,' was the brisk response. 'That is, if you remember to keep quite still.'

When the pinioning was completed, she had a last request to put.

'I shall be obliged,' she said to the governor, 'if you will be so good as to forbid anybody to take a cast of me for exhibition at Madame Tussaud's establishment.'

'I will do my utmost to prevent it,' was the response.

Comforted with this promise (which, by the way, was not fulfilled, for it was more or less inevitable that she should have a niche in that Valhalla of criminality, the Chamber of Horrors), she then offered the surgeon a handkerchief.

'Please cover my face,' she said. 'I do not want the public to stare at me.'

With the passage of every moment, the hour of doom was drawing nearer. All being in readiness for the final act in the drama, the grim procession was assembled, each in the properly appointed place. First, Mr Sheriff Abbott, with want of office; then Mr Keene, the prison governor, and Mr Moore, his deputy; then the chaplain, reading the opening words of the burial service; then, with turnkeys on either side of them, Frederick Manning, in a frock coat, and Maria Manning, in a black satin gown; just behind them, Mr Harris, the surgeon; and, lastly, a trio of ghoulish figures hovering like ill-omened vultures in the rear, Calcraft and a couple of his assistants.

Eighty years ago, things at such times were done differently. No half a dozen steps from the condemned cell to the gallows drop. Instead, and with what suggests a refinement of cruelty, the Mannings were located in a part of the prison that required them to traverse a long corridor and mount a steep flight of stairs. At one spot, too, in a stone-flagged passage, they had to walk over quivering planks, beneath which their graves had already been dug.

The scaffold had been erected on the flat-topped tower above the prison entrance. While the twin nooses that dangled from the cross beam were adjusted, Frederick Manning, in a state of collapse, had to be held up by a couple of turnkeys. Maria Manning, however, stood there without a tremor.

In that last moment, the chaplain made a fresh effort to extract from her an admission of guilt.

'I have nothing to say,' she declared firmly.

The prison bell tolled nine. At a nod from the governor, Calcraft, stepping aside, pulled back a lever. Instantly the trap-doors on which the doomed pair, trussed and helpless, had stood a moment earlier, gaped apart, and they fell crashing through them. As they disappeared into the void, the huge mob below set up a shuddering roar of mingled triumph and execration.


A black flag fluttered in the breeze. Patrick O'Connor was avenged.

ROBIN SQUIRE

# Patrick Mahon
# The Possible Innocent

Often the only witness of a murder is the victim, and therefore beyond giving evidence. Unless a murderer makes a full confession of his actual crime, a great part of the history of the murder is pure conjecture. One reads that the police only need to show means, motive and opportunity to bring a charge of murder; the final decision that condemns the defendant is the jury's, and the police are probably thoroughly glad that it does. In such cases the jury must decide whether the defendant is a liar or is telling the truth. In spite of all warnings to the contrary, the defendant's life to the date of the trial must cause a bias in his favour or against him.

Patrick Mahon was one of the two professional criminals whose cases are analysed in this book.[1] Unlike Steinie Morrison, who was simply a thug, Mahon had what are usually called 'advantages'. He was handsome, middle-class, with enough organizing ability to make a success of various positions of commercial responsibility. Perhaps his professional opportunities were not as good as he would have liked, nor as profitable, because Mahon had a couple of very expensive hobbies. He liked to play the generous fellow, to be the first to stand a round of drinks, and he was a dedicated Don Juan. Putting up the required front for both of these activities took more money than he could earn, and so he turned to crime to boost his income. It was petty crime at first—a dud cheque here, a confidence trick there. He was caught often and often went to prison to serve at first short, and then longer sentences. Finally, possibly because he had learnt a few tricks in prison and possibly because he grew impatient of the small returns gained from small crimes, he set out to rob a bank.

This bank incorporated the manager's living quarters. A young servant girl, hearing a noise, went to investigate, with more courage than caution. Mahon practically battered her to death. He received five years hard—plenty of time to think things over.

This departure into violence gives us an interesting sidelight on

[1] Classic Murders (*London—Foulsham, 1970*). *The other cases are those of Crippen, Thompson and Bywaters, A.A. Rowse, Major Armstrong and Steinie Morrison.*

Mahon's character, all the more interesting because it could indicate one of two things. Either he was a man who panicked easily, or he was ruthless and violent to the point of being completely amoral. As the story of Mahon develops you will see that either theory would have been tenable. The choice is yours, but the story will read differently according to that choice. Certainly, Mahon could have floored the poor child with one straight left; instead of which he was lucky to avoid a charge of attempted murder at the very least.

Mahon was married. Every time he came out of prison, his wife was waiting for him. She supported herself while he was 'inside', kept the home going, and was ready to welcome him back. She gave him what so many ex-criminals lack—the background to a fresh start, if he were inclined to take advantage of it.

When Mahon returned from his five-year stretch, he found that his wife had been working for a prominent London firm, and she used her influence to get him a job as sales manager with the company. This suited Mahon admirably, and he did very well at it. Good-looking, outgoing and friendly, his extrovert personality was ideally suited to this kind of occupation. He was an almost instant success.

Mrs Mahon was undoubtedly a very long-suffering woman, as the wives of habitual criminals must of necessity be. She was prepared to put up with a lot, but there was one thing that she would not tolerate— her husband being unfaithful to her.

It was, of course, a naïve expectation. Suspecting Patrick was up to his old philandering tricks, Mrs Mahon lost patience, and she engaged the services of a private detective.

Women of Mrs Mahon's type, especially in the early 1930's, hired prived detectives for one reason only—to obtain evidence for a divorce. it appears that Mrs Mahon had finally had enough of her husband, because, even if divorce was no longer the unthinkable step it had been in the Victorian and Edwardian periods, it was still serious enough. And a divorced woman still did not find all social doors open to her.

In briefing her detective, Mrs Mahon handed him a railway cloak-room ticket, saying that she 'found it lying around' and that it belonged to her husband—investigation, please.

The ticket was for a suitcase. In wanting to know the contents, Mrs Mahon may have been motivated by one of several factors. She may genuinely have thought that this suitcase belonged to Mahon's girl friend, conveniently lodged in a station luggage office, to be taken out at a moment's notice on the way to a 'dirty weekend' in some cosy hotel.

Mahon spent a considerable time away from home, not always on his employers' behalf, even though he claimed that it was. Mrs Mahon had checked and found several days unaccounted for. On the other hand, she may have suspected that Patrick had gone back to his burglarious ways and that the suitcase contained the 'swag', neatly hidden. She may even have guessed at a more serious crime—Mahon's behaviour couldn't have been exactly normal during the previous week or two.

In any case, the little detective pattered happily off to the station cloakroom and presented the ticket.

Whatever fiction, films and TV would have us believe, the life of a private detective is normally abysmally dull, mostly concerned with standing in wet, windy streets watching the blank wall of a house until the bedroom light goes out, or drinking cup after cup of rather terrible coffee, while watching a 'suspect' fare far better on steak and chips. It must undoubtedly have been the high spot of the little man's career when he received in exchange for the ticket an overnight bag with the initials E.B.K. and opened it there and then on the luggage office counter. Inside he found a butcher's knife and a quantity of woman's clothing, heavily bloodstained.

It is curious how often in the accounts of factual crime, one comes across the words 'and then the murderer made his fatal mistake'. Many psychologists believe that criminals carrying a burden of guilt, often subconsciously, and subconsciously desire discovery and therefore punishment. So blatant are some of these blunders that one wonders if this cannot be true: Crippen with his mistress dressed in the dead wife's clothes; Major Armstrong with the scone; Rouse with his curious remark about a bonfire as he walked away from his own blazing car. All these are errors so stupid that one wonders how people even with limited intelligence (and in most cases the general intelligence of the murderer seems to have been average, if not above average) could have imagined that their chances of getting away with the crime could possibly have been furthered by them. By these errors, they literally threw their own lives away.

Admittedly, Mrs Mahon may not simply have found the ticket 'lying around', as she claimed. It might have been, for instance, in a jacket pocket, and a wife, looking for evidence against a husband, can dig fairly deep. But the fact remains that the ticket was there to be found, and Mrs Mahon found it.

However, we have left our private detective at the railway station with his grisly find. He quickly closed the bag, and probably his eyes as well, and hot-footed it to the nearest police station, carrying the bag—the bag with the initials E.B.K.

E.B.K. Emily Beilby Kaye. A woman of about thirty-five, un-married, not particularly good-looking, but placid, easy-going, a thoroughly nice person, employed by a company with whom Mahon did business. He met her during a routine call at her company's office and apparently dated her casually, as he had probably dated a great many other women in similiar circumstances. They hired a punt and went on the river to Staines. In a quiet backwater he seduced her, and found that she was not a virgin.

It must be emphasized here that, although Mahon subsequently made a number of statements, we have no way of knowing how far they were true. The only other witness, as so often in these cases, was beyond being questioned. It was the fashion of the day to presume that a murderer, by definition, must be the devil incarnate, and that the victim, also by definition, must be the 'innocent victim'. One might say, with justification, that the victim's behaviour is irrelevant to the issue, since there are no acceptable grounds for murder, and the British courts do not recognize 'justifiable homicide'. Certainly murder was not justified in this case, but Mahon did make attempts to present himself in as favourable a light as possible by emphasizing Emily Kaye's willing part in the affair. She was, after all, no dewy-eyed teenager. She was an adult woman of some sophistication, and could hardly have been raped on those leafy reaches of the Thames, even on a week-day.

Actually Mahon's statements had the reverse effect. He was accused of trying to 'black the name of the dead'.

Today we might have difficulty in understanding the emphasis placed on the loss of Miss Kaye's virginity. But even forty years ago, premarital intercourse was very rare, and no 'nice' spinster was supposed even to know of the existence of sex. Of course, men had mistresses, but they tended to be 'of a certain class', and a kept woman was a lonely figure, not accepted in the society she might otherwise claim as her own.

However, Emily Kaye did not seem at all reluctant to indulge in an affair with Mahon. She was apparently genuinely in love with him, although he did say in one of his subsequent statements that 'he liked her in many ways, but never cared for her tremendously'. This was a fairly common case of a man wanting a casual affair purely on a sexual basis, and a woman who wanted love, marriage and the continued protection of a normal, secure relationship. This was undoubtedly heightened by the fact that she was no longer young and could consider her future chances of marriage virtually non-existent.

Mahon had some money dealings with Miss Kaye, during which he claimed that she speculated in French francs on his behalf, this being a common practice at the time. He claimed that he scraped up the money, and they shared the proceeds fifty-fifty. Twice she gave him a £100 bank note, which he cashed without the usual counter-signature on the back, because he suspected some kind of trap. How he cashed the notes without a signature is not revealed. There were people at the time, of course, who were of the opinion that this story of speculation in francs was untrue, and that he had simply bled the poor girl for money, as people in his position often do. And it may, of course, be true. Emily Kaye could hardly confirm or deny it at the time of Mahon's arrest.

At that time Patrick Mahon had everything going for him. He had a job he liked and in which he was successful, a comfortable home and a log-suffering wife, an obliging mistress who loved him more that he loved her, and a little extra money on the side. It couldn't have worked better for him if he had planned it that way, as possibly he did. If things had continued in this way, Patrick Mahon would probably never have stood in the dock at the Old Bailey.

Then two unfortunate things happened. Emily Kaye became pregnant, and she lost her job. The two facts are probably interlinked—no employer would retain on his staff a woman who became pregnant, whether she be married or unmarried. And, unmarried, she certainly would have no chance whatever of gaining a decent post again, because no firm would give her a reference in such circumstances.

To say that Emily Kaye was desperate would be a understatement. Although long past the Victorian era, when illegitimate children were treated from birth as the criminals that many of them by force of circumstances became, society in the 1930's was still not prepared to accept the 'fallen women', even as a fit subject for rehabilitation. Sex was still considered an appetite which, once indulged, was awakened to a voracious degree. A woman who had once engaged in sex as a *pleasure*, rather than as a marital duty, was simply not to be trusted where one's husbands, brothers and sons were concerned. Lady Chatterley was a warning to everyone whose views were advanced enough to read it—if they could get a copy.

An unmarried mother, even if her child was secreted in a foundling home or put out for adoption, could expect only the roughest deal from life. Domestic service at cut-rate wages was the best that she could expect. Many people still held that such women, by their godless behaviour, had no right to enter a church to attend divine service.

Emily Kaye was a well-educated woman wo had held an executive position at a reasonably decent wage. She would not have taken kindly to working as a skivvy for some woman who, considering herself to be the soul of rectitude, would grind the fact of her 'sin' into her every time she committed the slightest domestic offence. Patrick was the father of her child. Patrick should marry her, and they would emigrate to South Africa, where the irregular origins of their union would not be known.

They would make a fresh start, and everything would be wonderful, if only . . .

If only Patrick loved her. This was the single fact that stopped the dream from being feasible. Patrick was quite unwilling to leave a job he liked and a wife who provided a background he found convenient. He may even have been in love with his wife in his own way. Certainly he owed her gratitude, which he may or may not have felt. He had indulged in a casual affair which had grown out of all proportion and had fathered a bastard, which was the last thing in the world he wanted to happen. And now he was being badgered by a desperate woman who had, under the circumstances, become an expert in applying pressure.

This is perhaps the moment to consider what today would appear to be the obvious solution. Illegal abortions were, of course, obtainable. Decently and aseptically performed, they were crashingly expensive, disguised as appendicectomies in highly priced nursing homes. Back-street abortions were notorious in their danger, and improperly cleaned knitting needle being the most commonly used instrument. The death rate from septicaemia was very high. Pregnant women drank hot gin and nutmeg, hoping that the resultant effects would dislodge the foetus. It seldom did.

But even if abortion was considered, and we don't know that it was, this would not have been part of Emily's plan at all. Whether she wanted the baby or not, what she wanted most was Patrick, and she was determined to have him.

Patrick was a man who lacked decision. This is shown by his behaviour throughout the whole affair. He seemed incapable of simply saying to Emily Kaye; 'No, I won't leave my wife and marry you. No, I won't go abroad with you. I don't love you enough to live with you for the rest of your life.' He simply let the matter drift, the situation worsening day by day. As his character weakness revealed itself, Emily's strength grew, and she showed herself increasingly as a woman of great force and staying power.

At about this time, she found out—probably searched and found out—that Mahon had served five years for the attack on the servant girl during the unsuccessful bank robbery attempt. She used this as a weapon against him. If he did not go abroad with her, she would tell his employers about it and, for good measure, go to Mrs Mahon and reveal the fact of her pregnancy. She now had Mahon completely at her mercy and could apparently force his hand in any direction she wished.

It may seem extraordinary that a woman could do such a thing to a man she confessed to love. But it must be remembered that in desperation both men and women can reach the state in which they feel that if only they could get together in happier circumstances, they can 'make up' for what they have done, and everything will be forgiven and forgotten. Human nature can be extraordinarily naïve. She may noot have meant ot use her knowledge—it might only have been a threat. But she was desperate, and desperate people do extraordinary things.

(It must be re-emphasized here that all this information has been assembled from Mahon's statements, there being no other relevant witnesses. A great deal of this must be conjecture, but the narrative seems to follow a logical pattern.)

Stirred to action by the threats, Mahon bought Emily Kaye an engagement ring and put it about among their mutual friends that Emily was engaged to a certain Derek Patterson, with whom she would shortly be sailing to South Africa. The prosecution at his trial made much of this as evidence of a murder plan, and indeed it does have a ring reminiscent of Crippen's *modus operandi*. Howeer, Emily Kaye was satisfied that at last Mahon was falling in with her plans and that they would shortly be going to South Africa.

Then the plan languished. Mahon had excuses—his firm was involved in litigation and he was duty-bound to stay until it was settled. Emily's pregnancy was well advanced. Might it not be better to wait in England until after the child was born and then go to South Africa? She wouldn't want to have the baby on board ship, would she?

Wait—where? Emily Kaye gave up her flat and left herself homeless in an attempt to force his hand. (It is noticeable that she did not carry out her threat to inform his employers or his wife. If such a threat had indeed been made, it was an empty one.) They agreed on a compromise. They would rent a bungalow for a while and see if they could work things out together.

Mahon maintained that the bungalow was Emily's idea and that she believed she would be able to convince him within a short space of time that they could live happily together for the rest of their lives. This little excursion into marital bliss, she hoped, would make Patrick really fall in love with her.

In all events it was Mahon who rented the bungalow outside Eastbourne, although he claimed that it was Emily who found the advertisement and pursuaded him to investigate its possibility. It was a small place, rather primitive, but not without charm. It seemed an ideal place for a secluded love affair. Or a murder.

After a few days at the bungalow, Emily Kaye re-opened the subject of South Africa. To her, this Eastbourne holiday, was only an interval. She clung to her plan that they should go away together to start a new life. She was determined on it, and she would not let it go. She may have resolved not to bring up the subject while they were at the bungalow; after all, she had determined to show Mahon what a good wife she would make and how happy they would be together. But here they were, at it again, she nagging at him to make the arrangements, see to passports and other details. The birth of a baby does not wait for plans to be made, and she was heavily pregnant.

Mahon went to London ostensibly to get passports, but he did not get them. Perhaps he did not intend to get them but was simply drifting again. He went back to the bungalow, and there was a blazing row about it. Emily Kaye tried to force his hand by insisting that he write resigning membership of a club of which he was a member. She herself wrote other letters which would commit him to his departure to South Africa. When he refused to do what she asked, she wrote the letter of resignation herself and begged him to sign it. He refused.

At this, claimed Mahon, she became so enraged that she threw a coal axe at him, hitting him on the shoulder. The shaft of the axe broke on the bedroom door, which indicates that it would have been thrown with some violence. She dashed at him, clawing at his face and neck, and he grappled with her to ward off the attack.

It was the custom of the day to consider all men strong and all women 'frail', but Emily Kaye was well-built and probably mad with desperation. The force and suddenness of the attack from a woman who had done little but plead and threaten up to this point, may have surprised Mahon considerably and thrown him off-balance. Remembering that we only have Mahon's statements to go on, all this may well have been true. Certainly they could have struggled, and certainly Emily Kaye could have fallen to the floor, hitting her head on the coal cauldron, as he claimed. The prosecution brought forward the point that the cauldron was flimsy in structure and was not damaged, as one would expect, from the weight of a falling body, although a few spots of blood were afterwards found on it. Mahon fell on top of her.

In his statements Mahon said: 'I cannot remember anything but a nightmare of terror, for I saw blood beginning to flow from her head, where she hit it against the coal cauldron ... I was so distraught that I cannot say ... whether I strangled her or whether she died by the fall. I cannot clearly remember the next few hours ... I think I wandered in madness round the garden for some time.'

These are curious statements on the face of it, the statements of a man who was possibly temporarily out of his mind with rage and pain, and who possibly suffered a blackout during and after the event. One would expect a man to remember whether he had strangled someone or not, and surely the marks of strangulation would have been visible on her neck, if they were there to be seen. 'I think I wandered around the garden in madness for some time.' This might very well have been the actual truth, and he may have had no clear recollection of what he was doing for several hours after the murder.

When he want back into the bungalow, he removed Emily's body into the smaller bedroom. He covered it with her fur coat and stuffed clothes under the head, from which he claimed, 'blood had flowed *and was still flowing*'. As any student of criminology knows, this was a very possible sign that Emily Kaye was still alive, because the dead do not bleed, unless the skull had been fractured, and blood had gathered in some cranial cavity to be spilled out when the body was moved. But if she was still alive, Mahon threw away his chance of life by not realizing the fact and fetching help immediately.

He then proceeded to throw away his life even more thoroughly. He told no-one and made plans to dispose of the body. And with its disposal went all his chances of a plea of self-defence, of accidental death, or even of manslaughter, because with it went all the evidence in his favour, if such evidence there was. And with the manner of its disposal went any shred of sympathy that he might ever have received from any quarter, and he could well have been hanged on this fact alone.

Up to this point we have been considering a very ordinary story, duplicated thousands of times in all ages and in every locality. A man gets himself into serious woman-trouble, quarrels with her, and she dies during that quarrel, or is murdered. Except for the fact that we will never be sure whether this was a case of premeditated murder or not, what makes the Mahon case a classic?

Until the actual death of Emily Beilby Kaye, it is possible to understand, although not of course condone, the progressions of Mahon's action. He acted according to his temperament, as far as the evidence reveals it. Even if he did murder the woman, this could be part of his psychological picture. Remember the bank robbery and the servant girl. He was undoubtedly capable of murder if he felt himself cornered.

The Mahon case deserves its place in the annals of crime because Mahon's subsequent actions were so extraordinary and inexplicable that they can be fitted into no known psychological pattern. He possibly was completely mad; he may have been in a situation that tried him beyond sanity. The reporters of the time who stated that he was a fiend incarnate who gloried in his actions and who actively *enjoyed* his subsequent actions were begging the issue, as we know it today. To get anything in the way of enjoyment out of the situation, Mahon must surely have been insane.

So we have Patrick Mahon with a dead body on his hands, no matter how she died. Probably far fewer murderers would be caught if the human body were easier to dispose of. We will never know why Mahon did not take the obvious course of burying the body, since the bungalow was isolated and his actions would not have been observed. He had taken the bungalow for two months under a false name. The address he had given may also have been false. He would have had a fair chance of getting away with the whole affair.

We don't know when he set to work on the body, but Emily died on April 15th. Mahon subsequently claimed that he went to London on the 17th and bought a butcher's knife and a small saw to aid his disposal operations. Actually it was proved that he bought them on the 12th, and this single fact did more to hang him than any other, because it was argued that it proved premeditation. Mahon's argument was that the knife and saw were normal household impliments and that he bought them quite openly, thinking that they might be useful, after seeing them in a shop window. He made a great impression on the shop assistant because it was closing time and Mahon insisted on being served, being a bit unpleasant about it. He had lied to the police, he said, because he felt the truth might be incriminating. He constantly made contradictory statements.

Either before he started to dismember the body, or before he had finished the operation, Mahon went up to London to keep a date with a girl he had met casually in a Richmond cinema. He took her back to the bungalow, and they actually had intercourse in the room next to the one in which Emily's body was lying. The girl displayed mild curiosity about the fact that one of the doors in the bungalow was locked, but Mahon said that he kept valuable books in there, and she seemed satisfied with the explanation. She was not interested in books. So sure was he of her lack of curiosity that he left her alone in the bungalow while he went to the Plumpton races for the day! She was no Bluebeard's wife—she left the bungalow without discovering the secret of the locked room.

Now Mahon entered on a very busy period. He had to make an appearance at the office, spend part of his time with his wife, and return to the bungalow to dispose of a dead body.

He decided to burn it. This, on the face of it, might seem a feasible idea. Bodies, after all, do burn. But he was in a small bungalow, with a small grate in a small sitting room. He apparently did manage to burn the head, hands and feet.

By all accounts, almost a thousand fragments of bone were subsequently recovered from the fireplace and were identified, together with the other fragments as belonging to a woman of Emily Beilby Kaye's physical description.

This presupposed an extraordinary amount of activity. We can imagine Mahon returning evening after evening from the office or from his home to return to his task. The whole business began to become impossibly tedious. He boiled the flesh in an attempt to get rid of it, although how anyone in their right senses could imagine that this would have the slightest effect cannot be imagined.

Despairing of ever disposing of the remains of the body, Mahon stuffed them into various pieces of luggage. Taking the case with initials E.B.K. on it, he travelled to London and then to Richmond, throwing pieces of Emily Beilby Kaye's flesh out of the window at intervals. Then, apparently, he went home, because it was at home that his wife found the cloakroom ticket.

Of course, with the ticket in the hands of the police, it was a very short time before Mahon found himself in custody. Confronted with the case and its grisly contents, Mahon explained that he was fond of dogs and carried meat for them. The inspector said that the blood was human, and that he had better think of a more plausible story.

Mahon sat silently for a long time, and then he said: 'I wonder if you can realize how terrible it is for one's body to be active and one's mind to fail to act.' He paused again and added: 'I am considering what my position is.'

It wasn't good, of course. He made a statement in which he claimed that Emily Kaye had died accidentally after their quarrel and struggle. He also said that he had bought the knife and saw *after* her death and had used them to dismember the body, but this was later disproved at the trial.

Patrick Mahon was tried at Lewes Assizes, with Mr Justice Avory presiding. He was defended by Mr Cassels, and the prosecution was led by Sir Henry Curtis Bennett.

Trials are supposed to be held without prejudice, but it is doubtful if anyone in the courtroom or any member of the general public really believed that Mahon could be found anything but guilty. The hangman's noose was already around his neck, in a figurative sense, before he entered the dock.

Several interesting points were brought out in the evidence, none of them doing Mahon's case any good. Bernard Spilsbury, by that time Sir Bernard, brought forward evidence aleady dealt with in this account. He had found, among other things, a two-gallon saucepan of boiled flesh, more boiled flesh in a hat-box, a saucer of dripping in the fireplace, sawn-up pieces of spine in a trunk, and the thousand pieces of splintered bone previously mentioned. There were, in all, thirty-seven pieces of boiled flesh.

Again, we can only wonder why, even at this stage, he didn't bury the lot. We can imagine Mahon, in a kind of demented frenzy, trying to dispose of this mass of bones and flesh which would *not* disappear, which would *not* render itself disposable. And yet, in that frenzy, it did not seem to occur to him to dig a hole and at least get the lot out of his sight and certainly more safely hidden.

Questioned later about his pathetic attempts to burn the remains he said: 'It was horrible.' About the boiling of the flesh, he said: 'That was horrible, too'. He was not a highly articulate man, and he probably meant exactly that. He probably plumbed the depths of horror in those few days.

One of the features of the Mahon trial was the fact that Mr Justice Avory frequently interposed questions to Mahon to clear up various points. As far as the press, the public, and possibly the jury were concerned, Mahon was already guilty and the trial a mere formality. But Avory seemed to be at some pains to ensure that proceedings were scrupulously fair—and could be seen to be fair. He was particularly concerned with establishing the actual relationship between Mahon and Emily Kaye, and constantly had to bring Mahon back to the point during cross-examination. At one time Mahon broke down and sobbed while describing the quarrel and fight which led to Emily Kaye's death, and was brought back to the point by the judge.

Hampered by Mahon's wandering, contradictory statements, Mr Justice Avory established a curious and indicative point. Mahon, it seemed, had taken the bungalow in the name of Mr and Mrs Waller and had rented it for two months, although he had only apparently planned to be there with Emily Kaye for one weekend. He claimed, when cross-examined by Sir Henry Curtis Bennett for the prosecution that the false name had been Miss Kaye's idea.

He also said that after the weekend was finished he intended to take his wife down to the bungalow for a holiday, as she had been unwell.

Would she come down as Mrs Waller? Asked Sir Henry. Wasn't he known as Waller in local shops?

Not necessarily, replied Mahon.

Here Mr Justice Avory intervened. Suppose a letter came to the bungalow addressed to him as Mr Waller, what had he intended to do?

Mahon replied that he would have told her everything. He had intended to make a clean breast of his affair with Emily Kaye.

This reply possibly gives us the strongest clue to Mahon's character— that everything would come miraculously right, that he could explain, smile, apologize, and people would understand and forgive.

Much of the evidence stressed Mahon's inherent weakness of character. Asked by Curtis Bennett why he simply didn't say to Emily Kaye that he couldn't see her again and that the relationship must end, he answered lamely that he had said that.

| Curtis Bennet: | 'Why go (to the bungalow) at all with Miss Kaye?' |
| Mahon: | 'Because I gave her a promise.' |
| Curtis Bennet: | 'Weakness on your part?' |
| Mahon: | 'Yes, weakness on my part.' |

The world is full of socially inadequate people who make their charming way through the world, and often their inadequacies go undiscovered. When the crunch comes, they react in their individual ways—get drunk; take a tranquillizer; go to bed with a hot-water bottle on their stomach; or go into a nursing home with a nervous breakdown.

Few of them react as Mahon reacted, battering a servant girl, or pounding into a thousand pieces the bones of a woman for whose death he was undoubtedly responsible, whether he actually went to the bungalow intending to kill her or not.

He might well have bought the knife and saw as a second line of attack. It seems very probable that he really thought he could persuade this strong-minded, determined woman that he really didn't want to marry her, and have her go away quietly, without fuss, to oblige him, as he had persuaded so many other people to oblige him. Things nearly always worked out for Patrick Mahon. Perhaps they would work out just once more.

During his closing speech, Mr Cassels for the defence pleaded with the jury to ignore the fact that Mahon was an immoral man and patently a liar. He was charged with murder and on murder alone. Mr Justice Avory, while he said everything possible in Mahon's favour, which, let's face it, was very little, also touched on the fact of Mahon's conflicting statements. After all, if a man wants to be believed when he tells what on the face of it sounds a very unlikely story, he has a better chance if he starts off by being a truthful person.

The jury deliberated for an hour before bringing in a verdict of 'Guilty'. Mahon, possibly forced to face reality for the first time in his life, almost collapsed on hearing the deaths sentence, murmuring an almost inaudible protest.

There was an appeal, as there usually is, but it hardly got off the ground. Mahon took his final days in prison very badly and had to be dragged to the scaffold to die.

And with him died the only hope of ever learning the true solution to the case. We will never know whether a patholological liar finally turned to telling the truth, unlikely though that truth may have been, or whether Patrick Mahon really planned one of the most inept murders in history, and quite the most inefficient attempts at the disposal of a body in the annals of modern crime.

RAYMOND RUDORFF

# The Case of the Papin Sisters

> Have you ever reflected for an instant on the deadly and justified hatreds
> and murderous—yes, murderous—desires than can seize us when, with
> a disdain that hurls us beyond the pale of humanity, we hear our masters
> crying out 'he has a servant's soul ... that's a servant's sentiment'
> whenever they want to describe something low and base? Well then,
> what do you expect us to become in such a hell?
>
> Octave Mirbeau, *Diary of a Chambermaid*.

'I'll scratch her eyes out!' A common female threat, often heard and
seldom taken seriously. An expression of woman's anger and perhaps
of some innate, atavistic, feline ferocity. The case of the two Papin sisters
in 1933 is one of the rare instances in which such a threat was carried
out in an apparently gratuitous, sudden, volcanic explosion of female
fury that baffled psychiatrists, fascinated anarchists and surrealists in
France and inspired a recent film and the well-known play *The Maids*
by Jean Genet. It is certainly one of the most awesome recorded
occurrences of motiveless ferocity and has yet to be satisfactorily
explained.

On the evening of February 2, 1933, Monsieur Lancelin, an honorary
attorney in the small French provincial town of Le Mans, had been
invited out to dinner with his wife and daughter, aged twenty-seven.
As M. Lancelin had been out all day, he had gone alone to the friends'
house, where he was to be joined by his family. After waiting in vain
and telephoning his house without receiving any reply, he excused
himself before his hosts, and went back home. The front door had been
shut from the inside and all the windows were dark, except for a faint
glow in an upstairs room, which belonged to two maids, both sisters,
named Christiane and Lea Papin, aged twenty-eight and twenty-one
respectively. Unable to enter his own house, Lancelin then called the
police. A police inspector went around to force the door open and to
investigate. After searching the ground floor this is what he found on
the first-floor landing:

'The corpses of Madame and Mademoiselle Lancelin were lying
stretched out on the floor and were frightfully mutilated. Mademoiselle

Lancelin's corpse was lying face downward, head bare, coat pulled up and with her knickers down, revealing deep wounds in the buttocks and multiple cuts in the calves. Madame Lancelin's body was lying on its back; the eyes had disappeared, she seemed no longer to have a mouth and all the teeth had been knocked out.

'The walls and doors were covered with splashes of blood to a height of 2 metres, 20 centimetres. On the floor, there were found fragments of bone and teeth, one eye, hair pins, a handbag, a key-ring, an untied parcel, numerous bits of white faience and a coat-button.'

Further investigation led to the finding of a kitchen knife, covered with blood, a damaged pewter lid, the pot itself, which was dented although it was so massive and heavy, and a blood-stained hammer. In a room on the second floor, the two servant-maids were found naked, huddled together in one of two single beds. The elder of the two girls, Christiane, immediately confessed to the murders:

'When Madame came back to the house, I informed her that the iron was broken again and that I had not been able to iron. When I told her this, she had wanted to jump on me. At that moment, my sister and I and our two mistresses were on the first-floor landing. When I saw Madame Lancelin was going to jump on me, I leaped at her face and scratched her eyes out with my fingers. No, I made a mistake when I said that I leaped on Madame Lancelin. It was on Mademoiselle Lancelin that I leaped and it was her eyes that I scratched out. Meanwhile, my sister Lea had jumped on Madame Lancelin and scratched her eyes out in the same way. After we had done this, they lay and crouched down on the spot. I then rushed down to the kitchen to fetch a hammer and a knife. With these two instruments, my sister and I fell upon our two mistresses; we struck at the head with the knife, hacked at the bodies and legs and also struck with a pewter pot which was standing on a little table on the landing. We exchanged one instrument for another several times. By that I mean that I would pass the hammer over to my sister, so she could hit with it, while she handed me the knife, and we did the same with the pewter pot. The victims began to cry out but I don't remember that they said anything. When we had done the job, I went to bolt the front door and I also shut the vestibule door. I shut these doors because I wanted the police to find out our crime before our master. My sister and I then went and washed our hands in the kitchen because they were covered with blood. We then went up to our room, took off all our clothes which were stained with blood, put on a dressing gown, shut the door of our room with a key and lay down in the same bed. That's where you found us when you broke the door down. I have no regrets or, rather, I can't tell you whether I have any or not. I'd rather have had the skin of my mistresses than that they should have had mine or my sister's. I did not plan my crime and I didn't feel any hatred towards them but I don't put up with the sort of gesture that Madame Lancelin was making at me that evening.'

Lea Papin confirmed her sister's statement:

'Like my sister, I affirm that we had not planned to kill our mistresses. The idea suddenly came to us when we heard Madame Lancelin scolding us. I don't have any more regrets for the criminal act we have committed than my sister does. Like her, I would rather have had my mistresses' skin that their having ours.'

The immediate pretext for the explosion of violence is known. The day before the murders, Madame Lancelin had paid the maids' monthly wages, holding back five francs from Lea's wages as she had put the electric iron out of order. The next day, the sisters were ironing in the empty house when there was a short-circuit in the iron and all the lights fused. Christiane had anxiously asked Lea 'what will Madame do to us when she gets back?' and it seems certain that when Madame Lancelin was told of the accident, she must have made some gesture of irritation, particularly as she had had to have the iron repaired only a short time previously, although at Lea's expense.

It seemed a trifling incident. Madame Lancelin had lost her temper —after all, the mishap with the iron *was* irritating—and had probably raised her hand to slap Lea or Christiane without thinking. Both maids, perhaps Christiane first, had reacted with unbelievable savagery. Had they hated their mistresses? When they came before the examining magistrate, prior to being committed for trial, Lea had repeated that neither she nor her sister had nourished any feelings of hatred towards their employers although they were sometimes severe. She explained:

'Life with the Lancelins was hard. We never went out. Madame was haughty and distant. She only spoke to us when she wanted to scold us. She was always spying on us behind our backs and counting the lumps of sugar that remained in the basin. When housework was done in the morning, Madame Lancelin would put on white gloves and run her fingers over the furniture to see if the dusting had been done carefully and whether any speck of dust remained. If we had the misfortune to break the slightest thing, she at once took it out of our wages. It couldn't go on. It had to come to an end. We were too unhappy.'

In the light of Lea's statement, it might seem that this was a case of sudden rebellion against a tyrannical and overbearing mistress. But it was soon obvious that the case was far more complex and unusual. According to one newspaper, when she was arrested, Christiane had said 'I'm not mad. I know what I've done' and then added: 'We've been servants for long enough. We've showed them our power'. This indicated a sudden furious reaction against the mistress and a complete breakdown of the master-servant relationship, but the sexual nature of some of the wounds inflicted, and the horrible way in which the two sisters had had an equal share in the butchery, pointed to no ordinary outbreak of resentment.

Let us consider once again what had taken place on the evening of February 2nd, when Madame Lancelin and her daughter came home to find the lights out and the iron out of order again. According to the sisters, the mother had lost her temper for a moment and raised her hand in anger. Christiane and Lea had then, almost simultaneously, flown at the mother and daughter with almost unbelievable violence, since they both succeeded in gouging and scratching out the eyes of two women, neither of whom was in any way feeble or decrepit, and who presumably had made some attempt to defend themselves. The horror of the scene needs no emphasising. Then, while the two blinded women were crouching and moaning with pain and terror, Christiane had gone down to the kitchen to fetch a knife and a hammer, and had proceeded to cut and lacerate them with sustained ferocity and with the equal participation of her sister. Not only did they exchange weapons but they also made use of the pewter pot on the landing, using both the pot and its lid to batter their two victims almost beyond recognition. There was no sign that Lea had been egged on by her elder sister. What was so strange and seemingly inexplicable was the way in which they had acted in unison, as though one sister were the living replica of the other. To the examining magistrate, the prison doctors and psychiatrists, and the court at the trial, nearly eight months later, the exact nature of the relationship between the sisters assumed vital significance.

The popular press made the most of the case. In shrieking, black headlines, the girls were described as 'the monsters of Le Mans', the 'diabolical sisters' and 'the lambs who had become wolves'. Some papers hinted at the victims having had 'wounds which it is impossible for us to describe' although the court observed a certain discretion as to the injuries that had been inflicted. Not surprisingly, much was made of the supposed lesbianism of the sisters, especially after it was known that the girls had been found naked in bed together after committing the murders. Nor was this all, for they soon gave other signs of being bound together by ties stronger than those of 'normal' sisterly affection.

After the sisters had been arrested and taken to the police station, they were interrogated by the public prosecutor, the examining magistrate, the police inspector and a doctor in forensic medicine. As mentioned, their two statements were practically identical, with both Lea and Christiane agreeing that they had no hatred towards their mistresses for, as they said 'they were the bosses, weren't they?' But the examining magistrate went on to ask for certain precisions of details: had not Madame and Mademoiselle Lancelin come back unexpectedly from a shopping expedition, although it had been arranged that they were to go straight on to join Monsieur Lancelin at a friend's house where they were to have dinner? Yes, they had. Doubtless, they had wished to unload their parcels and make themselves up before going out again. But why had the packet of meat, that had been found near the bodies on the landing, been taken upstairs with them when the kitchen was on the ground floor? Had there been something to make the two women hurry up the stairs, forgetting to put down the parcel? Neither Christiane nor Lea could say. The prosecutor suggested that the bodies had been moved, and suggested that Lea Papin had not killed the mother, as she had stated. Instead, she was trying to assume an equal responsibility for the murders as a gesture of solidarity with Christiane, and in order to share her eventual fate. The examining magistrate insisted that it must have been Christiane who had killed both mother and daughter before Lea had come on the scene. Lea passionately insisted that Madame Lancelin had not been dead when she had struck her, and that she had also attacked the daughter with the kitchen knife. The forensic doctor then pointed out that Mademoiselle Lancelin had ben mutilated with the knife after death, but Lea maintained her statement obstinately.

The sisters later changed their statements slightly, but always the substance was the same. They had both taken part in the killings, afterwards they had remarked to one another *'C'est du propre'* (a remarkable understatement: 'What a pretty business' might be the best equivalent expression in English), washed themselves and gone to bed to wait for the police after locking the doors.

Christiane confirmed that Lea had attacked Madame Lancelin and said that she had urged her to 'tear her eyes out'. Lea repeatedly made a point of insisting that she had 'hit as hard as her sister'. Although it was to be alleged that Christiane, being the oldest and most experienced, had dominated her sister and egged her on or even commanded her to take part in the killing, there could be no proof of this. What seemed so astonishing and even incredible was that the two girls could have been seized simultaneously by the same outbreak of murderous fury, and could have acted in such perfect accord. According to their confessions, they had used two knives. Christiane had fetched the first from the kitchen, but as it was not sharp enough, Lea went in turn to get another, used for carving, from the dining-room. They way in which they spoke of exchanging weapons while engaged in their grisly deed seemed a sign of some common compulsion for each to behave exactly the same as the other, as though they felt that they had to be 'twin sisters' in everything—and, perhaps, more than sisters. The way in which they both spoke of the murders implied that they were both conscious of some tremendously strong link between them—a link which went far beyond the fact that they were sisters, eight years apart in age, and both employed in a same occupation in a same household.

Even stranger was Christiane's behaviour in prison before the trial. Once she had been taken to her cell, she burst into tears, screamed threats and howled like a dog. Another inmate of the cells later stated that she called for her 'darling Lea' all night like a lover separated from his adored mistress, and a warder testified that she had rolled on the ground, screaming obscene words as though tormented by sexual desire. She went on hunger strike and had to be forcibly fed, was threatened with the straitjacket, repeatedly begged for her sister to be sent to her and, according to another prisoner, even confessed to having killed both Madame and Mademoiselle Lancelin. At another time, Christiane confided to another prisoner 'at one time, I must have been Lea's husband'. Once she had made a threatening gesture towards her warder, as though to scratch out the woman's eyes, and at another time she had made as though to tear her own eyes out, and was imprisoned in a straitjacket as a result. But the most spectacular incident took place when the two sisters were reunited in the prison. According to several witnesses who were present, when Lea came into the cell, Christiane had leapt upon her and hugged her until she was almost choking and had to be separated by force. When the girls were sitting on the bed in the cell, Christiane tried to tear Lea's blouse from her and cried out beseechingly: 'Say yes to me, Lea! Say yes to me!' She had then tried to kiss Lea on the mouth and had to be restrained while Lea was taken away again.

According to other accounts, the sight of Lea had been enough to send Christiane into a fit of hysteria. She had pulled up her own skirts, showing her thighs, and urged Lea to come to her, in an unequivocal fit of desire. But it should be noted also that Lea herself remained relatively calm, and generally passive.

In view of such behaviour, it seems all the more surprising that the three doctors who had been appointed to examine the sisters should have come to the conclusion in their report that: 'no equivocal explanation can be given for the affection uniting the two sisters, nor is there ar. / question of an attachment of a sexual nature'. They also suggested that Lea's feelings for Christiane was 'filial'. In other words, the elder sister had become a 'mother figure'.

In the light of Christiane's behaviour, once she was separated from Lea, it might be supposed that the elder sister was insane. Was she not also said to have crawled around her cell on all fours, and to have licked the walls, while howling more like an animal in pain or bereavement for the loss of its mate than as a human? And then, there was this strange insistence on the idea of reincarnation . . . Besides claiming that she had probably been Lea's husband in some previous life, Christiane had also declared that Madame and Mademoiselle Lancelin were no longer dead since they had been reincarnated. But insanity seemed too convenient an explanation and it was rejected. After the director of the lunatic asylum at Le Mans had examined both girls, he had declared, in agreement with another doctor: 'Christiane and Lea are in no way depraved. They are not suffering from any mental illness and are in no way labouring under the burden of a defective heredity. From an intellectual, affective and emotive point of view they are completely normal'.

There are many examples of perfectly 'normal' people doing 'abnormal' things under some exceptional stress. History is rich in examples of the atrocities committed upon masters and mistresses by servants, slaves and serfs who have been persecuted and humiliated beyond endurance. Sometimes, as the French Revolution and, more recently, outbreaks of anti-colonial rebellion, have shown, even people who have never themselves suffered from the dominating class have committed acts of horrifying atrocity. But any such feeling of persecution and humiliation seems to have been absent in the case of the Papin sisters.

Both Christiane and Lea continued to puzzle the medical and legal experts who examined them in the months before the trial. They both agreed that the attitude shown towards them by the Lancelin family was perfectly correct. Their wages were normal; in the seven years they had worked in the household, they had saved twenty-four thousand francs; they were given the same food as their masters, and they slept in a heated room, provided with electricity (something that was by no means to be taken for granted in provincial France in the early Thirties). They had the freedom to leave whenever conditions became unbearable but never once did it appear that they had thought of leaving. Christiane agreed that Madame Lancelin was a finicky mistress but, without the resentment shown by Lea when she had spoken of Madame Lancelin 'spying' on them and checking the lumps of sugar left in the sugar-basin, she found such finickiness 'quite right', speaking as a professional maid who took pride in a job well done. She gave no sign of having suffered from a feeling of inferiority due to her social condition, nor of having nourished any class-hatred towards her mistress or master. At one point, when she was being questioned, she did claim that she had been 'attacked' on the night of the murders and that she had struck a blow of 'vengeance and fury'. When asked why she had torn out her victim's (or victims'?) eyes, she replied that she did not know. Without any sign of emotion, she then proceeded to show by gestures how she had done it, adding: 'when I tore out the first eye, I threw it down the stairs'. Lea was asked why she had mutilated Mademoiselle Lancelin so horribly and was seen to smile faintly as she replied: 'to revenge myself'. Upon being further questioned, she elucidated only to the extent of saying that what she had meant had been that she had only wanted to revenge herself on Madame Lancelin for having intervened in the scuffle on the landing, and for having made it more violent. Did this mean that it had been the younger of the two mistresses who had raised her hand at Christiane? The objective truth could never be established. To return to Lea, she never had had any complaint to make about her mistress before this 'attack', as she called it. Yes, Madame was a strict and demanding mistress but 'if we had had anything against her we wouldn't have stayed'. And did she love her masters? Well 'we served them and that's all. We never spoke to them.'

Nothing abnormal was revealed by the medical examination, except for the fact that after the crime both sisters ceased to menstruate. But neither girl had ever suffered from any special illnesses, convulsions or fits at any time. There were no records of any mental breakdowns or nervous crises. Moreover, neither Christiane nor Lea had ever had any sexual relationships—with men, at least. They were both virgins.

It was agreed that they both had retained a full sense of responsibility for their actions. Christiane answered the questions put to her rapidly and correctly. The only sign of any inner emotion was an occasional faint smile. Her memory seemed perfect and she seemed fully aware of the gravity of her deed. What was strange was her ready willingness to repeat her description of the murder in all its gory detail. Lea, who persistently gave the impression of being the more delicate of the two, showed a certain timidity when answering questions but she never seemed to be holding anything back. Both girls had preserved their ethical notions of good and evil.

They constantly repeated a closely similar version of what had occurred and denied any premeditation. Christiane once admitted 'if I hadn't been taken by surprise, things wouldn't have gone so far'. As for the sustained fit of ferocity which had led her and Lea to hack and slash the victims, she could only explain it by the 'black state of anger' which had seized her. She was quite calm about her prospects: 'I shall be punished—my head cut off, even. I've killed. Too bad for me'. In response to further questioning, she said that she had neither thought of marriage nor hoped for it. She had no friends, had never felt attracted by the idea of friendships with men, and had been quite content to live alone with her sister. The only future plans she had ever made had been to 'set up by herself one day'.

Religion meant nothing to either sister. Lea also declared that she had never worried about sex, that she had never had any men friends and that she had never been tempted by the prospect of having any. The only person towards whom she seemed to have had any lasting resentment was her mother, who had been much given to nagging and scolding both sisters.

The only thing left to the puzzled examining doctors, psychiatrists and lawyers was to examine the past lives of the sisters.

At the time of the crime, the mother was still alive and aged 54. She had been married to a drunkard who used to beat her and had been living apart from him with her daughters since 1913. She had three daughters and the eldest, Emilie, had became a nun. Like Lea and Christiane, the mother had also been in domestic service.

Christiane was born in 1905. After being brought up at first by a sister of her father, she had been placed in the convent of the Good Shepherd at Le Mans when aged 7 and she had remained there until the age of 15. She had been reluctant to leave the convent for she had wanted to stay there with her sister Emilie. She had been trained in embroidery work, was generally well esteemed and seemed to have behaved quite normally. When she came out, her mother had found her a situation as a maid in a family where she remained for three years. She then went on to work in several other households but, each time, it was her mother who had found her the post. Whenever her mother had decided that she, and Lea later, were not being paid good enough wages, she had taken them away and looked for a new situation. In 1926, Christiane had gone to the Lancelin household, where her sister was already working. Her previous employers had all given her good references. They had written that she was gentle-mannered, honest, agreable, and hard-working and that she preferred embroidery to household chores. She had not been observed displaying any noticeable signs of temper, although on two or three occasions, she had been noticed to show signs of repressed anger or resentment after being rebuked for some slight fault or omission in her work. But generally, she had been good-natured, even gay, deferential and willing. She was thought to be an intelligent girl.

Lea had at first been brought up by an uncle before being put in an orphanage where she stayed until she was thirteen. Like Christiane, she had been considered to be a good, honest, hard-working girl—perfect material for a maid, in fact. Once though, there had been an incident when she had made a threatening remark to the Sister Superior in charge of the establishment. She had then gone on to work in domestic service with her mother before serving a series of families in succession. She had later gone to work for the Lancelins, where she was soon afterwards joined by Christiane. The two girls had kept very much to themselves. Not only did they never enter into conversation with the Lancelins' neighbours but they did not even speak to the servants working in nearby households. Everybody who saw them thought they were hard-working, honest and sober-minded, but rather taciturn and gloomy.

Towards the end of 1929, there came a break between the two sisters and their mother. The mother was later to testify that the girls would no longer look at her when she met them, and that they seemed anxious to get away from her. Sometimes she would go up to one of them, or both, but would be ignored when she spoke to them. To the examining experts, before the trial, Christiane complained of her mother's behaviour; her mother had been nagging and trying to dominate her daughters. Not only did she take them away from their houses when she thought they were not being paid enought, but she would also take their wages, either putting them into savings accounts in their own names, or simply keeping them for herself.

Could this first revolt against maternal domination have been the beginning of a greater revolt against the Papin sisters' condition of life? So far, both sisters had lived passively, going wherever they were sent and doing what they were told. A servant is, of course, by definition, a person who 'does what she is told'. Two years later, Christiane made another positive act: in September that year, she went with Lea to the Town Hall to see the municipal authorities in an attempt to obtain the emancipation in law of Lea—still a minor—to free her from the domination of the mother and to enable her to be able freely to dispose of her own earnings. The scene that took place in the Town Hall must have been a strange one. Both the *commissaire-central* and the mayor of Le Mans only had vague memories of the event but from what they could recall, both the girls had seemed agitated and had spoken rather incoherently. It seems that at one point in the interview, Christiane had spoken of 'being persecuted' to the mayor. 'Persecuted' by whom? Christiane made a vehement outburst, accusing the mayor of not doing his duty by defending them. The astonished mayor had referred them to the *commissaire* who was equally at a loss to know what to do. It was found that the mother was well esteemed in the neighbourhood and known to be hard-working and honest. What could have got into the two daughters? The *commissaire central* was so struck by the sisters' behaviour that he even advised Monsieur Lancelin to separate them. The life they were leading did not seem quite normal, for they seemed to go to no amusements such as cinemas or dances, had no friends of either sex, went out together, attended mass regularly, it was true, but always seemed to be quite indifferent to the world around them. They were inseparable. However, Monsieur Lancelin was quite unconcerned and said that he was perfectly satisfied with his two maids and the matter was dropped there.

At the trial, Lancelin was to declare that both girls had given entire satisfaction in their work. He had found Christiane to be rather a nervous girl, somewhat excitable it was true, but still intelligent and hard-working. She liked to call upon Lea to help her, almost as though she thought her younger sister was a kind of personal servant. As for Lea, well, she seemed to have a rather limited intelligence, and there was something mechanical about the way she worked, without ever entering into conversation with her employers. She appeared to be under the complete domination of her older sister, and had never been heard to complain. Monsieur Lancelin also remarked that for some time recently she had seemed to be getting thinner. His brother-in-law had once remarked to him that she no longer seemed to hear what was being said to her and had a 'strange look' in her eyes.

Other witnesses also testified that, at about the same time, there seemed to be a change in the general behaviour of the sisters who were even more sombre-looking and reserved than usual. But, as Monsieur Lancelin said: 'they were polite and we felt that any remarks would be badly received as our household chores were very well done. As we had no reason to criticise or complain, we were patient with them'.

But on one occasion, Madame Lancelin's patience had deserted her—although only for a moment. The incident occurred in 1930: Lea had been working in Madame's room, tidying up, but as she was about to go, her mistress noticed a piece of paper that had fallen out of a waste-paper basket, lying on the carpet. Madame Lancelin called Lea back and took her by the left shoulder, pinching it hard, as she made the girl go down on her knees to pick up the piece of paper before letting her go. This was most unusual behaviour on the part of the mistress. Lea was so surprised and resentful that she discussed the incident with her sister that evening. As she was to admit, she had said: 'Next time, I'll defend myself'.

The day before the murder, three years later, Christiane had gone to the local grocer's shop to buy some bread. The woman owning the shop later declared that Christiane had not been very talkative and seemed even more reserved than she had been about a year before. She had also given the impression of being very highly strung and excited. In retrospect, it would seem that a storm was brewing. All that was needed was the spark that would set it off.

The trial of the sisters Papin was held on September 29, 1933, at the assize court of Le Mans. It was extensively reported by the French press but, in the months that had elapsed since the crime, a certain change of attitude could be noticed in the articles of several reporters who had followed the case. Although some papers still spoke of the 'eye-gougers of Le Mans' and the 'enraged lambs', several writers stressed the mysterious, seemingly inexplicable aspect as much as the almost unprecedented atrocity of the murders.

Naturally enough, the appearance of the sisters attracted much comment. Both were impassive, their heavy-lidded eyes generally looking downwards, their somewhat thick, peasant-like but by no means coarse features never showing the slightest trace of emotion. Dressed elegantly they might have been very attractive—but there was one great essential missing: life itself, lifeless demeanour, as though 'all their life was directed inwards'. They might have been creatures from another world, robots in human form. During the thirteen-hour hearing which only ended at twenty-five minutes past one the following morning, Christiane never once lifted her eyes although at one moment a camera caught her with a strangely, almost beatific smile playing about her lips, as though she was savouring some secret feeling of inner contentment. Lea looked younger than ever, with her dark coat buttoned up to the neck and her hands thrust deep in her pockets. She gazed vacantly into space and was almost inaudible when she spoke.

During the entire hearing, the President of the court never failed to show his utter incomprehension of the sisters' behaviour. He spoke softly and earnestly to them like an anxious father trying to elicit the truth from two recalcitrant children. 'What did you have against the Lancelin family?' he asked, almost pleadingly. 'There has been mention of social hatred, that of the employee against the employer. But this was not the case, since you suffered from no feeling of inferiority. As you rightly said: "a servant's profession is as good as any other". You had no preconceived ideas against your employer in his quality as employer. Nor had your mind been inflamed by certain reading matter ...'

The mention of reading matter was interesting. The political climate in France at the time was stormy. Anarchism and fascism were in the air. It was the year before the Stavisky affair and the bloody riots of Left versus Right, two years before the formation of France's leftist Popular Front government. To many provincial middle-class families, the two sisters might well have seemed agents of that 'Red Terror' the right-wing papers were writing so much about.[1] In another effort

[1] Not only in France. At the time of the Popular Front in France, the English *Sunday Dispatch* came out with the following headline: FRANCE AND BELGIUM RAPIDLY GOING RED: SCENES OF HORROR, Rioting, Bloodshed and Misery, etc. etc. (*Sunday Dispatch*, June 21, 1936).

at comprehension, the presiding judge remarked that the sisters might have been able to reproach the Lancelins for having been rather distant in their attitude towards their servants for 'they might perhaps —I said perhaps—have kept the manners of a certain old-fashioned kind of bourgeoisie. Perhaps they had not realized that times have changed.'

Weighing his words carefully, the judge told Lea that he was bound to ask Christiane and Lea whether there had been anything of a sexual nature in their relationship. It seemed strange, for instance, that they never went out, that they never had any kind of a relationship with men, that they would shut themselves up in their room on Sundays and, of course, the fact that they had both been found lying in the same bed by the police. But Christiane's reply was clear-cut and brief:

'There was nothing else between us.'

The details of the crime were gone over again. Christiane said that she had not had any argument before the murders with her mistress. Madame Lancelin had seized her by the arm to make her go downstairs but 'she didn't say anything to me. It was I who attacked her. I knocked her out with the pewter pot.' The judge then went on: 'you knocked Madame Lancelin down with a blow from a pewter pot. As she cried out your sister came running. What did you say to her?' Answer: 'I told Lea to tear her eyes out'. There was a sensation in the court. Another thrill of horror was to run through the entire court-room when Lea was being questioned. In reply to the question as to whether she loved her employers, she simply answered: 'we served them and that was all. We never talked with them'. The presiding judge then asked: 'When your sister saw that Madame Lancelin wanted to get up again did she say to you: "Tear her eyes out"?' Lea: 'Yes'. Judge: 'You came rushing up. You knocked her out by banging her head against the floor and then you tore her eyes out. How?' Quietly but unemotionally, in a matter-of-fact tone that did not fail to horrify the spectators present, Lea replied: 'With my fingers'. And what did she then do? She slashed the body of Mademoiselle Lancelin, who, it was established, was already dead. Had Lea any excuses for her action, any explanations, any regrets? There was no reply.

The jury were shown the instruments used in the murders. Particular attention was paid to the heavily dented pewter pot which bore witness to the violence which the sisters had displayed in striking their victims. The forensic doctor was called upon to give evidence and he declared that never before, in the whole of his career, had he ever seen bodies so horribly mutilated. His revelations concerning the wounds sent the spectators into a turmoil. Shouts of 'death to them!' were heard and the presiding judge had to threaten to clear the court-room. The psychiatrists were then called. The first, a Dr Schwarzimmer, declared that neither sister could be said to be suffering from any mental illness. The only explanation he could give for their ferocity was a sudden explosion of anger. In the view of the law as it stood, they had been entirely responsible for their actions. He was confirmed in his opinion by two other analysts. All the defence could plead was that the sisters had been suffering from a form of alienation. Dr Logre, a well-known analyst, speaking on behalf of the accused, stressed the eyewitness accounts of Christiane's strange behaviour in prison and the disproportion between the almost ridiculously trivial motive for the murders and the unprecedented violence and ferocity shown in their execution. Moreover, did the nature of certain wounds inflicted point to an impulse of sadism? The court should consider the extraordinary bond between the sisters. It seemed that of the two Christiane was undoubtedly the strongest. Although Lea followed her in everything she did and said, it was as if she had abdicated her own individuality, until she was a lesser reflection of the other, and under her complete domination. He ended by requesting that there be further examination into the case but his request was rejected by the court.

The prosecution made an attack on certain 'Parisian newspapers' which, he said, had reported the case in such a way as to arouse more sympathy for the murderesses than for the victims. There had been certain insinuations against the Lancelin family, whose morality and respectability was above all suspicion. As for the motive for the crime, Madame Lancelin had not behaved in a provocative way nor had the crime been committed in an 'explosion of anger'. Christiane Papin had been lying, for the murders had been motivated by a long-nourished desire for vengeance. But vengeance for what? The prosecution could not say. Instead, it preferred to represent the two girls as beings who had given way to 'their most savage instincts'. Since they had behaved like wild beasts, let them be treated as wild beasts!

After an adjournment, the prosecutor declared that the crime that was being judged was 'the most horrible, and the most abominable ever recorded in the annals of justice'. There could be no doubt that Christiane and Lea Papin were both fully responsible for their actions. The solution to the enigma was plain: 'The Papin girls are bad-tempered but not mad. Mad dogs bite as a result of a morbid craving; snarling dogs, which can sometimes show affection, bit at random. The Papin girls are not mad dogs but simply snarling, bad-tempered dogs!' All the defence could do was insist that psychiatry was a complicated and haphazard science and that therefore, the question whether the sisters had been responsible or not for their deed was still open to debate. What did the court know, for instance, of the 'peasant mentality'? In addition, there was the fact only recently discovered, that the father of the Papin girls had once sexually assaulted the eldest sister, Emilie. But the court were unmoved by such arguments. Anyway, as the prosecution said, there was no way of checking the truth of the statement that the Papin father had been a sexual degenerate. There was to be no further enquiry into the state of mind of the sisters. It was an 'open-and-shut' case.

After retiring for an hour and three-quarters, the jury found both sisters guilty, Lea with extenuating circumstances. Christiane was sentenced to death. Her only reaction was to fall to her knees for a moment, before being lifted up by her lawyer. As for Lea, she was sentenced to ten years' hard labour. Neither sister appealed against the sentences, but Christiane's sentence was commuted to imprisonment for life, with hard labour. She refused to work, showed signs of insanity and was transferred to the psychiatric hospital at Rennes where she died in 1937. It was noticed that she never once called for her sister. Lea served her sentence, was released and lived in obscurity ever afterwards.


No satisfactory explanation for the murders has ever been put forward. French intellectuals of the surrealist or anarchist camps were fascinated by the case and hailed the murders as an 'acte gratuit' or else as a revolt against established authority. The two sisters were baptized 'the angels of the Revolution', which was all very poetical but hardly illuminating. The prosecution at the trial had mentioned 'vengeance' as a motive and it was on record that the sisters had said once 'we've had our revenge'. What made the case seem so inexplicable was that neither sister had had anything to complain of at the hands of their masters. The secret perhaps lay not so much in the behaviour of Madame, Monsieur or Mademoiselle, as in the very condition of the life that had been imposed from the beginning on the sisters. The psychiatrists had considered the girls from a medical, pathological aspect, with negative results. But some thirty years before, a man of letters who was also a sworn enemy of authority and who had marked anarchist sympathies, had written a novel which, in its way, may throw far more light upon the case than any amount of psychiatric investigation. The doctor and the psychiatrist deal with 'cases', but the novelist deals with living beings in the round. In this case, it is the imagination of the novelist that we perhaps need, if we are to understand the tragic life of the Papin sisters.

In 1900, Octave Mirbeau published a novel called *Diary of a Chambermaid* which purported to be a real-life account of her day-to-day existence in a French provincial middle-class household, interrupted by reminiscences of experiences in other households, by a young and attractive chambermaid called Celestine. The book explored the mentality and attitudes of the servant maid, her resignations, resentments and compensations. Especially interesting, with regard to the Papin case, was the way in which the author dwelt upon the impulses of sadism and perversity in Celestine—impulses which largely stemmed from her servant's condition. In one part of the novel, Celestine describes how she felt the need to attack and humiliate a mistress who had shown nothing but kindness to her. After leaving her service, Celestine sent back the clothes she had been given by her kindly mistress, accompanying them with a particularly spiteful and gratuitous note. Celestine was unable to explain to herself why she had done it, but noted that every now and again she was subject to these sudden urges to throw everything in the face of her employers. Later in the book, she recalls how she had once been working in a house in which the masters were celebrating the marriage of their daughter. All the wedding gifts were laid out on display, and Celestine jokingly asked the valet, Baptiste, what he would give the newly married couple as his own, personal offering:

'A can of petrol set alight under their bed ... That's my gift. And yours, Celestine?'—'My nails—in her eyes!'

Was the ferocity of the Papin sisters so gratuitous? It seems strange that no one had brought up the question of their social and professional status at the trial. Everyone had behaved as though they had taken it for granted that as maids, the sisters would be hard-working, docile, obedient and respectful and this very complacency may well furnish a clue. If there was a revolt, it was a revolt not against Madame Lancelin personally but against the whole condition of the sisters. What had their life consisted of? All their life, they had been taking orders; they had been brought up in convents and orphanages, and had spent their life between the work-shop, the chapel, the refectory and the dormitory before going directly into domestic service. They were to all intents and purposes born into a life of servitude, whatever others might call it. They could of course leave but what else could they do? They had only been trained as maids, and as servants they belonged to a class apart from ordinary, everyday humanity. No matter how kindly treated they might be by their masters and mistresses, they were beings who were doomed to live upon another plane, in a social dimension in which their individual personalities could be summed up in the words 'docile', 'hard-working', 'obedient' and 'honest'.

Their only compensation was their relationship to each other. They may well have been lesbians. The defence at the trial had mentioned a sexual assault made on Emilie, the oldest sister, by their father who was a known drunkard. Christiane and Lea may also have suffered in infancy from such abuse. It is easy to imagine them growing up with the firm conviction that 'all men are pigs'. This might explain their indifference to men, and lack of heterosexual preoccupations. Their attitude to others was passive and the whole orientation of their lives seems to have been *inwards*. Their mother had made use of them from their earliest childhood and any maternal feelings they might ever have had soon vanished. They appeared to have a sense of persecution, as shown in Christiane's outburst in front of the mayor in her endeavour to emancipate Lea. They had only themselves to rely upon for human warmth and in the hothouse atmosphere generated by their years of togetherness in their small room in the Lancelins' house, they may in time have become lovers, leading a secret life apart from a world which had only treated them as ciphers and towards which they felt no loyalty or attraction.

We can only imagine what had happened on that fatal evening in February 1933, when the sisters had been left alone in the house. Why had their mistresses come upstairs, holding a packet of meat in their hands without first going to the kitchen? Perhaps this is over-stressing what may be only an insignificant detail, but could it have been that Madame and Mademoiselle Lancelin had in some way discovered the 'secret life' that Lea and Christiane Papin had been leading in their little room—their refuge during the long, slow Sundays that succeeded one another so monotonously in that small, deadly dull provincial town? There was a strangely remote quality about both sisters that had struck many witnesses of the trial. The sisters might have been visitors from some other world. In a way, all their lives long, they *had* been living in another world. The tragedy was that only once, in an outburst of sudden ferocity, had they briefly broken through into that 'other world' from which they had been predestined to live apart.

# WILLIAM BOLITHO

# *The Self-Help of G.J. Smith*

Sir, In answer to your application my parentage and age &c. My mother
was a Buss horse, my father a Cab driver my sister a Roughrider over
the Artic regions, my brothers were all galant sailors on a steam-roller.

We have but little to set against this claim of George Joseph Smith
to be the issue of a phantasmagoria and not a human family. His
birth certificate states that he was born at 92 Roman Road, Bethnal
Green, London, on the 11th January 1872. His father, the 'Cab
driver', according to this meagre document, was also an insurance
agent: an insecure category that may (risking something on the
observed unspontaneity of a mass-murderer's imagination) include
the practice of flower and figure painting, which, in one of his marriage
explanations, George Joseph claimed for him. Beyond this cloudy
genealogy it is vain to seek. The very surname is clueless, for all
family trees lose themselves among the Smiths. If ants have names
for each other, they must use a tiny equivalent for Smith. It has no
handle for the curious to meddle with. It is a name unlimited by
space or time; it is an anonymity that may cover an earl or a gipsy
evangelist, and is a sort of evasion of the laws of heredity. 'Smith'
suited the fantastic figure of this man who hated identification. With
it, his only heirloom, he could wander undetectably in the depths of
any directory; he could enjoy some of the privilege of the disembodied
spirit. He escapes the unplatonic ties of family, and promotes himself
out of commonplace crime to the company of Mr Hyde, and Spring-
Heeled Jack; a phantasm haunting the hinder terraces of the Lower
Middle Class, a subject for a new Tale of Wonder and Imagination,
where, instead of Hermits, are Respectable Spinsters; instead of
Dungeons, the shadows of boarding-house basements; instead of skulls,
a more gruesome terror of Tin Baths.

From the obscure bourn from which he came to his first appearance
in the light of record is nine years. Our knowledge of this first
appearance is solely due to his own negligent confidence to a woman
in days before his character had set. At nine years old he was sent

to a reformatory, where he stayed until he was sixteen. Meagre as it is, the information has many implications. A reformatory boy is indeed seldom different from other boys when he goes in. When he comes out, he is a type. It is a punishment for acts which proverbially—and in certain classes of society, practically—are recognized as natural to the growing male: theft, cruelty, various destructions of property. In the complicated social system of England there is a contradictory attitude towards this phenomenon. If the family is rich, it is excused, or in certain circumstances even praised, as natural and a sign of health. Thus the theft of growing fruit, the breaking of windows or fences, is not only pardoned, but often encouraged by jocular reminiscence and approving laughter. Graver deeds are punished privately by the family. When the family is poor, or only callous, the boy taken in any such act (in Smith's days) was certain of from four to seven years' imprisonment in a reformatory. An apple off a barrow, a stone through a window, a broken street lamp: any of these acts may have brought on Smith his sentence. If he had been out of his teens, such offences would have entailed a fine or a few weeks' hard labour. But for philanthropic reasons such leniency is considered against the interests of the growing boy, if he is poor, and it is usual to send him to imprisonment for such period of his boyhood as may remain. This imprisonment, of course, was quite different from that inflicted on the adult; in addition to the manual work of prisons, the reformatory boy had to work at his books, and while there was no ticket-to-leave or remission system for good behaviour, corporal punishment, practically abolished for the grown prisoner, was an important part of the reformatory method for the youngsters. This system, devised for the betterment of the lower classes, the correction of their faults, and to assist them to bring up their families hard-working members of the State, does not always succeed. The boys on their release may be divided into two categories: those who have either outgrown the destructive stage without damage to property in their confinement, or whom the wholesome lesson of the power of the forces of order has discouraged from ever again trying to oppose it; and those who from a feeling of revolt, or because of hereditary tares, are incorrigible and henceforth for the rest of their days are integrally attached to the police system as criminals.

The first class are set to the credit side of our system; they are assured that no stigma attaches to them for their past, and all they have to do is to persuade a trades union to recognize their irregular apprenticeship in the reformatory workshop and admit them to the practice of the trade they have been taught. The second class are our failures; nothing more can be done for them. But they may be certain that their future sentences will usually be longer than those given to other criminals who have not had advantages to excuse them.

Smith, we can detect from circumstantial evidence, particularly his correspondence, left the Reformatory in a state somewhat intermediary between reclamation and total loss. He was certainly neither cowed nor inspired sufficiently to make his peace with society. But unlike the majority of 'bad cases', he had used his head during the seven years, and had learnt something important and useful beyond the beggarly R's and the amateur woodwork. He was released with a precise knowledge of the ethics, and even of the vocabulary, of that good world that governs reformatories. Where else than from a good-hearted clerical visitor could he have learnt to compose such a sentence: 'I vow to take advantage of every future day that the great powers have ordained, until the miserable past is absolutely outlived and a character established which will be worthy of your appreciation.' Or: 'Possibly many years are before us all wherein peace and goodwill will always keep the past at bay, and a Christian brotherly feeling established.' This peak-faced urchin from Bethnal Green has remembered word for word, almost to intonation, what he heard on Sundays from his spiritual father, even to the characteristic nervous shrinking from New Testament onomatology. Certainly the young delinquent did something more than pick his nose during these seven years of reformation. He had acquired what no foreigner can ever hope to do, the practice of that difficult English undenominationalism under which our State Christianity hides itself against the double onslaught of the Education Act and Higher Criticism. He had mastered the right tone in which to speak of the past, the attitude towards the future expected of one on whom so much State money had been spent. In fact, the root theory of reform was in him. Of all his studies, the concept of 'making good', social atonement in its simplest form—to make a good living out of reach of the law—was the firmest embedded. As to the way to achieve it, he had not been so well instructed. The only rule he retained of this latter part of the curriculum was that an alibi, moral, local, or historical, always requires two witnesses.

With this baggage—it might have made him a masterly writer of begging-letters—he had also acquired at some time in between the imperceptible chinks of ceaseless routine one of those devastating egoisms with which, whether they arise out of fear or vice, all mass-murderers are afflicted. Besides their habit of living in a constructed lie, besides the lust of killing which is a mysterious but constant symptom, this damned class are invariably selfish to a degree of which the greatest actor can have no conception: passions that can be more justly compared with that of a mother for a sickly child than with any lesser love between the sexes. Such egotisms are not the growth of a day, nor within the reach of anyone who has not searched the bottom of possible miseries. To love oneself like a Troppmann or Smith is a lifelong paroxysm in which the adoration of Saint John of the Cross, the jealousy of Othello, the steadfastness of a Dante is imitated; if there were a measure of intensity, I would dare say, excelled. In other forms of love admiration may be a necessary factor. The love of a Smith for himself needs no such prop. It absorbs every globule of his being, so that when it is present God and Man alike have no part in him. His self-compassion, self-pity, wakened by what self-knowledge of wretchedness we do not know, sucked the meaning out of every existence but his own. In the life of Burke we suspected it. In the story of Troppmann we deduced its growth. In the case of Smith we see this demoniac Narcissism itself.

From the day of his release for two years Smith's history runs quite underground again. But there are two manholes. In 1890 he serves a week's imprisonment for a petty theft. In 1891 a London Court sent him to six months' hard labour for stealing a bicycle—at that time a luxury peculiarly seductive to a young man of nineteen. Then the trace of his woes and adventures disappears entirely. Possibly he had enlisted. There is some vague allusion to Army Service in what his first wife remembered of his confidences; and once he claimed to a boarding-house keeper to have been a gymnasium instructor. There was some vague allure of the corporal about his walk; some trace of pipe-clay and the button-stick about his later elegance. His unnaturally tough biceps were shaped by some other process than ordinary toil.

Then comes another official memento of his crooked track, the most important since the record of the Reformatory. In 1896, in the name of George Baker, he received twelve months' hard labour for larceny and receiving. This event is strictly analogous to the breaking of the cocoon that frees the fully-grown night-moth. The man has separated himself definitely from the caterpillar that was G. J. Smith, to begin a series of lives in other names, each separate in environment both personal and local and only joined by the hidden chain of his own identity. A double life is not enough for him: henceforth he will make of every year, sometimes every month, a separate life, in which his own history, his name, his profession, as well as the set of personages in which it is spent, is completely changed. He has embarked on a serial adventure in which each episode is complete in itself, whose master-plot is known only to himself: a life divided into impervious compartments. Other men may have mysteries in their life—every incident in his was a separate secret.

This development is simultaneous to his discovery of Woman. Every criminal out of his teens sooner or later collides with the Riddle of Women, and his fate depends, more critically than that of honest men, on the answer he gives it. He may be tangled in the sentimental obstructions of a woman who fears the code, and then be caught in one of the three perilous policies of taciturnity, desperation or reformation. If she is of the same turn he has to share her dangers, and double his own. But if he has even a part of the exalted egotism of Smith he is more surely doomed. He will then try to use women. He will embark on the forbidden and hopeless enterprise of exploiting all this ore lying to his hand: half humanity, with half humanity's property, and all humanity's spending. It is a grave moment in life when it suddenly appears that the ranks of the enemy are not solid; that besides men who fight, punish, resist, there are also women who may be persuaded to love. It is the moment also, if he but knew it, to rush back into the thick of the battle and, doing and receiving evils that he understands, continue open war. All music is there to warn him, the prickings of his own blood, the recesses of his earliest memory, that here is a temple in which sacrilege is desperately dangerous. But this outlying Smith, or George Baker, has no caution. From the day he met his first woman he set eagerly to exploit her. Somewhere in the tunnel he had developed the canaille virility of a Guardsman whose odour, heightened by hair pomade, blacking and tobacco, lures women out of the kitchen like a pack after aniseed. After a short fumbling with the elementary difficulties of the jealousies and timidity, he had his first team of hussies at work for him: their part being to pilfer from their masters and hand over the goods. We do not know what blunder led to the first failure of the scheme. The method, not the idea, was afterwards improved.

In this first essay Smith had come to taste, probably for the first time in his life, the strongest mental pleasure in our civilization—the joys of property. They are peculiarly dangerous to a man of his type. Even the minute quantity of superfluity that his love-slaves put into their master's hands intoxicated him. He had always before lived on the bread-line. None of his earnings had lasted longer than the shortest way from hand to mouth. His first exploitation of women opened to him a new world, garnished with reserve stores against the bitter surprises of life. It furnished his imagination with savings-bank books, cash-boxes, and money laid by. New avenues opened beyond him at the end of which shimmered title-deeds, scrip, fascinating intrinsically and still more in the promise they contained of the final salvation of his only darling, his adored, his own self.

The tiger had tasted blood; or just as accurately, George Joseph had experienced conversion, from the despairing vagrancy of a prison-dweller on leave, to a life of hopeful motive. Smith was a born possessor. The mere routine of acquisition sensually excited him. He picked up the jargon of property law as the Renaissance learned Greek, with the meticulous enthusiasm of a grammarian. Women, even when they kill, always give something. In his first brush with them he brought back that hobby of the lonely, that consolation of the fearful: Avarice. In its strange and twisted ways the neophyte was at once expert.

On his release he appeared in Leicester eager to begin his first hoard. We have mislaid the chain of little reasons that made him open a sweet-shop. But we are allowed for a long time to watch him through a plate-glass window, serving children bull's-eyes and all the assortment of morsels of aniline and sugar for which they wait from Saturday to Saturday in modern towns; or paper bags of broken biscuits and cake refuse; enjoying a till and a lease; practising himself, as if they were sonnets, in the petty art of writing business letters, with Re and Yours to hand, acknowledging kind receipts and begging to state. But after closing hours when the last shelf had been counted and tidied, he would sally out with his chest rigidly squared in search of more women, to see if they had any more to give him. So he came upon one Caroline Thornhill and married her in the symbolic name of George Oliver Love. In his marriage declaration, he promoted his father to one of the most eminent ranks in society that he knew, that of detective.

But if every incipient miser was a business man, the banks would shut their paying desks. Love and Company were bankrupt in six months. The only asset saved was Mrs Caroline Love. He took her to London and set her to work, after his first manner. He attended to the postal and receiving departments, that is, he wrote letters of recommendation to employers for her and took what she stole from them.

In the course of this business he came to discover the seaside. It delighted him. From Brighton they went to Hove, from Hove to Hastings, finding everywhere business easier, people more gullible. Smith had found his America. Everywhere around him were rolling prairies of single women, so tame that the hunting male could approach them with the wind. This English seaside has not been methodically explored, yet it is as fascinating in its way as the labyrinths of the vast industrial towns of which it is a sub-continent. The scheme is different, the manner of life and customs are different. Instead of the regular pulse of nine hours between factory and tene-ment—the regular circulation of the traffic arteries that pump the crowd fresh and living into the vessels of production in the early morning, and the network of veins that conducts their sluggish stream back to the sleeping cells at night, soiled, fatigued—at the seaside there are two other steady tides, at ten o'clock and four, towards the sea. To enable hundreds of thousands to look at the water at the same time, it has been fitted with a T-shaped road, made up of a concrete walk along the shore, and an iron and concrete jetty, a shorter arm, jutting at right angles into the sea. At the end of this jetty is a round glass booth of great size, which is the point of concentration of the whole life of the town. Here music of a special kind is performed: songs in which lifelong love is praised, and marches and dances. At the back of the towns the downs have been trimmed, and small plots of grass planted for the game of golf. In many places other plots of land have been fenced off for the other game of lawn-tennis. In these two amusements the majority of the better-class visitors pass their time, sometimes waiting for long periods for an opportunity to play. But in the lesser world of Smith these artificial distractions fill small place; most of its time is spent in the morning and afternoon walk on the sea-roads, or in station round the official music and the private choirs that are spaced along the main-road and the shore.

With these changed institutions of seaside life naturally goes a large alteration of social custom. The rigid observance of the English social code, a variety largely influenced by ascetic Christianity as well as by climatic, feudal and other conditions, depends so much on mutual policing that the slightest removal from the circle where he is known and by which his conduct is ruled produces a considerably relaxation in behaviour of the normal Englishman; and still more in that of the normal Englishwoman. This dissolvent comes into play in the seaside holiday, which like the annual orgy of many African tribes, the majority of our population periodically observed. It is a counterpart of the bodily release from the abominable round of drudgery to which the nation, by an unhappy development, is for the most part condemned, whose only intermission is this yearly visit to the free air of the sea. Once a year we must have leisure to breathe smokeless air. Probably the temporary abandonment of the corset of the innumerable niceties of conduct is as necessary to our naturally adventurous, unconventional, and even lyrical race, as the physical relief.

In this world Smith, for the first time introduced by the hazard of his business, felt so suited that he seldom afterwards operated elsewhere. He perceived the extraordinary advantage, to a man working irregularly and out of the organization, of a *milieu* in which freedom from work is the rule, discretion and change of identity conventional, and where sudden comings and goings cause no remark. But he had particularly noticed the possibilities of the changed rules of conduct among the women. In London, or even on Sunday nights in Leicester, their approach was always difficult, often impossible. But at the seaside, provided a minimum of *nous*, that principal barrier between the sexes—the need of a formal introduction—was down. Further, those venerated guardians of British morality, the board and lodging house and hotel-keepers, are disarmed at the seaside. This law of liberty stretching in depth as well as area, not only was his power of action on the servile class of women he had known hitherto greatly enlarged, but another stratum of the sex, higher and therefore richer than anything he had aspired to, was here within his reach. His first turn on the glistening promenades convinced him of this. But before we can follow him in his new discovery, we must press him back again, like a jack-in-the-box, into his cell for another two years' hard labour. Mrs Love had ended the second episode in the usual way.

Silvio Pellico, Baron Trenck, and half a score other innocent and learned men have informed us of their sufferings in prison life. But, that I know of, no genuine thief has published his impressions of confinement. Yet there must be a difference of view, if only because the latter must be deprived of the moral snobbery that so comforted Pellico. From such observations (usually facetious!) as we find strayed among the memoirs of prison governors and the like, it would appear that there are three periods in the course of a long sentence: first, when the guilty prisoner is crushed with despair and hardly able to live; second, when the routine soothes, and the time-shortening effect of monotony emerges; third, when the man begins to count, and the long chagrin of calendar-crossing sets in. Conscripts know this abominable occupation; schoolboys know it. In any old barracks the plasterers find little sums pencilled on the wall: so many days endured, so many to come before '*la classe*'. And insomniacs know, what convicts in their last months know, the precise length of an hour, the speed of the minute-hand. Perhaps these degrees are well known to all judges and enter into their standards for measuring the days, months, years, they apportion with such easy assurance to any variety of guilt. But the enormous mental constructions that men, by nature ungeared with reality, must be rearing in the silence of four walls, the strange and idiotic plans they must make in such a waking dream, we can only guess at. Happiest certainly of all those who, like Love, doing his 730 days for theft by receiving from his wife, have walled up along with them all that they adore, if it is only their wretched selves.

He was released in 1902, to find that Mrs Love had fled to Canada. He must have pondered much on this circumstance, for a voyage to Canada becomes henceforth an integral ornament of his lies. Possibly he tried to make up his mind to follow her, seeing no other way of making a living, for one forgets more than one learns in a cell. But gradually what he had observed at the seaside came back to him; then he bethought himself of other women, more convenient to his hand. He left the Canadian voyage lying in his mental life, complete enough for him to have a working belief in its accomplishment ever afterwards; and returned to the exploitation of other women.

In 1899 he already had conquered his first middle-class spinster; perhaps this was one of the reasons for Mrs Love's denunciation. She was a boarding-house keeper in London, whom he met at the seaside. He married her at once, and some time after his release returned to her. When she was sucked dry, he went on to others. For eight years he proceeded from spinster to spinster, leaving behind him a litter of closed saving-bank accounts. Some he got rid of at once, who bored or irritated him, by a set technique of taking them to a public exhibition, pretexting a bodily need that would separate them for a minute, and disappearing. Some were worth the troublesome business of marriage; for some the promise sufficed. Smith led in these years a leisured life. He began to frequent public libraries, and soon was praising himself his his literary taste. Some mysterious reminiscence of his father gave him a peg for believing he was an innate connoisseur of the arts. He indulged this talent by allowing himself a certain sum for buying an occasional piece of old furniture, which he would afterwards sell, and stood such losses as he met with in this traffic with equanimity. Second-hand dealing brought him in direct touch with more women. It satisfied his pride and fed his real business.

In 1908, as an incident in another episode, the details of which are totally lost, he became for a few weeks a servant in a West End club, then was dismissed for inefficiency. The next year with some £90, the largest gain he had yet made—it came from a Brighton conquest—he adventured to Bristol, and there opened a second-hand shop. For some time the idea of a settled base, as far as possible from London, without being out of reach of the hunting grounds of the coast, had occurred to him. Here he married his next-door neighbour, a Miss Pegler, marking the special nature of the union and his intention to make it permanent, by using the name of Smith.

Sooner or later Smith was bound to arrive at this end. Even the foxes need a base. It was the necessary complement of that hoard whose quest always now obsessed him. It would be a hiding-place in case of need, and the necessary fixed point from which he could estimate the pleasures and pains of his episodic adventures. He did not intend to make it more. He told Miss Pegler, besides the customary fable of his rich aunt, the truth that he intended to carry on his business of travelling about the country, with sundry warnings against curiosity, which she usually dutifully heeded. But from the foundation of this little fort henceforward directly developed the plot of his fate. These fantastic creatures of reverie, as long as they do not meddle with the humdrum of the world, seem for a time safe. But as soon as they leave the air, their story begins its last inevitable chapters. It is the phase which we have seen at its acute form in Burke, when confident in his security he had got to a pitch of madness; a stage at which Troppmann toys insolently with a whole family that he counts already dead and done with; when a deep illusion of relief takes possession of them and they stand-down the sentries. In Smith this feeling of confidence took the form of founding this home-base with a wife in Bristol, both a feature of his life of petty swindler, which it capped and ended, and the first stage of his career of murder, which it began.

For with a home, Smith indulged himself in another of his dreams; he bought his first house. The superfluity that began with his first use of women had grown to a hoard of £240, which he used towards the purchase price of a cottage in Southend, whither, giving up the Bristol shop, they then removed. At last he could enjoy title-deeds, the process of transfer, the full consciousness of possession. It spoiled him for work. This was no Casanova, drawn by an everlasting curiosity and passion to seek new women all his life. Smith, like all his class of women-exploiters, was nothing but a lady-killer, a man essentially monogamous, whom sexual novelty inwardly disgusts and repels, who persists in the hunt only for the money or boasting it can give him. It may be that an intuition of this kernel of monogamy in these false Don Juans is the sting or the prize that makes their success. Sensuality in both sexes is as rare as a real passion for rare foods, or wines, or jewels. Smith, having his property and his Pegler, stayed at home in his own house. He fell into a shirt-sleeve life, and in the evening, instead of a lingering promenade past basement grids, or along sea-fronts, he would sit over a dish of sausages or potter with paint and nails, saving money, not making it. His great pleasure was to go over the grocer's book and feel the head of a family. Occasionally he would visit the Saturday afternoon auctions and listen knowingly to the remarks of the dealers, or drop in to a workman's flat just to take a look at a sideboard that had been in the family for years. But saving halfpennies on the kitchen bills by itself will not pay them. In spite of all his niggling thrift at length Smith was forced to let the house and go back to lodgings in Bristol, then to raise money on his sacred deeds on mortgage from the Woolwich Insurance Company from whom he had bought it. The raising of these first loans gave him so

THE SELF-HELP OF G. J. SMITH 121

much pleasure in the officialism, the documents, testimonies, receipts, application forms they entailed, that he almost missed their disagreeable meaning. When the money was spent he roused himself for another raid on the women. With temper, as a man is aroused from sleep on a cold morning. Pegler and his next victim had to know it.

It was not necessary for him, it proved, to journey to his usual grounds by the seaside. In Bristol itself, somewhere in an evening walk, in the bare street, or under trees by some forlorn cricket-ground—I do not know—he brushed acquaintance with Bessie Constance Annie Mundy. She was then thirty-three years old, a full spinster, of that unhappy breed plentiful in late Victorian families. A full and critical study of her class, like that of most other phases of English social life of the nineteenth—early-twentieth century, has not yet been made, though their bizarre originality will doubtless tempt many an investigator in future centuries. Here will suffice a brief muster of general characteristics, in order to explain the fall of Miss Mundy to the power of Smith, and to a certain extent the seemingly impossible, but in reality very frequent, liability of the Mundy class to the Smith class. Fundamentally, though not obtrusively, the class of women to which she belonged was an economic product of the immense days of English trade, which beginning coincidently with the downfall of the French Empire created a huge new middle-class. The absorption of this into the rudimentary *schema* of the English eighteenth-century aristocracy forms practically the whole of the modern social history of our race and its institutions. The men of this new bourgeoisie were somewhat easily assimilated to the elder, petty gentry of the country, who, with a beautiful tolerance unknown in any other country, and which in its earliest stages excited the contemptuous wonder of Napoleon Bonaparte (ever a snob), received them as readily, if not as eagerly, as Early Christian Missionaries baptized the Goths into civilization. The generic title of nobility, 'gentleman', was extended to them with such philosophical and ethical explanations—and notably false etymology—as made the process plausible. Accepted as spiritual equals, the neophytes pressed their assimilation earnestly in manners and ways of thought. The mercantile gentlemen sent their sons to these special schools with which the Renaissance had equipped the country gentlemen, schools specifically designed to the needs of this latter, where, by internal discipline and the almost exclusive study of the classics, the English lesser noblesse had been raised, if not to the cultural level of the French, at any rate far above that of the rough clod-hoppers and Junkers of other northern countries. In this unlikely melting-pot the new-comers lost many of the qualities that had made their fathers' fortunes, in exchange for a culture which at its highest adds something Greek to the common round of rustic amusements and tasks. As far as the lowest borders of the middle-class the ideal, in short, became the country gentleman; and instead of a sharp, spectacled exporter with a pen over his ear, the popular image of England became that bluff, prosperous English squire, John Bull. Only one of the consequences of this development interests us: its effect on the status of women, and particularly on the creation of that class or order, the English genteel spinster. The English squire, for whom the quasi-totality of Englishmen who could read and write now strove to be mistaken, had the ascetic views on women natural to an open-air, uncourtly life, and this accordingly became the standard of the middle-class of the nation. The brother had become a gentleman, the sister, naturally, a lady. If the boy had to pretend that the shot-gun was his main tool and not a pen, though his high stool, six days in the week, was his only hunter, the girls had to perform the far more difficult make-belief of being the châtelaines of the gloomy town houses their fathers necessarily continued to live in, and model their conduct, their outlook, their ways upon that of fortunate prototypes who had fields, servitors, gardens, and all the multifarious occupations of the country-side. As direct consequence sprang into existence a class of women who had nothing to do, whom their chosen norm of behaviour forbade anything, which would differentiate them from their country model, and thus 'be unladylike'. Barred from Court and salon, as well as hunt-meet and the still-room, they were bereft of any reason for existence, except the passive wait for marriage. But not all could marry. From time to time (it is one of the strongest fascinations of the English nineteenth century) educators and reformers sought to fill this vacuum. The most notable of them, Ruskin, inspired these middle-class spinsters to a doughty attempt to interest themselves in Art, particularly Italian and Mediaeval Art, which has lasted almost until our own days. In that pre-war year with which we are concerned there had finally evolved a type out of all these influences to which Miss Mundy, and thousands of others, rigorously conformed. Over a superfluity, a complete uselessness, if such a word can be applied with a full sense of sympathy and pity, as no Stamboul odalisque ever was useless, they had bravely trained a tenuous decoration of books and tastes and principles: the *Rosary* and Tosti's *Good-bye*, and *Sesame and Lilies*, with Way-Farer Anthologies and Botticelli prints, and limp-leather editions of the poets, with fifty other like motives, which in their combination have a certain, essentially tragic, poise. For underneath the garland was a misery and a lack, all the more tormenting because in most cases it was unconscious and undefined, of that Reality which three generations of fantastic theorizing of men had in no way disposed of. Some of them escaped it by working in the one ironical way possible to Ladies, by educating another generation of girls to their own sad situation. But thousands more, like Miss Mundy, whose circumstances allowed of it, carried their load of meaningless days and years wherever hazard took them, over the whole of England and to watering-places, boarding-houses and pensions over the western half of Europe. The loveless, superfluous middle-class spinster is that institution round which George Joseph Smith, that other typical product of our civilization, has for some time been prowling.

The father of Miss Mundy was a bank manager in a country town, an intelligent and capable man who left his daughter a comfortable legacy of £2,500. This sum, invested and controlled by her uncle, produced £8 a month and some small additional fraction, which he held as a reserve for her. It sufficed for a simple life which she spent in various boarding-houses up and down the country, passing from one to the other at the hazard of the season or the movements of her friends. She was a tall, educated woman, extremely reserved, who accepted her nomadic fate, her daily round of perfectly meaningless acts, outwardly with complete resignation. Into such a life, in which the only object is to stay 'respectable', the intrusion of a Smith is almost supernatural. It is as if through the gate of a quiet convent, in the hours of the night, there should burst with shouts and torches the monstrous and obscene band of a Callot orgy. What unbelievable forces urging her towards a share in real life, beyond the round of shop-gazing and the prattle of her likes, must have been massing up behind the dam of her education and reserve before such a meeting could take place! What abominable science in this man of the unexplainable sufferings of a woman's heart before he could dare to sidle up, cough, raise his hat, look at her eyes and begin to tell her what he thought of the weather!

We need not resort to the absurd fable that Smith completely deceived her. Truth loves economy; there is no need to make her a fool, or him a genius. There is a simpler likelihood that he did not try to conceal his rank or the (unspecified) badness of his past. The first would have been useless in a country where a man cannot open his mouth without betraying his breeding. The second, presented without details, might have been necessary as a counterweight to the first. A proletarian such as Smith's opening vowels must have announced, whose life had been a humdrum, would neither have dared to accost Miss Mundy, nor would she have carried the acquaintance farther. When she set out to see the evening alone;

when she noticed at the turning that a man was following her; and after the first flurry slacked her pace, then stopped against the railing and waited; when she saw him come near with a swagger in his arms and hesitation in his feet, and saw the soldier's shoulders and the shape of biceps in his coat-sleeves, the carefully jutted chin, it was not expectation, be sure, of a talk with an industrious artisan that made her breathing an embarrassing pleasure and prompted her little bow. It was a messenger who brought a ticket to life, the great ball of pain and change from which she had been lawfully but unjustly excluded. He must prove he had lived.

So, as soon as she could help him to it, the bold spectre must have declared that he had a wild past. They parted late, she to notice the change in her room, as if all the furniture had been moved and ornamented, from the black hygienic bedstead to the row of pocket poets in limp leather. He, to exercises of deductive arithmetic, working from half-perceived rings and a brooch to the unknown resources of ladies that *were* ladies. Sleep sound, both of you; don't worry that the other will not keep the rendezvous. Henceforth your lives, and your deaths, are welded together.

In two days they were kissing. In three they were off to Weymouth. No half-human plausibility could have seduced her at this speed. The population of fifty genteel boarding-houses had been pushing her to it for ten years. Her decision had been under steam for ten years; Smith's knuckles only needed to touch the throttle. Nor was it a mad flight; her companion's grudging of the marriage fees could not dissuade her from two rooms, the first night, and four days later a permission from the registrar to Henry Williams, thirty-five, bachelor, picture-restorer, son of Henry John Williams, commercial traveller, and Bessie Constance Mundy, to sleep as they pleased thereafter. She, indeed, not Life, had the last word in the bargain after all, and wrung her contract, in the exact prescribed terms of lifelong support and faithfulness, out of the very jaws of the adventure. The same evening Smith was mollified for his expense and trouble by learning the value of his prize. Hereupon he sat down after supper and wrote to his bride's trustee recalling to him that £8 a month on £2,500 left odd shillings in hand, which in the course of years must now amount to no less than £138, for which he would be obliged to request early remittance, at your earliest possible convenience. A postscript in the hand of his niece informed the trustee both of her adventure and its triumphant success.

This stage is summed up by the lover himself, in his admirably personal style, in another letter to her trustee uncle.

14 Rodwell Avenue, Weymouth,
29th August, 1910.

Dear Sir,
My wife and self thank you very much for your letter to-day with kind
expressions. In *re* banks, undoubtedly to transact the business there would
be rather awkward. Thus we suggest it would be better if you will be
good enough to forward a money order instead of cheques—however it
will suit the circumstances. Any time we change our address we should
let you know beforehand. Bessie hopes you will forward as much money
as possible at your earliest (by registered letter). Am pleased to say Bessie
is in perfect health, and both looking forward to a bright and happy future.
Believe me, yours faithfully
H. Williams

On this was added, in her hand: 'I am very happy indeed—Bessie
Williams.'

This letter was the beginning of a month's postal struggle between
the trustee and Smith, in which each called in the aid of solicitors.
As for Bessie Williams, her will is asleep, either from the exhaustion
of the upheaval, or because her uncle's goodwill, having been risked
in the greater, did not count with her in the lesser injury her husband
was doing to it. Meanwhile, the subject of his past was tacitly dropped
between them, with the phraseology of courtship; indeed his romantic
sins seemed to fade into nothing but a busy and painstaking greed
for money. He was always absent-minded, always waiting for the
post, or preparing another letter for it. The solicitor they visited
together deposes that she sat silent at the interviews. She was probably
puzzled, but inwardly convinced, since the marriage certificate was
there, that in the end it would be all right.

The moment that the money came, at last, Smith had used all the
time he had to spare for her. He cashed it in gold and disappeared.
It was part of his terrible thrift that he never left a woman without
writing back to her some vague excuse, as if to save her for an
uncertain, unplanned future use. Although he had thoroughly convinced himself that there was not the dimmest possibility of touching
through her the locked-up capital of her fortune, over which the
raging uncle was mounting a fierce guard with all the power of the
law on his side, yet the mysterious man did not neglect his usual
leave-taking. But in this case, besides the disturbing recommendations
to save money, more precise and more menacing than ever before—

Ask your uncle about a week before the 8th to always send your cash in
a money order so that you can change it at the P.O. Pay the landlady
25s. weekly for board and lodging and take my advice and put 30s. out
of the £8 into the Savings Bank—so it will come handy for illness or

> other emergencies or for us when I return. If you do not I shall be
> angry when I return.

—there was a new and dreadful variation in the pretext for the
desertion. In his flights from other women, Smith had never gone
beyond a vague plea of 'urgent business'. But to this poor devil he
made a charge (that she had infected him with venereal disease) that
showed a bloody hatred, already full grown. We are now at last
treading near that lust of killing, that apparition from the depths,
whose fullest meaning will appear in the case of Haarmann. Such an
insult, unnecessary as well as untrue, could not be an accident tacked
on to the hurried lie of a coarse rogue. It is an act, a corporal violence,
like the thong of a whip laid across her face, the apparently senseless,
but by no means causeless, worrying of a sheep by a vicious dog.
The passivity, the meekness of this educated woman had aroused
some other nameless devil in him besides his biting fear-born avarice.
Other dupes were to him only jumping figures in a cash-book. This
most unhappy woman was to him flesh and blood. She had landed
on the island of his egotism; he was afraid he was not alone.

Shaking off her presence with the blow he went back to his realities,
the pasteboard wife he had contrived for himself, the mortgages and
the deeds. A week after his sin, he was in the office of the Insurance
Company, with a bag of sovereigns, asking to pay off £93 of the
mortgage. He began to play at dealing again, and took Miss Pegler-
Smith to Southend, then Walthamstow, then Barking Road, London,
then back to Bristol again, his fort. For two years he seems to have
lived without another victim. The Mundy episode had scared him—
without any obvious cause, for even a novice would know that he
would never hear from her again.

She showed the letter to her landlady; then when she was able to
travel her brother came and fetched her away.

In February 1912, Smith had no more money. The presentiment,
or whatever it was, fatigue or inertia, that had kept him in his own
quarters for two years, notwithstanding, must be thrown off and
another slinking adventure begun. He handed over the bare shop to
his creature (she sold the goodwill for £5) and he disappeared again.
She watched his train out of sight 'steaming in an easterly direction',
and then packed up and returned to her mother's. Another of Smith's
hoards put away neatly until wanted.

On the 14th of March in the same year, Bessie 'Williams' is a guest
at the house of Mrs Tuckett, a boarding-house called 'Norwood' at
Weston-super-Mare. Mrs Tuckett knows what is the matter with her,
for Bessie's aunt has told her the story. She is always called Miss

Mundy. She is treated with firm kindness, as if she was an invalid; sent out for a walk at regular hours; encouraged to eat a lot. On this day she went out at eleven to do a small commission for Mrs Tuckett. She returned late, at past one o'clock, 'very excited'. As soon as she had gone out she had met her husband. He was looking over the sea; she went up and touched him. He turned round and said: 'All a mistake.' Mrs Tuckett listened to this with pressed lips and sent a wire with the news of the catastrophe to Miss Mundy's aunt. At three o'clock the man himself arrived, unendingly loquacious. While he was talking, Mrs Tuckett sat still and stiff; Bessie, in her chair, thinking of something else. When his spring grew sluggish, Mrs Tuckett asked him, hard and dry, why he had left his wife at Weymouth? He replied with a new gush, sideways, that he had been looking for her for twelve months, 'in every town in England'. Mrs Tuckett said that she did not understand the necessity seeing that he knew the address of her relations. He answered quickly that, as a matter of fact, it was her brother or her uncle who had finally put him on the track.

He lied. The meeting on the front, however it might seem to show traces of human handiwork, was the freak product of nature, or Destiny, who had arranged her cosmic time-tables to suit, to ruin this pair. One of them, possibly both, did not desire the meeting, before it was malevolently thrust upon them by Providence. But, now it was accomplished, neither would call the bluff of the Gods and fly for their lives. Each reaccepted the other as food for that hungry imagination each lived marooned with, a character to be woven into the story each was living: Bessie had her human, handsome man again to be reformed, submitted to: Smith recovered a good business project to be carried to success by strict attention and diligence. That very afternoon he took her to a solicitor, signed a note acknowledging a 'loan' of the £150 with interest at 4 per cent. It was his idea of perfect reconciliation. Hers was to sit still and nod to all this queer simple lover proposed. In the enthusiasm of a man who returns from a long holiday, Smith turned to arrears of work and with the same candid methods as before tried his best to reconcile the family. An ordinary explanation might be difficult, but could they resist the straight thing from a solicitor? So his version of the return went to the uncle and brother, emphatically adorned with mention of the 4 per cent, under the stamped heading and over the signature of Messrs. Baker & Co., solicitors. But Smith's veneration of the law and all the actions of its limbs is not necessarily shared by honest men. His stamped and witnessed excuses only alarmed the relatives.

That night Bessie said to Mrs Tuckett: 'I suppose I may go back to my husband?' The good woman, angry but helpless, replied: 'You are over thirty, I cannot hold you back.' Man and wife they went away, promising to come back that night, but did not return. Instead, Smith sent a letter which did more credit to his reformatory teachers of what was the 'right thing' than his picked-up superstition about solicitors' letters. In it is, in solution, the whole of his views on the British middle-class, their ethics, their customs and their numerous soft spots. It must be read in full.

Weston-super-Mare,
15.3.12.

Dear Madam,

In consequence of the past and the heated argument which possibly would have occurred if wife and self had to face you and your friends this evening, thus, for the sake of peace we decided to stop away and remain together as man and wife should do in the apartments which I have chosen temporarily. Later on I will write a long letter to all Bessie's friends clearly purporting all the circumstances of the whole affair solely with the intention of placing all your minds at rest concerning our welfare. All I propose to state at present beside that which has already been stated by Bessie and myself before the solicitors that it is useless as the law stands and in view of all the circumstances together with the affinity existing between my wife and self for any person to try and part us and dangerous to try and do us harm or endeavour to make our lives miserable. It appears that many people would rather stir up strife than try and make peace. As far as Bessie and I are concerned the past is forgiven and forgotten. Bessie has not only stated that on her oath to the solicitors; but has also given it out to me in a letter written by herself to me which I shall always prize. Thus my future object and delight will be to prove myself not only a true husband but a gentleman and finally make my peace step by step with all those who has been kind to Bessie. Then why in the name of heaven and Christianity do people so like to constantly interfere and stir up past troubles. It would be more christian like and honourable on their part to do their best to make peace. There is time yet to make amends and if people will only let us alone and with the help of the higher powers which has united us twice, Bessie shall have a comfortable settled home and be happy with me. I trust there is many many years of happiness before us. I thank with all my heart all those who have been kind to my wife during my absence.

Yours respectfully,
H. Williams

In this witness to the influence of three pillars of Smith-society on Smith's soul, the parson, the magistrate, and the solicitor, it is only needful to comment that the cautious threat, without which hardly any letter of the man is complete, would not imply any physical reprisal, but only to bring the law on them. Pleased with this effort an ' still full of zeal, Smith went on to write another to the brother, which begins with the peerless lines: 'Dear Sir—I know not how I shall offend in dedicating my unpolished lines to you nor how you will censure me for using so strong a prop for supporting so grave a burden ...' To this Bessie had added a postscript—her correspondence from the moment of the reunion was all at the tail of her husband's screeds—in which was the terrible phrase heavy with all the besotted illusions of her whole life: 'I know my husband better now than ever before. I am perfectly happy.'

Meanwhile the succubus, gravely satisfied with the 'steps' he had taken, now devoted himself to a long examination of that trust-fund. Before making any definite plans on it he consulted the supreme oracle of his world: counsel's opinion, which made it clear that the mutual wills he had devised were useless, and that the only way to be certain of laying hands on it was that its owner should die, quickly, before the trustees, set on 'stirring up strife and unpleasantness', exercised their power of using it to buy an annuity for her. Those sinister 'higher powers' were closing in on Smith now, like policemen, to march him to that bourn in which he and Bessie will never again come upon each other by accident.

They were now at Herne Bay. In this climax, in which he would show all that he was, all that he had grown to, all that he had been taught, Smith will not desert the wide sands where he was most at ease. On 20th May he hires a house in the High Street. To the clerk of the owner, Miss Rapley (afterwards an important witness against him), he is talkative and conciliatory: 'My wife is a cut above me,' he confides to Miss Rapley. 'Her friends did not at all approve of her marriage. My wife had a private income paid monthly. I have not anything except that; I dabble in antiques.' At the end of his confidences, he was allowed to pay in advance for the rent instead of producing banker's references. The house, one suspects, must have been hard to let, possibly because of the old-fashioned absence of a bath, or he would not have been accepted as a tenant, for her made a doubtful impression on shrewd Miss Rapley.

Mutual wills were drawn up and executed on 8th July. The next day Smith went to the shop of Hill, ironmonger, and bargained for a tin bath. £2 was the price asked. He got it for £1 17s. 6d. It had no taps or fittings, but had to be filled and emptied with a bucket.

One more thing remains, before the end. On the day following Smith took Bessie to a young doctor, and stated to him that she had had some sort of a fit the previous day, and had lost consciousness. It is most probably that Smith meant a 'fainting fit', which may or may not have had some foundation in fact. The doctor decided that he meant an epileptic fit; passed him leading questions on the symptoms, to which

Smith agreed. This lesson on epilepsy Smith retained for future use. The woman did not remember anything so serious having happened to her; she had always been healthy; since Mr Williams said so, it must have come and gone outside her consciousness. All that she remembered was a headache. With a prescription for bromide of potassium they went home.

The next night, past midnight, Smith returned to the surgery and rang the night-bell. His wife had had another fit: please to come at once. When the two men reached the bedroom, Mrs Williams was sitting up, hot and flushed. It was a Senegalian night; she complained of the heat. At three next afternoon Smith and she went again to the dispensary; she looked in perfect health. Smith said she was much better. That same night she wrote to her uncle: 'Last Tuesday night I had a bad fit . . . My whole system is shaken. My husband has provided me with the best medical men, who are . . . attending me day and night. I have made my will and left all to my husband. That is only natural as I love my husband . . .'

This letter can only mean that the romantic obedience she was playing at had ended in her quite laying aside the use of her brain: a perilous thing for any human being, in any circumstances. Reason, sublime and faithful ally in all the snares with which our life is so beset, is never to be jilted, even for Love, even for Piety, even for that fidgety gossip, Conscience—who indeed had nothing to say to this poor woman dreaming with all her might, on the brink of the gulf. Nor was the killer himself, in these last days, better guided. As completely as his victim he had abandoned good sense. In its place he was plying himself with all the mental drugs to which his miserable life had made him addict, soaking himself with illusions, to tone his will for the infernal leap just ahead. Until now he had practised only sharp dealing, of a size and shape indeed that society particularly despises, but still possible for the trained imagination of a prison-formed egotist to accept as equally meriting the name 'business' as company-promotion or munition-manufacture. But now he had come to a profound verge where ordinary self-deception must fail, to a limit over which, if ever he was to sleep again, he must be aided by a wilder, stronger illusion. To the making of this hypnosis in the few days that remain, he intensifies all his ways of thinking, as an athlete prepares his muscles for a record test. Everything that could recall to him the Reality, the personality of the woman beside him, he rigidly put out of mind. At all costs he must regard her as 'raw material', and crush out every reminder of her humanity. To this end he calls in the aid of every drop of disgust and contempt which in his nature of *faux-homme-aux-femmes* he felt for all women but one. For fear she should 'put him under an obligation', he insists on doing all the housework himself, this lazy man. He does the shopping and insists on her staying in bed late, so that he can hate her. He had all the mean tidiness of routine of the incipient miser; he encouraged a hundred daily irritations of it; and he carefully concealed from her the way he liked things done, so that she could offend him. For the last few days he even paid the bills out of his own pocket, though every day he got nearer his last penny. The way of a murderer and a boa-constrictor are opposite. Where the one sweetens with his saliva, the other must carefully contrive to hate. To the same end, he refused to listen to any account of her life since they parted, pretexting his sensitive remorse; he definitely cut her strand by strand from life in his mind and memory before he killed her. Above all, he insisted with himself that it was business, business; and for this he forced himself to think only on the ledger-side of what he was doing. For this he haggled over the bath; if for the first time in his life he had bought a second-hand object without huckstering it would have been to recognize to himself that this was not business, but murder. In the nights he called up the ethics they had taught him, clause by clause; the pettifogging religion of the police-courts, the casuistry of evidence, that makes or unmakes a crime; and cited to himself many social examples of crimes that were not crimes; recalled from his soldier days that killing need be no murder. So with nourishing of contempt, watering of hatred, with artificial incomprehension, with the exercise of his life-system of thought, he diligently prepared himself to kill. If he had more difficulty than those whose cases we have examined before, it may be an illusion due to our lack of knowledge, unjustly favouring him or depreciating his breed-mates; it may be that this man, the most odious of all mass-murderers, in reality had less aptitude for the trade than the rest.

Then on Saturday morning, so that the inquest could pass without her relatives being able to hear the news and attend (owing to the absence of Sunday mails), he calls his wife at seven o'clock and suggests to her she should take a bath. There was a reason apparently why this should be not opportune; but intent on her Griselda-play she obeys. He had placed the bath, not in its natural place—an empty room over the kitchen where there was but one flight of stairs to mount with the water-buckets—but in another room, a flight farther: because the kitchen room had a bolt, the other, none.

At eight o'clock the same doctor as before, summoned by a note, enters the house, is met by Williams, and taken to the bathroom. In it, cold and naked, lies Bessie Mundy, drowned. A square piece of Castile soap was clutched in her right hand. Williams was calm and very ready with his dates and hours. Another who had found murder easier than he expected! His story was that he had gone out to fetch herrings for breakfast; when he returned his wife was dead. With this story the coroner and his jury, in spite of a letter of cautious warning from the brother, agreed. Smith's behaviour must now carefully be watched; there is much to learn from it. He has two problems, one inward—the struggle with himself, to keep his nerves straight and his heart on ice; the other objective—to carry out his simple plot to delude the police. The second is obviously the easier. He has only to stick to his pat story of the earlier visits to the doctor and point resignedly to the bath. But even so there are flaws in it, bad flaws, which in the presence of the letter from Herbert Mundy the coroner must have been uncommonly dense not to see. Why did Smith not lift her at once out of the water? Why did he wait for the doctor to find her with her face submerged? Why should the bath be placed in an inconvenient room without a lock? And especially, how could a woman of her stature he drowned, unaided, in a bath too small for her? The plan over which some have wasted intellectual admiration was only the elementary cunning of a second-rate mind; with any intelligence to contend with, Smith would have ended his career of murderer at his first kill. His inward problem, too, has a nasty repercussion. He is in the quandary: I dare not feel any pity for her: how am I to show it? Show it he ought to, and here he is a failure. The clerk of the landlord, Miss Rapley, related later Smith's awful complaisance; in her presence he made a bad pretence of weeping and talked about the 'lucky thing my wife had made her will'. Everyone he had to relate the happening to had the same impression: the woman who came to lay out the body, who found it lying naked on the bare boards; the undertaker, whom Smith instructed to bury is wife in a common grave, in the cheapest manner possible; the relations, to whom again he sent grossly unconvincing letters, packed with sentences such as 'Words cannot describe the great shock, and I am naturally too sad to write more': enough to rouse the suspicions of a Bessie Mundy herself. But Smith is caught in his own gin, from which neither here nor in later murders can he shake free; he has set his mind to think his victims into business items. Without this he could not have done away with them, and it is impossible to feign without trying to feel. For this reason he is obliged to keep the money advantage of her death so constantly in his mind that it slips out to Miss Rapley; for this reason he is obliged to huckster the very coffin; for this reason he cannot squeeze out even one sympathetic word to her relations; for this reason he is obliged to plunge at once into the most cold-blooded and suspicious attempts to collect her fortune. The family entered a caveat against the will; but later, discouraged by the coroner's verdict, and secretly afraid of the fellow snarling at the bottom of the affair, they yielded and Smith received the wage of his damnation. The day after, 'Williams' had vanished, and Smith was writing to his institutional wife, Edith Pegler, to join him in Margate. She told him she had searched for him everywhere, even calling at his accommodation address with the Insurance Company at Woolwich. At this he made as if he would strike her with his fist, then suddenly thinking of something else, contented himself with a warning never again to try to look into his affairs. He told her he had been to Canada again, done big business with a Chinese idol picked up for and song and sold for over £1,000, and went to write business letters.

With the money, the tormented man now began an intricate and fundamentally idiotic series of transactions, transferring his money (split up in innumerable cheques) from one bank and from one end of the country to the other, as if he was afraid it would melt away, or be traced; really, to beguile his mind by the pretence of constant business. When he was tired of this form of the game of Patience, he embarked on an equally miscellaneous series of property transactions, an orgy of buying and selling, signing and releasing, and entering and transferring, which lasted for months, dealt with some ten small houses and ended, as far as an outsider in such matters can judge, with a net loss of over £700. Another idea then seized him—its origin is sufficiently obvious—he would have no more houses, but an annuity, that brought money in regularly. On this he spent what remained of the woman's money, to bring in £76 1s. a year. Then some time later, he thought better of it, and tried to release the money again for some other series of operations he had thought out, but after its wild excitements the fortune of Bessie Mundy had reached immobility. The purchase of an annuity cannot be repented.

To the agent who had sold him this annuity (Mr Plaisance), Smith, in October 1913, brought new business, and at the same time made an enigmatic promise to buy another £500 worth of annuity 'out of land transactions in Canada' the following January. For this business he was obliged to return to his real name, and even to forgo all mythology and produce his birth certificate. So the next episode, his marriage with Alice Burnham, is played out in the name of Smith. It was this young woman, a stout merry nurse, in the best of health and spirits, whose life Smith insured with Plaisance. At first Smith wanted the sum to be £1,000, payable at death; but learning that marriage would make the premium on this amount out of his means, he contented himself with one for £500 on a twenty-year endowment.

His confidence in the 'Canadian' deal shows that he had fully made up his mind to continue in the trade for which Bessie Mundy had paid his apprenticeship. To make it pay, he was resolved to turn to the most common and dangerous method of life-insurance, which has hanged innumerable murderers before him. The exploitation of death ranges from the horrible sale of the body itself, as with Burke, which solves the problem of disposal of the body and covers its tell-tale witness to the cause of death; through the simple despoliation of the personal possessions of the victim—furniture in the case of Landru, trust funds in the example of Bessie Mundy—to the insurance fraud, which Smith was now premeditating. There is no other method to gain money by the death of a person who has no possessions, and Smith was, for whatever reason, unable to venture on another moneyed spinster. But the essence of mass-murder, to be profitable and safe, is that the victims must stand in a loosened relation to the rest of society. The wolf who knows his business only attacks the isolated members of the herds, the wanderers, the outliers. To strict observance of this principle, Burke owed his immunity. It was in a terrific attempt to snap the chains that bound Kinck to his fellow-men that Troppmann peopled the plain of Pantin with corpses. But the exploitation of life-insurance, while it allows on the one hand of the selection of poor strayers—riches being the most powerful chain to hold society's interest in a man's personal fate—yet the very act of giving a powerful commercial organization a direct interest that the victim should not die wakens an enemy whose determination and acumen is more dangerous to the assassin than all the Dogberrys of all the local inquest courts. Thus, while apparently cunning, it is the stupidest folly for a professional murderer to pick out a friendless victim and then give the victim's life over to the protection of a most powerful and interested corporation. It is a common folly, and tempted that stupid rogue, Smith. Nor indeed was his intended victim, this Alice Burnham, without friends. Her father was a retired coal-merchant, immensely more shrewd than the small shyster that thus pushed into his family circle; there were brothers, sisters, and a mother who loved her. Only over the girl herself, whom he had met in his accustomed manner at Portsmouth, had the murderer any advantage; not one, to be sure, of intellect, but given to him, an eligible male, by nature and the social system. Miss Burnham is a less enigmatic character than her predecessor, though hardly less tragic. She was a strong capable woman, hard-working in her profession, to whom celibacy with all its accompaniments was as irksome as it was despairing to Bessie Mundy. Every atom of Miss Burnham's body and her tastes repelled her from the state to which the customs of her country had condemned her. She was twenty-six years old when she accepted the company of this man, on whom she could have had less illusions even than Bessie. She was eager to risk all the smug-faced monotony of comfort and esteem, even the affection of her family, for the single chance of a natural life; and she was a cheerful gambler.

But first she made a bold attempt to impose her 'young man' (Smith was now 40) on her family. Smith cut a pitiable figure at the family home in Aston Clinton, where he was invited; the bluff father had met many such before, and concealed neither his contempt nor dislike for this stranger whose manner wavered always between brag and servility. The mother, whose ideas of the minimum qualifications of a husband were less exacting than those of Charles Burnham, tried to moderate her husband; but in the end the prospective son-in-law was kicked out, muttering threats, and Alice accompanied him to the station. That was the 31st October 1913. On the 4th November following they were married, without anyone of the family being present.

On retiring from business, Mr Burnham had presented each of his children with £40, the eldest son taking over the succession. To this sum Alice, from her savings, had added £60, and given the whole £100 to her father for save keeping. He paid her 4 per cent on it. This nest-egg Smith now set himself to collect, with his mixture of greed and legal stupidities. He poured forth a stream of letters to the father in his usual county-court cum lay-reader tone; he accused him of 'taking refuge in obdurateness, contempt, and remorse', and threatened 'to take the matter up without delay'. In the course of the correspondence, a postcard from Smith conveyed the genealogical information at the beginning of this study. Another ran, 'I do not know your next move, but take my advice and be careful.' Another pointed this vague threat (with sounds nastier to us who know the man's past than probably it was intended) with the explanation, 'I am keeping all letters that pass for the purpose of justice.' In the end, Burnham, dreading a long and vexatious law-case with this sinister sea-lawyer, yielded and sent the money.

By this ungainly procedure, Smith had achieved the opposite of what he no doubt intended, and set an estrangement between the daughter and her family. A similar action about a paltry sum owed by her sister completed the effect. But without meaning it, he had blundered into the only possible chance of the success of the deed he was planning—the isolation of the woman. The next act in his fixed repertory which he had composed from the circumstances of his first crime, after the habit of mass-murderers, was to take Alice Burnham on a trip to Blackpool. In the choice of this distant resort, he showed both a knowledge of geography and a nice science of the social usages. Blackpool in winter is out of season, yet the relaxation of censure and curiosity still might be hoped to prevail. The respectable by-roads of Herne Bay suited admirably in his former venture; but both the life and death of the gay little nurse would fit better into the setting of the People's Paradise of the North. And it was as far as possible from her family and any friends her infatuation for him could have left.

When they arrived in the cold grey air, there were no tunes from the merry-go-rounds to greet them; the shooting-galleries were quiet; the promenade empty and windy. They put up for their unseasonal honeymoon with a family named Crossley, in lodgings in Cocker Street. Previously Smith had tried elsewhere, but failed to find the convenience of a bathroom. In the Crossleys' house, for ten shillings a week, they could use the bath when they liked. All they had brought for luggage was a brownish hold-all and a paper parcel. The Crossleys were good Lancashire folk, very anxious to please in this lodgerless month. Mrs Crossley agreed to cook the visitors' meals. They would buy the materials themselves. Smith knows no other method of preparing himself for great acts than to soak his mind in petty meannesses. He grumbles astonishingly at the departure of every penny. Mrs Smith seemed to the Crossleys charming; it is a pity that this Mrs Smith has a train-headache from the journey. But in spite of it and Mr Smith's noticeable stinginess, she insists on going out the same evening to the kinematograph.

Smith is desperately quick this time; he is afraid this lively little Alice will either escape him or ruin him. Nevertheless he does not scamp a detail of his plaster-of-Paris plan. The morning after their arrival, he takes her to the doctor; naturally this time he does not dare to talk of fits (she is a nurse), but insists that the railway-headache alarms him. The doctor is not at a loss: he prescribes a mild purgative.

Two days later, that was a Friday, they went out for a walk, leaving instructions for a bath to be prepared. The bath was to be for Mrs Smith. Smith had already inspected the bathroom. Before this look-round the bolt worked perfectly. It was above the kitchen. At tea-time, the evening meal, the Crossleys, the mother, the son, the grown-up daughter-in-law, were sitting round the kitchen table, when one of them noticed a great stain of water on the ceiling. They all looked at it and saw it enlarge and drip down the wall, behind a picture. Such a thing had never happened before. The elder woman said, 'Oh, Alice, go and tell Mrs Smith not to fill the bath so.' But the girl answered, 'Oh, mother, they will think we are grumbling already, and they not two days in the house.'

Then suddenly the pale Smith came into the kitchen. He lumped a package on to the table and said, 'I have brought these eggs for our breakfast in the morning.' The girl got up to take them, wiping her mouth with her napkin. Smith then went upstairs. They heard him call shrilly, 'Alice, put the light out.' The daughter-in-law, who had this Christian name, thought he was speaking to her, rose and went up to him. He said, 'No, I was speaking to my wife, Alice, to put the light out.' The living Alice went back into the kitchen. Then Smith, who was standing on the mat on the bathroom landing, said suddenly again, 'My wife will not speak to me.' Good Mrs Crossley stood up at this sort of scream, and said, 'Oh, what is it?' 'Fetch Dr Billing in a hurry,' he said.

Mrs Crossley: Dr Billing lives quite near. I ran for him and he came to my house for a few minutes. I waited on the stairs and when he came down I asked him what was wrong, and he said, 'Oh, she is drowned. She is dead.' Smith was upstairs on the landing then. I went back to the kitchen and my daughter, called Mrs Haynes, came in. After the doctor had gone, Smith came down into the kitchen. I said to him, 'How dreadful: what an awful thing this is!' He said he would not be surprised at anything that would happen afterwards.

Behind this stiffness that shocked we may catch a glimpse of a soul clinging with all its might to unreality, a wretch, terror-stricken to the heart, striving with all his might to believe that he had simply done a good stroke of business. Under the watersplash on the ceiling, amidst the remnant of an evening meal, the two eyed each other, he helpless to relax his grip, not daring even to pretend to cry, she with an angry uneasiness growing every second. They are both tongue-tied. He breaks it off finally, in a new tone. 'Now, Smith, you cannot stop here to-night.' He can only say, 'Why?' 'Because I'll take good care not to have a callous fellow like you in the house.' He gulps, but does not protest, except, 'When they're dead, they're dead.' He had to write his letters in the next-door house that night. Across the post-card on which he left with her his address, Mrs Crossley wrote, in spite of the inquest, in spite of the verdict, the memento, 'Wife died in bath. We shall see him again.'

This bungler had succeeded again. The mere fact that the woman had died in a bath and that no one as yet had heard of this stealthy form of murder seemed alone to be in his favour. Hangdog and perpetually busy, he fixed his affairs, collected the money from the company without a murmur, and paid over to Plaisance the promised £500. Acting more near instinct than by free thought he repeated the chain of his acts as he had devised them in the former case, down to their least detail. He had prepared the doctor, prepared her parents, killed on Friday to avoid their presence, made up the same trumpery alibi of a small purchase outside. Now he completed the chain, sold the dead woman's jewels and clothing and cleared out to another seatown, then sent for the Bristol wife, with another tale of dealings in Canada.

The success of this second murder must have confirmed the man in the complicated unreality he had adjusted round himself. He no longer found it hard to believe that he was a bold business man, successful in a very serious line, who must, after all, look after his health. He became exacting with Pegler; with those annuities locked in his private drawer, he dared to begin to believe he had done it 'all for her.' The thought of another long sea-voyage to Canada, to find another valuable antique, oppressed him more than it did his companion; he had made symbols like this for everything in his life and used them even in his private thoughts. Every day he seemed more cynical about the hardness of the world. He pitied himself profoundly, because his nature was a handicap. He confided to his wife sometimes parts of what he had suffered in his last journey: how a certain man had tried to humiliate him about his birth, how the miserable suspicions of boarding-house keepers and the like just showed you. So by these symbolisms he managed to relieve himself of the only burden that weighed, the memory of humiliations, the scratches on his pride. Then he would spend hours reading the small print on the backs of his annuities and checking his old house-accounts. At intervals he would be stung with the recollection of what he had lost and he would leave the Bristol house for a week's trip. But never as far as Canada—lesser affairs in the earlier manner. Matters of savings, small deals with servants and the like.

At last those higher powers, who had so whimsically rejoined him and Bessie together, again intervened. At Clifton, near the spot where a man he knew named Henry Williams once met a girl called Mundy, he fell in with Miss Margaret Lofty, a small, wistful shape, who was walking in the cool of the evening to calm certain private anguishes. She was the daughter of a clergyman, dead for years, a lady's companion no longer young. A year before, she had been happy, but the man she was engaged to had turned out to be a married man and now she was alone. She was struck by Smith's eyes, eyes that showed he, too, had suffered, eyes that gave her the sensation of 'having been there before'. She learned that his name was 'Lloyd', a man beneath her station, of course, but a God-fearing, handsome fellow who understood.

She clung to him as if she were drowning. She made a show to him of all her accomplishments, fell in eagerly with all his ideas. When he talked about insurance and how it was a principle of his to make provision for the future, she picked up all its mechanism in an hour or two's quiet chat. He complimented her on her intelligence, regretted he had not had himself the advantage of much education. A shy and retiring man, he was too nervous to meet her family, which suited her, as she felt a tiny grudge against mother and sister for their uncomprehension in the terrible affair the year before, and now they might not understand. At thirty-eight a woman's affairs are her own concern, and seldom easy to tell. She told them nothing about Lloyd, and made up an innocent story about a new position (which was true after all) when she went away to be married. After she had gone to see the insurance-manager (she struck him as 'having the business at her finger's ends') and taken out a policy for £700, 'Lloyd' had the licence ready. They took train to Bath and the same day were man and wife.

Miss Lofty drew out her life savings, £19, and advanced it to her husband. This money carried them to London, where Smith, who knew the neighbourhood from one of his former existences, had booked lodgings into the superior district of Highgate. Coroner's juries would push complaisance to its limits in such a neighbourhood. But when they arrived at the address, Smith-Lloyd had a great shock. He stumbled across the war.

For during all these years while the man intent in his own cult pursued his private ritual of murder, a mightier killing was being prepared, a world-wide massacre, one of whose immense circuits of force lay through the very house he had selected for his last crime. As absent-minded as a weasel on the blood-scent, possibly until this moment he had never heard of the war. It was the 17th December 1914, the miraculous year. The day before, his own hunting-grounds, Scarborough, Whitby, were shelled by German cruisers. Two months before the London mob in a patriotic ecstasy had sacked the German shops, and every unfortunate German in the country was still trembling. Amongst them the mistress of the very house that he had chosen. On his first visit he had noticed her attitude. Little in a woman's manner ever escaped that professional eye. So automatically he had swelled in *his* manner, played the masterful. When she asked timidly for references, he did not give her an easy lie, but pulled six shillings out of his pocket and tapped them on the desk. She was afraid to refuse them; but more afraid, in such times, when every one of her actions was dangerous, to step even for an inch outside the safety of law. When he returned with the woman, this foreign woman had fortified herself with a supreme reinforcement, a real detective, friend of the family. It was this man (Dennison) who met the couple when they arrived and told Smith-Lloyd, with one of those precognitional glances of which those of his calling have the secret, to be off, and quickly.

The couple went out in silence, at hazard, when Smith had been paid his deposit. In a side-road near by, Bismark Road, they found another place, kept by Miss Blatch. His formula, for a moment checked, begins to run: 'Have you a bath?' They are accepted. Then Mrs Lloyd sits down to send the letter mentioning an illness; then they visit the nearest doctor, then the preparation of the bath, and the full canon of the slaying: with this exception, that there was a splash, a sigh, a strange visit of the man to the harmonium where he played 'something' for a few minutes.[1] Mrs Lloyd is dead. There is again the rushing

[1] *According to Miss Blatch, the tune that Smith played was 'Nearer My God to Thee'.*

through the house, the terror of the landlady, the calls, the doctor's dash upstairs, the splashing in the bathroom, the policeman's knock on the door; evidence; a grim man who has a clear story and a bad manner, a word-for-word repetition in the coroner's court. Letters, packings, bargainings with grave-diggers, another £700 safely received.

But this time something more. A coincidence, one of those queer logical figures with which the stream of becoming sometimes playfully diversifies its course, one of life's punning rhymes, which science hates and art abhors, but which fascinate the attention of mankind. Smith, painstaking imitator of nature, who had modelled his ferocity on her accidents, had unthinkingly composed a perfect, a triple coincidence. He had been betrayed by the first law of murder: repetition. Let but one man stumble upon this coincidence of the bath, and Smith, by it alone, like an incurable poison, will die as surely and cruelly as Bessie Mundy.

That man was Charles Burnham. He noticed an account of the Highgate inquest in a Sunday newspaper, the *News of the World*, which is a collection of the happenings of the week, curious, dramatic, horrible and comic, immensely diffused among the English masses. 'Death' and 'Bride' are index-words to the tastes of the readers of this journal; their conjunction in one case gave the news a good place in the paper. Almost with greed, this quiet unhurrying man, lying in not hopeless ambush for the return of the phantom who had destroyed his daughter, caught the devilish assonance, the infernal rhyme with all the circumstances of his own loss. The description of this Highgate mystery made Burnham's long-waited revenge as simple then as the pull of a trigger; he cut out the printed account, pinned it to that in his possession of his own daughter's end, and sent them both to the police.

Thereafter there are two feverish activities running side by side, one out of sight and below the other. The figure of a man grown greyish, with an intangible history, working at accounts, very intent on the business of settling his wife's affairs with solicitor, Somerset House, the Insurance Company; and below him, like hounds out of sight in a sunken road, the detectives grappling with his faint and twisted trail back into the past. All that Smith may have noticed in this fortnight is a slight clogging of his affairs, an almost imperceptible increase of the customary delays, the shadow of obscure inhibitions behind the Insurance Company's formal letters. All his senses were sharpened in the darkness in which he worked. At times, deep in his correspondence, he would pause and listen as if through their typed formalities he could hear a far-off noise of running steps. Sometimes for two days in succession he would stop on his way to the solicitor's office and turn back thoughtfully: then for long hours fight with himself to pull back to the *business standpoint.* On the 1st of February 1915, as he left the solicitor's office, he saw with a great start that three soberly-dressed men wanted to speak to him. They came round him so close that he felt their coats, and one said something about Alice Burnham. As in an accident, it was too sudden for him to have any fear. If he had heard 'Miss Mundy' he might have screamed; but the man said, 'Alice Burnham', a name that only recalled a long and nasty business affair, in which he was in the right, quite in the right, and no jury would give a verdict against him. So, without any blink he admitted that he did know her, that he was the George Smith who had married her at the Portsmouth Registry Office: what about it? He was arrested at once on a charge of causing a false entry in the marriage register. He did not need the customary caution not to say more.

England found time to try the man at the Old Bailey; for the nine days between 22nd June 1915 and the 1st July his affairs competed for public interest with the first defeats of the Russians in Galicia and the first victories of the Italians in the Dolomites. A prosy judge, a high-spirited defender (Marshall Hall), let out the regulated driblets of information allowed by English law on the surly, absent-minded mystery fenced in their midst in dock. Under the weight of contrasts, Smith's deeds seemed more terrible than the crash of armies, his tin baths more evil things than bridge-destroying artillery, this minor devil more sinister than all the hell outside.

At times he would take his own part and yell at them. The whole court would stare at him with amazement as if his chop-law was speaking with tongues, and his blind belief in his own innocence—because they could not tell him the precise method he had killed, whether by pulling the feet, or by holding the heads—a thing never heard of in experience. But to this, and other last consolations of the mass-murderer—the inanimation of his victims, all trace of whose living personalities had long been expelled from his brain: the joy in the legal bickerings, so much to his taste: the sense of consideration and elevation that the dock confers—Smith, like Burke, like Troppmann, now left himself entire. Alone in the court he neglected to look at the iron coincidence, three women identically killed, for identical motives after marriage with the same man, and attached importance to the cunning details which the recurrence contemptuously destroyed. Alone in the court, like a rigid juryman, he refused to believe in his own guilt, because a coincidence was not evidence.

These fundamental errors of thought no doubt sustained him in the condemned cell in which, a safe for precious objects, he was carefully preserved for death by hanging. Irreality has lordly rewards for her devotees, whether solipsists or drug fiends or murderers. In her humblest, more eerie form which had rotted the mass-murderer's imagination, she stood staunch by Smith to his end; if, on the scaffold, with the ropes round his elbows and a bag over his mouth, his legs failed, it was a physical, not a moral, terror that prevailed.

## ALAN HYND
# The Case of the Man who Came to Dinner, etc.

According to doctors who examined her, Walburga Oesterreich was a nymphomaniac in the classic tradition. In the words of a certain Hollywood producer, she was an *over-sexed* nymphomaniac.

In 1903, Walburga and her husband Fred were jointly engaged in operating an apron factory in Milwaukee. Fred Oesterreich, an arrogant man who made Simon Legree look like a missionary, was noted for blustering through the work-rooms of the factory, making certain that his employees were giving him 61 minutes work per hour. Mrs Oesterreich would follow her husband around when he lashed the help to greater effort, picking up egos and returning them to their owners. Had the workers taken a vote on whom they hoped the brick factory building would fall, there is little doubt as to who would have won.

The Oesterreichs were childless (no fault of Walburga), and life in their home—a mustard-colored frame structure that looked as if it had been planned by an architect who had undergone several changes of mind—was average. Average, that is, for a household where the husband, sensing if not identifying certain basic inferiorities within himself, frequently became overstimulated by alcohol and assaulted his wife.

Police had to drop in on the Oesterreichs occasionally, simply to satisfy themselves that Mrs Oesterreich—a lady with well-developed vocal chords, among other things—wasn't getting her head bashed in by the burly Mr Oesterreich. Official concern for the lady's welfare, however, seemed somewhat unnecessary. Mrs Oesterreich could protect herself and, after seventeen years of marital tiffs, had attained a certain knee dexterity and a good pitching arm, the latter useful for throwing small articles of furniture.

One day there walked into the apron factory, and into the lives of Fred and Walburga Oesterreich, an improbable little personality who, as somebody once said, bore an extraordinary resemblance to nobody in particular. His name was Otto Sanhuber. Otto, a wizened introvert with rumbled hair, eyeglasses, receding chin, and watery-blue eyes, stood not quite five feet tall; he was only seventeen but somehow looked older. An employee of the Singer Sewing Machine Company, whose product was used in the apron factory, he had come to repair a machine.

Walburga Oesterreich, beckoning the boy to follow her as she led the way to the machine to be repaired, started Otto on the first steps of a bizarre journey that was to be unique in the annals of crime. Otto Sanhuber, that day in 1903, entered upon a phase of human existence and experience that was, if it accomplished nothing else, to contribute impressive evidence to the theory that truth is stranger than fiction.

Women of Mrs Oesterreich's type usually see in certain men qualities not discernible to the average person. Whatever it was she was looking for, she saw it in little Otto Sanhuber. Yet, even girls Otto's own age, down by the Milwaukee beer vats, had passed him up as utterly uninteresting; but here was a woman, more than twice his age, who wanted to put him under lock and key—and eventually was to do precisely that.

Walburga was as unhurried as she was skillful in weaving her web about the unsuspecting Otto. She saw to it that there was plenty of repair work to be done on the sewing machines in the apron factory; there was so much repair work, in fact, that Mrs Oesterreich was suspected, in the light of subsequent events, of personally putting some of the sewing machines out of commission.

One day a machine that Mrs Oesterreich kept at home, in the bedroom of all places, suddenly broke down. The lady went through the motions of asking her husband what she should do about the broken machine. 'Why,' answered Oesterreich, 'get that kid to fix it—that kid who's been coming around the factory.' By virtue of that suggestion, Fred Oesterreich was never able technically to dispute the fact, after his wife and little Otto put an intrigue in motion, that he hadn't asked for it.

Oesterreich was one of those men who fancied himself so attractive to a woman that he couldn't imagine any female, once she had come to know him intimately, being interested in anyone else. Thus it was three years before he so much as suspected that there was more than friendship between his wife and the little sewing-machine repair-boy. The first inkling of what was happening came to Oesterreich when it suddenly occurred to him that the sewing machine in his wife's bedroom had been breaking down with suspicious consistency.

When Oesterreich suggested to his wife that she should get a new machine, Walburga replied, 'No, I like *this* one.' Not only her answer, but the way she lowered her eyes when she gave it, caused Fred to suspect that something was amiss.

Mrs Oesterreich divined what was in her husband's mind, according to a statement that Sanhuber himself was one day to make, and she suggested to Otto that they take a trip together. When Mrs Oesterreich resolved the only obstacle to the trip that Otto could think of—money—they were off. They went to Chicago and registered at a hotel under assumed names, but were unable to shake off the feeling that they were being followed.

The travelers left Chicago for St Louis, but Mrs Oesterreich saw, wherever she went, a man she had also frequently observed in Chicago. Instead of becoming alarmed over the obvious fact that her husband had put a private detective on her trail, she did what in theatrical parlance is known as a slow burn. She returned to Milwaukee with Sanhuber, bade him a temporary adieu at the railroad station, went home, and cracked her husband over the head with a silver candlestick.

'That,' she said, 'will learn you to have me followed.'

Oesterreich's reaction could hardly be described as normal. He fell on his knees, kissed the hem of his wife's skirt, and vowed that he could not live without her. 'All right,' she said, 'we'll forget the whole thing.' But Walburga Oesterreich was not a woman of her word. One day when her husband was at the apron factory and she stayed at home, supposedly not feeling well, she sneaked Otto Sanhuber into the house. 'I have,' she informed Otto, 'fixed everything.'

By 'everything' the lady meant that she had arranged affairs so that Otto was going to live right in the house with her and her husband—without the husband knowing it. Otto was to live in an unused portion of the attic, reached through a trap door over, of all places, the master bedroom.

He would be supplied with every physical need, including a specially shaded lamp by which to read at night; he would not be obliged to work or, presumably, worry. He could come down through the trap door whenever his 40-year-old paramour gave him the signal—three scratches with her fingernails on the bottom of the door. There would, of course, be certain restrictions to his life. He would not be permitted to leave the house or come back into it except at night, and then only when Fred Oesterreich was out, attending a lodge meeting or working late at the factory.

Otto would, on the other hand, have unlimited freedom when Oesterreich was not on the premises. The Oesterreichs did not keep a maid, because the apron-manufacturer was too stingy to hire one. That gave little Otto the run of the place during the day, whether Mrs Oesterreich was at the factory or at home. She pointed out to Otto how cozy it would be, of a snowy winter day, when she, feigning illness, packed her husband off to the apron factory and remained behind to be with Otto until nightfall.

If Fred and Walburga Oesterreich were peculiar people by ordinary standards, they were pleasantly normal compared to Sanhuber. Otto was simply entranced with the idea of being a prisoner of love. He was an emotionally short-circuited youth who had begun life in a foundling home and who, until he had met Walburga Oesterreich, had been destined to go through life as a square peg in a round hole. What Otto Sanhuber really needed was five to ten years' treatment by an alienist, as psychiatrists were called in those days. Lacking such treatment, and fearing to face the realities of life, a future in an attic sounded just great to Otto. After àll, he'd have no responsibilities and all of his physical wants, including an overly active sex life, guaranteed in advance. Then, too, he entertained a vague ambition to be a writer; certainly his paramour's proposition would afford him the solitude popularly supposed to be a prerequisite for successful authorship.

And so Otto Sanhuber, at the age of nineteen, moved into the unused portion of the attic of the big mustard-colored house in Milwaukee to begin an existence that was not to come to light for many years. He just dropped from sight—the sight of everyone except Walburga Oesterreich.

There were, to be sure, certain complications. From all accounts, Otto had, despite his frail stature, an appetite of Falstaffian dimension. It is a matter of record that he did not grow so much as half an inch, or put on a pound of weight, after his seventeenth year—perhaps because of the glandular demands of Walburga Oesterreich; but it wasn't that he didn't try. His paramour would sneak up to him large supplies of tinned meat and fish, whole cheeses, boxes of crackers, loaves of bread, whole bolognas and liverwursts, vegetables, mayonnaise, and bottles of milk and beer. Yet Otto was always hungry.

Sometimes, just before the Oesterreichs went out for the evening, Mrs Oesterreich would run up to the bedroom, scratch three times on the trap door, and unsnap it. When the Oesterreichs closed the front door behind them, Otto would rush downstairs and raid the icebox.

On occasion, when Mrs Oesterreich brought out a left-over roast for supper, her husband would look at it in a puzzled sort of way. 'Whatever happened to all the meat on this thing?' he would ask. 'We didn't eat *that* much last night.' Mrs Oesterreich would explain that Oesterreich himself had fallen upon the roast after returning from a party the night before but had been too drunk to remember.

Sometimes, in the watches of the night, Oesterreich, who did not enjoy untroubled sleep, would lie tossing in the big double bed he shared with his wife and hear a sound of some kind directly above in the attic.

'What,' he would ask, bolting upright in bed, 'was that?'

'Go back to sleep, Fred,' his wife would say. 'It's only your imagination.'

One night there was a loud thump above. '*That,*' said Oesterreich, 'wasn't my imagination!'

'It's probably something that tipped over,' said Mrs Oesterreich. 'I'll attend to it tomorrow. Now go to sleep.' Fred Oesterreich seems to have loved his sleep more than his suspicions. He obeyed his wife's command.

There was a small window in that portion of the attic where Otto Sanhuber domiciled; it was practically opaque with dust, but Mrs Oesterreich warned Sanhuber never to go near it. One summer evening, while Fred Oesterreich was burning rubbish in the back yard, he happened to glance up at the attic window at the precise moment that Otto chose to disobey the injunction of his mistress. What Fred Oesterreich saw at the window wasn't very distinct, but it moved.

Oesterreich rushed into the house. 'I just saw something in the attic!' he shouted. 'Somebody's up there!'

Walburga had a way of looking at Fred Oesterreich that made him feel foolish. As for him, he was too enamored of the woman, too afraid that she would run off with a man again, to cross her.

Walburga ventured the opinion that her husband was going out of his mind, probably from drink. Oesterreich became alarmed; he had never considered such a possibility before. But now that his wife pointed out certain things, he had to admit that he had been involved in some fairly outrageous observations. He had imagined that food was disappearing from the icebox, that liquor was stolen from his cellar, and that cigars were vanishing from his humidors. He had imagined that he heard rats and mice in the attic coughing and clearing their throats. And now he had just imagined that he had seen a face in the attic window.

Thereafter Fred Oesterreich, thoroughly alarmed at the prospect of approaching insanity, didn't dare mention to his wife that he thought he still heard queer noises in the attic and that he was under the impression that his cigars and liquor and the food from the icebox were disappearing. Then, rationalizing the whole improbable business, he said the house was haunted—and he decided to move.

Otto, who had been in the attic more than three years now, with only an occasional outside airing, was greatly disturbed; he had just gotten the attic fixed up to his liking. But he was only 23, and comparatively adjustable.

The new house, which Oesterreich hoped would put an end to his vague but deeply disturbing troubles, did no such thing. For three years more he still heard strange noises in the attic; edibles, potables, and smokes continued to vanish. He consulted a doctor who suggested a long trip. Business at the apron factory, however, demanded Oesterreich's uninterrupted presence there, and a trip was out of the question. Instead, he changed houses again. Otto went right along— now in his seventh year as a bat-man.

Otto, up there in the attic, was removed in more ways than one from contact with the life that ebbed and flowed around him. During his first years in seclusion, he had not gotten around to fulfilling his ambition to be a writer. He had spent those years reading—everything from history to philosophy. But now, when he wasn't eating or sleeping, he was writing. He moved in a world of plots and counterplots and sacred and profane love. He specialized in adventure stories, most of them set in the South Seas.

Walburga, who encouraged Otto in his ambition to be a successful, if obscure, author, made an occasional suggestion about a love scene, drawing on her own rich fund of experience. She also took the manuscripts to a typing agency and sent them off to magazines under a pen name—hiring a post-office box for all correspondence on the literary level.

At first, Otto drew only rejection slips from editors. He was such a prolific creator that he eventually accumulated enough slips to paper, had he so desired, his attic quarters. Then, around 1916, when Otto was 29 and in his eleventh year in the rafters, success came to him. Editors of pulp magazines found his South Seas stories exactly what they wanted; they were good escape fare for a country that wanted to look the other way from America's entry into the First World War. Walburga Oesterreich began to slip checks up to the hidden author, along with his food. He endorsed the checks over to the lady and became, after a fashion, self-supporting.

Although everything was progressing beautifully, there is evidence to support the belief that Otto, whose sense of hearing became very acute, issued an occasional protest to Mrs Oesterreich. It seems he heard a man other than her husband in her bedchamber. The lady denied this extra-infidelity; she was so completely domineering, and otherwise persuasive, that Otto soon abandoned his protests.

One night Fred, who had gone with his wife to a party, returned home alone and unexpectedly. He heard a noise in the kitchen and investigated. And he caught Otto Sanhuber poking around the icebox.

Although the apron-manufacturer had not laid eyes on Otto for a decade, he recognized him instantly. With magnificent self-control, he restrained himself from consigning little Otto to residence in a wheel chair; he merely gave him a thorough thrashing and threw him out of the house, little realizing that in so doing he was putting Otto out of the only home he had.

Sanhuber went to Los Angeles and got a job as a porter. But he couldn't, after his years in the attics, get used to the bright sunshine. He would probably have liked the place better today, with its smog. However, he still had a line of communication with Mrs Oesterreich—the post-office box that she had used in their dealings with the magazines. He contacted her and soon they were engaged in an enthusiastic correspondence.

Fred Oesterreich, it developed—upon discovering that Otto had been living in his attics—had been crushed by the weight of his wife's betrayal. But he had become too ill to protest; anyway, he loved the woman, no matter what she had done to him. He asked only one thing: that she never have anything to do with Otto Sanhuber again. Mrs Oesterreich, stepping up her correspondence with Otto, promised.

Fred became an increasingly unhappy man. When he walked through his apron factory he just didn't have the old energy to whip the help into maximum effort. Every time he looked at a Singer sewing machine he thought of Otto the repair-boy, and everytime he thought of Otto his heart began to pound. He went off his food; liquor and cigars no longer offered him enjoyment. He consulted three doctors about his condition. While they disagreed as to what was wrong with him, they were agreed on one thing: he needed a permanent change, business or no business. He asked his wife, who had just finished reading a letter from Otto in Los Angeles, where she thought they should go for a permanent change. This was asking for it for the second time.

The Oesterreichs settled themselves in a rambling house on North St Andrews Place, one of the more fashionable thoroughfares in the City of the Angels, in the summer of 1918. The change had a pronounced therapeutic effect on Oesterreich, now 55. He was soon in business as head of the Oesterreich Garment Company—aprons, dresses, lingerie. He offered his wife a full-time maid. She said no thanks, she could do with a cleaning woman a couple of times a week. She bustled with plans for Otto, whom she hadn't seen in two years, to resume his old status.

Then she discovered that there was a walled-off portion of the attic above, again, the master bedroom. While her husband was busy at the factory, the lady hustled workmen into the house and had them cut a secret entrance into the attic space by means of a trap door that opened off a shelf in one of the bedroom closets. Presently, Otto was back at the old stand, safely in out of the sunshine.

Whatever life in the Oesterreich house had been in Milwaukee, it was different in Los Angeles. Oesterreich never regained his old bounce and, although he still got drunk at night, he acted less quarrelsome. The neighbors, therefore, were quite unprepared for what happened a few minutes after 11 o'clock on the night of August 22, 1922, four years after the Oesterreichs had taken up residence on North St Andrews Place. Loud words—words between two men— began issuing from the premises. A woman screamed. Then there came the sounds of shots.

When police arrived they found Fred Oesterreich lying in the living room, fatally shot in the head and the chest. They found Mrs Oesterreich locked in a closet in her bedroom.

Walburga's story was that she and her husband, returning home from a party, had been set upon by an intruder. The intruder had slain her husband when the garment-manufacturer had grappled with him, then followed Mrs Oesterreich as she fled to her bedroom and locked her in the closet. An inventory of the murdered man's effects disclosed that a handsome diamond-studded watch was missing. Presumably the murderer had stolen it.

The chief of detectives, Herman Cline, was suspicious of practically everything and everybody. Especially of Mrs Oesterreich. The bullets that had killed her husband had come from a .25-caliber weapon. 'A lady's gun,' said Cline. 'Burglars don't use them. Let's look into this woman.'

Walburga couldn't, of course, stand much looking into. Nobody alive yet knew about Sanhuber's affinity for attics, except Otto himself and Mrs Oesterreich, and they weren't talking; but there was plenty for a man like Cline to find out back in Milwaukee. He learned that the lady had considerably less than a spotless reputation and that she had definitely not, as she was now attempting to lead Cline to believe, adored her husband.

Whatever Cline's suspicions, he was without evidence to hold Walburga, who three months after the murder, retained the services of Herman Shapiro, an attorney, to settle up her late husband's estate. Oesterreich, like many well-heeled heels, had left a complicated estate, worth almost a million dollars. 'Here,' said Mrs Oesterreich to lawyer Shapiro one day, dropping a diamond-studded watch in his hand. 'This belonged to my husband, and I want you to have it.'

In January, five months after the murder, Mrs Oesterreich disposed of the house on North St Andrews Place, saying it held too many terrible memories for her, and moved into a smaller place on North Beachwood Drive, with an attic.

She called a friend, an actor, and handed him a revolver. 'It wouldn't look good for me to have a .25-caliber revolver in my possession,' she explained, 'seeing that the man who murdered dear Fred had the same kind of gun. Please get rid of it for me.' Then she summoned another friend, a former neighbor, and gave him a .25-caliber revolver along with the same explanation and instructions.

The actor took his weapon and threw it in the LaBrea tar pits, a piece of real estate that was later to become joke fodder on the Jack Benny and Bob Hope radio programs. The ex-neighbor buried the second revolver in his yard.

Shortly after she moved to North Beachwood Drive, Mrs Oesterreich and attorney Shapiro prepared to make a trip to Milwaukee, on business relating to the garment-manufacturer's estate. Before leaving, Walburga instructed the attorney to go out and purchase a huge quantity of canned goods and leave it in the kitchen of her house. 'What do you want all that stuff for,' asked Shapiro, 'now that you're going on a trip?' Mrs Oesterreich divulged that she had an eccentric half brother, a vagrant, who often stopped by.

'I don't want him to be hungry,' the lady said to her counsel, 'if he stops by while I'm away.' Mrs Oesterreich and Shapiro were gone three weeks. When they returned, the canned goods had disappeared.

In July, 1923, eleven months after the murder of Fred Oesterreich, Chief of Detectives Cline learned that Mrs Oesterreich's attorney was walking around with a diamond-studded watch. Cline dropped into Shapiro's office and took a look at the watch. It was the one that the slayer had presumably made off with.

'Mrs Oesterreich,' said Shapiro, 'told me that she found the watch under a window seat after the murder. She was afraid to say anything about it because she didn't want any more publicity in the papers.' The story of the watch got in the papers, and clouds of suspicion about the head of Walburga grew darker than ever.

The two men to whom Mrs Oesterreich had given .25-caliber revolvers to dispose of—the actor and the ex-neighbor—now contacted Cline. Cline dug up the weapon that Mrs Oesterreich's ex-neighbor had buried under a rosebush. Ballistics tests proved it was not the gun that had killed Oesterreich. The second weapon, the one the actor had thrown into the LaBrea tar pits, could not be recovered.

Although he wasn't exactly wallowing in evidence, Cline arrested Mrs Oesterreich anyway, charging her with the murder of her husband, and hoped for a development that would result in a confession. The fact that the woman had been found locked in a closet didn't bother the chief of detectives; he maintained that she could have shot her husband, for whatever reason, and locked *herself* in the closet. The closet door locked and unlocked with an old-fashioned key, and the key was found on the outside of the closet, on the floor. Cline suspected that Mrs Oesterreich, after having locked the closet from the inside, had shoved the key through the quarter inch of space between the bottom of the door and the floor.

Walburga, languishing in jail, now had two attorneys—Shapiro, who was handling her fiscal matters, and Frank Dominquez, a well-known criminal lawyer. One day when Shapiro visited her, she asked him to do her a favor, to go to a closet in her bedroom, scratch three times on a panel above a shelf, and stand by: 'You will meet a man,' she said. 'He is my half brother—the vagabond I told you about. Have a talk with him and assure him I am all right and he will be taken care of.'

Otto Sanhuber was waiting for Shapiro when the attorney went into the closet. Otto, new nearing 40, had the color and personality of library-paste. He was soft-spoken, friendly, and possessed of a familiar approach. He called Shapiro by his first name, Mrs Oesterreich, he said, had often spoken of him.

The whole business, the murder of Fred Oesterreich, had been an accident of sorts, Otto told him. The Oesterreichs had come home, unexpectedly early and quarrelling, that night almost a year before. Otto, cavorting around the house, had decided to take a hand. He had confronted Fred Oesterreich. It just happened that he had a gun in his hand—a little .25-caliber weapon that he had somehow come into possession of. Fred Oesterreich had lunged for the gun, and, during a grapple, the weapon had gone off. Then, in sheer nervousness, Sanhuber had fired three more times. He had, being a creative writer, quickly concocted the robbery tale, locked Mrs Oesterreich in the bedroom closet, then retreated to his quarters in the attic.

Otto had harsh words to say about Herman Cline, the chief of detectives. He had, from his hiding-place, heard Cline questioning Mrs Oesterreich over and over again in the bedroom. 'I don't like that man,' said Otto, who looked incapable of disliking anybody. 'I think I'll take his name.'

The last remark of Otto's wasn't interpretable for several years.

Shapiro, the civil lawyer, consulted Dominquez, the criminal lawyer. 'What,' he asked, 'shall I tell Sanhuber to do?'

'Tell him,' said Dominquez, 'to get the hell out of that attic. I don't care where he goes—only get him out of that attic.'

Shapiro told him, and Otto dropped from sight. With Otto out of the attic, Walburga had little to fear. The murder charge against her collapsed.

Seven years passed. Walburga Oesterreich and attorney Shapiro had begun to get into disagreements. One day Mrs Oesterreich had appeared in Shapiro's office and threatened him. Shapiro had called the police. Then, in 1930, Shapiro got in touch with the authorities and said that he feared injury or possible death at the hand of Walburga Oesterreich and wished to make an affidavit about the murder of her husband.

Shapiro's affidavit introduced the authorities, for the first time, to the character the newspapers were to call the phantom of the attics. The affidavit further revealed that Otto Sanhuber had confessed to Shapiro that he had, emerging from the rafters that day seven years before, killed Fred Oesterreich. Sanhuber, the affidavit disclosed, was still around Los Angeles, working as a porter in an apartment house. He had, whimsically enough, taken the name of the now retired chief of detectives—Cline—only he spelled it differently; he was now known as Walter Klein.

Sanhuber, alias Walter Klein, soon found his thin wrists encased in official bracelets—Chief of Detectives Cline emerging from retirement to take a crack at him. Otto agreed to go before a grand jury and confess having killed Fred Oesterreich during a quarrel. After Shapiro had told him to get out of the attic, Otto told the grand jurors, he had gone to Vancouver, Washington. He had worked at odd jobs, not being able to continue his writing without the privacy of an attic.

Then he had dropped down to Portland, Oregon, where he had met and married a stenographer. He was still married. Otto accounted to his wife for the years he had spent in the Oesterreich attics by telling her he had met with an accident. This had the peculiar effect of making his mind a blank between the years of 1903, when he had first met Walburga Oesterreich, and 1922, when he had shot Fred.

On the basis of Otto's confession to the grand jury, both he and Walburga were indicted for the eight-year-old murder of the garment manufacturer. They were tried separately. Otto went first.

He was fortunate in his choice of attorneys; he got Earl Seeley Wakeman, a man who had never lost a murder trial. Otto repudiated his grand-jury confession, saying he had made it because of a misunderstanding of some sort. The jury found him guilty of manslaughter. This posed a unique legal problem. The right to prosecute for that particular crime was then outlawed by the statute of limitations after three years. How, then, could Otto be guilty as eight years had elapsed since the death of Fred Oesterreich? The answer was, he couldn't. So on a legal technicality, little Otto was set free. He and his wife quickly departed.

Now Walburga Oesterreich had her turn. She hired as her counsel Jerry Geisler, specialist in getting Hollywoodians out of the woods. The lady, now 63, blamed everything on Otto. The murder of her husband had followed the line of Otto's now repudiated confession. She had remained silent about the circumstances of the murder because she had not wished to expose her private life, meaning Otto and the attics, to the public. The jury didn't say 'yes' and it didn't say 'no'. It disagreed.

Walburga Oesterreich, temporarily freed by the hung jury, stepped from the front pages into obscurity.

In 1936, the district attorney moved to dismiss the indictment against her. The lady, reported to have lost her fortune, took up residence over a garage in the Wilshire district of Los Angeles.

The murder of Fred Oesterreich, then, remains technically unsolved. But, after all, a man *was* murdered. It does seem that justice might have been better served had *somebody* been at least saddled with a good stiff fine.

## HORACE BLEACKLEY

# The Love Philtre
## The Case of Mary Blandy, 1751-2

Who hath not heard of Blandy's fatal fame,
Deplored her fate, and sorrowed o'er her shame?
—*Henley*, a poem, 1827.

During the reign of George II—when the gallant Young Pretender was
leading Jenny Cameron toward Derby, and flabby, gin-besotted
England, dismayed by a rabble of half-famished Highlanders, was
ready to take its thrashing lying-down—a prosperous attorney, named
Francis Blandy, was living at Henley-upon-Thames. For nine years he
had held the post of town clerk, and was reckoned a person of skill in
his profession. A dour, needle-witted man of law, whose social position
was more considerable than his means or his lineage, old Mr Blandy,
like others wiser than himself, had a foible. His pride was just great
enough to make him a tuft-hunter. In those times, a solicitor in a
country town had many chances of meeting his betters on equal terms,
and when the attorney of Henley pretended that he had saved the large
sum of ten thousand pounds, county society esteemed him at his supposed value. There lived with him—in an old-world home surrounded
by gardens and close to the bridge on the London road—his wife and
daughter, an only child, who at this period was twenty-five years of age.

Mrs Blandy, as consequential an old dame as ever flaunted *sacque* or
nodded her little bugle over a dish of tea, seems to have spent a weary
existence in wringing from her tight-fisted lord the funds to support the
small frivolities which her social ambition deemed essential to their
prestige. A feminine mind seldom appreciates the reputation without
the utility of wealth, and the lawyer's wife had strong opinions with
regard to the propriety of living up to their ten-thousand-pound
celebrity. While he was content with the barren honour that came to
him by reason of the reputed *dot* which his daughter one day must
enjoy—pluming himself, no doubt, that his Molly had as good a chance
of winning a coronet as the penniless daughter of an Irish squireen—his
lady, with more worldly wisdom, knew the value of an occasional jaunt
to town, and was fully alive to the chances of rout or assembly hardby

at Reading. Thus in the pretty little home near the beautiful reach of river, domestic storms—sad object-lesson to an only child—raged frequently over the parental truck and barter at the booths of Vanity Fair.

Though not a beauty—for the smallpox, that stole the bloom from the cheeks of many a sparkling belle in hoop and brocade, had set its seal upon her face—the portrait of Mary Blandy shows that she was comely. Still, it is a picture in which there is a full contrast between the light and shadows. Those fine glistening black eyes of hers—like the beam of sunshine that illumines a sombre chamber—made one forget the absence of winsome charm in her features; yet their radiance appeared to come through dark unfathomable depths rather than as the reflection of an unclouded soul. With warmth all blood may glow, with softness every heart can beat, but some, like hers, must be compelled by reciprocal power. Such, in her empty home, was not possible. Even the love and devotion of her parents gave merely a portion of their own essence. From a greedy father she acquired the sacred lust, and learnt from infancy to dream, with morbid longing, of her future dower; while her mother encouraged a hunger for vain and giddy pleasure, teaching unwittingly that these must be bought at the expense of peace, or by the sacrifice of truth. To a girl of wit and intelligence in whose heart nature had not sown the seeds of kindness, these lessons came as a crop of tares upon a fruitful soil. But, as in the case of all women, there was one hope of salvation. Indeed, since the passion of her soul cried out with imperious command that she should fulfil the destiny of her sex, the love of husband and children would have found her a strong but pliable material that could be fashioned into more gentle form. Without such influence she was one of those to whom womanhood was insufferable—a mortal shape where lay encaged one of the fiercest demons of discontent.

Molly Blandy did not lack admirers. Being pleasant and vivacious—while her powers of attraction were enhanced by the rumour of her fortune—not a few of the beaux in the fashionable world of Bath, and county society at Reading, gave homage and made her their toast. In the eyes of her parents it was imperative that a suitor should be able to offer to their daughter a station of life befitting an heiress. On this account two worthy swains, who were agreeable to the maiden but could not provide the expected dower, received a quick dismissal. Although there was nothing exorbitant in the ambition of the attorney and his dame, it is clear that the girl learnt an evil lesson from these mercenary transactions. Still, her crosses in love do not seem to have sunk very deeply into her heart, but henceforth her conduct lost a little of its maidenly reserve. The freedom of the coquette took the place of the earnestness and sincerity that had been the mark of her ardent nature, and her conduct towards the officers of the regiment stationed at Henley was deemed too forward. However, the father, whose reception into military circles no doubt made the desired impression upon his mayor and aldermen, was well satisfied that his daughter should be on familiar terms with her soldier friends. Even when she became betrothed to a captain of no great fortune, he offered small objection on account of the position of the young man. Yet, although the prospect of a son-in-law who held the king's commission had satisfied his vanity, the old lawyer, who foolishly had allowed the world to believe him richer than he was, could not, or (as he pretended) would not, provide a sufficient dowry. Thus the engagement promised to be a long one. Fate, however, decided otherwise. Very soon her suitor was ordered abroad on active service, and the hope of marriage faded away for the third time.

In the summer of 1746, while no doubt she was sighing for her soldier across the seas, the man destined to work the tragic mischief of her life appeared on the scene. William Henry Cranstoun, a younger son of the fifth Lord Cranstoun, a Scottish baron, was a lieutenant of marines, who, since his regiment had suffered severely during the late Jacobite rebellion, had come to Henley on a recruiting expedition. At first his attentions to Miss Blandy bore no fruit, but he returned the following summer, and while staying with his grand-uncle, General Lord Mark Kerr, who was an acquaintance of the lawyer and his family, he found that Mary was off with the old love and willing to welcome him as the new. All were amazed that the fastidious girl should forsake her gallant captain for this little sprig from North Britain—an undersized spindle-shanks, built after Beau Diddapper pattern—in whose weak eyes and pock-fretten features love must vainly seek her mirror. Still greater was the astonishment when ten-thousand-pound Blandy, swollen with importance, began to babble of 'my Lord of Crailing,' and the little bugle cap of his dame quivered with pride as she told her gossips of 'my Lady Cranstoun, my daughter's new mamma.' For it was common knowledge that the small Scot was the fifth son of a needy house, with little more than his pay to support his many vicious and extravagant habits. Such details seem to have been overlooked by the vain parents in their delight at the honour and glory of an alliance with a family of title. In the late autumn of 1747 they invited their prospective son-in-law to their home, where, as no one was fonder of free quarters, he remained for six months. But the cruel fate that presided over the destinies of the unfortunate Mary intervened once more. Honest Lord Mark Kerr (whose prowess as a duellist is chronicled in many a page), perceiving the intentions of his unscrupulous relative, made haste to give his lawyer friend the startling news that Cranstoun was a married man.

This information was correct. Yet, although wedded since the year before the rebellion, the vicious little Scot was seeking to put away the charming lady who was his wife and the mother of his child. Plain enough were the motives. A visit to England had taught him that the title which courtesy permitted him to bear was a commercial asset that, south of the Tweed, would enable him to sell himself in a better market. As one of his biographers tells us, 'he saw young sparklers every day running off with rich prizes,' for the chapels of Wilkinson and Keith were always ready to assist the abductor of an heiress. Indeed, before his arrival at Henley, he had almost succeeded in capturing the daughter of a Leicestershire squire, when the father, who suddenly learnt his past history, sent him about his business. Still, he persisted in his attempts to get the Scotch marriage anulled, and his chances seemed favourable. Most of the relatives of his wife, who had espoused the losing side in the late rebellion, were fled in exile to France or Flanders. Moreover, she belonged to the Catholic Church, which at that time in stern Presbyterian Scotland had fallen upon evil days. Believing that she was alone and friendless, and relying, no doubt, upon the sectarian prejudices of the law courts, he set forth the base lie that he had promised to marry her only on condition she became Protestant. His explanation to the Blandys, in answer to Lord Mark's imputation, was the same as his defence before the Scottish Commissaries. The lady was his mistress, not his wife!

Miss Blandy took the same view of the case that Sophy Western did under similar circumstances. Human nature was little different in those days, but men wore their hearts on their sleeve instead of exhibiting them only in the Courts, and women preferred to be deemed complacent rather than stupid. Doubtless old lawyer Blandy grunted many Saxon sarcasms at the expense of Scotch jurisprudence, and trembled lest son-in-law Diddapper had been entangled beyond redemption. Still, father, mother, and daughter believed the word of their guest, waiting anxiously for the result of the litigation that was to make him a free man. During the year 1748 the Commissaries at Edinburgh decided that Captain Cranstoun and the ill-used Miss Murray were man and wife. Then the latter, being aware of the flirtation at Henley, wrote to warn Miss Blandy, and provided her with a copy of the Court's decree. Great was the consternation at the house on the London road. Visions of tea-gossip over the best set of china in the long parlour at Crailing with my Lady Cranstoun vanished from the old mother's eyes, while the town clerk forgot his dreams of the baby whose two grandfathers were himself and a live lord. Nevertheless, the young Scotsman

protested that the marriage was invalid, declared that he would appeal
to the highest tribunal, and swore eternal fidelity to his Mary. Alas, she
trusted him! Within the sombre depths of her soul there dwelt a fierce
resolve to make this man her own. In her sight he was no graceless
creature from the barrack-room, but with a great impersonal love she
sought in him merely the fulfilment of her destiny.

'In her first passion, woman loves her lover:
In all the others, all she loves is love.'

At this time Cranstoun's fortunes were in a parlous state. More than
half of his slender patrimony had been sequestered for the maintenance
of his wife and child, and shortly after the peace of Aix-la-Chapelle, his
regiment being disbanded, he was left on half-pay. Still, he did not waver
in his purpose to win the heiress of Henley.

On the 30th of September 1749, the poor frivolous old head, which
had sported its cap so bravely amidst the worries of pretentious poverty,
lay still upon the pillow, and Mary Blandy looked upon the face of her
dead mother. It was the turning-point in her career. While his wife was
alive, the old lawyer had never lost all faith in his would-be son-in-law
during the two years that he had been affianced to his daughter, in spite
of the rude shocks which had staggered his credulity. Cranstoun had
been allowed to sponge on him for another six months in the previous
summer, and had pursued his womenfolk when they paid a visit to
Mary's uncle, Serjeant Stevens, of Doctors' Commons. However, soon
after the death of his wife the patience of Mr Blandy, who must have
perceived that the case of the pretender was hopeless, seems to have
become worn out. All idea of the baron's grandchild faded from his
mind; the blear-eyed lover was forbidden the house, and for nearly
twelve months did not meet his trusting sweetheart.

Although a woman of her intelligence must have perceived that, but
for some untoward event, her relationship with her betrothed could
never be one of honour, her fidelity remained unshaken. Having passed
her thirtieth birthday, the dreadful stigma of spinsterhood was fast
falling upon her. If the methods of analogy are of any avail, it is clear
that she had become a creature of lust—not the lust of sensuality, but
that far more insatiable greed, the craving for conquest, possession,
the attainment of the unattainable, calling forth not one but all the
emotions of body and soul. A sacrifice of honour—a paltry thing in the
face of such mighty passion—would have been no victory, for such in
itself was powerless to accomplish the essential metamorphosis of her
life. In mutual existence with a lover and slave the destiny of this rare
woman alone could be achieved. Thus came the harvest of the tempest.
It was not the criminal negligence of the father in encouraging for

nearly three years the pretensions of a suitor, who—so a trustworthy gentleman had told him—was a married man, that had planted the seeds of storm. Nor did the filial love of the daughter begin to fade and wither because she had been taught that the affections, like anything which has a price, should be subject to barter and exchange. Deeper far lay the roots of the malignant disease—growing as a portion of her being—a part and principle of life itself. Environment and education merely had inclined into its stunted form the twig, which could never bear fruit unless grafted upon a new stalk! And while the sombre girl brooded over her strange impersonal passion, there rang in her ears the voice of demon-conscience, unceasingly—a taunting, frightful whisper, 'When the old man is in his grave you shall be happy.'

The esteem of posterity for the eighteenth century, to which belong so many noble lives and great minds, has been influenced by the well-deserved censure bestowed upon a particular epoch. The year 1750 marks a period of transition when all the worst characteristics of the Georgian era were predominant. For nearly a quarter of a century the scornful glance that the boorish little king threw at any book had been reflected in the national taste for literature. Art had hobbled along bravely on the crutches of caricature, tolerated on account of its deformity, and not for its worth. The drama, which had drifted to the lowest ebb in the days of Rich and Heidegger, was just rising from its mud-bank, under the leadership of Garrick, with the turn of the tide. Religion, outside the pale of Methodism, was as dead as the influence of the Church of England and its plurality divines. The prostitution of the marriage laws in the Fleet and Savoy had grown to be a menace to the social fabric. London reeked of gin; and although the business of Jack Ketch has been seldom more flourishing, property, until magistrate Fielding came forward, was never less secure from the thief and highwayman. Our second George, who flaunted his mistresses before the public gaze, was a worthy leader of a coarse and vicious society. Female dress took its form from the vulgarity of the times, and was never uglier and more indecent simultaneously. Not only was the 'modern fine lady,' who wept when a handsome thief was hung, a common type, but the Boobys and Bellastons were fashionable women of the day, quite as much alive as Elizabeth Chudleigh or Caroline Fitzroy. Such was the age of Miss Blandy, and she proved a worthy daughter of it.

In the late summer of 1750 the fickle attorney, who had become weary of opposition, consented to withdraw the sentence of banishment he had pronounced against his daughter's lover. Possibly he fancied that there was a chance, after all, of the Scotch lieutenant's success in the curious law-courts of the North, and perhaps a present of salmon, received from Lady Cranstoun, appeared to him as a favourable

eodore Gardelle disposes of the body of his murdered landlady.
e page 23)
*vgate Calendar*

The principal characters involved in the case of Dr. Crippen.

(see page 14)

*Police Gazette*, 1910

SCENE AT THE INQUEST.
INSPECTOR DEW.-"EACH PIECE OF FLESH WAS NO BIGGER THAN THAT BAG"

MR PAUL MARTINETTI

MRS PAUL MARTINETTI

BELLE ELMORE

MISS LE NEVE

DRESSED AS A BOY.

MR J E NASH    MISS LIL HAWTHORNE

INSPECTOR DEW LEAVES LIVERPOOL FOR CANADA.

MISS LE NEVE RESUMES HER PROPER CLOTHES

Apprehension and final judgment of the murderer and his lover.
(see page 17)
*Police Gazette*, 1910

LANDING AT QUEBEC.

GINNETT DENOUNCES CRIPPEN IN COURT.

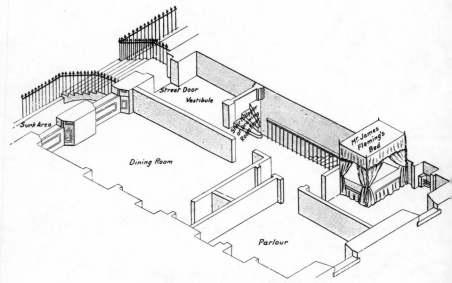

Isometrical view of street flat cf 17 Sandyford Place

Main floor and basement flat of 17 Sandyford Place.
(see page 30)

*Trial of Jessie M'Lachlan* (Hodge, 1911)

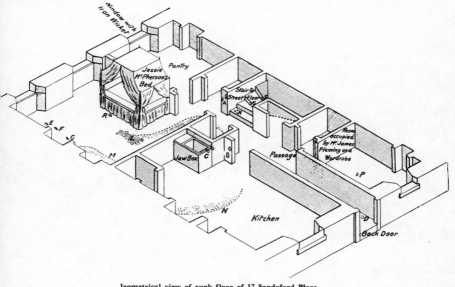

**Isometrical view of sunk floor of 17 Sandyford Place**

*A*—Finger marks.    *B*—Blood marks behind kitchen door.    *C*—Blood marks on jaw-box.    *D*—Spots of blood at back door.
*E F G*—Foot marks.    *H*—Drops of blood.    *L*—Where the body was found.    *M*—Dotted line showing margin of washed part of floor.
*N*—Do., do.    *P*—Spot of blood.    *R*—Droppings of blood.    *S*—Blood on breasts of steps.

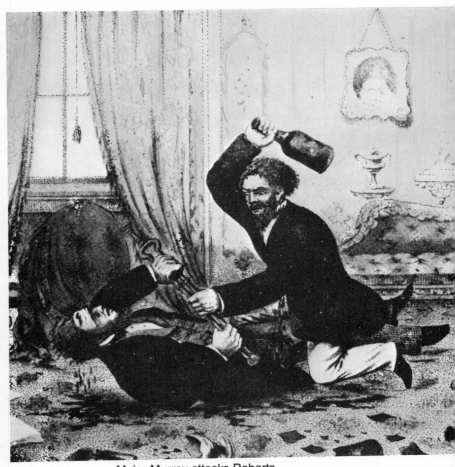

Major Murray attacks Roberts
with fire tongs and glass bottle.
(see page 60)
*From author's collection*

Police find remains of O'Connor's body
buried in house floor.
(see page 69)
*From author's collection*

# LA TRAGÉDIE DE LA RUE BRUYÈRE, AU MANS
— × × —

# LES DEUX SŒURS CRIMINELLES
## PRÉCISENT DEVANT LE JUGE D'INSTRUCTION
## LES CIRCONSTANCES DE LEUR FORFAIT

Pictures of the Papin sisters
after their apprehension and trial.
(see page 96)
*La Sarte*

"I am afraid my wife is dead," Smith told the doctor.
(see page 131)
*Sensational Crimes and Trials* (McGlennon, n.d.)

The execution of the murderess Mary Blandy in 1752.
(see page 175)
*Contemporary print*

The interior of Holmes's ''castle''
where charred human bones were found.
(see page 192)
*From author's collection*

The murder of Dr. Parkman of Boston
by Professor Webster of Harvard.
(see page 214)
*From author's collection*

James Hanratty sentenced to death in the notorious "A6 Murder."
(see page 234)
*Syndication International*

One of mass-murderer Williams's victims
escapes by sheets knotted together.
(see page 268)

*From author's collection*

augury. Consequently the needy fortune-hunter, who was only too
ready to return to his free quarters, paid another lengthy visit to Henley.
As the weeks passed, it was evident that the temper of the host and
father, whose senile humours were swayed by gravel and heartburn,
could not support the new ménage. Fearful lest the devotion of his
Molly had caused her to lose all regard for her fair fame, wroth that
the clumsy little soldier should have disturbed the peace of his household, the old man received every mention of 'the tiresome affair in
Scotland' with sneers and gibes. Vanished was the flunkey-optimism
that had led him to welcome once more the pertinacious slip of Scottish
baronage. Naught would have appeased him but prompt evidence that
the suitor was free to lead his daughter to the altar. Nothing could be
plainer than that the querulous widower had lost all confidence in his
unwelcomed guest.

The faithful lovers were filled with dismay. A few strokes of the pen
might rob them for ever of their ten thousand pounds. Their wishes were
the same, their minds worked as one. A deep, cruel soul-blot, trans-
mitted perhaps by some cut-throat borderer through the blood of
generations, would have led William Cranstoun to commit, without
scruple, the vilest of crimes. Those base attempts to put away his wife,
and to cast the stigma of bastardy upon his child, added to his endeavour to entrap one heiress after another into a bigamous marriage,
make him guilty of offences less only than murder. In his present
position he had cause for desperation. Yet, although utterly broken in
fortune, there was a rich treasure at his hand if he dared to seize it.
Were her father dead, Molly Blandy, whether as wife or mistress, would
be his—body, soul, and wealth. Within the veins of the woman a like
heart-stain spread its poison. All the lawless passion of her nature cried
out against her parent's rule, which, to her mind, was seeking to banish
what had become more precious than her life. Knowing that her own
fierce will had its mate in his, she believed that his obduracy could not
be conquered, and she lived in a dread lest she should be disinherited.
And all this time, day after day, the demon-tempter whispered, 'When
the old man is in his grave you shall be happy.'

Which of the guilty pair was the first to suggest the heartless crime
it is impossible to ascertain, but there is evidence, apart from Miss
Blandy's statement, that Cranstoun was the leading spirit. Possibly, nay
probably, the deed was never mentioned in brutal plainness in so many
words. The history of crime affords many indications that the blackest
criminals are obliged to soothe a neurotic conscience with the anodyne
of make-belief. It is quite credible that the two spoke of the projected
murder from the first (as indeed Miss Blandy explained it later) as an
attempt to conciliate the old lawyer by administering a supernatural

love philtre, having magical qualities like Oberon's flower in *A Midsummer Night's Dream*, which would make him consent to their marriage. Presently a reign of mystic terror seemed to invade the little house in the London road. With fear ever present in her eyes, the figure of the sombre woman glided from room to room, whispering to the frightened servants ghostly tales of things supernatural—of unearthly music that she had heard during the misty autumn nights, of noises that had awakened her from sleep, of the ghastly apparitions that had appeared to her lover. And to all these stories she had but one dismal interpretation—saying it had come to her from a wizard-woman in Scotland— they were signs and tokens that her father would die within a year! Those who heard her listened and trembled, and the words sank deep into their memory. So the winter crept on; but while all slunk through the house with bated breath, shrinking at each mysterious sound, the old man, doomed by the sorceress, remained unsuspicious of what was going on around him.

Not long before Christmas, to the great relief of his churlish host, the little Scotsman's clumsy legs passed through the front door for the last time, and he set out for his brother's seat at Crailing in the shire of Roxburgh. Yet, though his lengthy visit had come to an end, his spirit remained to rule the brain of the woman who loved him. Early in the year 1751 she received a box, containing a present from Cranstoun, a set of table linen, and some 'Scotch pebbles.' Lawyer Blandy viewed the stones with suspicious eyes, for he hated all things beyond the Cheviot Hills, but did not make any comment. The relationship between father and daughter had become cold and distant. Quarrels were constant in the unhappy home. Often in the midst of her passion she was heard to mutter deep curses against the old man. Indeed, so banished was her love that she talked without emotion to the servants of the likelihood of his death, in fulfilment of the witch's prophecy.

Some weeks later, when another consignment of the mysterious 'Scotch pebbles' had arrived for Miss Blandy, it was noticed that her conduct became still more dark and strange. Slinking through the house with slow and stealthy tread, she appeared to shun all eyes, as though bent upon some hidden purpose. A glance within the box from the North would have revealed the secret. When the crafty accomplice found that she was unable to procure the means of taking her father's life, he had been forced to supply her with the weapons. During the spring, the health of the old lawyer, who suffered more or less from chronic ailments, began to grow more feeble. His garments hung loosely upon his shrunken limbs, while the teeth dropped from his palsied jaws. The old witch's curse seemed to have fallen upon the home, and, to those who looked with apprehension for every sign and portent, it was

THE LOVE PHILTRE  163

fulfilled in many direful ways. Early in June, Ann Emmet, and old charwoman employed about the house, was seized with a violent illness after drinking from a half-emptied cup left at Mr Blandy's breakfast. A little later, Susan Gunnel, one of the maid-servants, was affected in a similar way through taking some tea prepared for her master. One August morning, in the secrecy of her own chamber, trembling at every footfall beyond the locked door, Mary Blandy gazed with eager, awe-struck eyes upon a message sent by her lover.

'I am sorry there are such occasions to clean your pebbles,' wrote the murderous little Scotsman. 'You must make use of the powder to them, by putting it into anything of substance, wherein it will not swim a-top of the water, of which I wrote to you in one of my last. I am afraid it will be too weak to take off their rust, or at least it will take too long a time.'

From the language of metaphor it is easy to translate the ghastly meaning. She must have told Cranstoun that the white arsenic, which he had sent to her under the pseudonym of 'powder to clean the pebbles,' remained floating on the surface of the tea. Possibly her father had noticed this phenomenon, and, not caring to drink the liquid, had escaped the painful sickness which had attacked the less cautious servants. But now she had found a remedy—'anything of substance!'—a safe and sure vehicle that could not fail. Louder still in the ears of the lost woman rang the mocking words, 'When the old man is dead you shall be happy.'

During the forenoon of Monday, the 5th of August, Susan Gunnel, the maid, met her young mistress coming from the pantry.

'Oh, Susan,' she exclaimed, 'I have been stirring my papa's water gruel'; and then, perceiving other servants through the half-open door of the laundry, she added gaily, 'If I was ever to take to eating anything in particular it would be oatmeal.'

No response came from the discreet Susan, but she marvelled, calling to mind that Miss Blandy had said to her sometime previously, noticing that she appeared unwell:

'Have you been eating any water gruel? for I am told that water gruel hurts me, and it may hurt you.'

Later in the day, her wonder was increased when she saw her mistress stirring the gruel in a half-pint mug, putting her fingers into the spoon, and then rubbing them together. In the evening the same mug was taken as usual to the old man's bedroom. On Tuesday night Miss Blandy sent down in haste to order gruel for her father, who had been indisposed all day, and such was her solicitude that she met the footman on the stairs, and taking the basin from his hands, carried it herself into the parlour. Early the next morning, while Ann Emmet, the old charwoman, was busy at her wash-tub, Susan Gunnel came from upstairs.

'Dame,' she observed, 'you used to be fond of water gruel. Here is a very fine mess my master left last night, and I believe it will do you good.'

Sitting down upon a bench, this most unfortunate old lady proceeded to consume the contents of the basin, and for a second time was seized with a strange and violent illness. Soon afterwards Miss Blandy came into the kitchen.

'Susan, as your master has taken physic, he may want some more water gruel,' said she. 'As there is some in the house you need not make fresh, for you are ironing.'

'Madam, it will be stale,' replied the servant. 'It will not hinder me much to make fresh.'

A little later, while tasting the stuff, Susan noticed a white sediment at the bottom of the pan. Greatly excited, she ran to show Betty Binfield, the cook, who bore no good-will towards her young mistress.

'What oatmeal is this?' asked Betty, significantly. 'It looks like flour.'

'I have never seen oatmeal as white before,' said the maid.

Carefully and thoroughly the suspicious servants examined the contents of the saucepan, taking it out of doors to view it in the light. And while they looked at the white gritty sediment they told each other in low whispers that this must be poison. Locking up the pan, they showed it next day to the local apothecary, who, as usual in those times, was the sick man's medical attendant.

Nothing occurred to alarm the guilty woman until Saturday. On that morning, in the homely fashion of middle-class manners, the lawyer, who wanted to shave, came into the kitchen, where hot water and a good fire were ready for him. Accustomed to his habits, the servants went about their work as usual. Some trouble seemed to be preying upon his mind.

'I was like to have been poisoned once,' piped the feeble old man, turning his bloodshot eyes upon his daughter, who was in the room.

'It was on this same day, the tenth of August,' he continued, in his weak, trembling voice, for his frame had become shattered during the last week. 'It was at the coffee-house or at the Lyon, and two other gentlemen were like to have been poisoned by what they drank.'

'Sir, I remember it very well,' replied the imperturbable woman, and then fell to arguing with her querulous father at which tavern the adventure had taken place.

'One of the gentlemen died immediately,' he resumed, looking at her with a long, reproachful glance. 'The other is dead now, and I have survived them both. But'—his piteous gaze grew more intense—'it is my fortune to be poisoned at last.'

A similar ordeal took place in a little while. At breakfast Mr Blandy seemed in great pain, making many complaints. As he sipped his tea, he declared that it had a gritty, bad taste, and would not drink it.

'Have you not put too much of the black stuff into it?' he demanded suddenly of his daughter, referring to the canister of Bohea.

This time she was unable to meet his searching eyes.

'It is as usual,' she stammered in confusion.

A moment later she rose, trembling and distressed, and hurriedly left the room.

There was reason for the old man's suspicion. Before he had risen from his bed, the faithful Susan Gunnel told him of the discovery in the pan of water gruel, and both agreed that the mysterious powder had been sent by Cranstoun. Yet, beyond what he had said at breakfast, and in the kitchen, he questioned his daughter no more! Still, although no direct charge had been made, alarmed by her father's hints she hastened to destroy all evidence that could be used against her. During the afternoon, stealing into the kitchen under pretence of drying a letter before the fire, she crushed a paper among the coals. As soon as she was gone the watchful spies—servants Gunnel and Binfield—snatched it away before it had been destroyed by the flames. This paper contained a white substance, and on it was written 'powder to clean the pebbles'. Towards evening famous Dr Addington arrived from Reading, summoned by Miss Blandy, who was driven on account of her fears to show a great concern. After seeing his patient the shrewd old leech had no doubt as to the symptoms. With habitual directness he told the daughter that her father had been poisoned.

'It is impossible,' she replied.

On Sunday morning the doctor found the sick man a little better, but ordered him to keep his bed. Startling proofs of the accuracy of his diagnosis were forthcoming. One of the maids put into his hands the packet of arsenic found in the fire, while Norton the apothecary produced the powder from the pan of gruel. Addington at once took the guilty woman to task.

'If your father dies,' he told her sternly, 'you will inevitably be ruined.'

Nevertheless she appears to have brazened the matter out, but desired the doctor to come again the next day. When she was alone, her first task was to scribble a note to Cranstoun, which she gave to her father's clerk to 'put into the post'. Having heard dark rumours whispered by the servants that Mr Blandy had been poisoned by his daughter, the man had no hesitation in opening the letter, which he handed over to the apothecary. It ran as follows:

> Dear Willy, My father is so bad that I have only time to tell you that if you do not hear from me soon again, don't be frightened. I am better myself. Lest any accident should happen to your letters be careful what you write.
>
> My sincere compliments.—I am ever, yours.

That evening Norton ordered Miss Blandy from her father's room, telling Susan Gunnel to remain on the watch, and admit no one. At last the heartless daughter must have seen that some other defence was needed than blind denial. Still, the poor old sufferer persisted that Cranstoun was the sole author of the mischief. On Monday morning, although sick almost to death, he sent the maid with a message to his daughter.

'Tell her,' said he, 'that I will forgive her if she will bring that villain to justice.'

In answer to his words, Miss Blandy came to her father's bedroom in tears, and a suppliant. Susan Gunnel, who was present, thus reports the interview.

'Sir, how do you do?' said she.

'I am very ill,' he replied.

Falling upon her knees, she said to him:

'Banish me or send me to any remote part of the world. As to Mr Cranstoun, I will never see him, speak to him, as long as I live, so as you will forgive me.'

'I forgive thee, my dear,' he answered. 'And I hope God will forgive thee, but thee should have considered better than to have attempted anything against thy father. Thee shouldst have considered I was thy own father.'

'Sir,' she protested, 'as to your illness I am entirely innocent.'

'Madam,' interrupted old Susan Gunnel, 'I believe you must not say you are entirely innocent, for the powder that was taken out of the water gruel, and the paper of powder that was taken out of the fire, are now in such hands that they must be publicly produced. I believe I had one dose prepared for my master in a dish of tea about six weeks ago.'

'I have put no powder into tea,' replied Miss Blandy. 'I have put powder into water gruel, and if you are injured,' she assured her father, 'I am entirely innocent, for it was given me with another intent.'

The dying man did not wait for further explanation, but, turning in his bed, he cried:

'Oh, such a villain! To come to my house, eat of the best, drink of the best that my house could afford—to take away my life, and ruin my daughter! Oh, my dear,' he continued, 'thee must hate that man, thee must hate the ground he treads on. Thee canst not help it.'

'Oh, sir, your tenderness towards me is like a sword to my heart,' she answered. 'Every word you say is like swords piercing my heart—much worse than if you were to be ever so angry. I must down on my knees and beg you will not curse me.'

'I curse thee, my dear!' he replied. 'How couldst thou think I could curse thee? I bless thee, and hope that God will bless thee and amend thy life. Go, my dear, go out of my room ... Say no more, lest thou shouldst say anything to thy own prejudice ... Go to thy uncle Stevens; take him for thy friend. Poor man,—I am sorry for him.'

The memory of the old servant, who repeated the above conversation in her evidence at Miss Blandy's trial, would seem remarkable did we not bear in mind that she went through various rehearsals before the coroner and magistrates, and possibly with the lawyers for the prosecution. Some embellishments also must be credited to the taste and fancy of Mr Rivington's reporters. Still, the gist must be true, and certainly has much pathos. Yet the father's forgiveness of his daughter, when he must have known that her conduct was wilful, although piteous and noble, may not have been the result of pure altruism. naturally, the wish that Cranstoun alone was guilty was parent to the thought. Whether the approach of eternity brought a softening influence upon him, and he saw his follies and errors in the light of repentance, or whether the ruling passion strong in death made the vain old man struggle to avert the black disgrace that threatened his good name, and the keen legal intellect, which could counsel his daughter so well, foresaw the coming escheatment of his small estate to the lord of the manor, are problems for the student of psychology.

During the course of the day brother leech Lewis of Oxford—a master-builder of pharmacopoeia—was summoned by the sturdy begetter of statesmen, and there was much bobbing of learned wigs and nice conduct of medical canes. Addington asked the dying man whom he suspected to be the giver of the poison.

'A poor love-sick girl,' murmured the old lawyer, smiling through his tears. 'I forgive her—I always thought there was mischief in those cursed Scotch pebbles.'

In the evening a drastic step was taken. Acting on the principle of 'thorough', which made his son's occupancy of the Home Office so memorable at a later period, the stern doctor accused Miss Blandy of the crime, and secured her keys and papers. Conquered by fear, the stealthy woman for a while lost all self-possession. In an agony of shame and terror she sought to shield herself by the pretence of superstitious folly. Wringing her hands in a seeming agony of remorse, she declared that her lover had ruined her.

'I received the powder from Mr Cranstoun,' she cried, 'with a present of Scotch pebbles. He had wrote on the paper that held it, "The powder to clean the pebbles with." He assured me that it was harmless, and that if I would give my father some of it now and then, a little and a little at a time, in any liquid, it would make him kind to him and to me.'

In a few scathing questions the worldly-wise Addington cast ridicule upon this weird story of a love philtre. Taking the law into his own resolute hands, with the consent of colleague Lewis he locked the wretched woman in her room and placed a guard over her. Little could be done to relieve the sufferings of poor ten-thousand-pound Blandy—who proved to be a mere four-thousand-pound attorney when it came to the test—and on Wednesday afternoon, the 14th of August, he closed his proud old eyes for ever. In her desperation the guilty daughter could think of naught but escape. On the evening of her father's death, impelled by an irresistible frenzy to flee from the scene of her butchery, she begged the footman in vain to assist her to get away. During Thursday morning—for it was not possible to keep her in custody without legal warrant—a little group of children saw a dishevelled figure coming swiftly along the High Street towards the river. At once there arose the cry of 'Murderess!' and, surrounded by an angry mob, she was driven to take refuge in a neighbouring inn. It was vain to battle against fate. That same afternoon the coroner's inquest was held, and the verdict pronounced her a parricide. On the following Saturday, in charge of two constables, she was driven in her father's carriage to Oxford Castle. An enraged populace, thinking that she was trying again to escape, surrounded the vehicle, and sought to prevent her from leaving the town.

Owing to the social position of the accused, and the enormity of her offence, the eyes of the whole nation were turned to the tragedy at Henley. Gossips of the day, such as Horace Walpole and Tate Wilkinson, tell us that the story of Miss Blandy was upon every lip. In spite of the noble irony of 'Drawcansir' Fielding, journalists and pamphleteers had no scruple in referring to the prisoner as a wicked murderess or a cruel parricide. Yet the case of Henry Coleman, who, during the August of this year, had been proved innocent of a crime for which he had suffered death, should have warned the public against hasty assumption. For six months the dark woman was waiting for her trial. Although it was the custom for a jailor to make an exhibition of his captive to anyone who would pay the entrance fee, nobody was allowed to see Miss Blandy without her consent. Two comfortable rooms were set apart for her in the keeper's house; she was free to take walks in the garden, and to have her own maid. At last, when stories of a premeditated escape were noised abroad, Secretary Newcastle, in a usual state of fuss, fearing that she might repeat the achievement of Queen Maud, gave orders that she must be put in irons. At first Thomas Newell, who had succeeded her father as town clerk of Henley four years previously, was employed in her defence, but he offended her by speaking of Cranstoun as 'a mean-looking, little, ugly fellow,' and so she dismissed him in favour of Mr Rives, a lawyer from Woodstock. Her old invincible courage had returned, and only once—when she learnt the paltry value of her father's fortune—did she lose self-possession. For a dismal echo must have come back in the mocking words, 'When the old man is in his grave you shall be happy.'

At last the magistrates—Lords Cadogan and 'New-Style' Maccles-field, who had undertaken duties which in later days Mr Newton or Mr Montagu Williams would have shared with Scotland Yard—finish their much-praised detective work, and on Tuesday, the 3rd of March 1752, Mary Blandy is brought to the bar. The Court meets in the divinity school, since the town-hall is in the hands of the British work-man, and because the University, so 'Sir Alexander Drawcansir' tells his readers, will not allow the use of the Sheldonian Theatre. Why the most beautiful room in Oxford should be deemed a fitter place of desecration than the archbishop's monstrosity is not made clear. An accident delays the trial—this second 'Great Oyer of Poisoning!' There in a small stone or other obstruction in the lock—can some sentimental, wry-brained undergraduate think to aid the gallows-heroine of his fancy?—and while it is being removed, Judges Legge and Smythe return to their lodgings.

At eight o'clock, Mary Blandy, calm and stately, stands beneath the graceful fretted ceiling, facing the tribunal. From wall to wall an eager crowd has filled the long chamber, surging through the doorway, flowing in at the open windows, jostling even against the prisoner. A chair is placed for her in case of fatigue, and her maid is by her side. A plain and neat dress befits her serene manner—a black bombazine short *sacque* (the garb of mourning), white linen kerchief, and a thick crape shade and hood. From the memory of those present her counten-ance can never fade. A broad high forehead, above which her thick jet hair is smoothed under a cap; a pair of fine black sparkling eyes; the colouring almost of a gipsy; cheeks with scarce a curve; mouth full, but showing no softness; nose large, straight, determined—it is the face of one of those rare women who command, not the love, but the obedience of mankind. Still it is intelligent, not unseductive, compelling; and yet, in spite of the deep, flashing eyes, without radiance of soul—the face of a sombre-hearted woman.

Black, indeed, is the indictment that Bathurst, a venerable young barrister who represents the Crown, unfolds against her, but only once during his burst of carefully-matured eloquence is there any change in her serenity. When the future Lord Chancellor declares that the base Cranstoun 'had fallen in love, not with her, but with her fortune', the woman's instinct cannot tolerate the reflection upon her charms, and she darts a look of bitterest scorn upon the speaker. And only once does she show a trace of human softness. When her godmother, old Mrs Mountenay, is leaving the witness-box, she repeats the curtsey which the prisoner had previously disregarded, and then, in an impulse of pity, presses forward, and, seizing Miss Blandy's hand, exclaims, 'God bless you!' At last, and for the first time, the tears gather in the accused woman's eyes.

Many abuses, handed down from a previous century, still render barbarous the procedure of criminal trials. The case is hurried over in one day; counsel for the prisoner can only examine witnesses, but not address the jury; the prosecution is accustomed to put forward evidence of which the defence has been kept in ignorance. Yet no injustice is done to Mary Blandy. Thirteen hours is enough to tear the veil from her sombre heart; the tongue of Nestor would fail to show her innocent; of all that her accusers can say of her she is well aware. Never for one moment is the issue in doubt. What can her scoffing, sceptic age, with its cold-blooded settiment and tame romance, think of a credulity that employed a love-potion in the guise of affection but with the result of death! How is it possible to judge a daughter who persisted in her black art, although its dire effects were visible, not once, but many times! Her defence, when at last it comes, is spoken bravely, but better had been left unsaid.

'My lords,' she begins, 'it is morally impossible for me to lay down the hardships I have received. I have been aspersed in my character. In the first place, it has been said that I have spoke ill of my father; that I have cursed him and wished him at hell; which is extremely false. Sometimes little family affairs have happened, and he did not speak to me so kind as I could wish. I own I am passionate, my lords, and in those passions some hasty expressions might have dropt. But great care has been taken to recollect every word I have spoken at different times, and to apply them to such particular purposes as my enemies knew would do me the greatest injury. These are hardships, my lords, extreme hardships!—such as you yourselves must allow to be so. It was said, too, my lords, that I endeavoured to make my escape. Your lordships will judge from the difficulties I laboured under. I had lost my father—I was accused of being his murderer—I was not permitted to go near him—I was forsaken by my friends—affronted by the mob—insulted by my servants. Although I begged to have the liberty to listen at the door where he died, I was not allowed it. My keys were taken from me, my shoe-buckles and garters too—to prevent me from making away with myself, as though I was the most abandoned creature. What could I do, my lords? I verily believe I was out of my senses. When I heard my father was dead and the door open, I ran out of the house, and over the bridge, and had nothing on but a half sack and petticoat, without a hoop, my petticoats hanging about me. The mob gathered about me. Was this a condition, my lords, to make my escape in? A good woman beyond the bridge, seeing me in this distress, desired me to walk in till the mob was dispersed. The town sergeant was there. I begged he would take me under his protection to have me home. The woman said it was not proper, the mob was very great, and that I had better stay a little. When I came home they said I used the constable ill. I was locked up for fifteen hours, with only an old servant of the family to attend me. I was not allowed a maid for the common decencies of my sex. I was sent to gaol, and was in hopes, there, at least, this usage would have ended, but was told it was reported I was frequently drunk—that I attempted to make my escape—that I never attended the chapel. A more abstemious woman,. my lords, I believe, does not live.

'Upon the report of my making my escape, the gentleman who was High Sheriff last year (not the present) came and told me, by order of the higher powers, he must put an iron on me. I submitted, as I always do to the higher powers. Some time after, he came again, and said he must put a heavier upon me, which I have worn, my lords, till I came hither. I asked the Sheriff why I was so ironed? He said he did it by command of some noble peer, on his hearing that I intended to make my escape. I told them I never had such a thought, and I would bear it with the other cruel usage I had received on my character. The Rev. Mr Swinton, the worthy clergyman who attended me in prison, can testify that I was very regular at the chapel when I was well. Sometimes I really was not able to come out, and then he attended me in my room. They likewise published papers and depositions which ought not to have been published, in order to represent me as the most abandoned of my sex, and to prejudice the world against me. I submit myself to your lordships, and to the worthy jury. I can assure your lordships, as I am to answer it before that Grand Tribunal where I must appear, I am as innocent as the child unborn of the death of my father. I would not endeavour to say my life at the expense of truth. I really thought the powder an innocent, inoffensive thing, and I gave it to procure his love. It was mentioned, I should say, I was ruined. My lords, when a young woman loses her character, is not that her ruin? Why, then, should this expression be construed in so wide a sense? Is it not ruining my character to have such a thing laid to my charge? And whatever may be the event of this trial, I am ruined most effectually.'

A strange apology—amazing in its effrontery!

Gentle Heneage Legge speaks long and tenderly, while the listeners shudder with horror as they hear the dismal history unfolded in all entirety for the first time. No innocent heart could have penned that last brief warning to her lover—none but an accomplice would have received his cryptic message. Every word in the testimony of the stern doctor seems to hail her parricide—every action of her stealthy career has been noted by the watchful eyes of her servants. And, as if in damning confirmation of her guilt there is the black record of her flight from the scene of crime. Eight o'clock has sounded when the judge has finished. For a few moments the jury converse in hurried whispers. It is ominous that they make no attempt to leave the court, but merely draw closer together. Then, after the space of five minutes they turn, and the harsh tones of the clerk of arraigns sound through the chamber.

'Mary Blandy, hold up thy hand . . . Gentlemen of the jury, look upon the prisoner. How say you: Is Mary Blandy guilty of the felony and murder whereof she stands indicted, or not guilty?'

'Guilty!' comes the low, reluctant answer.

Never has more piteous drama been played within the cold fair walls of the divinity school than that revealed by the guttering candles on this chill March night. Amidst the long black shadows, through which gleam countless rows of pallid faces, in the deep silence, broken at intervals by hushed sobs, the invincible woman stands with unruffled mien to receive her sentence. As the verdict is declared, a smile seems to play upon her lips. While the judge, with tearful eyes and broken voice, pronounces her doom, she listens without a sign of fear. There is a brief, breathless pause, while all wait with fierce-beating hearts for her reply. No trace of terror impedes her utterance. Thanking the judge for his candour and impartiality, she turns to her counsel, among whom only Richard Aston rose to eminence, and, with a touch of pretty fore-thought, wishes them better success in their other causes. Then, and her voice grows more solemn, she begs for a little time to settle her affairs and to make her peace with God. To which his lordship replies with great emotion:

'To be sure, you shall have proper time allowed you.'

When she is conducted from the court she steps into her coach with the air of a belle whose chair is to take her to a fashionable rout. The fatal news has reached the prison before her arrival. As she enters the keeper's house, which for so long has been her home, she finds the family overcome with grief and the children all in tears.

'Don't mind it,' she cries, cheerfully. 'What does it matter? I am very hungry. Pray let me have something for supper as soon as possible.'

That sombre heart of hers is a brave one also.

All this time William Cranstoun, worthy brother in all respects of Simon Tappertit, had been in hiding—in Scotland perhaps, or, as some say, in Northumberland—watching with fearful quakings for the result of the trial. Shortly after the conviction of his accomplice he managed to take ship to the Continent, and luckily for his country he never polluted its soil again. There are several contemporary accounts of his adventures in France and in the Netherlands, to which the curious may refer. All agree that he confessed his share in the murder when he was safe from justice. With unaccustomed propriety, our Lady Fate soon hastened to snap the thread of his existence, and on the 3rd of December of this same year, at the little town of Furnes in Flanders, aged thirty-eight, he drew his last breath. A short time before, being seized with remorse for his sins, he had given the Catholic Church the honour of enrolling him a proselyte. Indeed the conversion of so great a ruffian was regarded as such a feather in their cap that the good monks and friars advertised the event by means of a sumptuous funeral.

Worthy Judge Legge fulfils his promise to the unhappy Miss Blandy, and she is given six weeks in which to prepare herself for death. Meek and more softened is the sombre woman, who, like a devoted penitent, submits herself day after day to the vulgar gaze of a hundred eyes, while she bows in all humility before the altar of her God. Yet her busy brain is aware that those to whom she looks for intercession are keeping a careful watch upon her demeanour. For she has begged her godmother Mrs Mountenay to ask one of the bishops to speak for her; she is said to entertain the hope that the recently-bereaved princess will endeavour to obtain a reprieve. In the fierce war of pamphleteers, inevitable in those days, she takes her share, playing with incomparable tact to the folly of the credulous. Although the majority, perhaps, believe her guilty, she knows that a considerable party is in her favour. On the 20th of March is published 'A Letter from a Clergyman to Miss Blandy, with her Answer', in which she tells the story of her share in the tragedy. During the remainder of her imprisonment she extends this narrative into a long account of the whole case—assisted, it is believed, by her spiritual adviser, the Rev. John Swinton, who, afflicted possibly by one of his famous fits of woolgathering, seems convinced of her innocence. No human effort, however, is of any avail. Both the second and third George, knowing their duty as public entertainers, seldom cheated the gallows of a victim of distinction.

Originally the execution had been fixed for Saturday, the 4th of April, but is postponed until the following Monday, because the

University authorities do not think it seemly that the sentence shall be carried out during Holy Week. A great crowd collects in the early morning outside the prison walls before the announcement of the short reprieve, and it speaks marvels for the discipline of the gaol that Miss Blandy is allowed to go up into rooms facing the Castle Green so that she can view the throng. Gazing upon the assembly without a tremor, she says merely that she will not balk their expectations much longer. On Sunday she takes sacrament for the last time, and signs a declaration in which she denies once more all knowledge that the powder was poisonous. In the evening, hearing that the Sheriff has arrived in the town, she sends a request that she may not be disturbed until eight o'clock the next morning.

It was half-past the hour she had named when the dismal procession reached the door of her chamber. The Under-Sheriff was accompanied by the Rev. John Swinton, and by her friend Mr Rives, the lawyer. Although her courage did not falter, she appeared meek and repentant, and spoke with anxiety of her future state, in doubt whether she would obtain pardon for her sins. This penitent mood encouraged the clergyman to beg her declare the whole truth, to which she replied that she must persist in asserting her innocence to the end. No entreaty would induce her to retract the solemn avowal.

At nine o'clock she was conducted from her room, dressed in the same black gown that she had worn at the trial, with her hands and arms tied by strong black silk ribbons. A crowd of five thousand persons, hushed and expectant, was waiting on the Castle Green to witness her sufferings. Thirty yards from the door of the gaol, whence she was led into the open air, stood the gallows—a beam placed across the arms of two trees. Against it lay a step-ladder covered with black cloth. The horror of her crime must have been forgotten by all who gazed upon the calm and brave woman. For truly she died like a queen. Serene and fearless she walked to the fatal spot, and joined most fervently with the clergyman in prayer. After this was ended they told her that if she wished she might speak to the spectators.

'Good people,' she cried, in a clear, audible voice, 'give me leave to declare to you that I am perfectly innocent as to any intention to destroy or even hurt my dear father; that I did not know, or even suspect, that there was any poisonous quality in the fatal powder I gave him; though I can never be too much punished for being the innocent cause of his death. As to my mother's and Mrs Pocock's deaths, that have been unjustly laid to my charge, I am not even the innocent cause of them, nor did I in the least contribute to them. So help me, God, in these my last moments. And may I not meet with eternal salvation, nor be acquitted by Almighty God, in whose awful presence I am instantly to appear hereafter, if the whole of what is here asserted is not true. I from the bottom of my soul forgive all those concerned in my prosecution; and particularly the jury, notwithstanding their fatal verdict.'

Then, having ascended five steps of the ladder, she turned to the officials. 'Gentlemen,' she requested, with a show of modesty, 'do not hang me high.' The humanity of those whose task it was to put her to death, forced them to ask her to go a little higher. Climbing two steps more, she then looked round, and trembling, said, 'I am afraid I shall fall.' Still, her invincible courage enabled her to address the crowd once again. 'Good people,' she said, 'take warning by me to be on your guard against the sallies of any irregular passion, and pray for me that I may be accepted at the Throne of Grace.' While the rope was being placed around her neck it touched her face, and she gave a deep sigh. Then with her own fingers she moved it to one side. A white handkerchief had been bound across her forehead, and she drew it over her features. As it did not come low enough, a woman, who had attended her and who had fixed the noose around her throat, stepped up and pulled it down. For a while she stood in prayer, and then gave the signal by thrusting out a little book which she held in her hand. The ladder was moved from under her feet, and in obedience to the laws of her country she was suspended in the air, swaying and convulsed, until the grip of the rope choked the breath from her body.

Horrible! Yet only in degree are our own methods different from those employed a hundred and fifty years ago.

During the whole of the sad tragedy, the crowd, unlike the howling mob at Tyburn, maintained an awestruck silence. There were few dry eyes, though the sufferer did not shed a tear, and hundreds of those who witnessed her death went away convinced of her innocence. An elegant young man named Edward Gibbon, with brain wrapped in the mists of theology, who for three days had been gentleman commoner at Magdalen, does not appear to have been attracted to the scene. Surely George Selwyn must be maligned, else he would have posted to Oxford to witness this spectacle. It would have been his only opportunity of seeing a gentlewoman in the hands of the executioner.

After hanging for half an hour with the feet, in consequence of her request, almost touching the ground, the body was carried upon the shoulders of one of the sheriff's men to a neighbouring house. At five o'clock in the afternoon the coffin containing her remains was taken in a hearse to Henley, where, in the dead of night, amidst a vast concourse, it was interred in the chancel of the parish church between the graves of her father and mother.

So died 'the unfortunate Miss Blandy,' in the thirty-second year of her age—with a grace and valour which no scene on the scaffold has ever excelled. If, as the authors of *The Beggar's Opera* and *The History of Jonathan Wild* have sought to show, in playful irony, the greatness of the criminal is comparable with the greatness of the statesman, then she must rank with Mary of Scotland and Catherine of Russia among the queens of crime. Hers was the soul of steel, theirs also the opportunity.

In every period the enormity of a sin can be estimated only by its relation to the spirit of the age; and in spite of cant and sophistry, the contemporaries of Miss Blandy made no legal distinction between the crimes of parricide and petty larceny. Nay, the same rope that strangled the brutal cut-throat in a few moments might prolong the agony of a poor thief for a quarter of an hour. Had the doctors succeeded in saving the life of the old attorney, the strange law which in later times put to death Elizabeth Fenning would have been powerless to demand the life of Mary Blandy for a similar offence. The protests of Johnson and Fielding against the iniquity of the criminal code fell on idle ears.

Thus we may not judge Mary Blandy from the standpoint of our own moral grandeur, for she is a being of another world—one of the vain, wilful, selfish children to whom an early Guelph was king—merely one of the blackest sheep in a flock for the most part ill-favoured. As we gaze upon her portrait there comes a feeling that we do not know this sombre woman after all, for though the artist has produced a faithful resemblance, we perceive there is something lacking. We look into part, not into her whole soul. None but one of the immortals—Rembrandt, or his peer—could have shown this queen among criminals as she was: an iron-hearted, remorseless, demon-woman, her fair, cruel visage raised mockingly amidst a chiaroscuro of crime and murkiness unspeakable.

> a narrow, foxy face,
> Heart-hiding smile, and gay persistent eye.

In our own country the women of gentle birth who have been convicted of murder since the beginning of the eighteenth century may be counted on the fingers of one hand. Mary Blandy, Constance Kent, Florence Maybrick—for that unsavoury person, Elizabeth Jefferies, has no claim to be numbered in the roll, and the verdict against beautiful Madeleine Smith was 'Not proven'—these names exhaust the list. And of them, the first alone paid the penalty at the gallows. The annals of crime contain the records of many parricides, some that have been premeditated with devilish art, but scarce one that a daughter has wrought by the most loathsome of coward's weapons. In comparison with the murderess of Henley, even Frances Howard and Anne Turner were guilty of a venial crime. Mary Blandy stands alone and incomparable—pilloried to all ages among the basest of her sex.

Yet the world soon forgot her. 'Since the two misses were hanged,' chats Horace Walpole on the 23rd of June, coupling irreverently the names of Blandy and Jefferies with the beautiful Gunnings—'since the two misses were hanged, and the two misses were married, there is nothing at all talked of.' Society, however, soon found a new thrill in the adventures of the young woman Elizabeth Canning.

*For reasons of space, Bleackley's extensive bibliography is omitted. It was reprinted, with a generous tribute by the editor, William Roughead, in the Notable British Trials volume devoted to Mary Blandy (Hodge, 1914).*

# H. B. IRVING

# The Mysterious
# Mr Holmes[1]

## I   HONOUR AMONGST THIEVES

In the year 1894 Mr Smith, a carpenter, of Philadelphia, had patented
a new saw-set. Wishing to make some money out of his invention, Mr
Smith was attracted by the sign:

B. F. PERRY
PATENTS BOUGHT AND SOLD

which he saw stretched across the window of a two-storeyed house,
1,316 Callowhill Street. He entered the house and made the acquaintance of Mr Perry, a tall, dark, bony man, to whom he explained
the merits of his invention. Perry listened with interest, and asked for
a model. In the meantime he suggested that Smith should do some
carpenter's work for him in the house. Smith agreed, and on August
22, while at work there, saw a man enter the house and go up with
Perry to a room on the second storey.

A few days later Smith called at Callowhill Street to ask Perry about
the sale of the patent. He waited half an hour in the shop below, called
out to Perry who, he thought, might be in the rooms above, received
no answer and went away. Next day, September 4, Smith returned,
found the place just as he had left it the day before; called Perry again,
but again got no answer. Surprised, he went upstairs, and in the back
room of the second storey the morning sunshine, streaming through the
window, showed him the dead body of a man, his face charred beyond
recognition, lying with his feet to the window and his head to the door.
There was evidence of some sort of explosion: a broken bottle that had
contained an inflammable substance, a broken pipe filled with tobacco,
and a burnt match lay by the side of the body.

The general appearance of the dead man answered to that of
B. F. Perry. A medical examination of the body showed that death had

[1] *The Holmes-Pitezel Case*, by F. B. Geyer, 1896; *Holmes' Own Story*, Philadelphia, 1895; and
*Celebrated Criminal Cases of America*, by T. S. Duke, San Francisco, are the authorities for
this account of the case.

been sudden, that there had been paralysis of the involuntary muscles, and that the stomach, besides showing symptoms of alcoholic irritation, emitted a strong odour of chloroform. An inquest was held, and a verdict returned that B. F. Perry had died of congestion of the lungs caused by the inhalation of flame or chloroform. After lying in the mortuary for eleven days the body was buried.

In the meantime the Philadelphia branch of the Fidelity Mutual Life Association had received a letter from one Jephtha D. Howe, an attorney at St Louis, stating that the deceased B. F. Perry was Benjamin F. Pitezel of that city, who had been insured in their office for a sum of ten thousand dollars. The insurance had been effected in Chicago in the November of 1893. Mr Howe proposed to come to Philadelphia with some members of the Pitezel family to identify the remains. Referring to their Chicago branch, the insurance company found that the only person who would seem to have known Pitezel when in that city was a certain H. H. Holmes, living at Wilmette, Illinois. They got into communication with Mr Holmes, and forwarded to him a cutting from a newspaper, which stated erroneously that the death of B. F. Perry had taken place in Chicago.

On September 18 they received a letter from Mr Holmes, in which he offered what assistance he could toward the identification of B. F. Perry as B. F. Pitezel. He gave the name of a dentist in Chicago who would be able to recognize teeth which he had made for Pitezel, and himself furnished a description of the man, especially of a malformation of the knee and a warty growth on the back of the neck by which he could be further identified. Mr Holmes offered, if his expenses were paid, to come to Chicago to view the body. Two days later he wrote again saying that he had seen by other papers that Perry's death had taken place in Philadelphia and not in Chicago, and that, as he had to be in Baltimore in a day or two, he would run over to Philadelphia and visit the office of the Fidelity Life Association.

On September 20 the assiduous Mr Holmes called at the office of the Association in Philadelphia, inquired anxiously about the nature and cause of Perry's death, gave again a description of him and, on learning that Mr Howe, the attorney from St Louis, was about to come to Philadelphia to represent the widow, Mrs Pitezel, and complete the identification, said that he would return to give the company any further help he could in the matter. The following day Mr Jephtha D. Howe, attorney, of St Louis, arrived in Philadelphia, accompanied by Alice Pitezel, a daughter of the deceased. Howe explained that Pitezel had taken the name of Perry owing to financial difficulties. The company said that they accepted the fact that Perry and Pitezel were one and the same man, but were not convinced that the body

was Pitezel's body. The visit of Holmes was mentioned. Howe said
that he did not know Mr Holmes, but would be willing to meet him.
At this moment Holmes arrived at the office. He was introduced to
Howe as a stranger, and recognized as a friend by Alice Pitezel, a
shy, awkward girl of fourteen or fifteen years of age. It was then
arranged that all the parties should meet again next day to identify,
if possible, the body, which had been disinterred for that purpose.

The unpleasant duty of identifying the rapidly decomposing remains
was greatly curtailed by the readiness of Mr Holmes. When the party
met on the 22nd at the Potter's Field, where the body had been
disinterred and laid out, the doctor present was unable to find the
distinctive marks which would show Perry and Pitezel to have been
the same man. Holmes at once stepped into the breach, took off his
coat, rolled up his sleeves, put on the rubber gloves, and taking a
surgeon's knife from his pocket, cut off the wart at the back of the
neck, showed the injury to the leg, and revealed also a bruised thumb-
nail which had been another distinctive mark of Pitezel. The body
was then covered up, all but the teeth; the girl Alice was brought in,
and she said that the teeth appeared to be like those of her father.
The insurance company declared themselves satisfied, and handed to
Mr Howe a cheque for 9,175 dollars, and to Mr Holmes ten dollars
for his expenses. Smith, the carpenter, had been present at the
proceedings at the Potter's Field. For a moment he thought he detected
a likeness in Mr Holmes to the man who had visited Perry at Callowhill Street on August 22 and gone upstairs with him, but he did not
feel sure enough of the fact to make any mention of it.

In the prison at St Louis there languished in the year 1894 one
Marion Hedgspeth, serving a sentence of twenty years' imprisonment
for an audacious train robbery. On the night of November 30, 1891,
the ''Frisco' express from St Louis had been boarded by four ruffians,
the express car blown open with dynamite, and 10,000 dollars carried
off. Hedgspeth and another man were tried for the robbery, and
sentenced to twenty years' imprisonment. On October 9, 1894,
Hedgspeth made a statement to the Governor of the St Louis Prison,
which he said he wished to be communicated to the Fidelity Mutual
Life Association. In the previous July Hedgspeth said that he had met
in the prison a man of the name of H. M. Howard, who was charged
with fraud, but had been released on bail later in the month. While
in prison Howard told Hedgspeth that he had devised a scheme for
swindling an insurance company of 10,000 dollars, and promised
Hedgspeth that, if he would recommend him a lawyer suitable for
such an enterprise, he should have 500 dollars as his share of the
proceeds. Hedgspeth recommended Jephtha D. Howe. The latter

entered with enthusiasm into the scheme, and told Hedgspeth that he thought Mr Howard 'one of the smoothest and slickest' men he had ever known. A corpse was to be found answering to Pitezel's description, and to be so treated as to appear to have been the victim of an accidental explosion, while Pitezel himself would disappear to Germany. From Howe Hedgspeth learnt that the swindle had been carried out successfully, but he had never received from Howard the 500 dollars promised him. Consequently, he had but little compunction in divulging the plot to the authorities.

It was realized at once that H. M. Howard and H. H. Holmes were the same person, and that Jephtha D. Howe and Mr Holmes were not the strangers to each other that they had affected to be when they met in Philadelphia. Though somewhat doubtful of the truth of Hedgspeth's statement, the insurance company decided to set Pinkerton's detectives on the track of Mr H. H. Holmes. After more than a month's search he was traced to his father's house at Gilmanton, N.H., and arrested in Boston on November 17.

Inquiry showed that, early in 1894, Holmes and Pitezel had acquired some real property at Fort Worth in Texas and commenced building operations, but had soon after left Texas under a cloud, arising from the theft of a horse and other dubious transactions. Holmes had obtained the property at Fort Worth from a Miss Minnie Williams, and transferred it to Pitezel. Pitezel was a drunken 'crook', of mean intelligence, a mesmeric subject entirely under the influence of Holmes, who claimed to have considerable hypnotic powers. Pitezel had a wife living at St Louis and five children: three girls—Dessie, Alice, and Nellie—a boy, Howard, and a baby in arms. At the time of Holmes' arrest Mrs Pitezel, with her eldest daughter, Dessie, and her little baby, was living at a house rented by Holmes at Burlington, Vermont. She also was arrested on a charge of complicity in the insurance fraud and brought to Boston.

Two days after his arrest Holmes, who dreaded being sent back to Texas on a charge of horse-stealing, for which in that State the punishment is apt to be rough and ready, made a statement to the police, in which he acknowledged the fraud practised by him and Pitezel on the insurance company. The body substituted for Pitezel had been obtained, said Holmes, from a doctor in New York, packed in a trunk and sent to Philadelphia, but he declined for the present to give the doctor's name. Pitzel, he said, had gone with three of his children—Alice, Nellie and Howard—to South America. This fact, however, Holmes had not communicated to Mrs Pitezel. When she arrived at Boston, the poor woman was in great distress of mind. Questioned by the officers, she attempted to deny any complicity in the fraud, but her real anxiety was to get news of her husband and her three children. Alice she had not seen since the girl had gone to Philadelpha to identify the supposed remains of her father. Shortly after this Holmes had come to Mrs Pitezel at St Louis, and taken away Nellie and Howard to join Alice, who, he said, was in the care of a widow lady at Ovington, Kentucky. Since then Mrs Pitezel had seen nothing of the children or her husband. At Holmes' direction she had gone to Detroit, Toronto, Ogdensberg and, lastly, to Burlington in the hope of meeting either Pitezel or the children, but in vain. She believed that her husband had deserted her; her only desire was to recover her children.

On November 20 Holmes and Mrs Pitezel were transferred from Boston to Philadelphia, and there, along with Benjamin Pitezel and Jephtha D. Howe, were charged with defrauding the Fidelity Life Association of 10,000 dollars. Soon after his arrival in Philadelphia, Holmes, who was never averse to talking, was asked by an inspector of the insurance company who it was that had helped him to double up the body sent from New York and pack it into the trunk. He replied that he had done it alone, having learned the trick when studying medicine in Michigan. The inspector recollected that the body when removed from Callowhill Street had been straight and rigid. He asked Holmes what trick he had learnt in the course of his medical studies by which it was possible to re-stiffen a body once the *rigor mortis* had been broken. To this Holmes made no reply. But he realized his mistake, and a few weeks later volunteered a second statement. He now said that Pitezel, in a fit of depression, aggravated by his drinking habits, had committed suicide on the third storey of the house in Callowhill Street. There Holmes had found his body, carried it down on to the floor below, and arranged it in the manner agreed upon for deceiving the insurance company. Pitezel, he said, had taken his life by lying on the floor and allowing chloroform to run slowly into his mouth through a rubber tube placed on a chair. The three children, Holmes now stated, had gone to England with a friend of his, Miss Minnie Williams.

Miss Minnie Williams was the lady from whom Holmes was said to have acquired the property in Texas which he and Pitezel had set about developing. There was quite a tragedy, according to Holmes, connected with the life of Miss Williams. She had come to Holmes in 1893, as secretary at a drug store which he was then keeping in Chicago. Their relations had become more intimate, and later in the year Miss Williams wrote to her sister Nannie saying that she was going to be married, and inviting her to the wedding. Nannie arrived, but unfortunately a violent quarrel broke out between the two sisters, and

Holmes came home to find that Minnie in her rage had killed her sister. He had helped her out of the trouble by dropping Nannie's body into the Chicago lake. After such a distressing occurrence Miss Williams was only too glad of the opportunity of leaving America with the Pitezel children. In the meantime Holmes, under the name of Bond, and Pitezel, under that of Lyman, had proceeded to deal with Miss Williams' property in Texas.

For women Holmes would always appear to have possessed some power of attraction, a power of which he availed himself generously. Holmes, whose real name was Herman W. Mudgett, was thirty-four years of age at the time of his arrest. As a boy he had spent his life farming in Vermont, after which he had taken up medicine and acquired some kind of medical degree. In the course of his training Holmes and a fellow-student, finding a body that bore a striking resemblance to the latter, obtained 1,000 dollars from an insurance company by a fraud similar to that in which Holmes had engaged subsequently with Pitezel. After spending some time on the staff of a lunatic asylum in Pennsylvania, Holmes set up as a druggist in Chicago. His affairs in this city prospered, and he was enabled to erect, at the corner of Wallace and Sixty-third Streets, the four-storeyed building known later as 'Holmes Castle'. It was a singular structure. The lower part consisted of a shop and offices. Holmes occupied the second floor, and had a laboratory on the third. In his office was a vault, air-proof and sound-proof. In the bathroom a trap-door, covered by a rug, opened on to a secret staircase leading down to the cellar, and a similar staircase connected the cellar with the laboratory. In the cellar was a large grate. To this building Miss Minnie Williams had invited her sister to come for her wedding with Holmes, and it was in this building, according to Holmes, that the tragedy of Nannie's untimely death occurred.

In hoping to become Holmes' wife, Miss Minnie Williams was not to enjoy an exclusive privilege. At the time of his arrest Holmes had three wives, each ignorant of the others' existence. He had married the first in 1878, under the name of Mudgett, and was visiting her at Burlington, Vermont, when the Pinkerton detectives first got on his track; the second had married at Chicago, under the name of Howard; and the third at Denver, as recently as January, 1894, under the name of Holmes. The third Mrs Holmes had been with him when he came to Philadelphia to identify Pitezel's body. The appearance of Holmes was commonplace, but he was a man of plausible and ingratiating address, apparent candour, and able in case of necessity to 'let loose', as he phrased it, 'the fount of emotion'.

The year 1895 opened to find the much-enduring Holmes still a prisoner in Philadelphia. The authorities seemed in no haste to indict him for fraud; their interest was concentrated rather in endeavouring to find the whereabouts of Miss Williams and the children, and of one Edward Hatch, whom Holmes had described as helping him in arranging for their departure. The 'great humiliation' of being a prisoner was very distressing to Holmes.

> I only know the sky has lost its blue,
> The days are weary and the night is drear.

These struck him as two beautiful lines very appropriate to his situation. He made a New Year's resolve to give up meat during his close confinement. The visits of his third wife brought him some comfort. He was 'agreeably surprised' to find that, as an unconvicted prisoner, he could order in his own meals and receive newspapers and periodicals. But he was hurt at an unfriendly suggestion on the part of the authorities that Pitezel had not died by his own hand, and that Edward Hatch was but a figment of his rich imagination. He would have liked to be released on bail, but in the same unfriendly spirit was informed that, if he were, he would be detained on a charge of murder. And so the months dragged on. Holmes—studious, patient, injured, the authorities puzzled, suspicious, baffled—still no news of Miss Williams or the three children. It was not until June 3 that Holmes was put on his trial for fraud, and the following day pleaded guilty. Sentence was postponed.

The same day Holmes was sent for to the office of the District Attorney, who thus addressed him: 'It is strongly suspected, Holmes, that you have not only murdered Pitezel, but that you have killed the children. The best way to remove this suspicion is to produce the children at once. Now, where are they?' Unfriendly as was this approach, Holmes met it calmly, reiterated his previous statement that the children had gone with Miss Williams to England, and gave her address in London, 80 Veder or Vadar Street, where, he said, Miss Williams had opened a massage establishment. He offered to draw up and insert a cipher advertisement in the *New York Herald*, by means of which, he said, Miss Williams and he had agreed to communicate, and almost tearfully he added, 'Why should I kill innocent children?' Asked to give the name of any person who had seen Miss Williams and the children in the course of their journeyings in America, he resented the disbelief implied in such a question, and strong was his manly indignation when one of the gentlemen present expressed his opinion that the story was a lie from beginning to end. This rude estimate of Holmes' veracity was, however, in some degree confirmed when a cipher advertisement published in the *New York*

*Herald* according to Holmes' directions, produced no reply from Miss Williams, and inquiry showed that no such street as Veder or Vadar Street was to be found in London.

In spite of these disappointments, Holmes' quiet confidence in his own good faith continued unshaken. When the hapless Mrs Pitezel was released, he wrote her a long letter. 'Knowing me as you do,' he said, 'can you imagine me killing little and innocent children, especially without any motive?' But even Mrs Pitezel was not wholly reassured. She recollected how Holmes had taken her just before his arrest to a house he had rented at Burlington, Vermont, how he had written asking her to carry a package of nitro-glycerine from the bottom to the top of the house, and how one day she had found him busily removing the boards in the cellar.

## II  THE WANDERING ASSASSIN

The District Attorney and the Insurance Company were not in agreement as to the fate of the Pitezel children. The former still inclined to the hope and belief that they were in England with Miss Williams, but the insurance company took a more sinister view. No trace of them existed except a tin box found among Holmes' effects, containing letters they had written to their mother and grandparents from Cincinnati, Indianapolis, and Detroit, which had been given to Holmes to post but had never reached their destination. The box contained letters from Mrs Pitezel to her children, which Holmes had presumably intercepted. It was decided to make a final attempt to resolve all doubts by sending an experienced detective over the route taken by the children in America. He was to make exhaustive inquiries in each city with a view to tracing the visits of Holmes or the three children. For this purpose a detective of the name of Geyer was chosen. The record of his search is a remarkable story of patient and persistent investigation.

Alice Pitezel had not seen her mother since she had gone with Holmes to identify her father's remains in Philadelphia. From there Homes had taken her to Indianapolis. In the meantime he had visited Mrs Pitezel at St Louis, and taken away with him the girl, Nellie, and the boy, Howard, alleging as his reason for doing so that they and Alice were to join their father, whose temporary effacement was necessary to carry out successfully the fraud on the insurance company, to which Mrs Pitezel had been from the first an unwilling party. Holmes, Nellie and Howard had joined Alice at Indianapolis, and from there all four were believed to have gone to Cincinnati. It was here, accordingly, on June 27, 1895, that Geyer commenced his search.

After calling at a number of hotels, Geyer found that on Friday, September 28, 1894, a man, giving the name of Alexander E. Cook, and three children had stayed at an hotel called the Atlantic House. Geyer recollected that Holmes, when later on he had sent Mrs Pitezel to the house in Burlington, had described her as Mrs A. E. Cook and, though not positive, the hotel clerk thought that he recognized in the photographs of Holmes and the three children, which Geyer showed him, the four visitors to the hotel. They had left the Atlantic House the next day, and on that same day, the 29th, Geyer found that Mr A. E. Cook and three children had registered at the Bristol Hotel, where they had stayed until Sunday the 30th.

Knowing Holmes' habit of renting houses, Geyer did not confine his inquiries to the hotels. He visited a number of estate agents and learnt that a man and a boy, identified as Holmes and Howard Pitezel, had occupied a house No. 305 Poplar Street. The man had given the name of A. C. Hayes. He had taken the house on Friday the 28th, and on the 29th had driven up to it with the boy in a furniture wagon. A curious neighbour, interested in the advent of a newcomer, saw the wagon arrive, and was somewhat astonished to observe that the only furniture taken into the house was a large iron cylinder stove. She was still further surprised when, on the following day, Mr Hayes told her that he was not going after all to occupy the house, and made her a present of the cylinder stove.

From Cincinnati Geyer went to Indianapolis. Here inquiry showed that on September 30 three children had been brought by a man identified as Holmes to the Hotel English, and registered in the name of Canning. This was the maiden name of Mrs Pitezel. The children had stayed at the hotel one night. After that Geyer seemed to lose track of them until he was reminded of an hotel then closed, called the Circle House. With some difficulty he got a sight of the books of the hotel, and found that the three Canning children had arrived there on October 1 and stayed until the 10th. From the former proprietor of the hotel he learnt that Holmes had described himself as the children's uncle, and had said that Howard was a bad boy, whom he was trying to place in some institution. The children seldom went out; they would sit in their room drawing or writing; often they were found crying; they seemed homesick and unhappy.

There are letters of the children written from Indianapolis to their mother, letters found in Holmes' possession, which had never reached her. In these letters they ask their mother why she does not write to them. She had written, but her letters were in Holmes' possession. Alice writes that she is reading *Uncle Tom's Cabin*. She has read so much that her eyes hurt; they have bought a crystal pen for five cents which gives them some amusement; they had been to the Zoo in Cincinnati the Sunday before: 'I expect this Sunday will pass away slower than I don't know—Howard is two (*sic*) dirty to be seen out on the street to-day.' Sometimes they go and watch a man who paints 'genuine oil paintings' in a shoe store, which are given away with every dollar purchase of shoes—'he can paint a picture in one and a half minutes, ain't that quick!' Howard was getting a little troublesome. 'I don't like to tell you,' writes Alice, 'but you ask me, so I will have to. Howard won't mind me at all. He wanted a book and I got *Life of General Sheridan*, and it is awful nice, but now he don't read it at all hardly.' Poor Howard! One morning, says Alice, Mr Holmes told him to stay in and wait for him, as he was coming to take him out, but Howard was disobedient, and when Mr Holmes arrived he had gone out. Better for Howard had he never returned. 'We have written two or three letters to you,' Alice tells her mother, 'and I guess you will begin to get them now.' She will not get them. Mr Holmes is so very particular that the insurance company shall get no clue to the whereabouts of any member of the Pitezel family.

Geyer knew that from Indianapolis Holmes had gone to Detroit. He ascertained that two girls, 'Etta and Nellie Canning', had registered on October 12 at the New Western Hotel in that city, and from there had moved on the 15th to a boarding-house in Congress Street. From Detroit Alice had written to her grandparents. It was cold and wet, she wrote; she and Etta had colds and chapped hands: 'We have to stay in all the time. All that Nell and I can do is to draw, and I get so tired sitting that I could get up and fly almost. I wish I could see you all. I am getting so homesick that I don't know what to do. I suppose Wharton (their baby brother) walks by this time, don't he? I would like to have him here, he would pass away the time a good deal.' As a fact little Wharton, his mother and sister Dessie, were at this very moment in Detroit, within ten minutes' walk of the hotel at which Holmes had registered 'Etta and Nellie Canning'.

On October 14 there had arrived in that city a weary, anxious-looking woman, with a girl and a little baby. They took a room at Geis's Hotel, registering as Mrs Adams and daughter. Mrs Adams seemed in great distress of mind, and never left her room.

The housekeeper, being shown their photographs, identified the woman and the girl as Mrs Pitezel and her eldest daughter Dessie. At the same time there had been staying at another hotel in Detroit a Mr and Mrs Holmes, whose photographs showed them to be the Mr Holmes in question and his third wife. These three parties—the two children, Mrs Pitezel and her baby, and the third Mrs Holmes—were all ignorant of each other's presence in Detroit; and under the secret guidance of Mr Holmes the three parties, still unaware of their proximity to each other, left Detroit for Canada, arriving in Toronto on or about October 18, and registering at three separate hotels. The only one who had not to all appearances reached Toronto was the boy Howard.

In Toronto 'Alice and Nellie Canning' stayed at the Albion Hotel. They arrived there on October 19, and left on the 25th. During their stay a man, identified as Holmes, had called every morning for the two children, and taken them out; but they had come back alone, usually in time for supper. On the 25th he had called and taken them out, but they had not returned to supper. After that date Geyer could find not trace of them. Bearing in mind Holmes' custom of renting houses, he compiled a list of all the house agents in Toronto, and laboriously applied to each one for information. The process was a slow one, and the result seemed likely to be disappointing.

To aid his search Geyer decided to call in the assistance of the Press. The newspapers readily published long accounts of the case and por-traits of Holmes and the children. At last, after eight days of patient and untiring investigation, after following up more than one false clue, Geyer received a report that there was a house—No. 16 St Vincent Street—which had been rented in the previous October by a man answering to the description of Holmes. The information came from an old Scottish gentleman living next door. Geyer hastened to see him. The old gentleman said that the man who had occupied No. 16 in October had told him that he had taken the house for his widowed sister, and he recognized the photograph of Alice Pitezel as one of the two girls accompanying him. The only furniture the man had taken into the house was a bed, a mattress and a trunk. During his stay at No. 16 this man had called on his neighbour about four o'clock one afternoon and borrowed a spade, saying that he wanted to dig a place in the cellar where his widowed sister could keep potatoes; he had returned the spade the following morning. The lady to whom the house belonged recognized Holmes' portrait as that of the man to whom she had let No. 16.

At last Geyer seemed to be on the right track. He hurried back to St Vincent Street, borrowed from the old gentleman at No. 18 the very spade which he had lent to Holmes in the previous October, and got the permission of the present occupier of No. 16 to make a search. In the centre of the kitchen Geyer found a trap-door leading down into a small cellar. In one corner of the cellar he saw that the earth had been recently dug up. With the help of the spade the loose earth was removed, and at a depth of some three feet, in a state of advanced decomposition, lay the remains of what appeared to be two children.

A little toy wooden egg with a snake inside it, belonging to the Pitezel children, had been found by the tenant who had taken the house after Holmes; a later tenant had found stuffed into the chimney, but not burnt, some clothing that answered the description of that worn by Alice and Etta Pitezel; and by the teeth and hair of the two corpses Mrs Pitezel was able to identify them as those of her two daughters. The very day that Alice and Etta had met their deaths at St Vincent Street, their mother had been staying near them at a hotel in the same city, and later on the same day Holmes had persuaded her to leave Toronto for Ogdensburg. He said that they were being watched by detectives, and so it would be impossible for her husband to come to see her there.

But the problem was not yet wholly solved. What had become of Howard? So far Geyer's search had shown that Holmes had rented three houses, one in Cincinnati, one in Detroit, and one in Toronto. Howard had been with his sisters at the hotels in Indianapolis, and in Detroit the house agents had said that, when Holmes had rented a house there, he had been accompanied by a boy. Yet an exhaustive search of that house had revealed no trace of him. Geyer returned to Detroit and again questioned the house agents; on being pressed, their recollection of the boy who had accompanied Holmes seemed very vague and uncertain. This served only to justify a conclusion at which Geyer had already arrived, that Howard had never reached Detroit, but had disappeared in Indianapolis. Alice's letters, written from there, had described how Holmes had wanted to take Howard out one day and how the boy had refused to stay in and wait for him. In the same way Holmes had called for the two girls at the Albion Hotel in Toronto on October 25 and taken them out with him, after which they had never been seen alive except by the old gentleman at No. 18 St Vincent Street.

If Geyer could discover that Holmes had not departed in Indianapolis from his usual custom of renting houses, he might be on the high way to solving the mystery of Howard's fate. Accordingly he returned to Indianapolis.

In the meantime, Holmes, in his prison at Philadelphia, learnt of the discovery at Toronto. 'On the morning of the 16th of July,' he writes in his journal, 'my newspaper was delivered to me about 8.30 a.m., and I had hardly opened it before I saw in large headlines the announcement of the finding of the children in Toronto. For the moment it seemed so impossible that I was inclined to think it was one of the frequent newspaper excitements that had attended the earlier part of the case, but, in attempting to gain some accurate comprehension of what was stated in the article, I became convinced that at least certain bodies had been found there, and upon comparing the date when the house was hired I knew it to be the same as when the children had been in

Toronto; and thus being forced to realize the awfulness of what had probably happened, I gave up trying to read the article, and saw instead the two little faces as they had looked when I hurriedly left them—felt the innocent child's kiss so timidly given, and heard again their earnest words of farewell, and realized that I had received another burden to carry to my grave with me, equal, if not worse, than the horrors of Nannie Williams' death.'

Questioned by the district attorney, Holmes met this fresh evidence by evoking once again the mythical Edward Hatch and suggesting that Miss Minnie Williams, in a 'hellish wish for vengeance' because of Holmes' fancied desertion, and in order to make it appear probable that he, and not she, had murdered her sister, had prompted Hatch to commit the horrid deed. Holmes asked to be allowed to go to Toronto that he might collect any evidence which he could find there in his favour. The district attorney refused his request; he had determined to try Holmes in Philadelphia. 'What more could be said?' writes Holmes. Indeed, under the circumstances, and in the unaccountable absence of Edward Hatch and Minnie Williams, there was little more to be said.

Detective Geyer reopened his search in Indianapolis by obtaining a list of advertisements of houses to let in the city in 1894. Nine hundred of these were followed up in vain. He then turned his attention to the small towns lying around Indianapolis with no happier result. Geyer wrote in something of despair to his superiors: 'By Monday we will have searched every outlying town except Irvington. After Irvington, I scarcely know where we shall go.' Thither he went on August 27, exactly two months from the day on which his quest had begun. As he entered the town he noticed the advertisement of an estate agent. He called at the office and found a 'pleasant-faced old gentleman', who greeted him amiably. Once again Geyer opened his now soiled and ragged packet of photographs, and asked the gentleman if in October, 1894, he had let a house to a man who said that he wanted one for a widowed sister. He showed him the portrait of Holmes.

The old man put on his glasses and looked at the photograph for some time. Yes, he said, he did remember that he had given the keys of a cottage in October, 1894, to a man of Holmes' apearance, and he recollected the man the more distinctly for the uncivil abruptness with which he had asked for the keys; 'I felt,' he said, 'he should have had more respect for my grey hairs.'

From the old gentleman's office Geyer hastened to the cottage, and made at once for the cellar. There he could find no sign of recent disturbance. But beneath the floor of a piazza adjoining the house he found the remains of a trunk, answering to the description of that which the Pitezel children had had with them, and in an outhouse he discovered the inevitable stove, Holmes' one indispensable piece of furniture. It was stained with blood on the top. A neighbour had seen Holmes in the same October drive up to the house in the furniture wagon accompanied by a boy, and later in the day Holmes had asked him to come over to the cottage and help him to put up a stove. The neighbour asked him why he did not use gas; Holmes replied that he did not think gas was healthy for children. While the two men were putting up the stove, the little boy stood by and watched them. After further search there were discovered in the cellar chimney some bones, teeth, a pelvis and the baked remains of a stomach, liver and spleen.

Medical examination showed them to be the remains of a child between seven and ten years of age. A spinning top, a scarf-pin, a pair of shoes and some articles of clothing that had belonged to the little Pitezels, had been found in the house at different times, and were handed over to Geyer.

His search was ended. On September 1 he returned to Philadelphia.

Holmes was put on his trial on October 28, 1895, before the Court of Oyer and Terminer in Philadelphia, charged with the murder of Benjamin Pitezel. In the course of the trial the district attorney offered to put in evidence showing that Holmes had also murdered the three children of Pitezel, contending that such evidence was admissible on the ground that the murders of the children and their father were parts of the same transaction. The judge refused to admit the evidence, though expressing a doubt as to its inadmissibility. The defence did not dispute the identity of the body found in Callowhill Street, but contended that Pitezel had committed suicide. The medical evidence negatived such a theory. The position of the body, its condition when discovered, were entirely inconsistent with self-destruction, and the absence of irritation in the stomach showed that the chloroform found there must have been poured into it after death. In all probability, Holmes had chloroformed Pitezel when he was drunk or asleep. He had taken the chloroform to Callowhill Street as a proposed ingredient in a solution for cleaning clothes, which he and Pitezel were to patent. It was no doubt with the help of the same drug that he had done to death the little children, and failing the nitro-glycerine, with that drug he had intended to put Mrs Pitezel and her two remaining children out of the way at the house in Burlington; for after his trial there was found there, hidden away in the cellar, a bottle containing eight or ten ounces of chloroform.

Though assisted by counsel, Holmes took an active part in his defence. He betrayed no feeling at the sight of Mrs Pitezel, the greater part of whose family he had destroyed, but the appearance of his third wife as a witness he made an opportunity for 'letting loose the fount of emotion', taking care to inform his counsel beforehand that he intended to perform this touching feat. He was convicted and sentenced to death on November 2.

Before the trial of Holmes the police had made an exhaustive investigation of the myserious building in Chicago known as 'Holmes' Castle'. The result was sufficiently sinister. In the stove in the cellar charred human bones were found, and in the middle of the room stood a large dissecting table stained with blood. On digging up the cellar floor some human ribs, sections of vertebrae and teeth were discovered buried in quicklime, and in other parts of the 'castle' the police found more charred bones, some metal buttons, a trunk, and a piece of a watch chain. The trunk and piece of watch chain were identified as having belonged to Miss Minnie Williams.

Inquiry showed that Miss Williams had entered Holmes' employment as a typist in 1893, and had lived with him at the castle. In the latter part of the year she had invited her sister, Nannie, to be present at her wedding with Holmes. Nannie had come to Chicago for that purpose, and since then the two sisters had never been seen alive. In February in the following year Pitezel, under the name of Lyman, had deposited at Forth Worth, Texas, a deed according to which a man named Bond had transferred to him property in that city which had belonged to Miss Williams, and shortly after, Holmes, under the name of Pratt, joined him at Fort Worth, whereupon the two commenced building on Miss Williams' land.

Other mysterious cases besides those of the Williams sisters revealed the Bluebeard-like character of this latter-day castle of Mr Holmes. In 1887 a man of the name of Connor entered Holmes' employment. He brought with him to the castle a handsome, intelligent wife and a little girl of eight or nine years of age. After a short time Connor quarrelled with his wife and went away, leaving Mrs Connor and the little girl with Holmes. After 1892 Mrs Connor and her daughter had disappeared, but in August, 1895, the police found in the castle some clothes identified as theirs, and the janitor, Quinlan, admitted having seen the dead body of Mrs Connor in the castle. Holmes, questioned in his prison in Philadelphia, said that Mrs Connor had died under an operation, but that he did not know what had become of the little girl.

In the year of Mrs Connor's disappearance, a typist named Emily Cigrand, who had been employed in a hospital in which Benjamin Pitezel had been a patient, was recommended by the latter to Holmes. She entered his employment, and she and Holmes soon became intimate, passing as 'Mr and Mrs Gordon'. Emily Cigrand had been in the habit of writing regularly to her parents in Indiana, but after

December 6, 1892, they had never heard from her again, nor could any further trace of her be found.

A man who worked for Holmes as a handy man at the castle stated to the police that in 1892 Holmes had given him a skeleton of a man to mount, and in January, 1893, showed him in the laboratory another male skeleton with some flesh still on it, which also he asked him to mount. As there was a set of surgical instruments in the laboratory and also a tank filled with a fluid preparation for removing flesh, the handy man thought that Holmes was engaged in some kind of surgical work.

About a month before his execution, when Holmes' appeals from his sentence had failed and death appeared imminent, he sold to the newspapers for 7,500 dollars a confession in which he claimed to have committed twenty-seven murders in the course of his career. The day after it appeared he declared the whole confession to be a 'fake'. He was tired, he said, of being accused by the newspapers of having committed every mysterious murder that had occurred during the last ten years. When it was pointed out to him that the account given in his confession of the murder of the Pitezel children was clearly untrue, he replied, 'Of course, it is not true, but the newspapers wanted a sensation and they have got it.' The confession was certainly sensational enough to satisfy the most exacting of penny-a-liners, and a lasting tribute to Holmes' undoubted power of extravagant romancing.

According to his story, some of his twenty-seven victims had met their death by poison, some by more violent methods, some had died a lingering death in the air-tight and sound-proof vault of the castle. Most of these he mentioned by name, but some of these were proved afterwards to be alive. Holmes had actually perpetrated, in all probability, about ten murders. But, given further time and opportunity, there is no reason why this peripatetic assassin should not have attained to the considerable figure with which he credited himself in his bogus confession.

Holmes was executed in Philadelphia on May 7, 1896. He seemed to meet his fate with indifference.

The motive of Holmes in murdering Pitezel and three of his children and in planning to murder his wife and remaining children, originated in all probability in a quarrel that occurred between Pitezel and himself in the July of 1894. Pitezel had tired apparently of Holmes and his doings, and wanted to break off the connection. But he must have known enough of Holmes' past to make him a dangerous enemy. It was Pitezel who had introduced to Holmes Emily Cigrand, the typist, who had disappeared so mysteriously in the castle; Pitezel had been his partner in the fraudulent appropriation of Miss Minnie Williams' property in Texas; it is more than likely, therefore, that Pitezel knew something of the fate of Miss Williams and her sister. By reviving, with Pitezel's help, his old plan for defrauding insurance companies, Holmes saw the opportunity of making 10,000 dollars, which he needed sorely, and at the same time removing his inconvenient and now lukewarm associate. Having killed Pitezel and received the insurance money, Holmes appropriated to his own use the greater part of the 10,000 dollars, giving Mrs Pitezel in return for her share of the plunder a bogus bill for 5,000 dollars. Having robbed Mrs Pitezel of both her husband and her money, to this thoroughgoing criminal there seemed only one satisfactory way of escaping detection, and that was to exterminate her and the whole of her family.

Had Holmes not confided his scheme of the insurance fraud to Hedgspeth in St Louis prison and then broken faith with him, there is no reason why the fraud should ever have been discovered. The subsequent murders had been so cunningly contrived that, had the insurance company not put the Pinkerton detectives on his track, Holmes would in all probability have ended by successfully disposing of Mrs Pitezel, Dessie, and the baby at the house in Burlington, Vermont, and the entire Pitezel family would have disappeared as completely as his other victims.

Holmes admitted afterwards that his one mistake had been his confiding to Hedgspeth his plans for defrauding an insurance company —a mistake, the unfortunate results of which might have been avoided if he had kept faith with the train robber and given him the 500 dollars which he had promised.

The case of Holmes illustrates the practical as well as the purely ethical value of 'honour among thieves', and shows how a comparatively insignificant misdeed may ruin a great and comprehensive plan of crime. To dare to attempt the extermination of a family of seven persons, and to succeed so nearly in effecting it, could be the work of no tyro, no beginner like J. B. Troppmann. It was the act of one who having already succeeded in putting out of the way a number of other persons undetected, might well and justifiably believe that he was born for greater and more compendious achievements in robbery and murder than any who had gone before him. One can almost subscribe to America's claim that Holmes is the 'greatest criminal' of a century boasting no mean record in such persons.

In the remarkable character of his achievements as an assassin we are apt to lose sight of Holmes' singular skill and daring as a liar and a bigamist. As an instance of the former may be cited his audacious explanation to his family, when they heard of his having married a second time. He said that he had met with a serious accident to his head, and that when he left the hospital, found that he had entirely lost his memory; that, while in this state of oblivion, he had married again and then, when his memory returned, realized to his horror his unfortunate position. Plausibility would seem to have been one of Holmes' most useful gifts; men and women alike—particularly the latter—he seems to have deceived with ease. His appearance was commonplace, in no way suggesting the conventional criminal; his manner courteous, ingratiating and seemingly candid; and like so many scoundrels, he could play consummately the man of sentiment. The weak spot in Holmes' armour as an enemy of society was a dangerous tendency to loquacity, the defeat no doubt of his qualities of plausible and insinuating address and ever-ready mendacity.

LESLIE HALE

# Night Life in
# Manchester

In most trials for murder intelligent jurymen become conscious of gaps
in the evidence. Many of them are due to the application of our strict
rules which preclude hearsay and are designed to protect a prisoner
from questioning after his arrest or from making any but a voluntary
statement. Some are due to the reluctance of defence counsel to put
probing questions when he cannot be sure of a favourable answer. Some
may be due to the failure of the investigators to have observed correct
methods of inquiry. A strong prosecuting counsel should decline to call
evidence which he regards as tainted with suspicion. These gaps are
usually inevitable, but it is difficult to believe that they may not lead
to the possibility of speculation by the jury, who remain uninformed
about the reason for the omissions. The absence of evidence may seem
to have considerable significance and in this respect the defence are, in
this country, almost invariably at a considerable disadvantage. Whilst
the prisoner is protected by strict rules from unfair interrogation he is
provided with singularly inadequate resources for the preparation of an
answer to the case presented by the Crown. At the disposal of the prosecution are the whole resources of experts and unparalleled facilities
for investigating, checking and counterchecking every relevant fact.

The accused will usually be in prison, physically and financially
unable to conduct any investigation or to call expert evidence of
comparable value to that of the prosecution. He will be provided with
solicitor and counsel who will do their best to interview such witnesses
as the prisoner has indicated to them, but they have no power or duty
to conduct a widespread and systematic investigation. Their principal
chance of testing the accuracy of the evidence for the prosecution is by
cross-examination. It is a difficult and dangerous art, for able counsel
are naturally inhibited against putting a question which may produce
an unhelpful answer.

The case of Walter Graham Rowland is here presented, without
comment, just as it was to the jury at his trial in December 1946. He
was charged with the murder on the night of October 19th–20th, 1946,
of Olive Balchin. On Sunday morning October 20th, 1946, at about

eleven o'clock her body was found lying on some derelict land not far from Deansgate, one of the main streets of Manchester. She had been brutally murdered with heavy blows on the head from a hammer which was left lying near the body. Near by, too, was a piece of brown paper in which the hammer had been wrapped. She had bled very extensively and her hat and coat were heavily bloodstained. The injuries indicated that blood would have spurted considerably because arteries had been broken and the brain was exposed.

Olive Balchin was a woman of forty to fifty years of age, with yellow hair turning grey, and a few septic teeth in the lower jaw, who was known as a local prostitute. She had been dead for about twelve hours when her body was found. None of these facts was ever in dispute. There was never any question that Olive Blachin had been murdered, and on the spot where she was found. There was no question that the weapon was the bloodstained hammer.

Mr Edward Macdonald informed the police that he had sold a hammer of that type at his shop in Downing Street at about twenty to six on Saturday evening October 19th, only a few hours before the crime. He identified the hammer and the piece of brown paper in which he had wrapped it. The hammer was a leather-dressers' hammer with a figure four impressed upon it, and Mr Macdonald recognized it when he saw a photograph in the newspaper.

Mr Macdonald made a statement to the police on the day following the discovery of the body. In this he said that he had purchased the hammer on the Saturday morning and placed it on sale about three p.m.

'Between five p.m. and six p.m. that evening a customer came into the shop, and pointing to the leather-dressers' hammer in the window asked the price of it. I told him three shillings and sixpence, and pointed out to him that it was a special leather-dressers' hammer. He told me that was quite all right, as he only wanted it for general purposes.'

Mr Macdonald described the man as from twenty-eight to thirty-two years, five feet seven to eight inches tall, medium build, very pale, thin features, clean shaven, quiet-spoken, no hat, white soft collar and shirt, dark tie, dark suit, dark fawn cotton raincoat, clean and of respectable appearance.

A second witness, Mrs Elizebeth Copley, was employed as a waitress at the Queen's Café quite near the scene of the crime. She saw a man accompanied by two women enter the café at about ten thirty on the Saturday night. The two women she described as 'a very old woman; she was well over sixty', and 'the young girl Olive'. The old woman was 'not Welsh, more Irish'. She noticed that the man was carrying a thin brown-paper parcel. She described the man to the police as a man with black hair and fresh complexion and wearing a dark suit. He was not wearing a hat and she did not see a macintosh. She had seen the old lady before and the man on two occasions, but not the girl.

A third witness was a local licensed victualler, Norman Mercer, who, taking his dog for a walk in Deansgate at about midnight, saw a man and woman arguing at a point near to where the crime was committed. He identified the body as that of the woman he saw. He described the man as from thirty to thirty-five, five feet seven inches tall, of proportionate build, full round face, clean shaven, dark hair, dressed in a blue suit, of clean and tidy appearance.

On the night of Saturday–Sunday of the following week-end Walter Graham Rowland, who was staying in a transit dormitory, was awakened from his sleep by police officers. One of them said: 'Get dressed. I want to see you.' He sat up in bed and replied: 'You don't want me for murdering that bloody woman, do you?' He was cautioned and told that the inspector wanted to see him at headquarters. On arriving there the inspector told him that he answered the description of a man seen late on the Saturday night in company with the murdered woman. According to the inspector he said: 'I am admitting nothing because it's only a fool's game to do that. I can account for where I was. I was at home at New Mills when she was murdered. I did not come back to Manchester that night.' He was asked if he would care to say where he had spent the night of the 19th, and Rowland asked: 'Have you seen my mother?' (She lived at New Mills.) He then went on to admit that he did return from New Mills but only as far as Ardwick, which is in the south of Manchester. He said he had had some refreshment and spent the night at Grafton House in Hyde Road, and then corrected this to Number 36 Hyde Road.

Rowland was questioned at considerable length and provided, against himself, the first evidence of motive. He said he had known Olive for about eight weeks. He asked to see her photo and referring to the crime said: 'Things like that don't happen to decent women and whoever did it did not do it without a cause. You can't see what you have done in the dark. Let me see it and I'll tell you if it's the same woman.'

He was shown the photograph, which he recognized.

'Yes, that's her, but I have got a fighting chance and I'm going to hang on to it. I have got an uncontrollable temper, but that's not evidence, is it? I am sure I would not do that. It's possible the hammer was got to do a job with. I was not going to do a job that night. The fact that I went home proves that, unless you think I could do the job when I cane back. I am not admitting anything. I came back on the nine-thirty bus and got off at Ardwick. I was never near that place on Saturday night.'

NIGHT LIFE IN MANCHESTER 199

Questioned about his clothes he said he was wearing the same suit, a dark blue suit with a light blue pin stripe. 'I had a mac I borrowed from a man I only now as Slim. I have given it back to him.' Rowland then went on to volunteer the information that he'd found himself suffering from V.D. 'It was a blow to find out. I wanted to know where I got it. If I had been sure it was her, I'd have strangled her. I did think it was her. It's hard to say it was her now. Has she got V.D.? If she gave it to me she deserved all she got.'

Rowland then made a more detailed statement of his movements on the night of the crime. Now it was common ground that Rowland had travelled from Manchester on that Saturday evening to his mother's home at New Mills. There he had changed his clothes and returned by a bus which left New Mills, on time, at nine-thirty p.m. and was due in Stockport at ten-nine p.m. Ardwick lies on the route from Stockport to Manchester and he could have caught any number of buses to Ardwick, but in order to reach the café in Deansgate, in time to be observed by Mrs Copley, he must have caught the ten-five p.m. from Stockport. A police officer gave evidence of having performed this feat on a later date, the New Mills bus having arrived several minutes before time. The bus driver was unable to say what time he arrived on the night of the crime. There was no evidence of anyone having seen Rowland on the ten-five p.m. In his fuller statement Rowland said he had some drinks in Stockport, then caught a bus to Ardwick and went up Brunswick Street and had some supper in a fish-and-chip shop. He stayed the night at Hyde Road, signed the register and told the landlord he had got a job working on a building contract. He also said that the place he'd had the drinks at Stockport was 'the bottom Wellington'. He remembered seeing two police officers coming down the steps from the top Wellington to the bottom Wellington and leaving by the lower door. That was about half past ten. Subsequently Rowland recalled that it was at 81 Brunswick Street where he had stayed on the Saturday, and at 36 Hyde Road where he stayed on the Sunday.

According to Rowland's mother, who was called for the prosecution, she used to post his washing to the Manchester Post Office. He arrived home at seven thirty and told her the parcel, which she had posted on the Thursday, had not arrived. He was wearing his demob suit, which was the only one he possessed, and wore no hat or macintosh and was not carrying a parcel. He changed from a brown striped shirt and soft collar to a pale blue shirt with collar to match; and while he was washing and tidying she adjusted his coat, which contained no hammer. He left to catch the bus carrying a parcel of spare shirts. He never wore hair grease.

While he was in prison Rowland's clothes were removed for expert examination. In the turn-ups of the trousers was found material corresponding with a sample of the ground where the body was found. On the jacket were some grey hairs which could have come from Olive Balchin, but with no definite identity, a small bloodstain on the inside left heel of a shoe and a faint bloodstain on the paper round the washing.

This was the case against Rowland. It remains necessary to examine the evidence of identity. All three witnesses identified Rowland. He could have been the man who bought the hammer and would have had time to catch the bus for New Mills. Mr Macdonald had described a man of very pale face and thin features, on the dark side, wearing a white collar and white shirt. His mother said he was wearing a brown shirt and collar. Mrs Copley had said he was a dark man with black hair and a dark suit carrying one parcel which could have contained a hammer but not shirts. Mrs Copley had also described Olive as a young girl with tinted hair and wearing no hat. Mr Mercer had described a man of full round face and dark hair.

At the police court Mr Macdonald failed to point out Rowland at the first attempt. Mrs Cowley was taken to an identification parade and walked up and down three times and from five to ten minutes before picking correctly.

All three identification witnesses explained at the assizes, and for the first time, that Rowland's hair was greased and that made his fair hair look dark. His mother said he never used grease, declaring that he did not want to look like a cissy.

No attempt was made to explain how thin and pale-faced features had become full and round and fresh-complexioned later on.

For the defence a Stockport police sergeant testified that he and another officer had visited the Wellington Hotel at ten thirty-two on the Saturday night, had entered by that part which opens on a higher street, come down the steps into the lower half and left by the lower door. It was the sort of thing they did from time to time, but not systematically.

The landlord of the lodging-house testified that Rowland stayed at 81 Brunswick Street on the Saturday night, arriving about eleven fifteen, when he signed the register. He went out for fish and chips, returning within a few minutes, and the landlord locked up at about twenty to twelve. He identified Rowland's signature and the visitor's book had been submitted to expert examination. Rowland did not have a macintosh, but had a parcel which could contain shirts.

Those are the facts as given in evidence at Rowland's trial and they have been presented, necessarily abbreviated, but as fairly as possible and without any comment.

What would your verdict have been?

## SOLUTION: PART ONE

Rowland was found guilty and sentenced to death. No one seems to have had much doubt. One gap in the evidence is easy to explain. It shows not only the reason why Rowland was suspected but goes far to explain his reference to the murder when arrested and his chatty attitude to the police questions. Rowland had been through it all before. He had been arrested, charged, tried and convicted for murder previously. In a fit of temper, many years previously, he had struck and killed a boy. That information was properly kept from the jury. Mr Norman Birkett in his successful defence of Mancini realized that he could only explain his client's actions by revealing his criminal record, but it is a difficult and dangerous line.

The trial of Rowland presented many very unsatisfactory features. It took place far too soon after the crime to permit of a sufficiently full investigation by both sides.

Evidence is given that a well-known local prostitute is seen in a downstairs café in one of the busiest streets of Manchester on a Saturday night for half an hour in company with two people who have been there before. No evidence is forthcoming about the old lady with the Irish accent. We know nothing of what happened between eleven p.m. and midnight. It is surely material in testing Mrs Copley's recollection to know whether the woman existed. Rowland travelled that night by bus from Manchester to Stockport and then to New Mills, and returned, and all that time he must have had a brown-paper parcel containing a hammer. It was known to the prosecution precisely which four buses he must have travelled on. Did they not have conductors? Did not one recollect Rowland?

Rowland stayed somewhere on the Saturday night, if not at 81 Brunswick Street, where? His various beds were traced on other nights. The prosecution suggested that the evidence from Brunswick Street was faked. It was surprising, if it had been faked at the time, that Rowland forgot to give that address. It was still more surprising, if it were faked later, that the visitor's book survived examination by the forensic science laboratory. The signature could not have been made after Rowland's arrest.

The most astonishing absence of evidence is in relation to fingerprints. Here is a hammer found, within twelve hours of its use as a weapon, and apparently no clear fingerprints are traced. It is possible that when used as a weapon the hand might have been covered with something, possibly the brown paper, but that would have been drenched in blood. The brown paper was not. If Rowland bought the hammer, he handled it at the shop and again when he undid the parcel. No evidence about fingerprints seems to have been given. Finally we have the difficulty that from half past twelve at night, when Rowland said he was in bed in Ardwick and the police say he was standing over the battered body of his victim, his clothes stained with blood, he disappeared from view for many hours. We do not know where he went or how he got there, or how he removed the blood.

The case against Rowland was, on the face of it, a strong one. Most juries would probably have convicted. The evidence fits in very well and a picture emerges of Rowland as the sort of man who might well commit such a crime. If we sit down to dissect the evidence it has a different appearance. The evidence of the murder itself has to be set on one side, for it does not involve Rowland. The expert evidence is strongly in his favour. A woman is battered to death in circumstances where blood would be spurted and no trace of blood was found upon him that would not be found on every man who shaves. He possesses only one suit and that suit has not been cleaned. The soil in the turn-ups has no significance—there was no evidence of a struggle and he had visited that site since. The grey hairs might have been Olive's or might have been his mother's, but he admitted seeing Olive recently. The one piece of significant statement is contained in Rowland's chat with the police. He seems to have volunteered information about a macintosh he had borrowed and returned. That macintosh might well have received the bloodstains. It could have been folded and carried away from the scene. Rowland volunteered, too, the evidence of motive.

We are left with a case in which a strong alibi is furnished, confirmed by the probabilities of the omnibus services and by what happened at the Wellington Hotel, and which is refuted only by evidence of identity. Mrs Copley's evidence was confused on a number of points and, however honest, could well have referred to three different people. Mr Macdonald's evidence was strong and convincing. Mr Mercer's attention was drawn to the couple and his evidence was clearly and honestly given. The long history of miscarriages of justice due to mistakes of identity shows why such evidence, however sincere, should never be completely relied upon, particularly in relation to a person seen once.

That was the case of Rowland, and at the end one is left with the question that always presents itself. If Rowland didn't do it, who did? He was a bad man, a man with a record, a man with a bitter grievance, a man with an uncontrollable temper. Who more likely than he to commit the crime?

It is a question to which there is an answer.

## PART TWO

On January 22nd, 1947, David John Ware confessed in writing to the Governor of Liverpool Prison that he 'killed Olive Balshaw [*sic*] with a hammer on a bomb site in the Deansgate, Manchester, on Saturday October 19th, about ten p.m. We had been in a picture-house near the Bellevue Stadium earlier in the evening. I did not know her before that night.'

Two days later Ware was interviewed in prison by the officers who had been in charge of the Rowland case. He made a statement to them in his own handwriting. He said that he left Stoke-upon-Trent on Friday October 18th with money stolen from the Salvation Army Hostel, went to Longton and by bus to Uttoxeter, and then by train to Manchester, where he arrived at seven thirty, picked up a girl and spent the night with her. In the afternoon he bought a hammer for the purpose of robbery. He met Olive Balshaw about six, took her to a picture-house near Bellevue, came out at nine, had a cup of coffee opposite and they caught a bus to the city centre. He described in detail proceeding to the bomb site, said he caught her trying to pick his pocket and felt a desire to kill her. He persuaded her to go farther inside and took the brown paper off the hammer and threw it in a corner. He then described how he struck her down with the hammer near to the wall. 'Blood shot up in a thin spray. I felt it in my face and then I panicked, threw the hammer and left everything as it was. I ran and ran zigzagged up and down streets I didn't know, eventually getting to Salford Station.' He then described travelling by bus to Manchester and thence to Stockport, where he slept at a lodging-house, walking on the Sunday to Buxton and to Chapel-en-le-Frith, where he stayed at the institution, and hitch-hiking on the Monday to Sheffield where he voluntarily gave himself up for the theft from the Salvation Army.

Rowland appealed to the Court of Criminal Appeal, who declined to hear Ware's evidence, saying that could be investigated by the Home Office. They dismissed the appeal. The Attorney-General, Sir Hartley Shawcross, refused his fiat for the case to go to the House of Lords. The Home Secretary appointed Mr J. C. Jolly, K.C., to inquire into the confession and to report if there had been a possible miscarriage of justice.

Such an inquiry places the investigator in a position of very great difficulty. Public opinion greatly dislikes an inordinate delay of a capital sentence. The inquiry must be speedy. Evidence is heard in secret. There is no time or power to conduct a very full check of all relevant facts. Evidence is not given on oath. Decency demands that

Ware must be warned of the consequences of his confession and given an opportunity to withdraw, and the report, whatever it says, is almost certain to be criticized.

It must be said at once that there is much in Ware's confession which is singularly convincing. He did commit the theft on the Friday morning, he was in Manchester over the week-end and he did travel to Sheffield and give himself up, and the one obvious reason for giving himself up in Sheffield was the hope that he would thus escape the inquiry in Manchester.

The reference to the spurting of blood accords singularly with the medical evidence. Ware may have got his information from the newspapers on most points, but one is not entitled to reason both ways. One cannot point to discrepancies of time and name as invalidating the confession and then say that he derived it from accurate reports in the press. If the couple seen by Mr Mercer at midnight were not Olive and the murderer the crime may have been committed earlier.

There was evidence of someone who walked over the site at half past ten with a dog which suggests that it was probably later than that. If Ware's account were true he was probably wrong in fixing it as early as ten. He puts the purchase of the hammer within half an hour of the time given by Mr Macdonald.

The three witnesses to identity failed to recognize Ware, which is not surprising, because no one ever doubted that they honestly believed it was Rowland. Ware, of course, withdrew his confession. He made a new statement in which he put his arrival in Manchester from Uttoxeter as precisely twenty-four hours later, and described picking up the girl on the Saturday night. He describes staying on the Saturday night with the girl whom he picked up in Piccadilly, Manchester, between eleven and midnight. He paid twenty-five shillings for bed and breakfast for both. It was a residential hotel kept by a stout foreigner who he thought was Italian, and a man was there who was later with him in Liverpool prison. He gave very long details of his movements on the Sunday and said he spent that night at a lodging-house in Stockport.

Mr Jolly presented a report accepting Ware's withdrawal of the confession, and was satisfied that there were no grounds for thinking there was any miscarriage of justice. Mr Jolly's report adds a number of new mysteries to a mysterious case.

Inspector Hannam, who assisted in the inquiry, visited the lodging-house at Stockport. The police had visited the lodging-house to inspect the register subsequent to Ware's confession. When Inspector Hannam called it had been destroyed. Why on earth was this important document not preserved? We are told it was found to confirm Ware's statement that he was there on the 19th. Mr Jolly found this as corroboration

of his innocence. It was completely consistent with guilt. In the statement admitting his guilt he said he stopped at a lodging-house at
Stockport on the night of the murder. In the statement withdrawing
his confession he said he spent that night at the Italian's hotel and the
Sunday night at Stockport.

Ware did say in his earlier statement that he spent the Sunday night
at the institution at Chapel. Was that checked? Was he asked where he
was on the Friday? There is much in his later statement about what he
did in Manchester on the Sunday which could hardly have happened
that day. He went to a shoe-shop; he lunched at Woolworths who were
not open; he got in a cinema surprisingly early; and he thinks the public
house closed at ten thirty, which it does on a Saturday. Mr Jolly,
unfortunately, got the dates mixed up. In his report he says, speaking
of Ware's final statement: 'It appears to me to be extremely significant
that this was the first time Ware ever said anything about going to a
cinema in the afternoon (as distinct from the evening) of October
19th ...' Ware did not say anything of the kind. He said he didn't
arrive in Manchester till the evening.

In his first letter to the Governor he had said that he'd been with
Olive to a picture-house earlier in the evening.

On February 27th, 1947, Walter Graham Rowland was hanged at
Strangeways Prison, Manchester. He always protested his innocence.

David John Ware, after his release from prison, spent several periods
in mental institutions. He had been discharged from the Army suffering
from manic depression. On August 2nd, 1951, he surrendered himself
to the police at Bristol. He said: 'I have killed a woman. I don't know
what is the matter with me. I keep on having an urge to hit women on
the head.' This statement was true. He had attempted to murder a
woman by blows on the head with a hammer. He was found guilty but
insane.

CLEVELAND AMORY

# Dr Parkman Takes a Walk

To the student of American Society the year 1849 will always remain a red-letter one. In that year two events occurred at opposite ends of the country, both of which, in their own way, made social history. At one end, in Sutter's Creek, California, gold was discovered. At the other, in Boston, Massachusetts, Dr George Parkman walked off the face of the earth.

The discovery of gold ushered in a new social era. It marked the first great rise of the Western *nouveau riche*, the beginning of that wonderful time when a gentleman arriving in San Francisco and offering a boy fifty cents to carry his suitcase could receive the reply, 'Here's a dollar, man—carry it yourself,' and when a poor Irish prospector suddenly striking it rich in a vein near Central City, Colorado, could fling down his pick and exclaim, 'Thank God, now my wife can be a lady!'

Dr Parkman's little walk did no such thing as this. It must be remembered, however, that it occurred some three thousand miles away. Boston is not Sutter's Creek or Central City or even San Francisco. There has never been a 'new' social era in the Western sense in Boston's rock-ribbed Society, and it remains very doubtful it there ever will be one. The best that could be expected of any one event in Boston would be to shake up the old. Dr Parkman's walk did this; it shook Boston Society to the very bottom of its First Family foundations. Viewed almost a hundred years later it thus seems, in its restricted way, almost as wonderful as the Gold Rush and not undeserving of the accidental fact that it happened, in the great march of social history, in exactly the same year.

The date was Friday, November 23rd. It was warm for a Boston November, and Dr Parkman needed no overcoat as he left his Beacon Hill home at 8 Walnut Street. He wore in the fashion of the day a black morning coat, purple silk vest, dark trousers, a dark-figured black tie, and a black silk top hat. He had breakfasted as usual, and he left his home to head downtown toward the Merchants Bank on State Street. Dr Parkman was quite a figure as he moved along. His high hat and angular physique made him seem far taller than his actual five feet nine and a half inches. He was sixty years old and his head was almost bald, but his hat hid this fact also. To all outward appearances he was remarkably well-preserved, his most striking feature being a conspicuously protruding chin. Boston Parkmans have been noted for their chins the way Boston Adamses are noted for their foreheads or Boston Saltonstalls are noted for their noses, and the chin of old Dr Parkman was especially formidable. His lower jaw jutted out so far it had made the fitting of a set of false teeth for him a very difficult job. The dentist who had had that job had never forgotten it. He was proud of the china-white teeth he had installed. He had even kept the mold to prove to people that he, little Dr Nathan Keep, had made the teeth of the great Dr George Parkman.

Although he had studied to be a physician and received his degree Dr Parkman had rarely practiced medicine in his life. He was a merchant at heart, one of Boston's wealthiest men, and he spent his time in the Boston manner keeping sharp account of his money—and a sharp eye on his debtors. He had many of the traits of character peculiar to the Proper Bostonian breed. He was shrewd and hard, but he was Boston-honest, Boston-direct and Boston-dependable. Like so many other First Family men before his time and after Dr Parkman was not popular but he was highly respected. It was hard to like a man like Dr Parkman because his manners were curt and he had a way of glaring at people that made them uncomfortable. Without liking him, however, it was possible to look up to him. People knew him as a great philanthropist and it was said he had given away a hundred thousand dollars in his time. The phrase 'wholesale charity and retail penury' as descriptive of the Proper Bostonian breed had not yet come into the Boston lingo, though the day was coming when Dr Parkman might be regarded as the very personification of it. Certainly he had given away large sums of money with wholesale generosity—even anonymously— yet with small sums, with money on a retail basis, he was penny-punctilious. 'The same rule,' a biographer records, 'governed Dr Parkman in settling an account involving the balance of a cent as in transactions of thousands of dollars.'

Children in the Boston streets pointed out Dr Parkman to other children. 'There goes Dr Parkman,' they would say. People always seemed to point him out after he had passed them. There was no use speaking to Dr Parkman before he went by. If you weren't his friend, Dr George Shattuck, or his brother-in-law, Robert Gould Shaw, Esq., or a Cabot or a Lowell, or perhaps a man who owed him money—and then, as someone said, God help you—the doctor would ignore you. Dr Parkman had no need to court favor from anybody. The Parkmans cut a sizeable chunk of Boston's social ice in 1849, and they still do today.

Like other merchant-blooded First Families they were of course econ-omically self-sufficient. They hadn't yet made much of an intellectual mark on their city, but a nephew of the doctor, Francis Parkman, had just published his first book and was on his way to becoming what Van Wyck Brooks has called 'the climax and crown' of the Boston historical school. The Parkmans were in the Boston fashion well-connected by marriages. Dr Parkman's sister's marriage with Robert Gould Shaw, Boston's wealthiest merchant, was a typical First Family alliance. As for Dr Parkman's own wealth, some idea of its extent may be gathered from the fact that his son, who never worked a day in his life, was able to leave a will which bequeathed, among other things, the sum of five million dollars for the care and improvement of the Boston Common.

On the morning of that Friday, November 23rd, Dr Parkman was hurrying. He walked with the characteristic gait of the Proper Bos-tonian merchant—a gait still practiced by such notable present-day First Family footmen as Charles Francis Adams and Godfrey Lowell Cabot—measuring off distances with long, ground-consuming strides. Dr Parkman always hurried. Once when riding a horse up Beacon Hill and unable to speed the animal to his satisfaction he had left the horse in the middle of the street and hurried ahead on foot. On that occasion he had been after money, a matter of debt collection.

This morning, too, Dr Parkman was after money. He left the Mer-chants Bank and after making several other calls dropped into a grocery store at the corner of Blossom and Vine Streets. This stop, the only non-financial mission of his morning, was to buy a head of lettuce for his invalid sister. He left it in the store and said he would return for it on his way home. The time was half past one and Dr Parkman presumably intended to be home at 2:30, then the fashionable hour for one's midday meal. Ten minutes later, at 1:40, Elias Fuller, a merchant standing outside his counting room at Fuller's Iron Foundry at the corner of Vine and North Grove Streets, observed Dr Parkman passing him headed north on North Grove Street. Fuller was later to remember that the doctor seemed particularly annoyed about something and recalled that his cane beat a brisk tattoo on the pavement as he hurried along. What the merchant observed at 1:40 that day is of more than passing im-portance, for Elias Fuller was the last man who ever saw the doctor alive on the streets of Boston. Somewhere, last seen going north on North Grove Street, Dr George Parkman walked off the face of the earth.

At 8 Walnut Street Mrs Parkman, her daughter Harriet and Dr Parkman's invalid sister sat down to their two-thirty dinner long after three o'clock. Their dinner was ruined and there was no lettuce, but Mrs Parkman and the others did not mind. They were all worried about the master of the house. Dr Parkman was not the sort of man who was ever late for anything. Right after dinner they got in touch with Dr Parkman's agent, Charles Kingsley. Kingsley was the man who looked after the doctor's business affairs, usually some time after the doctor had thoroughly looked after them himself. Almost at once Kingsley began to search for his employer. First Family men of the prominence of Dr Parkman did not disappear in Boston—and they do not today—even for an afternoon. By night-fall Kinglsey was ready to inform Robert Gould Shaw. Shaw, acting with the customary dispatch of the Proper Bostonian merchant, went at once to Boston's City Marshal, Mr Tukey. Marshal Tukey did of course what Shaw told him to do, which was to instigate an all-night search.

The next morning the merchant Shaw placed advertisements in all the papers and had 28,000 handbills distributed. The advertisements and the handbills announced a reward of $3,000 for his brother-in-law alive and $1,000 for his brother-in-law dead. The prices, considering the times, were sky-high but Shaw knew what he was doing in Yankee Boston. Before long virtually every able-bodied man, woman and child in the city was looking for Dr Parkman. They beat the bushes and they combed the streets. Slum areas were ransacked. All suspicious characters, all persons with known criminal records, were rounded up and held for questioning. Strangers in Boston were given a summary one-two treatment. An Irishman, it is recorded, attempting to change a twenty-dollar bill, was brought in to the police headquarters apparently solely on the assumption that no son of Erin, in the Boston of 1849, had any business with a bill of this size in his possession.

Every one of Dr Parkman's actions on the previous day, up to 1:40, were checked. At that time, on North Grove Street, the trail always ended. Police had to sift all manner of wild reports. One had the doctor 'beguiled to East Cambridge and done in'. Another had him riding in a hansom cab, his head covered with blood, being driven at 'breakneck speed' over a Charles River bridge. Of the papers only the Boston *Transcript* seems to have kept its head. Its reporter managed to learn from a servant in the Parkman home that the doctor had received a caller at 9:30 Friday reminding him of a 1:30 appointment later in the day. The servant could not remember what the man looked like, but the *Transcript* printed the story in its Saturday night edition along with the reward advertisements. Most people took the caller to be some sort of front man who had appeared to lead Dr Parkman to a dastardly death. By Monday foul play was so thoroughly suspected that the shrewd merchant Shaw saw no reason to mention a sum as high as $1,000 for the body. Three thousand dollars was still the price for Dr Parkman alive but only 'a suitable reward' was mentioned in Shaw's Monday handbills for Dr Parkman dead. Monday's handbills also noted the possibility of amnesia but the theory of a First Family man's mind wandering to this extent was regarded as highly doubtful. Dr Parkman, it was stated, was 'perfectly well' when he left his house.

All that the Parkman case now needed to make it a complete panorama of Boston's First Family Society was the active entry of Harvard College into the picture. This occurred on Sunday morning in the person of a caller to the home of Rev. Francis Parkman, the missing doctor's brother, where the entire Family Parkman in all its ramifications had gathered. The caller was a man named John White Webster, Harvard graduate and professor of chemistry at the Harvard Medical School. He was a short squat man, fifty-six years old, who had a mass of unruly black hair and always wore thick spectacles. He had had a most ditinguished career. He had studied at Guy's Hospital, London, back in 1815, where among his fellow students had been the poet John Keats. He was a member of the London Geological Society, the American Academy of Arts and Sciences, and during his twenty-five years as a Harvard professor had published numerous nationally noted scientific works. His wife, a Hickling and aunt of the soon-to-be-recognized historian William Hickling Prescott, was 'well-connected' with several of Boston's First Families.

The Rev. Parkman was glad to see Professor Webster and ushered him toward the parlor expecting that his desire would be to offer sympathy to the assorted Parkmans there assembled. But Webster, it seemed, did not want to go into the parlor. Instead he spoke abruptly to the minister. 'I have come to tell you,' he said, 'that I saw your brother at half past one o'clock on Friday.' The minister was glad to have this report. Since Webster also told him he had been the caller at the Parkman home earlier that day it cleared up the mystery of the strange appointment as recorded in the *Transcript*. Webster explained he should have come sooner but had been so busy he had not seen the notices of Dr Parkman's disappearance until the previous night. The minister was also satisfied with this. Webster further declared that, at the appointment shortly after 1:30 which took place in his laboratory at the Medical School, he had paid Dr Parkman the sum of $483.64 which he had owed him. This, of course, explained why the doctor had last been seen by the merchant Fuller in such a cane-tattooing hurry. It had indeed been a matter of a debt collection.

When Professor Webster had left, Robert Gould Shaw was advised of his visit. Shaw was intimate enough in his brother-in-law's affairs to know that Webster had been owing Dr Parkman money for some time. He did not, however, know the full extent of Webster's misery. Few men have ever suffered from the retail penury side of the Proper Bostonian character as acutely as John White Webster.

The professor received a salary from Harvard of $1,200 a year. This, augmented by income from extra lectures he was able to give, might have sufficed for the average Harvard professor in those days. But Webster was not the average. His wife, for all her connections with Boston's First Families, was still a socially aspirant woman, particularly for her two daughters of debutante age. Mrs Webster and the Misses Webster entertained lavishly at their charming home in Cambridge. Professor Webster went into debt. He borrowed money here and he borrowed money there. But mostly he borrowed from Dr George Parkman.

Who better to borrow from? Dr Parkman, man of wholesale charity, Proper Bostonian merchant philanthropist. He had given Harvard College the very ground on which at that time stood its Medical School. He had endowed the Parkman Chair of Anatomy, then being occupied by the great Dr Oliver Wendell Holmes. He had himself been responsible for Webster's appointment as chemistry professor. There were no two ways about it. When Webster needed money the doctor was his obvious choice. As early as 1842 he had borrowed $400. He had then borrowed more. In 1847 he had borrowed from a group headed by Dr Parkman the sum of $2000. For the latter he had been forced to give a mortgage on all his personal property. He knew he had little chance to pay the debt but he was banking on the generosity of the 'good Dr Parkman'. A year later, in 1848, he even went to Dr Parkman's brother-in-law, the merchant Shaw, and prevailed upon him to buy a mineral collection for $1,200. This was most unfortunate. The mineral collection, like the rest of Webster's property, in hock to Dr Parkman and his group, was not Webster's to sell. By so doing he had made the doctor guilty of that cardinal sin of Yankeeism—the sin of being shown up as an easy mark. No longer was there for Webster any 'good Dr Parkman'. 'From that moment onward,' says author Stewart Holbrook, 'poor Professor Webster knew what it was like to have a Yankee bloodhound on his trail. His creditor was a punctilious man who paid his own obligations when due and he expected the same of everybody else, even a Harvard professor.'[1]

Dr Parkman dogged Professor Webster in the streets, outside his home, even to the classrooms. He would come in and take a front-row seat at Webster's lectures. He would not say anything; he would just sit and glare in the remarkable way of his. He wrote the professor notes, not just plain insulting notes but the awful, superior, skin-biting notes of the Yankee gentleman. He spoke sternly of legal processes. Meeting Webster he would never shout at him but instead address him in clipped

[1] 'Murder at Harvard', by Stewart Holbrook, *The American Scholar*, 1945.

Proper Bostonian accents. It was always the same question. When would the professor be 'ready' for him?

Dr Parkman even bearded Professor Webster in his den, in the inner recesses of the latter's laboratory at the Medical School. He had been there, in the professor's private back room—according to the janitor of the building—on Monday evening, November 19th, just four days before he had disappeared.

The janitor was a strange man, the grim New England village type, a small person with dark brooding eyes. His name was Ephraim Little-field. He watched with growing interest the goings-on around him. Following Webster's call on Rev. Francis Parkman, which established the farthest link yet on the trail of Dr Parkman's walk, it had of course been necessary to search the Medical School. Littlefield wanted this done thoroughly, as thoroughly for example as they were dragging the Charles River outside. He personally led the investigators to Webster's laboratory. Everything was searched, all but the private back room and adjoining privy. One of the party of investigators, which also included Dr Parkman's agent Kingsley, was a police officer named Derastus Clapp. Littlefield prevailed upon this officer to go into the back room, but just as Clapp opened the door Professor Webster solicitiously called out for him to be careful. There were dangerous articles in there, he said. 'Very well, then,' said Officer Clapp, 'I will not go in there and get blowed up.' He backed out again.

The whole search was carried on to the satisfaction of even Robert Gould Shaw who, after all, knew at firsthand the story of Webster's duplicity via the mineral collection. And who was the little janitor Ephriam Littlefield to dispute the word of the great merchant Robert Shaw? As each day went by the theory of murder was becoming more and more generally accepted, but in a Boston Society eternally geared to the mesh of a Harvard A.B. degree the idea of pinning a homicide on a Harvard man—and a professor at that—was heresy itself. One might as well pry for the body of Dr Parkman among the prayer cushions of the First Family pews in Trinity Church.

But Littlefield was not, in the socially sacrosanct meaning of the words, a 'Harvard man'. He was a Harvard janitor. Furthermore he was stubborn. He wanted the Medical School searched again. When it was, he was once more prodding the investigators to greater efforts. He told them they should visit the cellar of the building, down in the section where the Charles River water flowed in and carried off waste water from the dissecting rooms and privies above. The agent Kingsley took one gentlemanly sniff from the head of the stairs and refused to accompany the janitor and the other investigators any farther. The others, however, went on. As they passed the wall under Webster's back room the janitor volunteered the information that it was only the only place in the building that hadn't been searched. Why not, the men wanted to know. The janitor explained that to get there it would be necessary to dig through the wall. The men had little stomach left for this sort of operation and soon rejoined Kingsley upstairs.

Littlefield, however, had plenty of stomach. He determined to dig into the wall himself. Whether he was by this time, Monday, already suspicious of Professor Webster has never been made clear. He had, it is true, heard the Webster-Parkman meeting of Monday night the week before. He had distinctly overheard the doctor say to the professor in that ever-insinuating way, 'Something, Sir, must be accomplished.' Just yesterday, Sunday, he had seen Professor Webster enter the Medical School around noontime, apparently shortly after he had made his call on Rev. Francis Parkman. Webster had spoken to him and had acted 'very queerly'. Come to think of it, Littlefield brooded, Sunday was a queer day for the professor to be hanging around the School anyway. 'Ephraim,' writes Richard Dempewolff, one of the Parkman case's most avid devotees, 'was one of those shrewd New England conclusion-jumpers who, unfortunately for the people they victimize, are usually right. By putting two and two together, Mr Littlefield achieved a nice round dozen.'[1]

The janitor's wife was a practical woman. She thought little of her husband's determination to search the filthy old place under the private rooms of the Harvard professor she had always regarded as a fine gentleman. Her husband would lose his job, that would be what would happen. Just you wait and see, Mr Littlefield.

Mr Littlefield deferred to Mrs Littlefield and did wait—until Tuesday, five days after Dr Parkman's disappearance. On Tuesday something extraordinary happened. At four o'clock in the afternoon he heard Professor Webster's bell jangle, a signal that the janitor was wanted. He went to Webster's laboratory. The professor asked him if he had bought his Thanksgiving turkey yet. Littlefield did not know what to say. He replied he had thought some about going out Thanksgiving.

'Here,' said Webster, 'go and get yourself one.' With that he handed the janitor an order for a turkey at a near-by grocery store.

John White Webster had here made a fatal error. The call he had paid on Rev. Francis Parkman had been bad enough. It had aroused the searching of the Medical School and had brought Littlefield actively into the case. But as Webster later admitted he had been afraid

[1] *Famous Old New England Murders*, by Richard Dempewolff (Brattleboro, Vt.: Stephen Daye Press, 1942).

that sooner or later someone would have found out about his 1:30 Friday rendezvous with Dr Parkman and felt that his best chance lay in making a clean breast of it. For this action in regard to the janitor's Thanksgiving turkey, however, there could be no such defense. If he hoped to win the janitor over to 'his side', then he was a poor judge of human nature indeed. Harvard Janitor Ephriam Littlefield had worked for Harvard Professor John Webster for seven years—curiously the same length of time Professor John Webster had been borrowing from Dr Parkman—without ever receiving a present of any kind. And now, a Thanksgiving turkey. Even the deferentially dormant suspicions of Mrs Littlefield were thoroughly aroused.

Janitor Littlefield had no chance to begin his labors Wednesday. Professor Webster was in his laboratory most of the day. On Thanksgiving, however, while Mrs Littlefield kept her eyes peeled for the professor or any other intruder, the janitor began the task of crowbarring his way through the solid brick wall below the back room. It was slow work and even though the Littlefields took time off to enjoy their dinner—the janitor had characteristically not passed up the opportunity to procure a nine-pound bird—it was soon obvious he could not get through the wall in one day. That evening the Littlefields took time off again. They went to a dance given by the Sons of Temperance Division of the Boston Odd Fellows. They stayed until four o'clock in the morning. 'There were twenty dances,' Littlefield afterwards recalled, 'and I danced eighteen out of the twenty.'

Late Friday afternoon, after Professor Webster had left for the day, Littlefield was at his digging again. This time he had taken the precaution of advising two of the School's First Family doctors, Doctors Bigelow and Jackson, of what he was doing. They were surprised but told him since he had started he might as well continue. But they were against his idea of informing the dean of the School, Dr Holmes, of the matter. It would, they felt, disturb the dean unnecessarily.

Even a half-hearted First Family blessing has always counted for something in Boston, and Janitor Littlefield now went to work with renewed vigor. Again his wife stood watch. At five-thirty he broke through the fifth of the five courses of brick in the wall. 'I held my light forward,' he afterwards declared, 'and the first thing which I saw was the pelvis of a man, and two parts of a leg ... It was no place for these things.'

It was not indeed. Within fifteen minutes Doctors Bigelow and Jackson were on the scene. Later Dr Holmes himself would view the remains. Meanwhile of course there was the matter of a little trip out to the Webster home in Cambridge.

To that same police officer who had been so loath to get himself 'blowed up' in Webster's back room fell the honor of making the business trip to Cambridge and arresting the Harvard professor. Once bitten, Derastus Clapp was twice shy. There would be no more monkeyshines, Harvard or no Harvard. He had his cab halt some distance from the Webster home and approached on foot. Opening the outer gate he started up the walk just as Webster himself appeared on the steps of his house, apparently showing a visitor out. The professor attempted to duck back inside. Officer Clapp hailed him. 'We are about to search the Medical School again,' he called, moving forward rapidly as he spoke, 'and we wish you to be present.' Webster feigned the traditional Harvard indifference. It was a waste of time; the School had already been searched twice. Clapp laid a stern hand on his shoulder. Webster, escorted outward and suddenly noting two other men in the waiting cab, wanted to go back for his keys. Officer Clapp was not unaware of the drama of the moment. 'Professor Webster,' he said, 'we have keys enough to unlock the whole of Harvard College.'

Boston was in an uproar. Dr Parkman had not walked off the face of the earth. He had been pushed off—and by the authoritative hands of a Harvard professor! Even the *Transcript*, calm when there was still a hope the Parkman case was merely a matter of disappearance, could restrain itself no longer. I threw its genteel caution to the winds. There were two exclamation marks after its headline, and its editor called on Shakespeare himself to sum up the situation:

> Since last evening, our whole population has been in a state of the greatest possible excitement in consequence of the astounding rumor that the body of Dr Parkman has been discovered, and that Dr John W. Webster, Professor of Chemistry in the Medical School of Harvard College, and a gentleman connected by marriage with some of our most distinguished families, has been arrested and imprisoned, on suspicion of being the murderer. Incredulity, then amazement, and then blank, unspeakable horror have been the emotions, which have agitated the public mind as the rumor has gone on, gathering countenance and confirmation. Never in the annals of crime in Massachussetts has such a sensation been produced.
>
> In the streets, in the market-place, at every turn, men greet each other with pale, eager looks and the inquiry, 'Can it be true?' And then as the terrible reply, 'the circumstances begin to gather weight against him,' is wrung forth, the agitated listener can only vent his sickening sense of horror, in some expression as that of Hamlet—
> 'O, horrible! O, horrible! most horrible!'

There is irony in the fact that proud, staid Boston chose the time it did to provide American Society with the nineteenth century's outstanding social circus. Boston was at the height of its cultural attainments in

1849. In that year a scholarly but hardly earth-shaking book by a rather minor Boston author, *The History of the Spanish Literature* by George Ticknor, was the world literary event of the year and the only book recommended by Lord Macaulay to Queen Victoria. Yet just three months later, on March 19, 1850, Boston put on a show which for pure social artistry Barnum himself would have had difficulty matching. The Boston courtroom had everything. It had one of Boston's greatest jurists, Judge Lemuel Shaw on its bench; it had the only Harvard professor ever to be tried for murder, John White Webster, as its defendant; it had promised witnesses of national renown, from Dr Oliver Wendell Holmes on down; and in the offing, so to speak, it had the shades of Dr George Parkman, perhaps the most socially distinguished victim in the annals of American crime.

Nobody wanted to miss such a sight. Trains and stages from all parts of the East brought people to Boston. They wanted tickets. Everybody in Boston wanted tickets, too. Consequences of revolutionary proportions were feared if they could not be accommodated. Yet what to do? There was only a small gallery to spare, it having been decreed in typical Boston fashion that the main part of the courtroom would be reserved on an invitation basis. Finally, Field Marshal Tukey hit on the only possible solution, which was to effect a complete change of audience in the gallery every ten minutes during the proceedings. It took elaborate street barricades and doorway defenses to do the job, but in the eleven days of the trial, to that little gallery holding hardly more than a hundred souls, came a recorded total of sixty thousand persons. Considering that the constabulary of Boston assigned to the job numbered just fifteen men, this feat ranks as a monumental milestone in police annals.

From the suspense angle the trial, which has been called a landmark in the history of criminal law, must have been something of a disappointment. By the time it began, despite Webster's protestations of innocence, there was little doubt in the minds of most of the spectators as to the guilt of the professor. A few days after his arrest a skeleton measuring 70½ inches had finally been assembled from the grisly remains found lying about under the professor's back room, and while the sum total of this was an inch taller than Dr Parkman had been in happier days, there had been no question in the minds of the coroner's jury, of Dr Holmes, and of a lot of other people, but that Dr Parkman it was. The case against the professor was one of circumstantial evidence of course. No one had seen Webster and Parkman together at the time of the murder; indeed, during the trial the time of the murder was never satisfactorily established. But the strongest Webster adherents had to admit that it was evidence of a very powerful nature, as Chief Justice

Shaw could not fail to point out in his famous charge to the jury, an address which lawyers today still consider one of the greatest expositions of the nature and use of circumstantial evidence ever delivered.

There were a number of pro-Websterites. Harvard professor though he may have been, he was still the underdog, up against the almighty forces of Boston's First Families. Many of the Websterites had undoubtedly had experiences of their own on the score of Proper Bostonian retail penury and were ready to recognize that Dr Parkman had been so importunate a creditor that he had quite possibly driven the little professor first to distraction and then to the deed. They went to Rufus Choate, Boston's great First Family lawyer, and asked him to undertake the defense. After reading up on the case Choate was apparently willing to do so on the condition that Webster would admit the killing and plead manslaughter. Another First Family lawyer, old Judge Fay, with whom the Webster family regularly played whist, thought a verdict of manslaughter could be reached.

But Webster would not plead guilty. From the beginning he had made his defence an all but impossible task. He talked when he shouldn't have talked and he kept quiet when, at least by the light of hindsight, he should have come clean. On his first trip to the jail he immediately asked the officers about the finding of the body. 'Have they found the *whole* body?' he wanted to know. This while certainly a reasonable question in view of the wide area over which the remains were found was hardly the thing for a man in his position to be asking. Then, while vehemently protesting his innocence, he took a strychnine pill out of his waistcoat pocket and attempted to kill himself, an attempt which was foiled only by the fact that, though the dose was a large one, he was in such a nervous condition it failed to take fatal effect. At the trial Webster maintained through his lawyers that the body he was proved to be so vigorously dismembering during his spare moments in the week following November 23rd had been a Medical School cadaver brought to him for that purpose. This was sheer folly, and the prosecution had but to call upon the little dentist, Nathan Keep, to prove it so. Tooth by tooth, during what was called one of the 'tumultuous moments' of the trial, Dr Keep fitted the fragments of the false teeth found in Webster's furnace into the mold he still had in his possession. Charred as they were there could be no doubt they had once been the china-white teeth of Dr Parkman.

The spectators were treated to other memorable scenes. The great Dr Holmes testified twice, once for the State on the matter of the identity of the reconstructed skeleton and once for the defense as a character witness for the accused. Professor Webster's character witnesses were a howitzer battery of First Family notables, among them

Doctors Bigelow and Jackson, a Codman and a Lovering, the New England historian John Gorham Palfrey and Nathaniel Bowditch, son of the famed mathematician—even Harvard's president Jared Sparks took the stand for his errant employee. All seemed to agree that Webster, if occasionally irritable, was basically a kindhearted man, and President Sparks was thoughtful enough to add one gratuitous comment. 'Our professors,' he said, 'do not often commit murder.'

Credit was due Webster for his ability as a cadaver carver. He had done the job on Dr Parkman, it was established, with no more formidable instrument than a jackknife. A Dr Woodbridge Strong was especially emphatic on this point. He had dissected a good many bodies in his time, he recalled, including a rush job on a decaying pirate, but never one with just a jackknife. Ephraim Littlefield was of course star witness for the prosecution. The indefatigable little janitor talked for one whole day on the witness stand, a total of eight hours, five hours in the morning before recess for lunch and three hours in the afternoon. Only once did he falter and that on the occasion when, under cross-examination with the defense making a valiant attempt to throw suspicion on him, he was asked if he played 'gambling cards' with friends in Webster's back room. Four times the defense had to ask the question and four times Littlefield refused to answer. Finally, his New England conscience stung to the quick, he replied in exasperation, 'If you ask me if I played cards there *last winter*, I can truthfully say I did not.'

In those days prisoners were not allowed to testify, but on the last day of the trial Professor Webster was asked if he wanted to say anything. Against the advice of his counsel he rose and spoke for fifteen minutes. He spent most of those precious moments denying the accusation that he had written the various anonymous notes which had been turning up from time to time in the City Marchal's office ever since the disappearance of Dr Parkman. One of these had been signed CIVIS and Webster's last sentence was a pathetic plea for CIVIS to come forward if he was in the courtroom. CIVIS did not, and at eight o'clock on the evening of March 30th the trial was over.

Even the jury seems to have been overcome with pity for the professor. Before filing out of the courtroom the foreman, pointing a trembling finger at Webster, asked: 'Is that all? Is that the end? Can nothing further be said in defense of the man?' Three hours later the foreman and his cohorts were back, having spent, it is recorded, the first two hours and fifty-five minutes in prayer 'to put off the sorrowful duty'. When the verdict was delivered, 'an awful and unbroken silence ensued, in which the Court, the jury, the clerk, and the spectators seemed to be absorbed in their own reflections.'

Webster's hanging, by the neck until he was dead, proceeded without untoward incident in the courtyard of Boston's Leverett Street jail just five months to the day after he had been declared guilty. Before that time, however, the professor made a complete confession. He stated that Dr Parkman had come into his laboratory on that fatal Friday and that, when he had been unable to produce the money he owed, the doctor had shown him a sheaf of papers proving that he had been responsible for getting him his professorship. The doctor then added, 'I got you into your office, Sir, and now I will get you out of it.' This, said Webster, so infuriated him that he seized a stick of wood off his laboratory bench and struck Dr Parkman one blow on the head. Death was instantaneous and Webster declared, 'I saw nothing but the alternative of a successful removal and concealment of the body, on the one hand, and of infamy and destruction on the other.' He then related his week-long attempt to dismember and burn the body. Even the clergyman who regularly visited Webster in his cell during his last days was not able to extract from the professor the admission that the crime had been premeditated. He had done it in that one frenzy of rage. 'I am irritable and passionate,' the clergyman quoted Webster as saying, 'and Dr Parkman was the most provoking of men.'

The late Edmund Pearson, recognized authority on nonfictional homicide here and abroad, has called the Webster-Parkman case America's classic murder and the one which has lived longest in books of reminiscences. Certainly in Boston's First Family Society the aftermath of the case has been hardly less distinguished than its actual occurrence. To this day no Proper Bostonian grandfather autobiography is complete without some reference to the case. The Beacon Hill house at 8 Walnut Street from which Dr Parkman started out on his walk that Friday morning almost a hundred years ago is still standing, and its present occupant, a prominent Boston lawyer, is still on occasion plagued by the never-say-die curious.

Among Boston Parkmans the effect was a profound one. For years certain members of the Family shrank from Society altogether, embarrassed as they were by the grievous result of Dr Parkman's financial punctiliousness and all too aware of the sympathy extended Professor Webster in his budgetary plight. In the doctor's immediate family it is noteworthy that his widow headed the subscription list of a fund taken up to care for Webster's wife and children. Dr Parkman's son, George Francis Parkman, was five years out of Harvard in 1849. He had been, in contrast to his father, a rather gay blade as a youth and at college had taken part in Hasty Pudding Club theatricals; at the time of the murder he was enjoying himself in Paris. He returned to Boston a married man. He moved his mother and sister from 8 Walnut Street and took a house at 33 Beacon Street. From the latter house he buried his mother and aunt, and there he and his sister lived on as Boston Society's most distinguished recluses. His solitary existence never included even the solace of a job. Describing him as he appeared a full fifty years after the crime a biographer records:

> Past the chain of the bolted door on Beacon Street no strangers, save those who came on easily recognized business, were ever allowed to enter. Here George Francis Parkman and his sister Harriet, neither of whom ever married, practised the utmost frugality, the master of the house going himself to the market every day to purchase their meager provisions, and invariably paying cash for the simple supplies he brought home.
>
> The windows of his house looked out upon the Common but he did not frequent it ... He always walked slowly and alone, in a stately way, and attracted attention by his distinguished though retiring appearance ... In cool weather he wore a heavy coat of dark cloth and his shoulders and neck were closely wrapped with a wide scarf, the ends of which were tucked into his coat or under folds. He sheltered himself against the east winds of Boston just as he seemed, by his manner, to shelter his inmost self from contact with the ordinary affairs of men.[1]

Tremors of the Parkman earthquake continued to be felt by Boston Society often at times when they were least desired. Twenty years later, when Boston was privileged to play proud host to Charles Dickens, there was a particularly intense tremor. Dickens was asked which one of the city's historic landmarks he would like to visit first. 'The room where Dr Parkman was murdered,' he replied, and there being no doubt he meant what he said, nothing remained for a wry-faced group of Boston's best but to shepherd the distinguished novelist out to the chemistry laboratory of the Harvard Medical School.

A Webster-Parkman story, vintage of 1880, is still told today by Boston's distinguished author and teacher, Bliss Perry. He recalls that for a meeting of New England college officers at Williamstown, Massachusetts, his mother had been asked to put up as a guest in her house Boston's First Family poet laureate, diplomat and first editor of the *Atlantic*, James Russell Lowell. Unfortunately Lowell was at that time teaching at Harvard and for all his other accomplishments Mrs Perry would have none of him. He had to be quartered elsewhere.

'I could not sleep,' Mrs Perry said, 'if one of those Harvard professors were in the house.'

[1] *Famous Families of Massachusetts*, by Mary Caroline Crawford (Boston: Little Brown) © 1930.

# CHARLES FRANKLIN

# *Valerie Storie*

If this book needs a true heroine, here she is. Certainly Valerie Storie is a heroine in the etymological sense. She will go down in the history of crime as a brave and an avenging spirit.

What happened to her on that ghastly night of August 22–3, 1961, was enough to have broken most girls for life—mentally as well as physically. But not Valerie Storie. She not only survived appalling injuries, but she lived to avenge her lover who was murdered before her eyes, and is now taking up the threads of her life once more, paralysed from the waist down, but with a remarkable spirit of courage and confidence.

The public are used to horrors. Murders and rape constitute the staple diet of the majority of newspaper readers today. But the A6 Murder, of which Valerie Storie and Michael Gregsten were the victims sent a thrill of horror through the public such as it had rarely experienced before.

It was not the first time something like this had happened. But almost never before had a victim survived in such poignant and pitiful circumstances and able to give a vivid and detailed account of the kind of thing that happens when a familiar piece of violent fiction is projected into reality.

The man with the gun haunts our cinema and television screens. The A6 Murder showed what really happens when a psychopath gets hold of a gun. The scene has been documented for all time by the evidence of Valerie Storie.

Hanratty's bestial and purposeless crime was just the imitation by a dangerous moron of what he had seen countless times at the cinema and on the telly. Clever actors, playing brutal homicidal psychopaths abound on the screen and the goggle-box. Is it any wonder that they have imitators among real homicidal psychopaths?

Much has been written about this case, and it has been suggested that in hanging Hanratty, society has denied itself the opportunity of finding out why he did it.

Whatever mysteries remain about the A6 Murder, why Hanratty did it is surely not one of them. His action was purely imitative. He had seen it done so many times before—except for the rape.

The man with the gun has absolute power in given circumstances. He can command absolute obedience, instil absolute terror, dispense death and suffering at will. This sort of scene is frequently described in fiction, but hardly ever taken to its logical conclusion. The gunman is usually stopped in time by the forces of law and order.

In real life it is different. The gunman is rarely stopped before he presses the trigger.

We know that Hanratty was a psychopath, who can be described as an individual who is emotionally unstable to an abnormal degree, though not suffering from a specific mental disorder. In 1952 he was diagnosed at St Francis Hospital, Haywards Heath, as a mental defective. This does not mean that he was mad or a lunatic in the accepted sense.

A mental defective is a person who is uneducatable, unable to maintain himself in anything but the simplest of environments. Such a person is a moron and is generally described as feeble-minded. There are many such people in society. Most of them are quite harmless, and many, under proper guidance, can be useful people who can lead happy lives. Such persons have moral responsibility, and know the difference between right and wrong.

Hanratty knew perfectly well that he was committing a foul and bestial crime for no possible reason upon these two young people. He refused to plead diminished responsibility. The prosecution had great difficulty in securing his conviction and Hanratty was astute enough to gamble on this.

He was wrongly considered to be mad by many people. But the Home Secretary made an exhaustive investigation into his mental condition and 'failed to discover any sufficient ground to justify him in advising Her Majesty to interfere with the due course of the law'. It should be remembered that the Home Secretary in question, Mr R. A. Butler, is one of the most enlightened and humane men who have held the office this century, and he was acutely conscious of, even sympathetic with the powerful and growing abolitionist opinion today.

Unlike Edith Thompson, Ruth Ellis, Derek Bentley, Timothy Evans, and a disturbing number of other cases, the hanging of Hanratty was no propaganda for the abolitionists.

If you trace the events of the small hours of August 23rd in all their mad, terrifying reality, you can see how closely Hanratty was imitating the gunman of the screen, whom he had seen and envied so often and whose actions he copied in every detail, when at last he had a gun in his hand.

The fact that this was a purely imitative crime does not mean that the people who create gangster fiction, either in books or on the screen, are in any way responsible. I myself have written a great deal of crime fiction, though not of the sadistic kind involving rape and murder by which Hanratty seems to have been inspired.

It is as reasonable to blame the authors of this kind of fiction as it is to blame the makers of the gun which did the killing. If neither had existed, Hanratty would not have committed the A6 Murder, but he would have committed some other crime equally as bestial.

It is just as profitless to try and imagine the world without make-believe gangsters as it is to imagine it without guns, or without Hanrattys. They have to be accepted as part of civilization. We shall never be without them.

Valerie Storie and Michael Gregsten were civil servants who worked for the Department of Scientific and Industrial Research at the Road Research Laboratory at Slough. At the time of the murder she was twenty-three. He was fourteen years older, a married man with two children.

Four years before the murder, they fell in love and had been having quite a serious affair. Valerie Storie herself stated this a few months after the trial in some articles she wrote in the magazine *Today*.

They both had a common interest, motor rallying, and frequently went off together on rallies. She introduced him to her parents, but did not tell them at first that he was married. She says Gregsten was in love with her, but was devoted to his children, so the problem created by their love affair was practically unsolvable. A common enough situation.

Later her parents found out that Gregsten was married, but though they must have been grieved about it, they still made him welcome in their home on the Cippenham Estate, Slough.

The car Gregsten and Valerie Storie used for their motor rallying was a Morris Minor, 847 BHN, which was owned jointly by Gregsten's mother and aunt, from whom Gregsten borrowed it.

On the evening of August 22nd, the two lovers met after work and went to the Stories' home at Slough, and then on to the Old Station Inn at Taplow, a pretty Thames-side village near Maidenhead. They were working on plans for an eighty-mile car rally through the Chiltern Hills for the motor club at the place where they worked.

Towards none o'clock the pub started to fill up, and they left and drove to a place called Dorney Reach, not far away, and Gregston stopped the car in a cornfield, parking it with its back to the road.

They had often been here before, leaving the car in the field and strolling down to the river to watch the boats go through the lock—a pleasant spot for lovers on a summer's evening.

But the evening of August 22nd, 1961, was a chilly one, and they sat in the car with the windows up, still making plans for the rally. Valerie Storie says they were working out the system of penalty marks.

Just as it was getting dark there was a tap on the window at the driver's side. At first they were not alarmed, thinking perhaps it was someone from the farm wanting to drive a harvesting machine through the gateway.

Michael Gregsten wound down the window. They saw the figure of a man, neatly dressed, standing there, silhouetted against the darkening sky. The bottom half of his face was covered with a handkerchief. He poked a revolver through the window and said:

'This is a hold-up. I'm a desperate man. I've been on the run, so don't do anything silly.'

At first Valerie Storie couldn't take it seriously. It was a stupid joke. The gun couldn't be real.

But Gregsten, closer to the gunman, instantly sensed this was no joke, and that they had a dangerous homicide on their hands.

Hanratty demanded the car keys and told Gregsten to open the rear offside door. Gregsten obeyed and the intruder got in the back seat.

Both Gregsten and Valerie Storie were thoroughly scared by now and they had every reason to be.

Probably Hanratty's attitude, particularly at first, warned them subconsciously how extremely dangerous he was.

The armed gunman of fiction always has a purpose. He is anxious to execute a criminal exploit, or get away from one. His gun gives him power to force people to assist him in these ends. If the people he holds up do not try to foil him, generally speaking they don't get shot.

But the gunman *without* a purpose is another matter, and is infinitely more dangerous.

Hanratty was the gunman without a purpose. That was obvious as soon as he got into the car. He had held up two people with a gun, and then he didn't know what to do about it—apart from shooting them.

Gregsten and Valerie Storie were doomed from the start. It is only a mixture of good fortune and an indomitable courage that she is alive today, and that this dreadful story is able to be told.

The moment he got in the car, Hanratty betrayed the childlike mind of the moron at work. ('Be quiet, will you—I am finking'). He in fact behaved exactly as would the mental defective certified at St Francis Hospital in 1952.

Just before his execution, the *Observer* published medical records which disclosed Hanratty's mental state. The *Observer* was hotly criticized by Hanratty's solicitors for doing so.

Hanratty's defence had always been, and was to the end, that he did not do it. He wasn't the man. There are still people who think he was innocent. But the identification of him was positive enough to convince a jury, and I think the medical documents published by the *Observer* provide even further proof of identification.

The actions of the armed man who got into the back of Gregsten's car on the evening of August 22nd were consistent with the mentality of the man who was diagnosed as a mental defective in St Francis Hospital nine years previously. For anyone still wishing to believe in Hanratty's innocence of the crime, the documents the *Observer* published constituted an inconvenient disclosure.

Consider for a moment how the gunman acted when he first got these two people at his mercy. He was completely without purpose. Having perpetrated the initial outrage of holding them up with the gun, he didn't quite know what to do next. They offered him the car, their money, their watches. They would have done anything to have got rid of him. But he would not let them go. What did he want? The girl's body? Or just to cling on to the power the gun gave him? Both perhaps, though his lust for the girl was not apparent till later, till he had shot Gregsten. For undoubtedly killing Gregsten excited him sexually—a not uncommon psychopathic condition.

So at first they sat in the car for two wretched hours in that field. Hanratty said he hadn't eaten for two days and had slept rough, which was obviously untrue. He kept looking at his watch saying there was plenty of time, but obviously he wasn't clear what there was plenty of time for.

Every action, everything about him—even the nattiness of his dress which Valerie Storie observed—was consistent with Hanratty's character, mental state, and independently observed characteristics, and goes to confirm the fact that, whatever else might be said about this case, at least the right man was convicted.


The nightmare of the next few hours as told later by Valeria Storie is probably without parallel in the annals of human experience. People who suffer such appalling inhumanities at the hands of their fellow men are rarely able to give a vivid and detailed account of their sufferings.

The remarkable thing about this case was that when Valerie Storie recovered consciousness in hospital the next day her mind was clear as a bell, despite the awful injuries she had received. She could remember every tiny detail of what she and Gregsten suffered.

Hanratty sat in the back of the car, brandishing the revolver and his conversation gave an ominous indication of his mentality and intentions.

'This is like a cowboy's gun. I feel like a cowboy. I haven't had it very long. I have never shot anyone before.'

He made Gregsten drive further into the field and then demanded their watches and money. Gregsten gave him his wallet containing about three pounds. Valerie Storie took seven pounds out of her handbag before she gave Hanratty the bag, secreting the money inside her bra.

He told them that every policeman in England was looking for him, which was quite untrue, and that he intended to wait till morning, tie them up, take the car and leave.

About 10.30 a light came on in a nearby house and a man came out to put his bicycle away. This made Hanratty nervous and he told his victims that if the man should come up to the car, they must say nothing, or he would shoot the man and them also.

Another nerve-wracking hour passed with the couple in the front seats trying everything they knew to persuade him to go away and leave them.

At 11.30 Hanratty grew nervous. He forced Gregsten at gunpoint to drive out of the field and take the road to Slough.

Valerie Storie said that now she noticed an edge to Michael Gregsten's voice which told her how near to breaking point he was. As they continued their ghastly ride the two in front continually touched hands to try and comfort and reassure each other. It seems that Valerie Storie was the calmest of the three.

They went through Slough where she noticed that a clock showed a quarter-to-twelve. Behind them as they drove at gunpoint, they heard a clicking noise. Hanratty told them that he was putting the safety catch on and off. They were forbidden to look around in case they should see his face in the passing lights.

Near London Airport they stopped at a garage for petrol. The gunman was as precise in his instructions as they are in such circumstances on the screen.

'I want you to get two gallons. You are to stay in the car. I have the gun pointing at you and if you try to say anything else than to ask for two gallons, or give the man a note, or make any indication that anything is wrong, then I will shoot you.'

He gave Gregsten one pound of the money he had previously taken from him and Gregsten did as he was told. The unsuspecting attendant put in the petrol and gave him 10s. 3d. change.

Hanratty took the ten shilling note and gave Valerie Storie the threepence, saying: 'You can have that as a wedding present.' He insisted on believing that she and Gregsten were married, although they told him several times that they were not.

They then drove on, through Hayes and Harrow and across North-West London.

In Stanmore they stopped while Gregsten got out and got some cigarettes from a machine, Haratty holding the girl as a hostage in the car.

No doubt Gregsten hoped he might be able to summon assistance in some way, but there was nobody about, and nothing he could do, with this unpredictable gunman holding Valerie at his mercy. Hanratty had learnt his part well.

So the unhappy Gregsten returned to the car with the cigarettes, not dreaming of running away suddenly and deserting the girl he loved—as he undoubtedly could have done just then. And later, when her opportunity came to make a break for it, she refused to desert him. Afraid they undoubtedly were, but they showed great loyalty as well as courage on this awful night.

And so they drove on.

Valerie Storie lit two cigarettes, giving one to Gregsten, handing the other into the back for their captor to take. She noticed he was wearing black gloves. Although Hanratty took the cigarette, he said he did not like smoking—a further known characteristic of Hanratty's, one more link which built up to a definite identification.

They turned on to the A5, and Gregsten tried again to attract attention. He kept switching the reversing light on and off. A passing driver turned and pointed.

At this, Hanratty exclaimed: 'They must know something is wrong.' He made Gregsten stop and get out with him to examine the rear lights.

While they were doing this, Valerie Storie, herself a good driver, could easily have slipped into the driving seat and driven off and saved herself from the appalling thing that was done to her. But this extraordinarily brave girl could not bring herself to abandon the man she loved.

Who knows what would have happened if she had made a break for it at this point? The nervous, indecisive Hanratty would almost certainly have fired at the car, and only a very lucky shot could have hit the driver. Gregsten, if he had been quick enough, might have made a successful dive for the gun at the moment when Hanratty's attention was distracted, and the story might have had a very different ending.

But Hanratty had assured them that he would not harm them so long as they did as he told them, and Valerie Storie decided not to take a risk which would undoubtedly have provoked Hanratty to violence.

Besides, Gregsten scorned to desert her. So she scorned to desert him.

They got into the car again and Gregsten drove on to his death. But he still tried to attract the attention of passing cars by switching the reversing light on and off and flashing the headlamps from dipped beam to main beam.

'Every time we entered a built-up area we went slowly,' said Valerie Storie. 'And we had a plan that if we managed to see a policeman Mike would pretend there was something wrong with the steering and try to run the car on the pavement near a policeman. But there was no policeman. You never see one when you want one.' They did not see one policeman during the whole of this terrible journey.

And so they went to St Albans and on to the A6—the road that goes from London to Leicester, Derby, Manchester and Carlisle.

Hanratty said he was tired and said: 'I want a kip.' He told Gregsten to turn off the road and find somewhere where he could sleep. Twice they parked but found out they were on private property, so they went on.

Finally they came to a place known as Dead Man's Hill, where there was a layby which was separated from the road by a grass verge on which were some trees. Here Hanratty made Gregsten turn in and park, with the car pointing in the direction of Luton and turn all the lights out.

Again they begged him not to shoot them. He said if he had wanted to do that, he would have done so before.

'I want a kip,' he said. 'But first I must tie you up.'

He made Gregsten get out of the car, go round to the boot with him where he found a piece of cord which he gave to Gregsten and told him to get back into the driver's seat. Then he tied Valerie Storie's hands behind her and fastened them to the door handle, but she managed to keep her wrists apart so that she could easily get them free when she wanted to.

Hanratty then looked for something to tie Gregsten with. He decided to use the cord from the duffle bag containing some clean laundry.

The story of what happened then is best told in the girl's own words, at the trial.

'Somehow the duffle bag had got into the front of the car. The man said "Give me that bag up". Mike picked up the bag with both hands, turned towards the interior of the car to his left. He lifted the bag and as the bag was just about to go over the back of the seat, the man fired two shots in quick succession at Mike's head. The gun could not have been more than an inch or two from his head. There was a terrific noise and a smell of gunpowder.

'Mike fell forward and over the steering wheel and I could hear the blood pouring out of his head.

'For the first time that night, I screamed.

'Hanratty said: "Stop screaming!"

'I turned to him and said: "You shot him, you bastard! Why did you do that?"

'He said: "He frightened me. He moved too quick. I got frightened."

'My hands by this time were free of the rope and I was holding them together as if they were secure. Mike moved and flopped back against the seat. His head fell back. There was a look of surprise, disbelief in his face.

'I said to the man: "For God's sake let me get Mike to a doctor quick. I will do anything you want if you will let me take the car and get Mike to a doctor."

'He said: "Be quiet, I am finking."

'I said: "Let me move Mike. I will take the car. I will take you anywhere you want to go. Let me drive and find help for Mike."

'He said: "No, he's dead."

'I said: "Let me take Mike somewhere. I must try and get help."

'He said: "Be quiet, will you. I am finking." Then: "Turn round and face me. I know your hands are free."

'I obeyed.

'He looked at me. "Kiss me."

'I refused.

'While we were in this position facing each other, a car came from the direction of Luton towards Bedford lighting up the man's face. This was my first opportunity of really seeing what he looked like. He had very large, pale blue staring icy eyes. He seemed to have a pale face. I should imagine anyone would have, having just shot someone. He had brown hair, combed back, no parting.

'He said again: "Kiss me." I refused, and after he had asked several times, he pointed the gun at me and said: "If you don't, I will count five and I will shoot you."

'I said: "Please don't shoot me. Just let me go." And he started to count, so I let him kiss me very briefly.

'After that had happened, I sat back in the car. The gun was in his right hand as it had been the whole evening. I leaned across with my left hand and tried to grab the gun, but he was too strong.

'He said: "That was a silly thing to do. I thought you were sensible. I cannot trust you now."'

He took a cloth from the duffle bag and covered the dead man's face with it. Gregsten's body was slumped in the driving seat, his blood flowing down between the seat and the side of the car.

She continues:

'He said: "Come and sit in the back with me." I said: "No." Several times he asked me and several times I refused. He said: "Get out. Come and sit in the back with me. I will count five and if you have not got in, I will shoot."

'I got out of the car slowly, trying to play for time, hoping someone would come by. He was sitting in the car and opened the rear door for me, with the gun on me pointing at me all the time.

'He said: "Come on, get in." Again I refused. So he got out of the car and the gun was almost touching me, and he said: "Come on—get in." I got in the back. He followed and shut the door.

'The gun was resting on his lap. He tried to kiss me again. He tried to touch me. I managed to remove the seven pounds from my bra into my mackintosh pocket. He put the gun on the back window shelf of the car and took off one of his black gloves.'

Then he made her undo her brassiere, mauled her, and made her take off her knickers and lie back in the car while he undid his trousers and raped her.

'This lasted,' said Valerie Storie, 'only a very short time—a minute or so. He said: "You haven't had much sex, have you."'

She said afterwards that the rape itself seemed unimportant. The only thing she was thinking of was Gregsten slumped there just in front of them still bleeding.

Hanratty then made her pull Gregsten's body out of the car which she did by grasping him under the armpits. She dragged it round the back of the car to the edge of the concrete strip two or three yards behind the car. He made no attempt to help her, and was careful not to get any blood on himself.

He carefully wiped the steering wheel and covered up the blood-stained driving seat and made her start the engine and show him how the controls worked.

She went and sat beside Gregsten's body, her legs under her, her back to the car. She said she did not weep, but just sat there waiting for the murderer to go.

Minutes passed. He was still undecided whether to leave her, or to commit further outrage. He had already got into the car more than once.

She continues the story:

'He got out and came up to me and said: "I think I had better hit you on the head or get something to knock you out, or you will go for help."

'I said: "No, I won't. I won't move. Just go." I gave him £1 from my pocket. "Here you are. You can have that if you will go quick."

He said: "Where did you get that from?" I said it was just in my pocket. He took the pound and started to walk away.

'When he was about six or ten feet away he suddenly turned round and started to shoot. I felt one bullet hit me, then a second. I felt the use of my legs go and I fell over.'

One of the bullets had gone straight through her neck close to the spinal cord.

'He fired another two or three shots at me while I was lying on the ground. There was a pause and I heard a clicking as if he was reloading. Then he fired another three shots and they seemed to go over my head.

'I lay perfectly still. I heard him walk towards me, and I tried to stop breathing and pretend I was dead. I felt him touch me. whether it was with his hand or whether he kicked me, I do not know. He stood looking at me for a few seconds.'

Valerie Storie says in retrospect that this was the most terrifying moment of all.

Then he went away.

'I heard him walk back to the car, get in, slam the door, saw him put on the headlights. He drove off in the direction of Luton.

'I managed to turn over on to my back and thought what do I do now? I found I could not move. I thought of trying to roll along the layby and get on the road, but I could not move. I thought to myself, If I die now, no one will know who to look for, and with my right hand I tried to get up some little stones and I was trying to make out the words: Blue eyes, brown hair. But there were not any stones.

'I must have been lying there for almost half an hour when I heard a vehicle approach. As it got nearer I started to scream and shout for help. It just went by.'

She managed to pull off her petticoat and tried to wave it to attract attention.

It was now about three o'clock, some six hours after that tap on the car window in the cornfield at Dorney Reach. She presently lost consciousness.

'When next I opened my eyes it was light. I looked back and on the verge behind me, I saw a pair of legs, and I shouted for help.'

The man who found her was a young undergraduate engaged on a traffic census. He soon summoned help and before she was taken to hospital she was able to give a brief description of the murderer.

For six terrible hours he had sat behind her in the car talking, and it was natural that it was his voice which was indelibly imprinted on her mind—quietly spoken, youngish and Cockney, unable to pronounce 'th'. Thus 'things' were 'fings' and 'thinking' was 'finking'. This as much as anything put the noose around Hanratty's neck.

Valerie Storie woke up in hospital with the doctors bending anxiously over her and the police in the background not having much hope that a girl who had been so savaged and outraged would be coherent enough to help them much in their urgent inquiries—even if she could bear to talk about it.

But they were soon to discover this was no ordinary girl they were dealing with. By some strange fortune, her mind was crystal clear on every detail of her terrible experience. Despite her pain and her helplessness, a cold rage was burning inside her. One thought was uppermost in her mind—she wanted to avenge her lover's death. In those long weeks in hospital, through the nightmares and the suffering, she thought of little else.

Hanratty in that mad senseless night had smashed more than two lives. There was Gregsten's widow, left in an appalling situation with two fatherless children.

There were many who criticized Valerie Storie as she lay in hospital paralyzed, with an irreparable injury to her spinal column. Some even wrote poison pen letters to her, telling her she was a wicked woman who had got what she deserved and that she had wrecked a good man's life.

Anonymous phone calls were made to the hospital threatening her life. She was guarded night and day by police and dogs. Every night her bed was moved to a different position in case someone should try and shoot her through the window to silence her.

Who threatened her life? We shall never know. Hanratty denied everything to the end. It was most likely the act of deranged individuals who are called for the want of better words practical jokers.

Not only did the police guard her carefully, they also did their best to spare her feelings when questioning her by glossing over the more unpleasant details of that night of horror. But they were surprised to find that she was not to be hurried over her awful tale, and was meticulous in describing every little detail of what had happened. Her calm, matter-of-fact attitude helped the police enormously in their inquiries.

For her part she found them 'so patient, so understanding, so untiring and so human'.

As she lay in hospital, through all the pain and suffering she said she had only one thought—revenge. She knew no pity for Hanratty. She wanted him to be hanged for what he had done.

In October, barely two months after the outrage, she picked him out at an identification parade. Later he was identified by someone else in connection with the case and charged. Early the following year his trial took place—the longest and one of the most controversial murder trials in English history.

One of the controversies centred around the fact that in September, Valerie Storie picked out a different man at another identification parade—someone who had obviously nothing to do with the crime. She had plainly made a mistake, and this of course was held against the validity of her later evidence. She picked out Hanratty at a second identification parade.

At this second parade each of the men was asked to say 'Be quiet, will you, I am thinking.' At the first parade the men said nothing. It was hearing Hanratty speak those words—he had said them so many times during the night of the murder—that clinched it in her mind.

Upon the identification of the accused man by Valerie Storie the prosecution's case rested. Without it, there would have been no conviction. The defence were unable to shake her evidence in court and the jury believed her.

Although a jury's verdict is always accepted, providing there is no misdirection, lawyers said later that a trained legal mind would not have placed much weight upon her identification in view of the circumstances—the fact that she had once wrongly identified the killer and that when she did pick out Hanratty it was only from a fleeting glimpse of his face in the headlamps of a passing car.

This is only a technical point however, for legal opinion is that even if Hanratty should not have been convicted upon the evidence, there is very little doubt that he was the A6 killer. There was no miscarriage of justice.

The lay mind is more likely to believe that Valerie Storie's identification of Hanratty was good enough.

The legal critics are inclined to depreciate the value of her reliance upon the voice, saying that many Cockneys say 'fings' and 'fink', for 'things' and 'think'.

They forget that for nearly six hours Valerie Storie sat in the front seat of that car with the monster sitting behind her, talking all the time, forbidding them to turn round and look at him. For ever afterwards that voice must have haunted her mind. Could she ever forget it?

We all know how in ordinary experience people are readily identifiable by their voices. The telephone, if nothing else, has taught us this. We know our friends by their voices, and our enemies. And we know too those familiar strangers on the radio and television by their voices. When well-known radio people first began to appear on television we identified them quickly and infallibly by their voices—and they had only to say a few words. Their faces meant nothing to us.

It is pedantic, and indeed typical of the legal mind to discount identification by voice.

And then this 'fleeting glimpse of his face' in the lights of a passing car. There is no doubt that Valerie Storie took a very good look at him, when she was able to for the first time, in that terrible agonizing moment.

Her lover had just been murdered before her eyes. She was in no state of panic or hysteria. She was full of anger and hatred. She wanted to live, if only to bring the murderer to justice. She seemed to have had the most extraordinary presence of mind during those awful minutes, when Gregsten was shot and Hanratty raped her. She even removed the £7 from her brassiere before he started to maul her there.

She took a very good look at his face and was able to give a fair description of Hanratty as soon as she was found in the morning.

Why then did she pick out the wrong man at the first identification parade? We shall never know the answer to this. The fact that the man she picked out could have had no connection with the case and is therefore unknown makes it impossible to say whether he could have been mistaken for Hanratty.

A more interesting speculation arose from the fact that at the second identification parade, Valerie Storie took a full twenty minutes before she picked out Hanratty. Why did she take so long? Why did she not pick him out at once? people asked.

She later explained this by saying that she knew him at once, the moment she set eyes on him, but that she deliberately kept him in suspense, spinning out the torture for as long as possible before she picked him out.

She says she deliberately played cat-and-mouse with him at that parade. It was her revenge for what he had done to her and Gregsten.

If one can really believe this, then one's respect for this formidable young woman is greatly increased. Certainly no one can blame her for wanting to make him suffer, after what she and her lover had suffered at his hands. Though perhaps she need not have bothered. There can surely be no suffering which can be compared with the torture of a person awaiting execution.


The trial of James Hanratty at Bedford Assizes began on January 22nd, 1962, and lasted until February 17th. It was the longest murder trial in British legal history.

The Judge was Mr Justice Gorman and there was a jury of eleven men. The Crown was led by Mr Graham Swannick, Q.C., and Hanratty's counsel was Mr Michael Sherrard, who was then a junior member of the Bar. Although opinion is that Mr Sherrard defended Hanratty very well, he was not a Q.C., and some legal authorities have said that a person on a capital charge should always have leading counsel to defend him as well as a junior.

No question of expense enters into this. When Hanratty was committed for trial, the Magistrates at Ampthill authorized him legal aid which could have provided him with both senior and junior counsel, as is usual in capital charges.

Hanratty, however, had implicit faith in Mr Sherrard's ability to save him from the gallows, and insisted that he should conduct his defence without the benefit of senior counsel. Hanratty was entitled to make this vital decision, regardless of whether he was mentally equipped to do so. It was up to him also to decide what plea he should make. He had the benefit of legal advice of course, but the decision was his to make.

He was astute enough to see that the prosecution were going to have difficulty in establishing that he was the man, so he pleaded not guilty—a total denial. He maintained he wasn't the man, and said he was somewhere else at the time. In view of the circumstances and his own medical history, he could probably have made a successful plea of diminished responsibility, and ended his days in Broadmoor. But Hanratty decided to take a chance.

This sounds like the decision of a reasonably intelligent, if cunning person, and Hanratty certainly gave that impression in the witness box. He was cocky, even insolent.

However restrained he was in the courtroom, outside he was less reticent. While in Brixton Prison he boasted to a fellow prisoner that he was the A6 killer.

As the crime was on everyone's lips just then, too much evidence need not necessarily have been placed upon such a boast by a psychopath with delusions of criminal grandeur.

But Hanratty confided details of the crime which, at that time, only Valerie Storie, the police and the killer knew. He must therefore have been the killer.

This came out only in part at the trial. Owing to the peculiar nature of English courtroom procedure, which often acts very largely in the accused's favour, the whole story of the A6 killing and the circumstances surrounding it could not be told.

The whole story indeed has never been told, and may never be. But this damning piece of evidence against Hanratty, though not known to the Court, was known to the Home Secretary when he was considering the question of the reprieve, and no doubt it sealed Hanratty's fate.

Over a million words of evidence were spoken at this marathon of a trial. There were moments of drama among the long hours of weighty argument and apparently inconsequential testimony.

The high moment of the trial of course was the appearance of Valerie Storie to give her evidence, brightly dressed in tartan slacks and yellow sweater and seated in a wheelchair. No one who saw her and heard her could fail to be touched to the heart. She gave her evidence simply but with great conviction, and of course was handled with kid gloves by cross-examining counsel.

We have heard the story she told. The legal pundits don't give much credence to her evidence owing to the identification problem. This is a technical criticism and is part of an exposure of the glaring imperfections of the English legal system, always thought by most people to be little short of perfect.

What has been said now is that Hanratty should not have been convicted on the evidence submitted to the Court, though he would certainly have been if all the known facts had been presented to the Court. But they could not be owing to the laws and conventions by which English trials are bound. In the court procedure practised in most other countries all the facts about the A6 murder would have been known and an obviously guilty man would not so nearly have escaped justice, as Hanratty did.

This is an extremely serious criticism of English justice, and is but one of the controversies which arose out of this case.

An important and contentious point was brought up by the defence, when it alleged that the police investigations were directed not so much at finding out the truth but at discovering things which would implicate Hanratty.

This of course is usual in police practice. If the police suspect a person, their lines of inquiry are directed at discovering evidence against him. This is not necessarily unfair, nor could it be called disregarding the truth. If the facts the police uncover suggest that their suspect is innocent, then obviously they are not going to waste time on an investigation which is not going to result in a *prima facie* case.

The police were subjected to severe criticism by the defence particularly on their investigation into Hanratty's alibis, but as these alibis turned out to be false and were abandoned by the defence, much of the criticism, though it sounded formidable enough at the time, did not really amount to much when the case was considered in retrospect. It is true that the police were deliberately selective in their lines of investigation, but they were fully entitled to be, once having decided that Hanratty was their man.

One of the unsolved mysteries of the case was Hanratty's relationship with a man called Charles France.

France and his family lived in St Johns Wood and Hanratty had been staying there about the time of the A6 murder. France gave evidence for the prosecution to the effect that he was riding on a bus with Hanratty who asked him whether the back seat of the top of a bus was a good place to hide a gun. This was just where the murder weapon was later found.

France himself was a mental case and suffered from acute depression. He had always lived on the fringe of the underworld and undoubtedly knew of Hanratty's criminal aspirations.

His association with Hanratty worsened France's mental condition and three days before the trial he tried to commit suicide. Under psychiatric treatment France revealed that he was acutely worried about the great harm he had done his family by introducing Hanratty into his home. 'It could have been my wife and daughter that he killed.' France had an overwhelming guilt complex about the A6 murder.

A month after the trial ended and less than three weeks before Hanratty's execution, France finally succeeded in committing suicide, leaving letters expressing great bitterness towards Hanratty.

The inquest on him was adjourned until after Hanratty's execution on April 4th, 1962, because the disclosure might, the Coroner thought, prejudice Hanratty's chances of a reprieve.

When he did hold the inquest the Coroner refused to read the whole of the suicide letter saying: 'The rest of the letter I think is not in the public interest to read, but he explains that he had an association with a man, James Hanratty, and having been a witness at the trial of that man had played on his mind very much. He blames himself very much for having introduced the man to his family at all. It is a letter written with great bitterness and great feeling.'

What was the mystery of their relationship? The *Observer* said: 'If Mr Butler is the man of integrity we believe him to be he will make a public statement which fills in the gaps of the story of the A6 murder. The community has a right to know.'

But Mr Butler remained silent.

The letters mentioned by the Coroner were shown to Hanratty's solicitor, but whatever they contained, they did nothing to bring about a reprieve for Hanratty.

What was the final mystery of the A6 murder? Why did Charles France have this overwhelming sense of guilt about it? Was he instrumental in supplying Hanratty with the murder gun?

We know Hanratty's dearest wish in life was to be a gangster with a gun. If France had been able to help him realize his wish, he might well have held himself responsible for the horrible crime at Dead Man's Hill.

From his death cell Hanratty wrote: 'I can't say how sorry I am that things turned out this way, but it was not my fault. It was the fault of others. I am about to take the punishment for someone else's crime, but I will face it like a man.'

The final unanswered question is what was Hanratty doing in that lonely cornfield in Buckinghamshire that August evening with a gun in his hand?

He was miles away from his usual haunts. He was the nattily dressed Londoner. What was he doing at Dorney Reach?

Several theories have been advanced to explain this final mystery. It was even suggested that he might have been sent there to frighten Gregsten for some reason, and then went beserk. Another suggestion is that he had some sinister sexual motive which could only be fulfilled by the murder of a man and the rape of his woman. It is pretty certain that murdering Gregsten aroused Hanratty's sexual desires.

We are far from knowing all the dark mysteries which lurk in the human mind.

I think Hanratty's crime was an imitative one. He wanted to be the gangster of fiction. Having possessed himself of a gun for the first time in his life—his dearest wish—his encounter with this ill-starred pair in the cornfield was purely fortuitous. He may well have been wandering in this district with an idea of staging an armed hold-up at one of the big houses nearby.

It is not unusual for persons of a certain mentality to spy on couples in parked motor cars. Give such a person a gun, and anything can happen.

The case was resurrected again in the summer of 1963, when Mr Fenner Brockway, the Labour M.P. for Eton and Slough, produced a memorandum containing a confession by a Mr 'X' that it was he, not Hanratty, who committed the A6 Murder.

It was debated in the House of Commons on August 2nd, and the Home Secretary, Mr Henry Brooke, refused to reopen the case, saying that Mr X's confession had already been fully investigated by the Home Office a year previously.

'Not only was there every indication that this so-called confession was spurious,' said Mr Brooke, 'but it did not stand up to the known facts of the case.' There was no doubt in his mind that Hanratty was properly convicted. Neither indeed is there any doubt in the minds of most other people who have properly studied this case.

Commenting on Mr Brockway's memorandum, the *Observer* of July 14th, 1963, said that it 'contains little of significance that was not known to the authorities at the time of Hanratty's execution on April 4, 1962. In fact it does not begin to match the very real doubts that still characterize the case of Timothy Evans.'

Charles Sandell writing on August 4th, 1963 in the *News of the World*, a paper usually very well informed in these matters, said that he saw the confession a year previously and dismissed it as worthless. He continued: 'I hope we've heard the last of Mr X, the heartless publicity seeker whose phoney confession to the A6 Murder was debated in the Commons on Friday. I hope too that the people who swallowed his fantastic story will ignore him as he deserves.'

The 1963 move to re-open the case was, it seems to me, part of the campaign against capital punishment, the idea being to raise a doubt in people's minds about the guilt of an executed man. As many people are still doubtful of Hanratty's guilt, it was a very effective move.

Quite apart from the merits of this particular case, it is an extremely important and telling argument for the abolition of the death penalty, that once a man is executed there can be no reparation if it is subsequently discovered that a mistake has been made.

This argument is particularly effective just now when English legal procedure is coming under increasing criticism, and the belief is gaining ground that mistakes can, and are being made in the way justice is administered. And so the question is naturally being asked: Should we execute people who are condemned under our present out-of-date court procedure?

Of Hanratty's guilt I have little doubt myself. But as Louis Blom-Cooper points out in his book, *The A6 Murder*, many unanswered questions remain, Hanratty's guilt, however, not being one of them.


The mysteries of the A6 Murder case will perhaps never be explained. Criminologists will discuss it for years to come.

Let Valerie Storie, who because of it is fated to spend the rest of her life in a wheelchair, have the last word: 'We all do things in life which we should not do. Sometimes we escape unhurt. Sometimes we pay the price for it. For those who escape we say, they are the lucky ones.'

# THOMAS DE QUINCEY
# *Postscript:*
## *An Account of the Williams and M'Kean Murders*

*'With respect to the Williams murders, the sublimest and most entire in their excellence that ever were committed, I shall not allow myself to speak incidentally. Nothing less than an entire lecture, or even an entire course of lectures, would suffice to expound their merits.' So wrote De Quincey in his original 'lecture',* On Murder, Considered as One of the Fine Arts, *and in 1854 he fulfilled this promise with the* Postscript *which follows, adding for good measure the case of the M'Keans, 'bearing that relation . . . to the immortal works of Williams, which the* Aeneid *bears to the* Iliad.'

*Some commentators have pointed out that De Quincey is inaccurate in some of his details, but no matter, for here is one of the great masters of English prose in a virtuoso performance.*

It is impossible to conciliate readers of so saturnine and gloomy a class that they cannot enter with genial sympathy into any gaiety whatever, but least of all when the gaiety trespasses a little into the province of the extragavant. In such a case, not to sympathise is not to understand; and the playfulness, which is not relished, becomes flat and insipid, or absolutely without meaning. Fortunately, after all such churls have withdrawn from my audience in high displeasure, there remains a large majority who are loud in acknowledging the amusement which they have derived from this little paper; at the same time proving the sincerity of their praise by one hesitating expression of censure. Repeatedly they have suggested to me that perhaps the extravagance, though clearly intentional, and forming one element in the general gaiety of the conception, went too far.

I am not myself of that opinion; and I beg to remind these friendly censors that it is amongst the direct purposes and efforts of this *bagatelle* to graze the brink of horror and of all that would in actual realisation be most repulsive. The very excess of the extravagance in fact, by suggesting to the reader continually the mere aeriality of the entire speculation, furnishes the surest means of disenchanting him from the horror which might else gather upon his feelings. Let me remind such objectors, once for all, of Dean Swift's proposal for turning to account the supernumerary infants of the three kingdoms, which, in those days, both at Dublin and at London, were provided for in foundling hospitals, by cooking and eating them. This was an extravagance, though really bolder and more coarsely practical than mine, which did not provoke any reproaches even to a dignitary of the supreme Irish church; its own monstrosity was its excuse; mere extravagance was felt to license and accredit the little *jeu d'esprit*, precisely as the blank impossibilities of Lilliput, of Laputa, of the Yahoos, etc., had licensed those.

If, therefore, any man thinks it worth his while to tilt against so mere a foam-bubble of gaiety as this lecture on the æsthetics of murder, I shelter myself for the moment under the Telamonian shield of the dean. But, in reality, which (to say the truth) formed one motive for detaining the reader by this postscript, my own little paper may plead a privileged excuse for its extravagance, such as is altogether wanting to the dean's. Nobody can pretend for a moment, on behalf of the dean, that there is any ordinary and natural tendency in human thoughts which could ever turn to infants as articles of diet; under any conceivable circumstances this would be felt as the most aggravated form of cannibalism—cannibalism applying itself to the most defenceless part of the species. But, on the other hand, the tendency to a critical or æsthetic valuation of fires and murders is universal.

If you are summoned to the spectacle of a great fire, undoubtedly the first impulse is—to assist in putting it out. But that field of exertion is very limited, and is soon filled by regular professional people, trained and equipped for the service. In the case of a fire which is operating upon *private* property, pity for a neighbour's calamity checks us at first in treating the affair as a scenic spectacle. But perhaps the fire may be confined to public buildings. And in any case, after we have paid our tribute of regret to the affair, considered as a calamity, inevitably, and without restraint, we go on to consider it as a stage spectacle. Exclamations of—How grand! how magnificent! arise in a sort of rapture from the crowd.

For instance, when Drury Lane was burned down in the first decennium of this century, the falling in of the roof was signalised by a mimic suicide of the protecting Apollo that surmounted and crested the centre of this roof. The god was stationary with his lyre, and seemed looking down upon the fiery ruins that were so rapidly approaching him. Suddenly the supporting timbers below him gave way; a convulsive heave of the billowing flames seemed for a moment to raise the statue; and then, as if on some impulse of despair, the presiding deity appeared not to fall, but to throw himself into the fiery deluge, for he went down head foremost; and in all respects, the descent had the air of a voluntary act. What followed? From every one of the bridges over the river, and from other open areas which commanded the spectacle, there arose a sustained uproar of admiration and sympathy.

Some few years before this event, a prodigious fire occurred at Liverpool; the *Goree*, a vast pile of warehouses close to one of the docks, was burned to the ground. The huge edifice, eight or nine storeys high, and laden with most combustible goods, many thousand bales of cotton, wheat and oats in thousands of quarters, tar, turpentine, rum, gunpowder, etc., continued through many hours of darkness to feed this tremendous fire. To aggravate the calamity it blew a regular gale of wind; luckily for the shipping it blew inland, that is to the east; and all the way down to Warrington, eighteen miles distant to the eastward, the whole air was illuminated by flakes of cotton, often saturated with rum, and by what seemed absolute worlds of blazing sparks, that lighted up all the upper chambers of the air. All the cattle lying abroad in the fields through a breadth of eighteen miles, were thrown into terror and agitation. Men, of course, read in this hurrying overhead of scintillating and blazing vortices the annunciation of some gigantic calamity going on in Liverpool; and the lamentation on that account was universal. But that mood of public sympathy did not at all interfere to suppress or even to check the momentary bursts of rapturous admiration, as this arrowy sleet of many-coloured fire rode on the wings of hurricane, alternately through open depths of air or through dark clouds overhead.

Precisely the same treatment is applied to murders. After the first tribute of sorrow to those who have perished, but, at all events, after the personal interests have been tranquillised by time, inevitably the scenical features (what æsthetically may be called the comparative *advantages*) of the several murders are reviewed and valued. One murder is compared with another; and the circumstances of superiority, as, for example, in the incidence and effects of surprise, of mystery, etc., are collated and appraised. I, therefore, for *my* extravagance claim an inevitable and perpetual ground in the spontaneous tendencies of the human mind when left to itself. But no one will pretend that any corresponding plea can be advanced on behalf of Swift.

In this important distinction between myself and the dean, lies one reason which prompted the present postscript. A second purpose of the postscript is to make the reader acquainted circumstantially with three memorable cases of murder which long ago the voice of amateurs has crowned with laurel, but especially with the two earliest of the three, viz., the immortal Williams murders of 1812. The act and the actor are each separately in the highest degree interesting; and as forty-two years have elapsed since 1812, it cannot be supposed that either is known circumstantially to the men of the current generation.

Never, throughout the annals of universal Christendom, has there indeed been any act of one solitary insulated individual armed with power so appalling over the hearts of men as that exterminating murder by which, during the winter of 1811–12, John Williams, in one hour, smote two houses with emptiness, exterminated all but two entire households, and asserted his own supremacy above all the children of Cain. It would be absolutely impossible adequately to describe the frenzy of feelings which, throughout the next fortnight, mastered the popular heart—the mere delirium of indignant horror in some, the mere delirum of panic in others. For twelve succeeding days, under some groundless notion that the unknown murderer had quitted London, the panic which had convulsed the mighty metropolis diffused itself all over the island. I was myself at that time nearly three hundred miles from London; but there, and everywhere, the panic was indescribable. One lady, my next neighbour, whom personally I knew, living at the moment, during the absence of her husband, with a few servants in a very solitary house, never rested until she had placed eighteen doors (so she told me, and, indeed, satisfied me by ocular proof), each secured by ponderous bolts, and bars, and chains, between her own bedroom and any intruder of human build. To reach her, even in her drawing-room was like going as a flag of truce into a beleaguered fortress; at every sixth step one was stopped by a sort of portcullis. The panic was not confined to the rich; women in the humblest ranks more than once died upon the spot from the shock attending some suspicious attempts at intrusion upon the part of vagrants meditating probably nothing worse than a robbery, but whom the poor women, misled by the London newspapers, had fancied to be the dreadful London murderer. Meantime this solitary artist, that rested in the centre of London, self-supported by his own conscious grandeur, as a domestic Attila, or 'Scourge of God'—this man that walked in darkness, and relied upon murder (as afterwards transpired) for bread, for clothes, for promotion in life—was silently preparing an effectual answer to the public journals; and on the twelfth day after his inaugural murder he advertised his presence in London, and published to all men the absurdity of ascribing to *him* any ruralizing propensities, by striking a second blow and accomplishing a second family extermination. Somewhat lightened was the *provincial* panic by this proof that the murderer had not condescended to sneak into the country, or to abandon for a moment, under any motive of caution or fear, the great metropolitan *castra stativa* of gigantic crime seated for ever on the Thames. In fact, the great artist disdained a provincial reputation;

and he must have felt, as a case of ludicrous disproportion, the contrast between a country town or village, on the one hand, and, on the other, a work more lasting than brass—a χτημα ἐξ αετ—a murder such in quality as any murder that *he* would condescend to own for a work turned out from his own *studio*.

Coleridge, whom I saw some months after these terrific murders, told me that, for *his* part, though at the time resident in London, he had not shared in the prevailing panic; *him* they affected only as a philosopher, and threw him into a profound reverie upon the tremendous power which is laid open in a moment to any man who can reconcile himself to the abjuration of all conscientious restraints, if at the same time thoroughly without fear. Not sharing in the public panic, however, Coleridge did not consider that panic at all unreasonable; for, as he said most truly, in that vast metropolis there are many thousands of households composed exclusively of women and children; many other thousands there are who necessarily confide their safety, in the long evenings, to the discretion of a young servant girl; and, if she suffers herself to be beguiled by the pretence of a message from her mother, sister, or sweetheart, into opening the door, there, in one second of time, goes to wreck the security of the house. However, at that time, and for many months afterwards, the practice of steadily putting the chain upon the door before it was opened prevailed generally, and for a long time served as a record of that deep impression left upon London by Mr Williams. Southey, I may add, entered deeply into the public feeling on this occasion, and said to me, within a week or two of the first murder, that it was a private event of that order which rose to the dignity of a national event.

Yet, first of all, one word as to the local scene of the murders. Ratcliffe Highway is a public thoroughfare in a most chaotic quarter of eastern or nautical London; and at this time (viz. in 1812), when no adequate police existed except the *detective* police of Bow Street—admirable for its own peculiar purposes, but utterly incommensurate to the general service of the capital—it was a most dangerous quarter. Every third man at the least might be set down as a foreigner. Lascars, Chinese, Moors, Negroes, were met at every step. And, apart from the manifold ruffianism shrouded impenetrably under the mixed hats and turbans of men whose past was untraceable to any European eye, it is well known that the navy (especially, in time of war, the commercial navy) of Christendom is the sure receptacle of all the murderers and ruffians whose crimes have given them a motive for withdrawing themselves for a season from the public eye. It is true that few of this class are qualified to act as 'able' seamen; but at all times, and especially during war, only a small proportion (or nucleus) of each ship's company consists of such men—the large majority being mere untutored landsmen. John Williams, however, who had been occasionally rated as a seaman on board of various Indiamen, &c., was probably a very accomplished seaman. Pretty generally, in fact, he was a ready and adroit man, fertile in resources under all sudden difficulties, and most flexibly adapting himself to all varieties of social life. Williams was a man of middle stature (five feet seven and a half to five feet eight inches high), slenderly built, rather thin, but wiry, tolerably muscular, and clear of all superfluous flesh. A lady who saw him under examination (I think at the Thames Police Office) assured me that his hair was of the most extraordinary and vivid colour—viz. bright yellow, something between an orange and a lemon colour. Williams had been in India; chiefly in Bengal and Madras, but he had also been upon the Indus. Now, it is notorious that in the Punjab horses of a high caste are often painted—crimson, blue, green, purple: and it struck me that Williams might, for some casual purpose of disguise, have taken a hint from this practice of Sind and Lahore, so that the colour might not have been natural. In other respects his appearance was natural enough, and—judging by a plaster cast of him which I purchased in London—I should say mean as regarded his facial structure. One fact, however, was striking, and fell in with the impression of his natural tiger character—that his face wore at all times a bloodless ghastly pallor. 'You might imagine,' said my informant, 'that in his veins circulated not red life-blood, such as could kindle into the blush of shame, of wrath, of pity—but a green sap that welled from no human heart.' His eyes seemed frozen and glazed, as if their light were all converged upon some victim lurking in the far background. So far his appearance might have repelled; but, on the other hand, the concurrent testimony of many witnesses, and also the silent testimony of facts, showed that the oiliness and snaky insinuation of his demeanour counteracted the repulsiveness of his ghastly face, and amongst inexperienced young women won for him a very favourable reception. In particular, one gentle-mannered girl, whom Williams had undoubtedly designed to murder, gave in evidence that once, when sitting alone with her, he had said, 'Now, Miss R., supposing that I should appear about midnight at your bedside armed with a carving knife, what would you say?' To which the confiding girl had replied, 'Oh, Mr Williams, if it was anybody else, I should be frightened. But, as soon as I heard *your* voice, I should be tranquil.' Poor girl; had this outline sketch of Mr Williams been filled in and realized, she would have seen something in the corpselike face, and heard something in the sinister voice, that would have unsettled her tranquillity for ever. But nothing short of such dreadful experiences could avail to unmask Mr John Williams.

Into this perilous region it was that, on a Saturday night in December, Mr Williams, whom we must suppose to have long since made his *coup d'essai*, forced his way through the crowded streets, bound on business. To say was to do. And this night he had said to himself secretly that he would execute a design which he had already sketched, and which, when finished, was destined on the following day to strike consternation into 'all that mighty heart' of London, from centre to circumference. It was afterwards remembered that he had quitted his lodgings on this dark errand about eleven o'clock P.M.: not that he meant to begin so soon; but he needed to reconnoitre. He carried his tools closely buttoned up under his loose roomy coat. It was in harmony with the general subtlety of his character, and his polished hatred of brutality, that by universal agreement his manners were distinguished for exquisite suavity; the tiger's heart was masked by the most insinuating and snaky refinement. All his acquaintances afterwards described his dissimulation as so ready and so perfect that, if, in making his way through the streets, always so crowded on Saturday night in neighbourhoods so poor, he had accidentally jostled any person, he would (as they were all satisfied) have stopped to offer the most gentlemanly apologies: with his devilish heart brooding over the most hellish of purposes, he would yet have paused to express a benign hope that the huge mallet buttoned up under his elegant surtout, with a view to the little business that awaited him about ninety minutes further on, had not inflicted any pain on the stranger with whom he had come into collision. Titian, I believe, but certainly Rubens, and perhaps Vandyke, made it a rule never to practise their art but in full dress—point-ruffles, bag-wig, and diamond-hilted sword; and Mr Williams, there is reason to believe, when he went out for a grand compound massacre (in another sense, one might have applied to it the Oxford phrase of *going out as Grand Compounder*), always assumed black silk stockings and pumps; nor would he on any account have degraded his position as an artist by wearing a morning gown. In his second great performance, it was particularly noticed and recorded, by the one sole trembling man who under killing agonies of fear was compelled (as the reader will find) from a secret stand to become the solitary spectator of his atrocities, that Mr Williams wore a long blue frock, of the very finest cloth, and richly lined with silk. Amongst the anecdotes which circulated about him, it was also said at the time that Mr Williams employed the first of dentists and also the first of chiropodists. On no account would he patronize any second-rate skill. And, beyond a doubt, in that perilous little branch of business which was practised by himself he might be regarded as the most aristocratic and fastidious of artists.

But who meantime was the victim to whose abode he was hurrying? For surely he never could be so indiscreet as to be sailing about on a roving cruise in search of some chance person to murder? Oh no; he had suited himself with a victim some time before, viz. an old and very intimate friend. For he seems to have laid it down as a maxim that the best person to murder was a friend, and, in default of a friend, which is an article one cannot always command, an acquaintance: because, in either case, on first approaching his subject, suspicion would be disarmed, whereas a stranger might take alarm, and find in the very countenance of his murderer elect a warning summons to place himself on guard. However, in the present case, his destined victim was supposed to unite both characters: originally he had been a friend; but subsequently, on good cause arising, he had become an enemy. Or more probably, as others said, the feelings had long since languished which gave life to either relation of friendship or of enmity. Marr was the name of that unhappy man who (whether in the character of friend or enemy) had been selected for the subject of this present Saturday night's performance. And the story current at that time about the connexion between Williams and Marr—having (whether true or not true) never been contradicted upon authority—was that they sailed in the same Indiaman to Calcutta, and that they had quarrelled when at sea. But another version of the story said—No: they had quarrelled after returning from sea; and the subject of their quarrel was Mrs Marr, a very pretty young woman, for whose favour they had been rival candidates, and at one time with most bitter enmity towards each other. Some circumstances give a colour of probability to this story. Otherwise it has sometimes happened, on occasion of a murder not sufficiently accounted for, that, from pure goodness of heart intolerant of a mere sordid motive for a striking murder, some person has forged, and the public has accredited, a story representing the murderer as having moved under some loftier excitement: and in this case the public, too much shocked at the idea of Williams having on the single motive of gain consummated so complex a tragedy, welcomed the tale which represented him as governed by deadly malice, growing out of the more impassioned and noble rivalry for the favour of a woman. The case remains in some degree doubtful; but, certainly, the probability is that Mrs. Marr had been the true cause, the *causa teterrima*, of the feud between the men. Meantime the minutes are numbered, the sands of the hour-glass are running out, that measure the duration of this feud upon earth. This night it shall cease. Tomorrow is the day which in England they call Sunday, which in Scotland they call by the Judaic name of 'Sabbath'. To both nations, under different names, the day has the same functions; to both it is a day of rest. For thee also, Marr, it shall be a day of rest; so is it written; thou, too, young Marr, shalt find rest—thou, and thy household, and the stranger that is within thy gates. But that rest must be in the world which lies beyond the grave. On this side the grave ye have all slept your final sleep.

The night was one of exceeding darkness; and in this humble quarter of London, whatever the night happened to be, light or dark, quiet or stormy, all shops were kept open on Saturday nights until twelve o'clock at the least, and many for half an hour longer. There was no rigorous and pedantic Jewish superstition about the exact limits of Sunday. At the very worst, the Sunday stretched over from one o'clock A.M. of one day up to eight o'clock A.M. of the next, making a clear circuit of thirty-one hours. This, surely, was long enough. Marr, on this particular Saturday night, would be content if it were even shorter, provided it would come more quickly; for he has been toiling through sixteeen hours behind his counter. Marr's position in life was this—He kept a little hosier's shop, and had invested in his stock and the fittings of his shop about £180. Like all men engaged in trade, he suffered some anxieties. He was a new beginner; but already bad debts had alarmed him, and bills were coming to maturity that were not likely to be met by commensurate sales. Yet, constitutionally, he was a sanguine hoper. At this time he was a stout, fresh-coloured young man of twenty-seven; in some slight degree uneasy from his commercial prospects; but still cheerful, and anticipating—(how vainly!)—that for this night, and the next night, at least, he will rest his wearied head and his cares upon the faithful bosom of his sweet, lovely young wife. The household of Marr, consisting for five persons, is as follows: First, there is himself, who, if he should happen to be ruined in a limited commercial sense, has energy enough to jump up again, like a pyramid of fire, and soar high above ruin many times repeated. Yes, poor Marr, so it might be if thou wert left to thy native energies unmolested; but even now there stands on the other side of the street one born of hell who puts his peremptory negative on all these flattering prospects. Second in the list of this household stands his pretty and amiable wife; who is happy after the fashion of youthful wives, for she is only twenty-two, and anxious (if at all) only on account of her darling infant. For, thirdly, there is in a cradle, not quite nine feet below the street, viz. in a warm, cosy kitchen, and rocked at intervals by the young mother, a baby eight months old. Nineteen months have Marr and herself been married;

and this is their first-born child. Grieve not for this child, that it must keep the deep rest of Sunday in some other world; for wherefore should an orphan, steeped to the lips in poverty when once bereaved of father and mother, linger upon an alien and a murderous earth? Fourthly, there is a stoutish boy, an apprentice, say thirteen years old, a Devonshire boy, with handsome features, such as most Devon-shire youths have;[1] satisfied with his place; not overworked; treated kindly, and aware that he was treated kindly, by his master and mistress. Fifthly, and lastly, bringing up the rear of this quiet house-hold, is a servant girl, a grown-up young woman; and she, being particularly kind-hearted, occupied (as often happens in families of humbles pretensions as to rank) a sort of sisterly place in her relation to her mistress. Mary, the female servant, felt a sincere and unaffected respect for a mistress whom she saw so steadily occupied with her domestic duties, and who, though so young, and invested with some slight authority, never exerted it capriciously, or even showed it all conspicuously. According to the testimony of all the neighbours, she treated her mistress with a shade of unobtrusive respect on the one hand, and yet was eager to relieve her, whenever that was possible, from the weight of her maternal duties, with the cheerful voluntary service of a sister.

To this young woman it was that, suddenly, within three or four minutes of midnight, Marr called aloud from the head of the stairs—directing her to go out and purchase some oysters for the family supper. Upon what slender accidents hang oftentimes solemn life-long results! Marr, occupied in the concerns of his shop, Mrs Marr, occupied with some little ailment and restlessness of her baby, had both forgotten the affair of supper; the time was now narrowing every moment as regarded any variety of choice; and oysters were perhaps ordered as the likeliest article to be had at all after twelve o'clock should have struck. And yet upon this trivial circumstance depended Mary's life. Had she been sent abroad for supper at the ordinary time of ten or eleven o'clock, it is almost certain that she, the solitary member of the household who escaped from the exterminating tragedy, would *not* have escaped; too surely she would have shared the general fate. It had now become necessary to be quick. Hastily, therefore, receiving money from Marr, with a basket in her hand, but unbonneted, Mary tripped out of the shop. It became afterwards, on recollection, a heart-chilling remembrance to herself that, precisely

---

[1] An artist told me in this year, 1812, that, having accidentally seen a native Devon-shire regiment (either volunteers or militia), nine hundred strong, marching past a station at which he had posted himself, he did not observe a dozen men that would not have been described in common parlance as 'good-looking.'

as she emerged from the shop-door, she noticed, on the opposite side of the street, by the light of the lamps, a man's figure; stationary at the instant, but in the next instant slowly moving. This was Williams, as a little incident, either just before or just after (at present it is impossible to say which), sufficiently proved. Now, when one considers the inevitable hurry and trepidation of Mary under the circumstances stated, time barely sufficing for any chance of executing her errand, it becomes evident that she must have connected some deep feeling of mysterious uneasiness with the movements of this unknown man; else, assuredly, she would not have found her attention disposable for such a case. Thus far she herself threw some little light upon what it might be that, semi-consciously, was then passing through her mind: she said that, notwithstanding the darkness, which would not permit her to trace the man's features, or to ascertain the exact direction of his eyes, it yet struck her that, from his carriage when in motion, and from the apparent inclination of his person, he must be looking at No. 29. The little incident which I have alluded to as confirming Mary's belief was that, at some period not very far from midnight, the watchman had specially noticed this stranger; he had observed him continually peeping into the window of Marr's shop, and had thought this act, connected with the man's appearance, so suspicious that he stepped into Marr's shop and communicated what he had seen. This fact he afterwards stated before the magistrates; and he added that subsequently, viz. a few minutes after twelve (eight or ten minutes, probably, after the departure of Mary), he (the watchman), when re-entering upon his ordinary half-hourly beat, was requested by Marr to assist him in closing the shutters. Here they had a final communication with each other; and the watchman mentioned to Marr that the mysterious stranger had now apparently taken himself off; for that he had not been visible since the first communication made to Marr by the watchman. There is little doubt that Williams had observed the watchman's visit to Marr, and had thus had his attention seasonably drawn to the indiscretion of his own demeanour; so that the warning, given unavailingly to Marr, had been turned to account by Williams. There can be still less doubt that the bloodhound had commenced his work within one minute of the watchman's assisting Marr to put up his shutters; and on the following consideration: That which prevented Williams from commencing even earlier was the exposure of the shop's whole interior to the gaze of street passengers. It was indispensable that the shutters should be accurately closed before Williams could safely get to work. But, as soon as ever this preliminary precaution had been completed, once having secured that concealment from the public eye, it then became of still greater importance not to lose a moment by delay than previously it had been not to hazard anything by precipitance. For all depended upon going in before Marr should have locked the door. On any other mode of effecting an entrance (as, for instance, by waiting for the return of Mary, and making his entrance simultaneously with her) it will be seen that Williams must have forfeited that particular advantage which mute facts, when read into their true construction, will soon show the reader that he must have employed. Williams waited, of necessity, for the sound of the watchman's retreating steps; waited, perhaps, for thirty seconds; but, when that danger was past, the next danger was lest Marr should lock the door: one turn of the key, and the murderer would have been locked out. In, therefore, he bolted, and by a dexterous movement of his left hand, no doubt, turned the key, without letting Marr perceive this fatal stratagem. It is really wonderful and most interesting to pursue the successive steps of this monster, and to notice the absolute certainty with which the silent hieroglyphics of the case betray to us the whole process and movements of the bloody drama, not less surely and fully than if we had been ourselves hidden in Marr's shop, or had looked down from the heavens of mercy upon this hell-kite that knew not what mercy meant. That he had concealed from Marr his trick, secret and rapid, upon the lock, is evident; because else Marr would instantly have taken the alarm, especially after what the watchman had communicated. But it will soon be seen that Marr had *not* been alarmed, In reality, towards the full success of Williams it was important, in the last degree, to intercept and forestall any yell or shout of agony from Marr. Such an outcry, and in a situation so slenderly fenced off from the street, viz. by walls the very thinnest, makes itself heard outside pretty nearly as well as if it were uttered in the street. Such an outcry it was indispensable to stifle. It *was* stifled; and the reader will soon understand *how*. Meantime, at this point, let us leave the murderer alone with his victims. For fifty minutes let him work his pleasure. The front-door, as we know, is now fastened against all help. Help there is none. Let us, therefore, in vision, attach ourselves to Mary; and, when all is over, let us come back with *her*, again raise the curtain, and read the dreadful record of all that has passed in her absence.

The poor girl, uneasy in her mind to an extent that she could but half understand, roamed up and down in search of an oyster shop; and, finding none that was still open within any circuit that her ordinary experience had made her acquainted with, she fancied it best to try the chances of some remoter district. Lights she saw gleaming or twinkling at a distance, that still tempted her onwards; and thus, amongst unknown streets poorly lighted,[1] and on a night of peculiar darkness, and in a region of London where ferocious tumults were continually turning her out of what seemed to be the direct course, naturally she got bewildered. The purpose with which she started had by this time become hopeless. Nothing remained for her now but to retrace her steps. But this was difficult; for she was afraid to ask directions from chance passengers whose appearance the darkness prevented her from reconnoitring. At length by his lantern she recognized a watchman; through him she was guided into the right road; and in ten minutes more she found herself back at the door of No. 29, in Ratcliffe Highway. But by this time she felt satisfied that she must have been absent for fifty or sixty minutes; indeed, she had heard, at a distance, the cry of *past one o'clock*, which, commencing a few seconds after one, lasted intermittently for ten or thirteen minutes.

In the tumult of agonizing thoughts that very soon surprised her, naturally it became hard for her to recall distinctly the whole succession of doubts, and jealousies, and shadowy misgivings that soon opened upon her. But, so far as could be collected, she had not in the first moment of reaching home noticed anything decisively alarming. In very many cities bells are the main instruments for communicating between the street and the interior of houses; but in London knockers prevail. At Marr's there was both a knocker and a bell. Mary rang, and at the same time very gently knocked. She had no fear of disturbing her master or mistress; *them* she made sure of finding still up. Her anxiety was for the baby, who, being disturbed, might again rob her mistress of a night's rest. And she well knew that, with three people all anxiously awaiting her return, and by this time, perhaps, seriously uneasy at her delay, the least audible whisper from herself would in a moment bring one of them to the door. Yet how is this? To her astonishment—but with the astonishment came creeping over her an icy horror—no stir nor murmur was heard ascending from the kitchen. At this moment came back upon her, with shuddering anguish, the indistinct image of the stranger in the loose dark coat whom she had seen stealing along under the shadowy lamp-light, and too certainly watching her master's motions: keenly she now reproached herself that, under whatever stress of hurry, she had not acquainted Mr Marr with the suspicious appearances. Poor girl! she did not then know that, if this communication could have

---

[1] I do not remember, chronologically, the history of gaslights. But in London, long after Mr Winsor [a German] had shown the value of gas-lighting, and its applicability to street purposes, various districts were prevented, for many years, from resorting to the new system, in consequence of old contracts with oil-dealers, subsisting through long terms of years.

availed to put Marr upon his guard, it had reached him from another quarter; so that her own omission, which had in reality arisen under her hurry to execute her master's commission, could not be charged with any bad consequences. But all such reflections this way or that were swallowed up at this point in overmastering panic. That her double summons *could* have been unnoticed—this solitary fact in one moment made a revelation of horror. One person might have fallen asleep, but two—but three—*that* was a mere impossibility. And, even supposing all three together with the baby locked in sleep, still how unaccountable was this utter—utter silence! Most naturally at this moment something like hysterical horror overshadowed the poor girl, and now at last she rang the bell with the violence that belongs to sickening terror. This done, she paused; self-command enough she still retained, though fast and fast it was slipping away from her, to bethink herself that, if any overwhelming accident *had* compelled both Marr and his apprentice-boy to leave the house in order to summon surgical aid from opposite quarters—a thing barely supposable—still, even in that case Mrs Marr and her infant would be left, and some murmuring reply, under any extremity, would be elicited from the poor mother. To pause, therefore, to impose stern silence upon herself, so as to leave room for the possible answer to this final appeal, became a duty of spasmodic effort. Listen, therefore, poor trembling heart; listen, and for twenty seconds be still as death! Still as death she was; and during that dreadful stillness, when she hushed her breath that she might listen, occurred an incident of killing fear, that to her dying day would never cease to renew its echoes in her ear. She, Mary, the poor trembling girl, checking and overruling herself by a final effort, that she might leave full opening for her dear young mistress's answer to her own last frantic appeal, heard at last and most distinctly a sound within the house. Yes, now beyond a doubt there is coming an answer to her summons. What was it? On the stairs—not the stairs that led downwards to the kitchen, but the stairs that led upwards to the single storey of bedchambers above—was heard a creaking sound. Next was heard most distinctly a footfall: one, two, three, four, five stairs were slowly and distinctly descended. Then the dreadful footsteps were heard advancing along the little narrow passage to the door. The steps—oh heavens! *whose* steps?—have paused at the door. The very breathing can be heard of that dreadful being who has silenced all breathing except his own in the house. There is but a door between him and Mary. What is he doing on the other side of the door? A cautious step, a stealthy step it was that came down the stairs, then paced along the little narrow passage—narrow as a coffin—till at last the step pauses at the door. How hard the fellow breathes! He, the solitary murderer, is on one side the door; Mary is on the other side. Now, suppose that he should suddenly open the door, and that incautiously in the dark Mary should rush in, and find herself in the arms of the murderer. Thus far the case is a possible one—that to a certainty, had this little trick been tried immediately upon Mary's return, it would have succeeded: had the door been opened suddenly upon her first tingle-tingle, headlong she would have tumbled in, and perished. But now Mary is upon her guard. The unknown murderer and she have both their lips upon the door, listening, breathing hard; but luckily they are on different sides of the door; and upon the least indication of unlocking or unlatching she would have recoiled into the asylum of general darkness.

What was the murderer's meaning in coming along the passage to the front-door? The meaning was this: separately, as an individual. Mary was worth nothing at all to him. But, considered as a member of a household, she had this value, viz. that she, if caught and murdered, perfected and rounded the desolation of the house. The case being reported, as reported it would be all over Christendom, led the imagination captive. The whole covey of victims was thus netted: the household ruin was thus full and orbicular; and in that proportion the tendency of men and women, flutter as they might, would be helplessly and hopelessly to sink into the all-conquering hands of the mighty murdered. He had but to say 'My testimonials are dated from No. 29 Ratcliffe Highway,' and the poor vanquished imagination sank powerless before the fascinating rattlesnake eye of the murderer. There is not a doubt that the motive of the murderer for standing on the inner side of Marr's front-door whilst Mary stood on the outside was a hope that, if he quietly opened the door, whisperingly counterfeiting Marr's voice, and saying, What made you stay so long? possibly she might have been inveigled. He was wrong; the time was past for that; Mary was now maniacally awake; she began now to ring the bell and to ply the knocker with unintermitting violence. And the natural consequence was that the next-door neighbour, who has recently gone to bed and instantly fallen asleep, was roused; and by the incessant violence of the ringing and the knocking, which now obeyed a delirious and uncontrollable impulse in Mary, he became sensible that some very dreadful event must be at the root of so clamorous an uproar. To rise, to throw up the sash, to demand angrily the cause of this unseasonable tumult, was the work of a moment. The poor girl remained sufficiently mistress of herself rapidly to explain the circumstance of her own absence for an hour, her belief that Mr and Mrs Marr's family had all been murdered in the interval, and that at this very moment the murderer was in the house.

The person to whom she addressed this statement was a pawn-broker; and a thoroughly brave man he must have been; for it was a perilous undertaking, merely as a trial of physical strength, singly to face a mysterious assassin, who had apparently signalized his prowess by a triumph so comprehensive. But, again, for the imagination it required an effort of self-conquest to rush headlong into the presence of one invested with a cloud of mystery, whose nation, age, motives, were all alike unknown. Rarely on any field of battle has a soldier been called upon to face so complex a danger. For, if the entire family of his neighbour Marr had been exterminated—were this indeed true—such a scale of bloodshed would seem to argue that there must have been two persons as the perpetrators; or, if one singly had accomplished such a ruin, in that case how colossal must have been his audacity! probably, also, his skill and animal power! More-over, the unknown enemy (whether single or double) would, doubt-less, be elaborately armed. Yet, under all these disadvantages, did this fearless man rush at once to the field of butchery in his neighbour's house. Waiting only to draw on his trousers, and to arm himself with the kitchen poker, he went down into his own little back-yard. On this mode of approach, he would have a chance of intercepting the murderer; whereas from the front there would be no such chance, and there would also be considerable delay in the process of breaking open the door. A brick wall, 9 or 10 feet high, divided his own back premises from those of Marr. Over this he vaulted; and, at the moment when he was recalling himself to the necessity of going back for a candle, he suddenly perceived a feeble ray of light already glimmering on some part of Marr's premises. Marr's back-door stood wide open. Probably the murderer had passed through it one half-minute before. Rapidly the brave man passed onwards to the shop, and there beheld the carnage of the night stretched out on the floor, and the narrow premises so floated with gore that it was hardly possible to escape the pollution of blood in picking out a path to the front-door. In the lock of the door still remained the key which had given to the unknown murderer so fatal an advantage over his victims. By this time the heart-shaking news involved in the outcries of Mary (to whom it occurred that by possibility some one out of so many victims might still be within the reach of medical aid, but that all would depend upon speed) had availed, even at that late hour, to gather a small mob about the house. The pawnbroker threw open the door. One or two watchmen headed the crowd; but the soul-harrowing spectacle checked them, and impressed sudden silence upon their voices, previously so loud. The tragic drama read aloud its own history, and the succession of its several steps—few and summary. The murderer was as yet altogether unknown; not even suspected. But there were reasons for thinking that he must have been a person familiarly known to Marr. He had entered the shop by opening the door after it had been closed by Marr. But it was justly argued that, after the caution conveyed to Marr by the watchman, the appearance of any stranger in the shop at that hour, and in so dangerous a neighbourhood, and entering by so irregular and suspicious a course (*i.e.* walking in after the door had been closed, and after the closing of the shutters had cut off all open communication with the street), would naturally have roused Marr to an attitude of vigilance and self-defence. Any indication, therefore, that Marr had *not* been so roused would argue to a certainty that *something* had occurred to neutralize this alarm, and fatally to disarm the prudent jealousies of Marr. But this 'something' could only have lain in one simple fact, viz. that the person of the murderer was familiarly known to Marr as that of an ordinary and unsuspected acquaintance.

This being presupposed as the key to all the rest, the whole course and evolution of the subsequent drama becomes clear as daylight: The murderer, it is evident, had opened gently, and again closed behind him with equal gentleness, the street-door. He had then advanced to the little counter, all the while exchanging the ordinary salutation of an old acquaintance with the unsuspecting Marr. Having reached the counter, he would then ask Marr for a pair of unbleached cotton socks. In a shop so small as Marr's there could be no great latitude of choice for disposing of the different commodities. The arrangement of these had no doubt become familiar to the murderer; and he had already ascertained that, in order to reach down the particular parcel wanted at present, Marr would find it requisite to face round to the rear, and at the same moment to raise his eyes and his hands to a level eighteeen inches above his own head. This movement placed him in the most disadvantageous possible position with regard to the murderer; who now, at the instant when Marr's hands and eyes were embarrassed, and the back of his head fully exposed, suddenly from below his large surtout had unslung a heavy ship-carpenter's mallet, and with one solitary blow had so thoroughly stunned his victim as to leave him incapable of resistance. The whole position of Marr told its own tale. He had collapsed naturally behind the counter, with his hands so occupied as to confirm the whole outline of the affair as I have here suggested it. Probable enough it is that the very first blow, the first indication of treachery that reached Marr, would also be the last blow as regarded the abolition of consciousness. The murderer's plan and *rationale* of murder started systematically from this infliction of apoplexy, or at least of a stunning sufficient to insure a long loss of consciousness. This opening step placed the murderer at his ease. But still, as returning sense might constantly have led to the fullest exposures, it was his settled practice, by way of consummation, to cut the throat. To one invariable type all the murders on this occasion conformed: the skull was first shattered; this step secured the murderer from instant retaliation; and then, by way of locking up all into eternal silence, uniformly the throat was cut. The rest of the circumstances, as self-revealed, were these: The fall of Marr might, probably enough, cause a dull confused sound of a scuffle, and the more so as it could not now be confounded with any street uproar—the shop-door being shut. It is more probable, however, that the signal for the alarm passing down to the kitchen would arise when the murderer proceeded to cut Marr's throat. The very confined situation behind the counter would render it impossible, under the critical hurry of the case, to expose the throat broadly; the horrid scene would proceed by partial and interrupted cuts; deep groans would arise; and then would come the rush upstairs. Against this, as the only dangerous stage in the transaction, the murderer would have specially prepared. Mrs Marr and the apprentice-boy, both young and active, would make, of course, for the street-door; had Mary been at home, and three persons at once had combined to distract the purposes of the murderer, it is barely possible that one of them would have succeeded in reaching the street. But the dreadful swing of the heavy mallet intercepted both the boy and his mistress before they could reach the door. Each of them lay stretched out on the centre of the shop floor; and the very moment that this disabling was accomplished the accursed hound was down upon their throats with his razor. The fact is that, in the mere blindness of pity for poor Marr on hearing his groans, Mrs Marr had lost sight of her obvious policy: she and the boy ought to have made for the back-door; the alarm would thus have been given in the open air; which, of itself, was a great point; and several means of distracting the murderer's attention offered upon that course which the extreme limitation of the shop denied to them upon the other.

Vain would be all attempts to convey the horror which thrilled the gathering spectators of this piteous tragedy. It was known to the crowd that one person had, by some accident, escaped the general massacre; but she was now speechless, and probably delirious; so that, in compassion for her pitiable situation, one female neighbour had carried her away, and put her to bed. Hence it had happened, for a longer space of time than could else have been possible, that no person present was sufficiently acquainted with the Marrs to be aware of the little infant; for the bold pawnbroker had gone off to make a communication to the coroner, and another neighbour to lodge some evidence which he thought urgent at a neighbouring police-office. Suddenly some person appeared amongst the crowd who was aware that the murdered parents had a young infant; this would be found either below-stairs, or in one of the bedrooms above. Immediately a stream of people poured down into the kitchen, where at once they saw the cradle—but with the bedclothes in a state of indescribable confusion. On disentangling these, pools of blood became visible; and the next ominous sign was that the hood of the cradle had been smashed to pieces. It became evident that the wretch had found himself doubly embarrassed—first, by the arched hood at the head of the cradle, which accordingly he had beat into a ruin with his mallet, and, secondly, by the gathering of the blankets and pillows about the baby's head. The free play of his blows had thus been baffled. And he had therefore finished the scene by applying his razor to the throat of the little innocent; after which, with no apparent purpose, as though he had become confused by the spectacle of his own atrocities, he had busied himself in piling the clothes elaborately over the child's corpse. This incident undeniably gave the character of a vindictive proceeding to the whole affair, and so far confirmed the current rumour that the quarrel between Williams and Marr had originated in rivalship. One writer, indeed, alleged that the murderer might have found it necessary for his own safety to extinguish the crying of the child; but it was justly replied that a child only eight months old could not have cried under any sense of the tragedy proceeding, but simply in its ordinary way for the absence of its mother; and such a cry, even if audible at all out of the house, must have been precisely what the neighbours were hearing constantly, so that it could have drawn no special attention, nor suggested any reasonable alarm to the murderer. No one incident, indeed, throughout the whole tissue of atrocities, so much envenomed the popular fury against the unknown ruffian as this useless butchery of the infant.

Naturally, on the Sunday morning that dawned four or five hours later, the case was too full of horror not to diffuse itself in all directions; but I have no reason to think that it crept into any one of the numerous Sunday papers. In the regular course, any ordinary occurrence, not occurring or not transpiring until 15 minutes after 1 A.M. on a Sunday morning, would first reach the public ear through the Monday editions of the Sunday papers, and the regular morning papers of the Monday. But, if such were the course pursued on this occasion, never can there have been a more signal oversight. For it is certain that to have met the public demand for details on the Sunday, which might so easily have been done by cancilling a couple of dull columns, and substituting a circumstantial narrative, for which the pawnbroker and the watchman could have furnished the materials, would have made a small fortune. By proper handbills dispersed through all quarters of the infinite metropolis, 250,000 extra copies might have been sold—that is, by any journal that should have collected *exclusive* materials, meeting the public excitement, everywhere stirred to the centre by flying rumours, and everywhere burning for ampler information. On the Sunday se'ennight (Sunday the *octave* from the event) took place the funeral of the Marrs: in the first coffin was placed Marr, in the second Mrs Marr, and the baby in her arms; in the third the apprentice-boy. They were buried side by side; and 30,000 labouring people followed the funeral procession, with horror and grief written in their countenances.

As yet no whisper was astir that indicated, even conjecturally, the hideous author of those ruins—this patron of gravediggers. Had as much been known on this Sunday of the funeral concerning that person as became known universally six days later, the people would have gone right from the churchyard to the murderer's lodgings, and (brooking no delay) would have torn him limb from limb. As yet, however, in mere default of any object on whom reasonable suspicion could settle, the public wrath was compelled to suspend itself. Else, far indeed from showing any tendency to subside, the public emotion strengthened every day conspicuously, as the reverberation of the shock began to travel back from the provinces to the capital. On every great road in the kingdom continual arrests were made of vagrants and 'trampers' who could give no satisfactory account of themselves, or whose appearance in any respect answered to the imperfect description of Williams furnished by the watchman.

With this mighty tide of pity and indignation pointing backwards to the dreadful past there mingled also in the thoughts of reflecting persons an under-current of fearful expectation for the immediate future. 'The earthquake,' to quote a fragment from a striking passage in Wordsworth—

The earthquake is not satisfied at once.

All perils, specially malignant, are recurrent. A murderer who is such by passion and by a wolfish craving for bloodshed as a mode of unnatural luxury cannot relapse into *inertia*. Such a man, even more than the Alpine chamois-hunter, comes to crave the dangers and the hairbreadth escapes of his trade, as a condiment for seasoning the insipid monotonies of daily life. But, apart from the hellish instincts that might too surely be relied on for renewed attrocities, it was clear that the murderer of the Marrs, wheresoever lurking, must be a needy man, and a needy man of that class least likely to seek or to find resources in honourable modes of industry; for which, equally by haughty disgust and by disuse of the appropriate habits, men of violence are specially disqualified. Were it, therefore, merely for a livelihood, the murderer, whom all hearts were yearning to decipher, might be expected to make his resurrection on some stage of horror, after a reasonable interval. Even in the Marr murder, granting that it had been governed chiefly by cruel and vindictive impulses, it was still clear that the desire of booty had co-operated with such feelings. Equally clear it was that this desire must have been disappointed: excepting the trivial sum reserved by Marr for the week's expenditures, the murderer found, doubtless, little or nothing that he could turn to account. Two guineas, perhaps, would be the outside of what he had obtained in the way of booty. A week or so would see the end of that. The conviction, therefore, of all people was that in a month or two, when the fever of excitement might a little have cooled down, or have been superseded by other topics of fresher interest, so that the new-born vigilance of household life would have had time to relax, some new murder, equally appalling, might be counted upon.

Such was the public expectation. Let the reader then figure to himself the pure frenzy of horror when in this hush of expectation, looking, indeed, and waiting for the unknown arm to strike once more, but not believing that any audacity could be equal to such an attempt as yet—whilst all eyes were watching—suddenly, on the twelfth night from the Marr murder, a second case of the same mysterious nature, a murder on the same exterminating plan, was perpetrated in the very same neighourhood. It was on the Thursday next but one succeeding to the Marr murder that this second atrocity took place; and many people thought at the time that in its dramatic features of thrilling interest this second case even went beyond the first. The family which suffered in this instance was that of a Mr Williamson: and the house was situated, if not absolutely in Ratcliffe Highway, at any rate immediately round the corner of some secondary street, running at right angles to this public thoroughfare. Mr Williamson was a well-known and respectable man, long settled in that district; he was supposed to be rich; and, more with a view to the employment furnished by such a calling than with much anxiety for further accumulations, he kept a sort of tavern which, in this respect, might be considered on an old patriarchal footing—that, although people of considerable property resorted to the house in the evenings, no kind of anxious separation was maintained between them and the other visitors from the class of artisans or common labourers. Anybody who conducted himself with propriety was free to take a seat and call for any liquor that he might prefer. And thus the society was pretty miscellaneous; in part stationary, but in some proportion fluctuating. The household consisted of the following five persons: 1, Mr Williamson, its head, who was an old man above seventy, and was well fitted for his situation, being civil, and not at all morose, but at the same time firm in maintaining order; 2, Mrs Williamson, his wife, about ten years younger than himself; 3, a little granddaughter, about nine years old; 4, a housemaid, who was nearly forty years old; 5, a young journeyman, aged about twenty-six, belonging to some manufacturing establishment (of what class I have forgotten; neither do I remember of what nation he was). It was the established rule at Mr Williamson's that exactly as the clock struck eleven all the company, without favour or exception, moved off. That was one of the customs by which, in so stormy a district, Mr Williamson had found it possible to keep his house free from brawls. On the present Thursday night everything had gone on as usual, except for one slight shadow of suspicion, which had caught the attention of more persons than one. Perhaps at a less agitating time it would hardly have been noticed; but now, when the first question and the last in all social meetings turned upon the Marrs and their unknown murderer, it was a circumstance naturally fitted to cause some uneasiness that a stranger, of sinister appearance, in a wide surtout, had flitted in and out of the room at intervals during the evening, had sometimes retired from the light into obscure corners, and by more than one person had been observed stealing into the private passages of the house. It was presumed in general that the man must be known to Williamson. And, in some slight degree, as an occasional customer of the house, it is not impossible that he *was*. But afterwards this repulsive stranger, with his cadaverous ghastliness, extraordinary hair, and glazed eyes, showing himself intermittingly through the hours from 8 to 11 P.M., revolved upon the memory of all who had steadily observed him with something of the same freezing effect as belongs to the two assassins in *Macbeth* who present themselves reeking from the murder of Banquo, and gleaming dimly, with dreadful faces, from the misty background, athwart the pomps of the regal banquet.

Meantime the clock struck eleven; the company broke up; the door of entrance was nearly closed; and at this moment of general dispersion the situation of the five inmates left upon the premises was precisely this: The three elders, viz. Williamson, his wife, and his female servant, were all occupied on the ground-floor. Williamson himself was drawing ale, porter, &c., for those neighbours in whose favour the house-door had been left ajar until the hour of twelve should strike; Mrs Williamson and her servant were moving to and fro between the back-kitchen and a little parlour; the little grand-daughter, whose sleeping-room was on the *first* floor (which term in London means always the floor raised by one flight of stairs above the level of the street), had been fast asleep since nine o'clock; lastly, the journeyman artisan had retired to rest for some time. He was a regular lodger in the house; and his bedroom was on the second floor. For some time he had been undressed, and had lain down in bed. Being, as a working man, bound to habits of early rising, he was naturally anxious to fall asleep as soon as possible. But, on this particular night, his uneasiness, arising from the recent murders at No. 29, rose to a paroxysm of nervous excitement which kept him awake. It is possible that from somebody he had heard of the suspicious-looking stranger or might even personally have observed him slinking about. But, were it otherwise, he was aware of several circumstances dangerously affecting this house: for instance, the ruffianism of this whole neighbourhood, and the disagreeable fact that the Marrs had lived within a few doors of this very house, which again argued that the murderer also lived at no great distance. These were matters of *general* alarm. But there were others peculiar to this house: in particular, the notoriety of Williamson's opulence—the belief, whether well or ill founded, that he accumulated in desks and drawers the money continually flowing into his hands; and, lastly, the danger so ostentatiously courted by that habit of leaving the house-door ajar through one entire hour—and that hour loaded with extra danger by the well-advertised assurance that no collision need be feared with chance convivial visitors, since all such people were banished at eleven. A regulation which had hitherto operated beneficially for the character and comfort of the house now, on the contrary, under altered circumstances, became a positive proclamation of exposure and defencelessness through one entire period of an hour. Williamson himself, it was said generally, being a large unwieldly man, past seventy, and signally inactive, ought, in prudence, to make the locking of his door coincident with the dismissal of his evening party.

Upon these and other grounds of alarm (particularly this, that Mrs Williamson was reported to possess a considerable quantity of plate), the journeyman was musing painfully, and the time might be within twenty-eight or twenty-five minutes of twelve, when all at once, with a crash, proclaiming some hand of hideous violence, the house-door was suddenly shut and locked. Here, then, beyond all doubt, was the diabolic man, clothed in mystery, from No. 29 Ratcliffe

Highway. Yes, that dreadful being, who for twelve days had employed all thoughts and all tongues, was now, too certainly, in this defenceless house, and would, in a few minutes, be face to face with every one of its inmates. A question still lingered in the public mind—whether at Marr's there might not have been *two* men at work. If so, there would be two at present; and one of the two would be immediately disposable for the upstairs work; since no danger could obviously be more immediately fatal to such an attack than any alarm given from an upper window to the passengers in the street. Through one half-minute the poor panic-stricken man sat up motionless in bed. But then he rose, his first movement being towards the door of his room. Not for any purpose of securing it against intrusion—too well he knew that there was no fastening of any sort—neither lock nor bolt; nor was there any such moveable furniture in the room as might have availed to barricade the door, even if time could be counted on for such an attempt. It was no effect of prudence, merely the fascination of killing fear it was, that drove him to open the door. One step brought him to the head of the stairs; he lowered his head over the balustrade in order to listen; and at that moment ascended from the little parlour this agonizing cry from the woman-servant, 'Lord Jesus Christ! we shall all be murdered!' What a Medusa's head must have lurked in those dreadful bloodless features, and those glazed rigid eyes, that seemed rightfully belonging to a corpse, when one glance at them sufficed to proclaim a death-warrant.

Three separate death-struggles were by this time over; and the poor petrified journeyman, quite unconscious of what he was doing, in blind, passive, self-surrender to panic, absolutely descended both flights of stairs. Infinite terror inspired him with the same impulse as might have been inspired by headlong courage. In his shirt, and upon old decaying stairs, that at times creaked under his feet, he continued to descend, until he had reached the lowest step but four. The situation was tremendous beyond any that is on record. A sneeze, a cough, almost a breathing, and the young man would be a corpse, without a chance or a struggle for his life. The murderer was at that time in the little parlour—the door of which parlour faced you in descending the stairs; and this door stood ajar; indeed, much more considerably open than what is understood by the term 'ajar'. Of that quadrant, or 90 degrees, which the door would describe in swinging so far open as to stand at right angles to the lobby, or to itself in a closed position, 55 degrees at the least were exposed. Consequently, two out of three corpses were exposed to the young man's gaze. Where was the third? And the murderer—where was he? As to the murderer, he was walking rapidly backwards and forwards in the parlour, audible but not visible at first, being engaged with something or other in that part of the room which the door still concealed. What the something might be the sound soon explained; he was applying keys tentatively to a cupboard, a closet, and a scrutoire, in the hidden part of the room. Very soon, however, he came into view; but, fortunately for the young man, at this critical moment the murderer's purpose too entirely absorbed him to allow of his throwing a glance to the staircase, on which else the white figure of the journeyman, standing in motionless horror, would have been detected in one instant, and seasoned for the grave in the second. As to the third corpse, the missing corpse, viz. Mr Williamson's, *that* is in the cellar; and how its local position can be accounted for remains as a separate question, much discussed at the time, but never satisfactorily cleared up.

Meantime, that Williamson was dead became evident to the young man; since else he would have been heard stirring or groaning. Three friends, therefore, out of four whom the young man had parted with forty minutes ago, were now extinguished; remained, therefore, 40 per cent (a large percentage for Williams to leave); remained, in fact, himself and his pretty young friend, the little grand-daughter, whose childish innocence was still slumbering, without fear for herself, or grief for her aged grand-parents. If *they* are gone for ever, happily one friend (for such he will prove himself indeed, if from such a danger he can save this child) is pretty near to her. But alas! he is still nearer to a murderer. At this moment he is unnerved for any exertion whatever; he has changed into a pillar of ice; for the objects before him, separated by just thirteen feet, are these: The housemaid had been caught by the murderer on her knees; she was kneeling before the fire-grate, which she had been polishing with black lead. That part of her task was finished; and she had passed on to another task—viz. the filling of the grate with wood and coals, not for kindling at this moment, but so as to have it ready for kindling on the next day. The appearances all showed that she must have been engaged in this labour at the very moment when the murderer entered; and perhaps the succession of the incidents arranged itself as follows: From the awful ejaculation and loud outcry to Christ, as overheard by the journeyman, it was clear that then first she had been alarmed; yet this was at least one and a half or even two minutes after the door-slamming. Consequently the alarm which had so fearfully and seasonably alarmed the young man must, in some unaccountable way, have been misinterpreted by the two women. It was said, at the time, that Mrs Williamson laboured under some dullness of hearing; and it was conjectured that the servant, having her ears filled with the noise of her own scrubbing, and her head half under the grate, might have confounded it with the street noises, or else might have imputed this violent closure to some mischievous boys. But, howsoever explained, the fact was evident that, until the words of appeal to Christ, the servant had noticed nothing suspicious, nothing which interrupted her labours. If so, it followed that neither had Mrs Williamson noticed anything; for, in that case, she would have communicated her own alarm to the servant, since both were in the same small room. Apparently the course of things after the murderer had entered the room was this: Mrs Williamson had probably not seen him, from the accident of standing with her back to the door. Her, therefore, before he was himself observed at all, he had stunned and prostrated by a shattering blow on the back of her head; this blow, inflicted by a crow-bar, had smashed in the hinder part of the skull. She fell; and by the noise of her fall (for all was the work of a moment) had first roused the attention of the servant, who then uttered the cry which had reached the young man; but before she could repeat it the murderer had descended with his uplifted instrument upon *her* head, crushing the skull inwards upon the brain. Both the women were irrecoverably destroyed, so that further outrages were needless; and, moreover, the murderer was conscious of the imminent danger from delay; and yet, in spite of his hurry, so fully did he appreciate the fatal consequences to himself, if any of his victims should so far revive into consciousness as to make circumstantial deposition, that, by way of making this impossible, he had proceeded instantly to cut the throats of each. All this tallied with the appearances as now presenting themselves. Mrs Williamson had fallen backwards with her head to the door; the servant, from her kneeling posture, had been incapable of rising, and had presented her head passively to blows; after which, the miscreant had but to bend her head backwards so as to expose her throat, and the murder was finished. It is remarkable that the young artisan, paralysed as he had been by fear, and evidently fascinated for a time so as to walk right towards the lion's mouth, yet found himself able to notice everything important.

The reader must suppose him at this point watching the murderer whilst hanging over the body of Mrs Williamson, and whilst renewing his search for certain important keys. Doubtless it was an anxious situation for the murderer; for, unless he speedily found the keys wanted, all this hideous tragedy would end in nothing but a prodigious increase of the public horror, in tenfold precautions therefore, and redoubled obstacles interposed between himself and his future game. Nay, there was even a nearer interest at stake; his own immediate safety might, by a probable accident, be compromised. Most of those who came to the house for liquor were giddy girls or children, who, on finding this house closed, would go off carelessly to some other; but, let any thoughtful woman or man come to the door now, a full quarter of an hour before the established time of closing, in that case suspicion would arise too powerful to be checked. There would be a sudden alarm given; after which, mere luck would decide the event. For it is a remarkable fact, and one that illustrates the singular inconsistency of this villain—who, being often so superfluously subtle, was in other directions so reckless and improvident—that at this very moment, standing amongst corpses that had deluged the little parlour with blood, Williams must have been in considerable doubt whether he had any sure means of egress. There were windows, he knew, to the back; but upon what ground they opened he seems to have had no certain information; and in a neighbourhood so dangerous the windows of the lower storey would not imporbably be nailed down: those in the upper might be free, but then came the necessity of a leap too formidable. From all this, however, the sole practical inference was to hurry forward with the trial of further keys, and to detect the hidden treasure. This it was, this intense absorption in one overmastering pursuit, that dulled the murderer's perceptions as to all around him; otherwise he must have heard the breathing of the young man, which to himself at times became fearfully audible. As the murderer stood once more over the body of Mrs Williamson, and searched her pockets more narrowly, he pulled out various clusters of keys, one of which, dropping, gave a harsh jingling sound upon the floor. At this time it was that the secret witness, from his secret witness, from his secret stand, noticed the fact of Williams' surtout being lined with silk of the finest quality. One other fact he noticed, which eventually became more immediately important than many stronger circumstances of incrimination: this was that the shoes of the murderer, apparently new, and bought probably with poor Marr's money, creaked as he walked, harshly and frequently. With the new clusters of keys, the murderer walked off to the hidden section of the parlour. And here, at last, was suggested to the journeyman the sudden opening for an escape. Some minutes would be lost to a certainty in trying all these keys, and subsequently in searching the drawers, supposing that the keys answered— or in violently forcing them, supposing that they did *not*. He might thus count upon a brief interval of leisure, whilst the rattling of the keys might obscure to the murderer the creaking of the stairs under the reascending journeyman. His plan was now formed. On regaining his bedroom, he placed the bed against the door by way of a transient retardation to the enemy, that might give him a short warning, and, in the worst extremity, might give him a chance for life by means of a desperate leap. This change made as quietly as was possible, he tore the sheets, pillowcases, and blankets into broad ribbons, and, after plaiting them into ropes, spliced the different lengths together. But at the very first he descries this ugly addition to his labours. Where shall he look for any staple, hook, bar, or other fixture, from which his rope, when twisted, may safely depend? Measured from the window-*sill*—*i.e.* the lowest part of the window architrave—there count but twenty-two or twenty-three feet to the ground. Of this length ten or twelve feet may be looked upon as cancelled, because to that extent he might drop without danger. So much being deducted, there would remain, say, a dozen feet of rope to prepare. But, unhappily, there is no stout iron fixture anywhere about his window. The nearest, indeed the sole, fixture of that sort is not near to the window at all; it is a spike fixed (for no reason at all that is apparent) in the bed-tester. Now, the bed being shifted, the spike is shifted; and its distance from the window, having always been four feet, is now seven. Seven entire feet, therefore, must be added to that which would have sufficed if measured from the window. But courage! God, by the proverb of all nations in Christendom, helps those that help themselves. This our young man thankfully acknowledges; he reads already, in the very fact of any spike at all being found where hitherto it has been useless, an earnest of providential aid. Were it only for himself that he worked, he could not feel himself meritoriously employed; but this is not so. In deep sincerity he is now agitated for the poor child, whom he knows and loves; every minute, he feels, brings ruin nearer to *her*; and, as he passed her door, his first thought had been to take her out of bed in his arms, and to carry her where she might share his chances. But, on consideration, he felt that this sudden awaking of her, and the impossibility of even whispering any explanation, would cause her to cry audibly; and the inevitable indiscretion of one would be fatal to the two. As the Alpine avalanches, when suspended above the traveller's head, oftentimes (we are told) come down through the stirring of the air by a simple whisper, precisely on such a tenure of a whisper was now suspended the murderous malice of the man below. No; there is but one way to save the child; towards *her* deliverance the first step is through his own. And he has made an excellent beginning; for the spike, which too fearfully he had expected to see torn away by any strain upon it from the half-carious wood, stands firmly when tried against the pressure of his own weight. He has rapidly fastened on to it three lengths of his new rope, measuring eleven feet. He plaits it roughly; so that only three feet have been lost in the intertwisting; he has spliced on a second length equal to the first; so that, already, sixteen feet are ready to throw out of the window; and thus, let the worst come to the worst, it will not be absolute ruin to swarm down the rope so far as it will reach, and then to drop boldly.

All this has been accomplished in about six minutes; and the hot contest between above and below is still steadily, but fervently, proceeding. Murderer is working hard in the parlour; journeyman is working hard in the bedroom. Miscreant is getting on famously downstairs; one batch of bank-notes he has already bagged, and is hard upon the scent of a second. He has also sprung a covey of golden coins. Sovereigns as yet were not; but guineas at this period fetched thirty shillings apiece; and he was worked his way into a little quarry of these. Murderer is almost joyous; and, if any creature is still living in this house, as shrewdly he suspects and very soon means to know, with that creature he would be happy, before cutting the creature's throat, to drink a glass of something. Instead of the glass, might he not make a present to the poor creature of his throat? Oh no! impossible! Throats are a sort of thing that he never makes presents of; business—business must be attended to. Really the two men, considered simply as men of business, are both meritorious. Like chorus and semi-chorus, strophe and anti-strophe, they work each against the other. Pull journeyman, pull murderer! Pull baker, pull devil! As regards the journeyman, he is now safe. To his sixteen feet, of which seven are neutralized by the distance of the bed, he has at last added six feet more; which will be short of reaching the ground by perhaps ten feet—a trifle which man or boy may drop without injury. All is safe, therefore, for him; which is more than one can be sure of for miscreant in the parlour.

Miscreant, however, takes it coolly enough: the reason being that, with all his cleverness, for once in his life miscreant has been over-reached. The reader and I know, but miscreant does not in the least suspect, a little fact of some importance, viz. that just now through a space of full three minutes he has been overlooked and studied by one who (though reading in a dreadful book and suffering under mortal panic) took accurate notes of so much as his limited opportunities allowed him to see, and will assuredly report the creaking shoes and the silk-mounted surtout in quarters where such little facts will tell very little to his advantage. But, although it is true that Mr Williams, unaware of the journeyman's having 'assisted' at the examination of Mrs Williamson's pockets, could not connect any anxiety with that person's subsequent proceedings, nor specially therefore with his having embarked in the rope-weaving line, assuredly he knew of reasons enough for not loitering. And yet he *did* loiter. Reading his acts by the light of such mute traces as he left behind him, the police became aware that latterly he must have loitered. And the reason which governed him is striking; because at once it records that murder was not pursued by him simply as a means to an end, but also as an end for itself. Mr Williams had now been upon the premises for perhaps fifteen or twenty minutes; and in that space of time he had dispatched, in a style satisfactory to himself, a considerable amount of business. He had done, in commercial language, 'a good stroke of business'. Upon two floors, viz. the cellar-floor and the ground-floor, he has 'accounted for' all the population. But there remained at least two floors more; and it now occurred to Mr Williams that, although the landlord's somewhat chilling manner had shut him out from any familiar knowledge of the household arrangements, too probably on one or other of those floors there must be some throats. As to plunder, he has already bagged the whole. And it was next to impossible that any arrear, the most trivial, should still remain for a gleaner. But the throats—the throats—there it was that arrears and gleanings might perhaps be counted on. And thus it appeared that, in his wolfish thirst for blood, Mr Williams put to hazard the whole fruits of his night's work, and his life into the bargain. At this moment, if the murderer knew all—could he see the open window above stairs ready for the descent of the journeyman, could he witness the life-and-death rapidity with which that journeyman is working, could he guess at the almighty uproar which within ninety seconds will be maddening the population of this populous district—no picture of a maniac in flight of panic or in pursuit of vengeance would adequately represent the agony of haste with which he would himself be hurrying to the street-door for final evasion. That mode of escape was still free. Even at this moment there yet remained time sufficient for a successful flight, and, therefore, for the following revolution in the romance of his own abominable life: He had in his pockets above a hundred pounds of booty—means, therefore, for a full disguise. This very night, if he will shave off his yellow hair, and blacken his eyebrows, buying, when morning light returns, a dark-coloured wig, and clothes such as may co-operate in personating the character of a grave professional man, he may elude all suspicions of impertinent policemen—may sail by any one of a hundred vessels bound for any port along the huge line of seaboard (stretching through 2400 miles) of the American United States; may enjoy fifty years for leisurely repentance; and may even die in the odour of sanctity. On the other hand, if he prefer active life, it is not impossible that, with *his* subtlety, hardihood, and unscrupulousness, in a land where the simple process of naturalization converts the alien at once into a child of the family, he might rise to the President's chair; might have a statue at his death; and afterwards a life in three volumes quarto, with no hint glancing towards No. 29 Ratcliffe Highway. But all depends on the next ninety seconds. Within that time there is a sharp turn to be taken; there is a wrong turn, and a right turn. Should his better angel guide him to the right one, all may yet go well as regards this world's prosperity. But behold! in two minutes from this point we shall see him take the wrong one; and then Nemesis will be at his heels with ruin perfect and sudden.

Meantime, if the murderer allows himself to loiter, the ropemaker overheard does *not*. Well he knows that the poor child's fate is on the edge of a razor; for all turns upon the alarm being raised before the murderer reaches her bedside.

And at this very moment, whilst desperate agitation is nearly paralysing his fingers, he hears the sullen stealthy step of the murderer creeping up through the darkness. It had been the expectation of the journeyman (founded on the clamorous uproar with which the street-door was slammed) that Williams, when disposable for his upstairs work, would come racing at a long jubilant gallop, and with a tiger roar; and perhaps, on his natural instincts, he would have done so. But this mode of approach, which was of dreadful effect when applied to a case of surprise, became dangerous in the case of people who might by this time have been placed fully upon their guard. The step which he had heard was on the staircase—but upon which stair? He fancied upon the lowest; and, in a movement so slow and cautious, even this might make all the difference; yet might it not have been the tenth, twelfth, or fourteenth stair? Never, perhaps, in this world did any man feel his own responsibility so cruelly loaded and strained as at this moment did the poor journeyman on behalf of the slumbering child. Lose but two seconds, through awkwardness or through the self-counteractions of panic, and for *her* the total difference arose between life and death. Still there is a hope; and nothing can so frightfully expound the hellish nature of him whose baleful shadow, to speak astrologically, at this moment darkens the house of life, as the simple expression of the ground on which this hope rested. The journeyman felt sure that the murderer would not be satisfied to kill the poor child whilst unconscious. This would be to defeat his whole purpose in murdering her at all. To an epicure in murder such as Williams, it would be taking away the very sting of the enjoyment if the poor child should be suffered to drink off the bitter cup of death without fully apprehending the misery of the situation. But this luckily would require time: the double confusion of mind—first, from being roused up at so unusual an hour, and, secondly, from the horror of the occasion when explained to her—would at first produce fainting, or some mode of insensibility or distraction, such as must occupy a considerable time. The logic of the case, in short, all rested upon the *ultra* fiendishness of Williams. Were he likely to be content with the mere fact of the child's death, apart from the process and leisurely expansion of its mental agony—in that case there would be no hope. But, because our present murderer is fastidiously finical in his exactions—a sort of martinet in the scenical grouping and draping of the circumstances in his murders—therefore it is that hope becomes reasonable, since all such refinements of preparation demand time. Murders of mere necessity Williams was obliged to hurry: but in a murder of pure voluptuousness, entirely disinterested, where no hostile witness was to be removed, no extra booty to be gained, and no revenge to be gratified, it is clear that to hurry would be altogether to ruin. If this child, therefore, is to be saved, it will be on pure aesthetical considerations.[1]

But all considerations whatever are at this moment suddenly cut short. A second step is heard on the stairs, but still stealthy and cautious; a third—and then the child's doom seems fixed. But just at that moment all is ready. The window is wide open: the rope is swinging free; the journeyman has launched himself; and already he is in the first stage of his descent. Simply by the weight of his person he descended, and by the resistance of his hands he retarded the descent. The danger was that the rope should run too smoothly through his hands, and that by too rapid an acceleration of pace he should come violently to the ground. Happily he was able to resist the descending impetus; the knots of the splicings furnished a succession of retardations. But the rope proved shorter by four or five feet than he had calculated: ten or eleven feet from the ground he hung suspended in the air; speechless for the present through long-continued agitation, and not daring to drop boldly on the rough carriage pavement, lest he should fracture his legs. But the night was not dark, as it has been on occasion of the Marr murders. And yet, for purposes of criminal police, it was by accident worse than the darkest night that ever hid a murder or baffled a pursuit. London, from east to west, was covered with a deep pall (rising from the river) of universal fog. Hence it happened that for twenty or thirty seconds the young

[1] Let the reader who is disposed to regard as exaggerated or romantic the pure fiendishness imputed to Williams recollect that, except for the luxurious purpose of basking and revelling in the anguish of dying despair, he had no motive at all, small or great, for attempting the murder of this young girl. She had seen nothing, heard nothing—was fast asleep, and her door was closed; so that, as a witness against him, he knew that she was as useless as any one of the three corpses. And yet he *was* making preparations for her murder when the alarm in the street interrupted him.

man hanging in the air was not observed. His white shirt at length attracted notice. Three or four people ran up, and received him in their arms, all anticipating some dreadful annunciation. To what house did he belong? Even *that* was not instantly apparent; but he pointed with his finger to Williamson's door, and said in a half-choking whisper—'*Marr's murderer, now at work!*'

All explained itself in a moment: the silent language of the fact made its own eloquent revelation. The mysterious exterminator of No. 29 Ratcliffe Highway has visited another house; and, behold! one man only had escaped through the air, and in his nightdress, to tell the tale. Superstitiously, there was something to check the pursuit of this unintelligible criminal. Morally, and in the interests of vindictive justice, there was everything to rouse, quicken, and sustain it.

Yes, Marr's murderer—the man of mystery—was again at work; at this moment perhaps extinguishing some lamp of life, and not at any remote place, but here—in the very house which the listeners to this dreadful announcement were actually touching. The chaos and blind uproar of the scene which followed, measured by the crowded reports in the journals of many subsequent days, and in one feature of that case, has never to my knowledge had its parallel; or, if a parallel, only in one case—what followed, I mean, on the acquittal of the seven bishops at Westminster in 1688. At present there was more than passionate enthusiasm. The frenzied movement of mixed horror and exultation—the ululation of vengeance which ascended instantaneously from the individual street, and then by a sublime sort of magnetic contagion from all the adjacent street—can be adequately expressed only by a rapturous passage in Shelley:

> The transport of a fierce and monstrous gladness
>     Spread through the multitudinous streets, fast flying
> Upon the wings of fear—From his dull madness
>     The starveling waked, and died in joy: the dying,
>     Among the corpses in stark agony lying,
>     Just heard the happy tidings, and in hope
> Closed their faint eyes: from house to house replying
>     With loud acclaim, the living shook heaven's cope
> And filled the startled earth with echoes.

There was something, indeed, half inexplicable in the instantaneous interpretation of the gathering shout according to its true meaning. In fact, the deadly roar of vengeance, and its sublime unity, *could* point in this district only to the one demon whose idea had brooded and tyrannized, for twelve days, over the general heart; every door, every window in the neighbourhood, flew open as if at a word of command; multitudes, without waiting for the regular means of egress, leaped down at once from the windows on the lower storey; sick men rose from their beds: in one instance, as if expressly to verify the image of Shelley (in v. 4, 5, 6, 7), a man whose death had been looked for through some days, and who actually *did* die on the following day, rose, armed himself with a sword, and descended in his shirt into the street. The chance was a good one, and the mob were made aware of it, for catching the wolfish dog in the high noon and carnival of his bloody revels—in the very centre of his own shambles. For a moment the mob was self-baffled by its own numbers and its own fury. But even that fury felt the call for self-control. It is evident that the massy street-door must be driven in, since there was no longer any living person to co-operate with their efforts from within, excepting only a female child. Crowbars dexterously applied in one minute threw the door out of hangings, and the people entered like a torrent. It may be guessed with what fret and irritation to their consuming fury a signal of pause and absolute silence was made by a person of local importance. In the hope of receiving some useful communication, the mob became silent. 'Now, listen,' said the man of authority, 'and we shall learn whether he is above-stairs or below.' Immediately a noise was heard as if of someone forcing windows, and clearly the sound came from a bedroom above. Yes, the fact was apparent that the murderer was even yet in the house: he had been caught in a trap. Not having made himself familiar with the details of William-son's house, to all appearance he had suddenly become a prisoner in one of the upper rooms. Towards this the crowd now rushed impetuously. The door, however, was found to be slightly fastened; and, at the moment when this was forced, a loud crash of the window, both glass and frame, announced that the wretch had made his escape. He had leaped down; and several persons in the crowd, who burned with the general fury, leaped after him. These persons had not troubled themselves about the nature of the ground; but now, on making an examination of it with torches, they reported it to be an inclined plane, or embankment of clay, very wet and adhesive. The prints of the man's footsteps were deeply impressed upon the clay, and therefore easily traced up to the summit of the embankment; but it was perceived at once that pursuit would be useless, from the density of the mist. Two feet ahead of you a man was entirely withdrawn from your power of identification; and, on overtaking him, you could not venture to challenge him as the same whom you had lost sight of. Never, through the course of a whole century, could there be a night expected more propitious to an escaping criminal;

means of disguise Williams now had in excess; and the dens were innumerable in the neighbourhood of the river that could have sheltered him for years from troublesome inquiries. But favours are thrown away upon the reckless and the thankless. That night, when the turning-point offered itself for his whole future career, Williams took the wrong turn; for, out of mere indolence, he took the turn to his old lodgings—that place which, in all England, he had just now the most reason to shun.

Meantime the crowd had thoroughly searched the premises of Williamson. The first inquiry was for the young grand-daughter. Williams, it was evident, had gone into her room; but in this room apparently it was that the sudden uproar in the streets had surprised him; after which his undivided attention had been directed to the windows, since through these only any retreat had been left open to him. Even this retreat he owed only to the fog, and to the hurry of the moment, and to the difficulty of approaching the premises by the rear. The little girl was naturally agitated by the influx of strangers at that hour; but otherwise, through the humane precautions of the neighbours, she was preserved from all knowledge of the dreadful events that had occurred whilst she herself was sleeping. Her poor old grandfather was still missing, until the crowd descended into the cellar; he was then found lying prostrate on the cellar floor: apparently he had been thrown down from the top of the cellar stairs, and with so much violence that one leg was broken. After he had been thus disabled, Williams had gone down to him, and cut his throat. There was much discussion at the time, in some of the public journals, upon the possibility of reconciling these incidents with other circumstantialities of the case, supposing that only one man had been concerned in the affair. That there *was* only one man concerned seems to be certain. One only was seen or heard at Marr's; one only, and beyond all doubt the same man, was seen by the young journeyman in Mrs Williamson's parlour; and one only was traced by his footmarks on the clay embankment. Apparently the course which he had pursued was this: He had introduced himself to Williamson by ordering some beer. This order would oblige the old man to go down into the cellar; Williams would wait until he had reached it, and would then 'slam' and lock the street door in the violent way described. Williamson would come up in agitation upon hearing this violence. The murderer, aware that he would do so, met him, no doubt, at the head of the cellar stairs, and threw him down; after which he would go down to consummate the murder in his ordinary way. All this would occupy a minute, or a minute and a half; and in that way the interval would be accounted for that elapsed between the alarming sound of the street-door as heard by the journeyman and the lamentable outcry of the female servant. It was evident also that the reason why no cry whatsoever had been heard from the lips of Mrs Williamson is due to the positions of the parties as I have sketched them. Coming behind Mrs Williamson—unseen therefore, and from her deafness unheard—the murderer would inflict entire abolition of consciousness while she was yet unaware of his presence. But with the servant, who had unavoidably witnesses the attack upon her mistress, the murderer could not obtain the same fullness of advantage; and *she* therefore had time for making an agonizing ejaculation.

It has been mentioned that the murderer of the Marrs was not for nearly a fortnight so much as suspected—meaning that, previously to the Williamson murder, no vestige of any ground for suspicion in any direction whatever had occurred either to the general public or to the police. But there were two very limited exceptions to this state of absolute ignorance. Some of the magistrates had in their possession something which, when closely examined, offered a very probable means for tracing the criminal. But as yet they had *not* traced him. Until the Friday morning next after the destruction of the Williamsons, they had not published the important fact that upon the ship-carpenter's mallet (with which, as regarded the stunning or disabling process, the murders had been achieved) were inscribed the letters 'J.P.' This mallet had by a strange oversight on the part of the murderer, been left behind in Marr's shop: and it is an interesting fact, therefore, that, had the villain been intercepted by the grave pawnbroker, he would have been met virtually disarmed. This public notification was made officially on the Friday, viz. on the thirteenth day after the first murder. And it was instantly followed (as will be seen) by a most important result. Meantime, within the secrecy of one single bedroom in all London, it is a fact that Williams had been whisperingly the object of very deep suspicion from the very first—that is, within that same hour which witnessed the Marr tragedy. And singular it is that the suspicion was due entirely to his own folly.

Williams lodged, in company with other men of various nations, at a public house. In a large dormitory there were arranged five or six beds. These were occupied by artisans, generally of respectable character. One or two Englishmen there were, one or two Scotchmen, three or four Germans, and Williams, whose birthplace was not certainly known. On the fatal Saturday night, about half-past one o'clock, when Williams returned from his dreadful labours, he found the English and Scotch party asleep, but the Germans awake: one of them was sitting up with a lighted candle in his hands, and reading aloud to the other two. Upon this, Williams said, in an angry and very peremptory tone, 'Oh, put that candle out; put it out directly; we shall all be burned in our beds.' Had the British party in the room been awake, Mr Williams would have roused a mutinous protest against this arrogant mandate. But Germans are generally mild and facile in their tempers; so the light was complaisantly extinguished. Yet, as there were no curtains, it struck the Germans that the danger was really none at all; for bedclothes, massed upon each other, will no more burn than the leaves of a closed book. Privately, therefore, the Germans drew an inference that Mr Williams must have had some urgent motive for withdrawing his own person and dress from observation. What this motive might be the next day's news diffused all over London, and of course at this house, not two furlongs from Marr's shop, made awfully evident; and, as may well be supposed, the suspicion was communicated to the other members of the dormitory. All of them, however, were aware of the legal danger attaching, under English law, to insinuations against a man, even if true, which might not admit of proof. In reality, had Williams used the most obvious precautions, had he simply walked down to the Thames (not a stone's-throw distant) and flung two of his implements into the river, no conclusive proof could have been adduced against him. And he might have realized the scheme of Courvoisier (the murderer of Lord William Russell)—viz. have sought each separate month's support in a separate well-concerted murder. The party in the dormitory, meantime, were satisfied themselves, but waited for evidences that might satisfy others. No sooner, therefore, had the official notice been published as to the initials J.P. on the mallet than every man in the house recognized at once the well-known initials of an honest Norwegian ship-carpenter, John Petersen, who had worked in the English dockyards until the present year, but, having occasion to revisit his native land, had left his box of tools in the garrets of this inn. These garrets were now searched, Petersen's tool-chest was found, but wanting the mallet; and, on further examination, another over-whelming discovery was made. The surgeon who examined the corpses at Williamson's had given it as his opinion that the throats were not cut by means of a razor, but of some implement differently shaped. It was now remembered that Williams had recently borrowed a large French knife of peculiar construction; and, accordingly, from a heap of old lumber and rags, there was soon extricated a waistcoat, which the whole house could swear to as recently worn by Williams. In this waistcoat, and glued by gore to the lining of its pockets, was found the French knife. Next, it was matter of notoriety to everybody in the inn that Williams ordinarily wore at present a pair of creaking shoes, and a brown surtout lined with silk. Many other presumptions seemed scarcely called for. Williams was immediately apprehended, and briefly examined. This was on the Friday. On the Saturday morning (viz. fourteen days from the Marr murders) he was again brought up. The circumstantial evidence was overwhelming. Williams watched its course, but said very little. At the close, he was fully committed for trial at the next sessions; and it is needless to say that, on his road to prison, he was pursued by mobs so fierce that, under ordinary circumstances, there would have been small hope of escaping summary vengeance. But upon this occasion a powerful escort had been provided; so that he was safely lodged in jail. In this particular jail at this time the regulation was that at five o'clock P.M. all the prisoners on the criminal side should be finally locked up for the night, and without candles. For fourteen hours (that is, until seven o'clock on the next morning) they were left unvisited, and in total darkness. Time, therefore, Williams had for committing suicide. The means in other respects were small. One iron bar there was, meant (if I remember) for the suspension of a lamp; upon this he had hanged himself by his braces. At what hour was uncertain: some people fancied at midnight. And in that case, precisely at the hour when, fourteen days before, he had been spreading horror and desolation through the quiet family of poor Marr, now was he forced into drinking of the same cup, presented to his lips by the same accursed hands.

The case of the M'Keans, which has been specially alluded to, merits also a slight rehearsal for the dreadful picturesqueness of some two or three amongst its circumstances. The scene of this murder was at a rustic inn, some few miles (I think) from Manchester; and the advantageous situation of this inn it was out of which arose the twofold temptations of the case. Generally speaking, an inn argues, of course, a close cincture of neighbours, as the original motive for opening such an establishment. But in this case the house individually was solitary, so that no interruption was to be looked for from any persons living within reach of screams; and yet, on the other hand, the circumjacent vicinity was eminently populous; as one consequence of which, a benefit club had established its weekly rendezvous in this inn, and left the pecuniary accumulations in their club-room, under the custody of the landlord. This fund arose often to a considerable amount, fifty or seventy pounds, before it was transferred to the hands of a banker. Here, therefore, was a treasure worth some little risk, and a situation that promised next to none. These attractive circumstances had, by accident, become accurately known to one or both of the two M'Keans; and, unfortunately, at a moment of overwhelming misfortune to themselves. They were hawkers, and until lately had borne most respectable characters; but some mercantile crash had overtaken them with utter ruin, in which their joint capital had been swallowed up to the last shilling. This sudden prostration had made them desperate: their own little property had been swallowed up in a large *social* catastrophe, and society at large they looked upon as accountable to them for a robbery. In preying, therefore, upon society, they considered themselves as pursuing a wild natural justice of retaliation. The money aimed at did certainly assume the character of public money, being the product of many separate subscriptions. They forgot, however, that in the murderous acts which too certainly they mediated as preliminaries to the robbery they could plead no such imaginary social precedent. In dealing with a family that seemed almost helpless, if all went smoothly, they relied entirely upon their own bodily strength. They were stout young men, twenty-eight to thirty-two years old: somewhat undersized as to height; but squarely built, deep-chested, broad-shouldered, and so beautifully formed, as regarded the symmetry of their limbs and their articulations, that, after their execution, the bodies were privately exhibited by the surgeons of the Manchester Infirmary as objects of statuesque interest.

On the other hand, the household which they proposed to attack consisted of the following four persons: 1, the landlord, a stoutish farmer—but *him* they intended to disable by a trick then newly introduced amongst robbers, and termed *hocussing, i.e.* clandestinely drugging the liquor of the victim with laudanum; 2, the landlord's wife; 3, a young servant-woman; 4, a boy, twelve or fourteen years old. The danger was that out of four persons, scattered by possibility over a house which had two separate exists, one at least might escape, and, by better acquaintances with the adjacent paths, might succeed in giving an alarm to some of the houses a furlong distant. Their final resolution was—to be guided by circumstances as to the mode of conducting the affair; and yet, as it seemed essential to success that they should assume the air of strangers to each other, it was necessary that they should preconcert some general outline of their plan; since it would on this scheme be impossible, without awaking violent suspicions, to make any communications under the eyes of the family. This outline included, at the least, one murder: so much was settled; but otherwise their subsequent proceedings make it evident that they wished to have as little bloodshed as was consistent with their final object. On the appointed day they presented themselves separated at the rustic inn, and at different hours. One came as early as four o'clock in the afternoon; the other not until half-past seven. They saluted each other distantly and shyly; and, though occasionally exchanging a few words in the character of strangers, did not seem disposed to any familiar intercourse. With the landlord, however, on his return about eight o'clock from Manchester, one of the brothers entered into a lively conversation, invited him to take a tumbler of punch; and, at a moment when the landlord's absence from the room allowed it, poured into the punch a spoonful of laudanum. Some time after this the clock struck ten; upon which the elder M'Kean, professing to be weary, asked to be shown up to his bedroom: for each brother, immediately on arriving, had engaged a bed. On this, the poor servant-girl presented herself with a bed-candle to light him upstairs.

At this critical moment the family were distributed thus: The landlord, stupefied with the horrid narcotic which he had drunk, had retired to a private room adjoining the public room, for the purpose of reclining upon a sofa; and *he*, luckily for his own safety, was looked upon as entirely incapacitated for action. The landlady was occupied with her husband. And thus the younger M'Kean was left alone in the public room. He rose, therefore, softly, and placed himself at the foot of the stairs which his brother had just ascended, so as to be sure of intercepting any fugitive from the bedroom above. Into that room the elder M'Kean was ushered by the servant, who pointed to two beds—one of which was already half occupied by the boy, and the other empty: in these she intimated that the two strangers must dispose of themselves for the night, according to any arrangement that they might agree upon. Saying this, she presented him with the candle; which he in a moment placed upon the table, and, intercepting her retreat from the room, threw his arms around her neck with a gesture as though he meant to kiss her. This was evidently what she herself anticipated, and endeavoured to prevent. Her horror may be imagined when she felt the perfidious hand that clasped her neck armed with a razor, and violently cutting her throat. She was hardly able to utter one scream before she sank powerless upon the floor. This dreadful spectacle was witnessed by the boy; who was not asleep, but had presence of mind enough instantly to close his eyes. The murderer advanced hastily to the bed, and anxiously examined the expression of the boy's features: satisfied he was not, and he then placed his hand upon the boy's heart, in order to judge by its beatings whether he were agitated or not. This was a dreadful trial; and no doubt the counterfeit sleep would immediately have been detected, when suddenly a dreadful spectacle drew off the attention of the murderer. Solemnly, and in ghostly silence, uprose in her dying delirium the murdered girl; she stood upright, she walked steadily for a moment or two, she bent her steps towards the door. The murderer turned away to pursue her; and at that moment the boy, feeling that his one solitary chance was to fly whilst this scene was in progress, bounded out of bed. On the landing at the head of the stairs was one murderer; at the foot of the stairs was the other: who could believe that the boy had the shadow of a chance for escaping? And yet, in the most natural way, he surmounted all hindrances. In the boy's horror, he laid his left hand on the balustrade, and took a flying leap over it, which landed him at the bottom of the stairs, without having touched a single stair. He had thus effectually passed one of the murderers: the other, it is true, was still to be passed; and this would have been impossible but for a sudden accident. The landlady had been alarmed by the faint scream of the young woman; had hurried from her private room to the girl's assistance; but at the foot of the stairs had been intercepted by the younger brother, and was at this moment struggling with *him*. The confusion of this life-and-death conflict had allowed the boy to whirl past them. Luckily he took a turn into a kitchen out of which was a back-door, fastened by a single bolt that ran freely at a touch; and through this door he rushed into the open fields. But at this moment the elder brother was set free for pursuit by the death of the poor girl. There is no doubt that in her delirium the image moving through her thoughts was that of the club, which met once a week. She fancied it no doubt sitting; and to this room, for help and for safety, she staggered along; she entered it, and within the doorway once more she dropped down and instantly expired. Her murderer, who had followed her closely, now saw himself set at libery for the pursuit of the boy. At this critical moment all was at stake; unless the boy were caught the enterprise was ruined. He passed his brother, therefore, and the landlady, without pausing, and rushed through the open door into the fields. By a single second perhaps, he was too late. The boy was keenly aware that, if he continued in sight, he would have no chance of escaping from a powerful young man. He made, therefore, at once for a ditch; into which he tumbled headlong. Had the murderer ventured to make a leisurely examination of the nearest ditch, he would easily have found the boy—made so conspicuous by his white shirt. But he lost all heart, upon failing at once to arrest the boy's flight. And every succeeding second made his despair the greater. If the boy had really effected his escape to the neighbouring farm-houses, a party of men might be gathered within five minutes; and already it might have become difficult for himself and his brother, unacquainted with the field paths, to evade being intercepted. Nothing remained, therefore, but to summon his brother away. Thus it happened that the landlady, though mangled, escaped with life, and eventually recovered. The landlord owed his safety to the stupefying potion. And the baffled murderers had the misery of knowing that their dreadful crime had been altogether profitless. The road, indeed, was now open to the club-room; and, probably, forty seconds would have sufficed to carry off the box of treasure, which afterwards might have been burst open and pillaged at leisure. But the fear of intercepting enemies was too strongly upon them; and they fled rapidly by a road which carried them actually within six feet of the lurking boy.

That night they passed through Manchester. When daylight returned, they slept in a thicket twenty miles distant from the scene of their guilty attempt. On the second and third nights, they pursued their march on foot, resting again during the day. About sunrise on the fourth morning they were entering some village near Kirby Lonsdale, in Westmorland. They must have designedly quitted the direct line of route; for their object was Ayrshire, of which county they were natives, and the regular road would have led them through Shap, Penrith, Carlisle. Probably they were seeking to elude the persecution of the stagecoaches, which, for the last thirty hours, had been scattering at all the inns and road-side *cabarets* hand-bills describing their persons and dress. It happened (perhaps through design) that on this fourth morning they had separated, so as to enter the village ten minutes apart from each other. They were exhausted and footsore. In this condition it was easy to stop them. A blacksmith had silently reconnoitred them, and compared their appearance with the descriptions of the hand-bills. They were then easily overtaken, and separately arrested. Their trial and condemnation speedily followed at Lancaster; and in those days it followed, of course, that they were executed. Otherwise, their case fell so far within the sheltering limits of what would *now* be regarded as extenuating circumstances that, whilst a murder more or less was not to repel them from their object, very evidently they were anxious to economize the bloodshed as much as possible. Immeasurable, therefore, was the interval which divided them from the monster Williams.

*They* perished on the scaffold: Williams, as I have said, by his own hand; and, in obedience to the law as it then stood, he was buried in the centre of a *quadrivium*, or conflux of four roads (in this case four streets), with a stake driven through his heart. And over him drives for ever the uproar of unresting London!

# SOURCES AND ACKNOWLEDGEMENTS

'Dr Parkman Takes a Walk' by Cleveland Amory, from *The Proper Bostonians* (New York: E. P. Dutton, Inc., 1947), reprinted by permission of the author and publisher. Copyright © 1947, 1975 by the author.

'The Love Philtre: the Case of Mary Blandy, 1751–2' by Horace Bleackley, from *Some Distinguished Victims of the Scaffold* (London: Kegan Paul, Trench, Trübner and Co. Ltd, 1905).

'The Self-Help of G. J. Smith' by William Bolitho, from *Murder for Profit* (London: Jonathan Cape Ltd, 1926).

'Postscript' by Thomas De Quincey, first published in the *Collective Edition* of the author's works, Vol. IV, 1854.

'Valerie Storie' by Charles Franklin, from *Woman in the Case* (London: Corgi, 1964), reprinted by permission of the author's agents, David Higham Associates Ltd.

'Night Life in Manchester' by Leslie Hale, from *Blood on the Scales* (London: Cape, 1960), reprinted by permission of the author.

'The Case of the Man Who Came to Dinner, etc.' by Alan Hynd, from *A Mad Passion for Murder*, ed. Hirsch (New York: Pyramid, 1966).

'The Mysterious Mr Holmes' by H. B. Irving, from *A Book of Remarkable Criminals* (London: Cassell and Co. Ltd, 1918).

'That Damned Fellow Upstairs' by Edmund Pearson, from *Masterpieces of Murder* (Boston: Little, Brown and Co., Inc.; London: Hutchinson Publishing Group Ltd, 1964), reprinted by permission of the publishers.

'The Sandyford Mystery' by William Roughead, from *Knaves' Looking Glass*, collected in *Classic Crimes* (London: Cassell and Co. Ltd, 1951), reprinted by permission of the author's agents, A. D. Peters and Co. Ltd.

'The Case of the Papin Sisters' by Raymond Rudorff, from *Monsters* (Sudbury: Neville Spearman Ltd, 1968), reprinted by permission of the publisher.

'Patrick Mahon: the Possible Innocent' by Robin Squire, from *Classic Murders* (Slough: Foulsham and Co. Ltd, 1970), reprinted by permission of the publisher.

'A Corpse for Company' by C. E. Vulliamy, from *Rocking Horse Journey* (London: Michael Joseph Ltd, 1952), reprinted by permission of the publisher.

'Maria Manning' by Horace Wyndham, from *Feminine Frailty* (London: Ernest Benn Ltd, 1929).

While every effort has been made to trace authors and copyright-holders, in a few cases this has proved impossible; the publishers would be glad to hear from any such parties so that these omissions can be rectified in future editions of the book.